THE FOURTH SESSION

St. Mary's
College of Maryland
Library

....

Presented by

Miss Lucy F. Spedden
and
Mrs. Louis K. McDorman

in
Memory
of

Mrs. Lucy V. Maddox, Principal
of St. Mary's Female Seminary
1900-1923

Xavier Rynne

�֎

THE
FOURTH
SESSION

�֎

THE DEBATES AND DECREES OF
VATICAN COUNCIL II
SEPTEMBER 14 TO DECEMBER 8, 1965

New York
Farrar, Straus and Giroux

The authors are grateful to the editors of *The New Yorker,* in whose pages some of the material in this book first appeared in somewhat different form.

FIRST PRINTING, 1966

Printed in the United States of America
by American-Book Stratford Press, Inc.

Contents

✠

List of Illustrations

✠

FRONT ENDPAPERS

Procession of Council Fathers in St. Peter's Square at the closing
ceremony, December 8, 1965   (*Photo by Roma Press from Pix*)
Pope Paul VI at the UN, October 4, 1965
(*Photo by Nancy Sirkis from Pix*)

BACK ENDPAPERS

Left, The closing ceremony of the Council, outside St. Peter's.

Right, Pope Paul after receiving a group of children, during
the closing ceremony. Cardinal Ottaviani is at his left.
(*Photos by Roma Press from Pix*)

Preface

✠

DURING the closing weeks of Vatican Council II, Cardinal Ottaviani wrote Pope Paul a letter in which he stated: "But I was always in the minority."* The enormity of this admission can only be appreciated by those who had personal experience of the cardinal during the years when he presided over the Holy Office and considered himself the last word on theological orthodoxy. The cardinal's statement might serve as an epitome *à rebours* of Vatican Council II. When the Council opened, his opinions were thought to represent the thinking of the majority of the Church's bishops and theologians. As the Council came to a close on December 8, 1965, it had been demonstrated beyond cavil that the Ottaviani position was repudiated in every one of the Council's documents.

Those who were dismayed by Pope Paul's recent appointment of Cardinal Ottaviani as head of the papal commission

See p. 224.

for the study of the problems of population, family and birth
control, would do well to repeat over and over again the
phrase, "I was always in the minority," until they grasp its
full significance. In this light it becomes clear that it was a
stroke of diplomatic genius on Pope Paul's part to cast the
cardinal in the role, as it were, of midwife presiding over
this labor.*

*   *   *

Amid the accolades and brickbats that have come our way
in the last four years, we are happy to report that the majority of readers seem to have recognized the *raison d'être* behind our "essay in theological journalism." To those who
received the impression that we favored one side rather than
the other, we can only say that this was the reaction we expected. This does not mean, however, that no attempt was
made to do justice to all sides. If honesty required us to call
a spade a spade, it was also occasionally necessary to call a
knave a knave.

We have tried to report the Council *wie es eigentlich
gesehen wurde,* as it was seen, from the inside as well as the
outside, even enabling the reader to look over the shoulder
of a Council secretary while recording the official acts of the
Theological Commission, as in the exchanges on pages 204-
225. Meanwhile the Pope has announced that one function of his new postconciliar Central Commission, again under the Secretary Generalship of Archbishop Pericle Felici,
will be to publish in full the *Acta* of Vatican Council II. In
entrusting this task to the Central Commission, the Pope saw
fit to quote the Ciceronian dictum on historical honesty: "Let
nothing false dare be said, and nothing true dare not be said.
Let all be written without suggestion of favor or dissimula-
tion" (*De Oratore,* XI, 15.)

* Cf. Pius XI, Encyclical *Casti connubii,* Dec. 31, 1930; Pius XII, *Allocution
to Italian Midwives,* Oct. 29, 1951; Paul VI, *Allocution to the Cardinals,* June
23, 1964. With the doctrine of the *magisterium* in this state, we do not intend
to propose immediately concrete solutions. See page 223.

It remains to be seen how the commission will carry out this instruction. In the past, he who edited the *Acta* of a Council determined who won or lost, at least for his own generation, and historians coming later usually had a hard time determining all the facts, before arriving at a definitive evaluation. It will be interesting to see how close we came to the official record of the facts as they actually happened—*wie es eigentlich geschehen ist.*

Whatever the Church was in 1962 when the Council started, it is now something else also; it is the same Church, and not the same; and as a final paradox, though the Council has ended, its work is only beginning.

* * *

Finally, we are happy to report that the dossier started by the Holy Office in 1962 and filed under the rubric "RYNNE XAVERIUS" now reposes—through the mysterious movement of history itself—under the more benevolent auspices of the newly named and organized Congregation for the Doctrine of the Faith.

—XAVIER RYNNE

THE FOURTH SESSION

I

Toward the Fourth Session

THE CRISIS in the Council as the Third Session adjourned at the end of 1964 was symptomatic of a much broader crisis in the Church at large, termed variously "crisis of authority," "crisis of obedience," "period of readjustment," and "the Johannine revolution." The word *aggiornamento,* used by John XXIII to describe the goal of the Council, apparently had much deeper implications than he perhaps had intended. As Dom Butler, the Abbot of Downside, put it: "At the beginning of the Vatican Council, no one knew which way the Church would renew herself. But by the end of the Third Session last winter, we realized that it was not going to be a superficial adjustment but a radical one. It meant a fundamental reappraisal of Catholicism. By then this was not only the view of a progressive minority, but it had captured the center of the Council."

To some the revelation of dissension in the higher ranks is seen as nothing less than a calamity to be avoided at all costs. In the eyes of others, it is good for the world to know that the Catholic Church is not the rigid and uniform monolith it has generally been assumed to be, if any progress is to be made in adjusting to today's pluralistic conditions. "Startling opinions are freely being expressed," Cardinal Heenan of Westminster noted, "but this proves what Catholicism has always contended—that liberty exists in the Church."

Another conclusion that emerged from the painful post-mortems following the Third Session was the realization, resisted at first but gradually becoming a conviction, that the Council could not possibly hope to achieve the ideal goal of uniformly "open," biblically-oriented, updated documents, equally admirable in all respects, for each of the areas on which it had proposed to issue a statement. There would have to be compromises. A certain scaling down of ultimate goals was inevitable. Beyond this, even before the Fourth Session got underway, a marked disposition was evident both in the commissions revising the texts as well as among the planners, to concentrate on proposals and measures that would expedite matters and bring the Council to as speedy and successful a conclusion as possible.

The record of achievement by the end of the Third Session was not very impressive when compared with the total program which the Council had laid out for itself and still expected to accomplish, despite the weightiness of such completed items as the Constitutions on the Liturgy and on the Church, both of which had consumed so much time. Another perhaps decisive reason for the quickening pace and more businesslike, practical attitude prevailing after the Third Session was the unmistakable desire on the part of Pope Paul, shared unquestionably by the vast majority of the bishops, though not necessarily by those who were most active or by the theologians, to end the Council in a Fourth and final session.

An invariable consequence of any débâcle is the search for scapegoats. There was no tendency to blame the Pope exclusively for what had happened. Rather indignation and ire were visited on his entourage and on conservative members of the Curia who had ready access to his person and used the occasion to urge their claims, knowing how scrupulously he would endeavor to give them satisfaction. By contrast, the majority were negligent about making their wishes known with the same regularity. Cardinal Ritter admitted as much when he observed, apropos of the postponed vote on Religious Liberty, "Our feeling of frustration . . . was heightened by the conviction that we were stalled by the delaying tactics of a very small minority. Indeed subsequent events showed how small a minority is opposed." The majority were equally remiss about mustering their strength to prevent the dilution of the texts on collegiality and ecumenism, which might have been avoided if they had acted in time. The brusqueness of Cardinal Tisserant's announcement postponing the Religious Liberty vote and the suddenness of the last-minute changes in ecumenism were particularly galling. No effort was made to save appearances by avoiding the impression that the majority had been outmaneuvered. Resentment was directed particularly at Cardinal Cicognani, Secretary of State, who saw the Pope every day, and Archbishop Felici, Secretary General of the Council, who saw him several times a week, both regarded as spokesmen for the Curial point of view. Unfortunately the rules of the Council failed to specify exactly how the Pope was to communicate with the Council. His wishes were generally channeled through the conservative Cicognani, but whether as Secretary of State or as president of the Coordinating Commission (consisting of the 12 Council Presidents and 4 Moderators), or the extent to which the Pope himself was personally involved, was not always made clear. This vagueness about channels of command tended to perpetuate an impression that there was a regrettable lack of *rapport* between Pope and bishops.

But the real difficulty brought to light by the experience of the first three sessions was the inability of the Council to express itself spontaneously and effectively. The speeches on the various issues were really not "debates" in any realistic sense since texts had to be submitted days in advance and orators were rarely allowed to extemporize remarks (as when Cardinal Ottaviani replied to Cardinal Frings' charges against the Holy Office in a short first paragraph added at the last moment) because this was normally forbidden by the rules. The interval between discussion and voting was too long. The only spontaneous method left was applause, which on occasion proved to be very effective, as when Bishop De Smedt gave his *relatio* following the postponement of the vote on religious liberty, but this too was normally forbidden by the Rules. The experiment of putting a number of propositions or questions to the Fathers in order to ascertain their reactions to a particular problem was not repeated after the Second Session because of the furor raised by the minority. The Pope gave in and disallowed an improvement that might have shortened the duration of the proceedings. The minority of course tenaciously clung to the predominance which they had gained and were able to retain in some of the conciliar commissions even after Pope Paul enlarged the membership. By their obstructionism they were rather successful in slowing down the work of the Council. Except when the Pope personally exerted himself to expedite matters, as he did in the case of the Theological Commission, it would otherwise have continued to block passage of the crucial Constitution on the Church during the Third Session.

But it would be pointless to deny that Pope Paul VI has been subjected to an almost unprecedented amount of criticism since taking office two and a half years ago. Censorious judgments not only about his conduct of the Council but about his character and person began to be aired during the

Second Session and reached a kind of climax in the indignation following the close of the Third. A new factor was that
no Pope, since 1870, had been so widely criticized by Catholics themselves. Both those on the left and those on the
right were disenchanted by his overly subtle attempt to steer
a middle course in treacherous waters. Yet, paradoxically, no
Pope has taken so much trouble to create a favorable image
of the papacy. Though words like "mysterious" and "enig-
matic" were frequently used to describe him, the truth of
the matter is that Paul has consciously reacted against what
he regards as the excessive aloofness of Pius XII. His first
encyclical, *Ecclesiam suam,* was quite informal in tone and
revealed more about the personality of its author than such
documents normally do. His weekly audiences on Wednes-
days were transformed into "fireside chats" in which he replied to a number of questions or problems hypothetically
raised by those present. The short talks from the window of
his apartment after leading the faithful in the *Angelus* at
noon on Sundays or important feastdays have been even more
newsy and chatty: for example, one Sunday in late spring he
informed his listeners, ". . . better news came from Santo
Domingo last night . . . ," as if to share with the crowds the
latest cables received by the Secretariat of State about the
Dominican crisis. Peace is almost invariably the theme of
these Sunday chats and the tone is generally optimistic or
hopeful, but in July, 1965 he struck a pessimistic note, saying: "People are going backward rather than forward on the
path of civilization and peace. It seems to us that the idea of
peace is in danger . . ."

In his message to the Catholic Press Association meeting
in New York, in May 1965, read by the editor of *L'Osservatore Romano,* Raimondo Manzini, the Pope declared: "We
are not ignorant of the difficulties which you encounter, but
we can assure you that we will do all we can to make your
task easier," and he referred specifically to the Pontifical
Commission for the press headed by "our venerable brother"

Archbishop O'Connor. This reassurance was not much of a consolation to the delegates who were fully aware what little the Commission and "our venerable brother" had done to facilitate accurate reporting of the Third Session. The failure of the Vatican, thus far, to establish an effective press office run by professional people (the staff of *L'Osservatore Romano** do what they can to ease the task of journalists covering the Vatican, but the paper itself is in need of a thorough updating) is a serious drawback not only to journalists but a hindrance to the Pope's efforts to make himself better understood. Journalists are not likely to forget the extraordinary press conference during the Third Session at which officials of the Council Press Office (also headed by Archbishop O'Connor) denied that any maneuvers had taken place behind the scenes and accused the press of distortions, only to have to back down a few days later and issue an apology of sorts. Nor the conference of the Secretary General of the Council, Archbishop Felici, shortly after the end of the Third Session, before the *Circolo di Roma,* in which he referred to the press as a kind of "fungus" that would have to be tolerated until the conciliar record could be published. The Pope even implied that the press in reporting the Third Session concentrated too much on secondary matters. The English theologian, Father Charles Davis, seems to have summed the matter up perfectly when he observed: "Journalists have made some wrong comments on the Council (though, considering the difficulties, they have done very well), but they were right to expect the interaction of groups, the clash of personalities, the tension of differing aims and outlooks and the struggle to reach agreement. To deny such factors is to engage in elaborate doublethink."

Pope Paul was of course dismayed by the sharp reactions accompanying the closing days. In February 1965 Father Caprile, S.J., one of the editors of the Jesuit periodical, *La*

* See the article on it in *The Times* (London), March 4, 1965.

Civiltà Cattolica, published a highly informative account of what had happened in which he sought to make clear that the Pope was trying to play the role of an "honest broker" reconciling conflicting factions, and had not intended to act brusquely, or arbitrarily, or uncharitably. The widespread assumption was that Caprile's article had been inspired by the Pope himself or at any rate was based on information which only he or somebody very close to him could have supplied about his motives and actions. Incidentally, it confirmed by and large what journalists had already reported about the drama of those days and sustained their contention that there was a struggle between opposing factions constantly going on behind the scenes centered on the Pope himself. It also insinuated, though in highly discreet language so as not to ruffle any feelings, that Tisserant's rejection of the vote on religious liberty could have been announced more diplomatically and the bishops might have received it with less shock if they had been prepared in advance for what was coming.*

In an audience with Canon Pézéril one day the Pope remarked: "I read in the newspapers that I cannot make up my mind, am restless, timid, and torn by conflicting advice . . . I may perhaps be slow. But I know what I want. After all, it is my privilege to think about matters first."**

On January 25, 1965 the Pope announced the names of 27 persons whom he was elevating to the cardinalate. In addition to expected names like those of Shehan of Baltimore and Heenan of Westminster, there was a certain amount of excitement over the inclusion of figures like the theologian Charles Journet, Monsignor Joseph Cardijn, a venerable

---

* See *La Civiltà Cattolica,* February 20, 1965 (also printed in OR, February 15, 1965), as well as Père R. Rouquette's comment in *Études,* April 1965, p. 566ff. According to Caprile, the Pope tried incessantly to make the language of Chap. III of *De Ecclesia,* on collegiality, as clear and precise as possible, "but without contradicting or destroying the work already accomplished by the majority . . ."

** René Laurentin, *Bilan de la 3e session,* Paris 1965, p. 295.

priest long associated with the Catholic Youth Movement, and the aged Italian parish priest Giulio Bevilacqua who had been the Pope's spiritual mentor. What raised eyebrows, however, was the fact that the list was headed by the octogenarian Patriarch Maximos IV Saigh of Antioch, who had long resisted repeated invitations to join the College of Cardinals but now was leading a movement among the remaining patriarchal heads of Eastern-rite Churches to join that body. The Pope's words when announcing this historic step were somewhat laconic and mystifying. He said that it was his intention to give to the Sacred College "an expression of more complete communion and more effective representation of authority, collegiality, experience of tradition, cultures and merit," by including particularly the Eastern patriarchs. He went on to remark, "The Roman Church cannot be a closed fold, immobile, self-centered and exclusive, but rather should be the indispensable center of a flock which is gathered together: yes, a single, open, and many-faceted flock of Christ, wonderfully characterized by the complementary nature of its constituent parts, unity and catholicity, authority and brotherhood, an identity of faith in the boundless and vast breadth of charity."

Patriarch Maximos issued a statement later the same day explaining more fully why he had accepted the appointment at long last and indicating that certain conditions had been met: the Eastern patriarchs would enter the College of Cardinals but they would not become members of the Roman clergy like the rest of the cardinals; they would retain their patriarchal sees as titles instead of accepting Roman titular or parish churches. This would help to impart an ecumenical dimension to an ecclesiastical post which the Orthodox had always tended to look down on as a purely Western institution and beneath their dignity. Maximos also implied that other concessions had been made, or would be made, but he did not disclose what they were. Despite the protests of some of his clergy (by Archbishop Zoghby in particular) who felt that his action amounted to a surrender of Eastern claims to autonomy, the aged prelate was duly invested with his new rank in the two consistories on February 22nd and 25th. When the papal decree governing the reorganization of the Sacred College was published (February 20th), it was seen that the Eastern patriarchs were accorded precedence over all other members except the six cardinal-bishops, occupants of sees in the immediate neighborhood of Rome who for centuries had always been cardinals and in some cases had traditional functions to perform. (The cardinal bishop of Ostia, for example, was traditionally Dean of the Sacred College and normally crowned the Pope.) The question was therefore left pending whether these posts would be abolished when the aged incumbents died, or whether they would be integrated and equated with the cardinal-patriarchs in some eventual reorganization. Pope Paul's reference to "collegiality" and the *ex officio* status of the new cardinal patriarchs raised the question whether he was perhaps planning to substitute an enlarged College of Cardinals for the proposed Senate of Bishops. The matter was not entirely cleared up, but several days later in a general audience the Pope made clear that in making the recent appointments it had not been his intention to "discount our brothers in the episcopate" who would be called upon to lend their assistance "according to needs and in various ways." In a later private audience he cut short speculation by making it clear that the College of Cardinals would not replace the proposed Senate. The two bodies were destined to fulfill separate and different functions.

When investing the new cardinals in a solemn consistory on February 25th, Pope Paul reminded them that "there is no authority in the Church which is not a service." The Dutch *De Volkskrant* observed that the new cardinals "did not bring the reformation of the Roman Curia any nearer: the dominance of the Italian element was still being maintained, with more than a quarter of the total number of cardinals still being Italians, and 24 out of the 34 Curial cardinals being Italians in the new college as opposed to 20 out of 29 in the old." *De Nieuwe Linie* thought that the College of Cardinals was no longer essential for the Catholic Church as it had once been, but that while a better scheme of Church government could be worked out it was not likely to be introduced at present. Apropos of rumors that Pope Paul had ordered the cardinals to simplify their costume and generally cut down on expensive display (a letter from Cardinal Tisserant bearing on this subject was circulated among his colleagues but did not become binding until September 1965), *The Times* (London) urged Rome not to go too far in cutting down on "pomp," because "the British are firm believers in pomp and colour on great occasions, [and] expect a little pomp from Rome . . . Ecumenical advances should not be the signal for too much drabness of display."

An important clue to the Pope's intentions regarding the Council was the fact that he threw himself into the campaign to make the introduction of the vernacular liturgy a success with unremitting vigor. It was announced that he would celebrate mass in Italian in various Roman parish churches throughout Lent, beginning on March 7th, the day the new regulations were to go into effect throughout the Catholic world. In a general audience on January 31st, he declared flatly that the faithful must change their mental outlook if they believed that mass was nothing but an external rite at which they were expected to be passively present. "One must realize," he said, "that a new process of spiritual education was begun with the Ecumenical Council. This is the Council's great innovation, and we must not hesitate to become first disciples, and then supporters of the school of prayer that is about to begin." Urging the Lenten preachers of Rome, on March 1st, to be careful about explaining the liturgical changes to the people who were being asked to alter the habits of a lifetime, he advised them also to alter their own method of preaching and adopt a less florid, simpler style. "Modern man," he maintained, "is intolerant of every form of awkwardness, exaggeration, affected elegance, pseudo-culture, and worldly substitutes for the Word of God." They should conform to the present-day demand for "plain, simple, essential, brief and intelligible language." On March 17th, in a general audience, he proceeded to analyze the reactions to introduction of the vernacular and called for further efforts to make it successful. Addressing the various groups of pilgrims and faithful present, he said: "If the public character of this meeting did not prevent it, we should like to ask you, as we do at other meetings of a private character, for your impressions regarding this great innovation . . . You understand that this liturgical change cannot take place without your willing and earnest cooperation. We desire this response of yours so much that, as you see, we are making it the theme of our words to you today . . ." Then, to bring home the fact that he meant business, he added: "Before it was enough to attend mass, today it is necessary to participate. Before some could perhaps doze or chat—today this is impossible, you must listen and pray." In any case all thought must be given up that the Church would ever go back to the old days. In Italy as elsewhere the change-over was effected with the minimum of disturbance. There was a certain amount of grumbling but not much more. The right-wing press attempted to foment a campaign to protest the changes, but this came to nothing. *Il Borghese* invited Italian Catholics to fight as the French had done and an open letter was sent to Cardinal Lercaro, president of the Liturgical *Consilium,* charging him with attempting to foist erroneous conceptions of the liturgy on the Church. More indignation was expressed over the Pope's gesture returning the Turkish flag captured by the Christians in the famous sixteenth-century sea battle of Lepanto. *Il Borghese* described this and other conciliatory gestures like the return of the head of St. Andrew to Greece, as a "macabre striptease" that would not stop short even of a denudation of essentials, while the neo-Fascist organ *Il Secolo* lamented that instead of waging war against heretics these days, the Church was eager to start a dialogue with communists who were but one step from power in Italy.*

In spite of fears expressed at the time that the Pope's proclamation of a new title for Mary, "Mother of the Church,"
at the close of the Third Session would arouse agitation for
more dogmas about Mary, the tendency today seems to be
toward greater soberness in mariology. Pope Paul can certainly claim some of the credit for promoting this new trend.
In a speech on February 2nd, the feast of the Presentation,
he mentioned the Mariological Congress in Santo Domingo
in March and referred to the "Christocentric and Church-
centered direction which the Council intends to give to our
doctrine and devotion toward our Lady." The same theme
was stressed in a farewell audience granted to Father Balic
prior to the latter's departure for the Congress. Father Tav-
ard absented himself from the gathering because of objections
to the "methods" of the Mariologists. However, the tone of
meeting appears to have been rather moderate and more
attention was paid to the ecumenical aspects of Marian theology, in keeping with the investigations of such theologians
as De Lubac, Rahner, Congar, Laurentin and the publicly-
expressed wishes of Pope Paul. The restraining hand of the
Pope is evident also in the pages of *L'Osservatore Romano*
which no longer prints as many extravagant Marian articles
by L. Ciappi and others as formerly.

While progress appeared to be made here as well as in a
limited number of other sectors, a series of widely reported
Wednesday general audiences from early spring until late
summer in which the Pope endeavored to unburden his
mind, as it were, regarding the worrisome problems with
which he was faced, provided few clues about what he intended to do but did throw light on the man psychologically
and the troubled state of the Church. The uniform theme
running through all these talks was the importance of maintaining internal unity in the Catholic Church while the

* Desmond O'Grady, *National Catholic Reporter*, March 3, 1965.

Council was laying down the norms for its updating or renewal, which he repeatedly declared to be necessary and inevitable. Nothing tortured him more, he disclosed on a number of occasions, than the spectacle of disunion and dissension where charity and harmony ought to reign. A group of pilgrims were told that the Pope had need of their prayers and consolation, because every moment he was obliged to "face and struggle with endless, enormous tasks, responsibilities and duties of his office." The burden at times "approaches a real agony."

Nothing could have been more Pauline in style than his quiet rehabilitation of Galileo Galilei more than three hundred years after the famous astronomer's forced recantation and humiliation by the Holy Inquisition in 1633. The rehabilitation took place at Pisa on June 10, 1965 in such an offhand and casual way that few newspapers reported it, and those that did were not quite sure whether it was a rehabilitation. There can be no question about it, however; it was. Paul VI admonished the crowd of over 100,000, gathered for the eucharistic congress in front of the twelfth-century marble baptistery of the cathedral, to "imitate the faith of Galileo, Dante and Michelangelo." Galileo was born in 1564, the year Michelangelo died, while Dante of course was much earlier, so that the Pope went out of his way to mention Galileo first. Did the Pope use the occasion merely because he happened to be in Pisa, Galileo's birthplace and the scene of his famous experiments? It is interesting that *L'Osservatore Romano* failed to comment on this historic moment, while covering the eucharistic congress in its usual fulsome manner. However, in view of the bold remark by Cardinal Suenens at the Third Session that "the Church could only afford one Galileo case," Paul's statement can only be considered deliberate.

The Pope's action was also foreshadowed by the mysterious release for posthumous publication in 1964 of a full-scale biography of Galileo written some thirty years earlier by the late Monsignor Pio Paschini, the dean of Roman ecclesiastical

historians. Publication was delayed so long because the manuscript had originally been impounded, on orders of the Holy
Office, despite the acknowledged reliability of the author.
The appearance of Paschini's work was hailed as a significant
event by the Vatican newspaper, but it of course failed to
make any reference to the circumstances surrounding the
manuscript's suppression. The English Jesuit historian, James
Brodrick, in his interesting monograph, *Galileo: the Man,
his Work, his Misfortunes* (1964), has referred to the seventeenth-century Pope Urban VIII as "wrong and stupid," and
to Galileo as "one of the brightest spirits in human history
till, broken in health and terrorized, he even offered to add
new chapters to his *Dialogue* in refutation of the Copernican
views." The decision of Paul VI to make honorable amends
for a long-standing scientific scandal was certainly admirable.
If he had announced the rehabilitation with more fan-fare,
however, there would not have been the feeling that he was
still deferring to the Curial tradition of never admitting an
error.

A certain amount of anxiety, or at least concern, about the
heavy agenda of the Fourth Session was expressed in his talk
to the cardinals on July 28th. "The number and nature of the
themes to be dealt with, their gravity and complexity, as well
as the fact that with this session the Council will officially
come to an end and its immense follow-up problems . . . all
these things fill our spirit with great concern and anxious
solicitude. It is easy to imagine the burden they place upon
us." The Council was described as "a renovating and decisive
movement in the life of the Church," and spiritual vigilance
was needed "if we want the Council to realize its purposes."
What worried him particularly was a "spirit of disquiet and
radical reformism," not in harmony with the spirituality of
the Council, "both in the field of doctrine and in that of
discipline."

On August 4th he spoke of "strange and confused opinions" that had been reaching him, "causing us to reflect, often

in surprise and sorrow, since these opinions come not only from the many who have not the good fortune to possess our faith, but frequently from the best among the people of God, faithful and dear to us, where ordinarily the Church's doctrine is cultivated with fervent study and thought and honored by a fruitfulness of Christian life." These words naturally conjured up the thought that respected figures like Cardinals Suenens or Lercaro, Bishops Ancel or Helder Camara, theologians like Rahner, De Lubac, Philips, or possibly even Bishop Colombo, had been urging on him courses of action that he considered to be too daring for the moment. He went on to castigate "echoes of errors, ancient and modern, already condemned by the Church and excluded from her heritage of truth," as well as "would-be scientific affirmations that call in question principles, laws and traditions to which the Church is solidly bound and which it is not to be supposed that she will ever disclaim." It would probably not be wide of the mark to see here another reference to pressure for modification of the rule of clerical celibacy. "If these confused views and unwise proposals were followed," the Pope said, "far from deriving that new virtue and aspect which is the aim of the *aggiornamento* sought by the Second Vatican Council, the Church would end by acquiring the likeness of the world, whereas it is the world that awaits from the Church a ray of light . . ." It was necessary to have "trust in holy Church and in the Chair of Peter in particular." Only this tribunal (he did not distinguish between Church and papacy but seemed to be thinking more of the latter) could "guarantee to each and all of the People of God the same truths, the same certitude, the same way of speech, that of yesterday, today and tomorrow." Vatican Radio and *L'Osservatore Romano* commented copiously on this new papal definition of *aggiornamento*. An earlier comment of the Vatican organ on his July 28th talk was probably the classic remark of the year: "The Pope says exactly what he says, nothing more and nothing less!"

The one impression to be gained from all these talks was that Pope Paul was firmly committed to gradualism as a policy of action and to middle-of-the-road solutions as a goal, in an age calling more and more for radical solutions to radical problems. Yet those who saw him privately were convinced that while his tone might sound edgy at times, he was as calm and collected as ever. He assured Père Antoine Wenger, editor of *La Croix,* for example: "One must not attach too much importance to passing crises or to external repercussions which are only a phenomenal aspect of the Council." For Paul, "the eyes of faith seek to grasp the reality of the Council, which is a mystery defying appearances. The plan of the Holy Spirit is not immediately evident in the various activities which constitute the material element of the Council. But we are convinced that this is a time of grace, an important moment in the time of the Church. It is like a striking of the hour, preceded and followed by silence."*

The relative uncertainty that prevailed with regard to the Pope's intentions toward the Council was enhanced by his failure to take any effective action to reform the Roman Curia, despite repeated references to the problem—two years after his famous address to the Curia (September 21, 1963). Because the minority were not only hostile to the cause of reform but firmly entrenched in Curial positions from which they would be able to block the work of the Council, reform of that body became, as Hans Küng declared, one of the "touchstones of conciliar success." What is more, not all the Pope's references to the subject were very encouraging. In his address to the cardinals on December 24, 1964, for example, it did not sound as though he had any extensive reform in mind when he characterized the Curia as "the indispensable instrument, the well-ordered unity, the exemplary crown around the throne of St. Peter." Hopes were raised when it

* A Wenger, *Vatican II: Chronique de la troisième session,* Paris, 1965, p. 461, cited by G. Caprile, S.J., in an article in *L'Osservatore Romano,* June 28–29, 1965.

became known that a letter had been circulated in early January 1965 by Cardinal Cicognani to all heads of Curial offices asking them to accept the projected reforms in good grace and to be careful about becoming involved in controversy with persons who criticized the Curia "because experience shows that such arguments tend to harm the Curia rather than help it." This could be interpreted as a mild reminder that the Pope wanted no more belligerent replies like Cardinal Ottaviani's rejoinder to Cardinal Frings on the floor of the Council. It could also be read as a muzzling of such people as Monsignor Romeo, Archbishop Staffa and others who in the early days of the Council had not hesitrated to equate attacks on the Curia with attacks on the very structure and foundations of the Church. In any case, since that time the leading spokesmen for the Curia have tended to keep their irritation to themselves and not make a public issue of it, except in the case of Cardinal Ottaviani who still allowed himself an occasional riposte. It was regarded as significant that Cicognani had pointed out "defects that were bound to occur in an organization as ancient as the Curia." Rather extensive information about the details of the projected reform were published by the Italian Catholic weekly *Vita* in its February 5, 1965 issue, but nothing was done to implement them.

It was inevitable that this lack of action should suggest that the Curial party around the Pope were much more powerful than they perhaps were in reality. The words and actions of certain Curial figures also seemed to be at variance with the policy of moderation and conciliation the Pope was trying to pursue. In a statement during the summer Cardinal Ottaviani declared himself as flatly opposed to the policy of carrying on a dialogue with communists and atheists which Pope Paul had espoused, in very guarded language of course, in his encyclical *Ecclesiam suam*. (The cardinal was to reverse himself somewhat, in a later interview, and declare that he was enchanted by the word *dialogue:* "Yes, yes . . . dialogue, a beautiful word. I like it.") In the spring the Pope had established a new Secretariat for Non-Believers, under Cardinal König of Vienna, to try and find a "basis for accommodation" with communists, atheists and all other non-believers. Ottaviani then added this revelation to our store of knowledge: "Let it never be forgotten that communists hold principles that are diametrically opposed to the Church."

More promising was the progress being made on other fronts. In spite of the momentary upset accompanying the close of the Third Session, the forward march of the ecumenical spirit in the Church Universal was not seriously impeded. So far as the Catholic side was concerned, this was due primarily to the ubiquitous activity of Cardinal Bea and his helpers in the Secretariat for Promoting Christian Unity. The fragile-looking, eighty-four year old German cardinal, who more than anybody else seemed to embody the true Johannine spirit, had in the course of a relatively short time made personal contact with almost every major Christian confession and seemed to be continually turning up at universities and cultural centers, from Harvard to Madrid, from Bombay to Patras. An agreement was reached to establish a joint commission to carry on formal discussions between the World Council of Churches and the Catholic Church. Similar agreements were made with the Lutheran and Presbyterian Churches, on various levels. The Pope exchanged Easter messages with the various eastern patriarchs, including Athenagoras I of Constantinople and Alexei of Moscow, both of whom were visited by special papal missions, while Athenagoras sent a delegation to explain the decisions of the Pan-Orthodox Conference to the Pope, a step hailed by the latter as "marking a new stage in relations between Rome and the East."

Cardinal Alfrink, of Utrecht, once declared: "In Holland my position sometimes compels me to warn against exaggerations. On the other hand I can and must speak a different language outside the country where the thinking of people has lagged behind"—Dutch Catholics have not only not lagged, but scored two significant triumphs over the Holy Office. In 1963 the chaplain of Catholic students at the University of Amsterdam, Father J. Van Kilsdonk, S.J., was censured for a speech he made the previous October before the St. Adalbert's Society. He claimed that the apostasy of Dutch intellectuals from the Catholic Church was due primarily to the reactionary attitudes of the Roman Curia. The Holy Office demanded that he be relieved of his post, but the Dutch hierarchy refused to bow to this order. After personal contacts with Cardinal Ottaviani, the Bishop of Haarlem announced on January 2, 1963 that "while the Holy Office continued to disapprove of the way in which Father Van Kilsdonk had spoken, in view of the steps already taken by the authorities in Holland and the ensuing controversy, the Holy Office allowed the bishop to take whatever measures he considered appropriate." A statement subsequently issued by the Dutch bishop declared simply that Father Van Kilsdonk was being retained in his chaplaincy.

A great deal of publicity attended this case. Another situation had been developing behind the scenes before it suddenly came to light in 1964 owing to an indiscretion. It concerned a Dutch woman psychiatrist, Dr. Anna Terruwe, whom the Holy Office accused in 1950 of giving professional advice contrary to Catholic morality. Many of her patients were seminarians and priests. At the request of the Holy Office the Dutch hierarchy questioned her about her doctoral thesis and teaching, but came to the conclusion that the charges against her were unfounded. Some time after this decision the Dutch Jesuit Father Sebastian Tromp, an official of the Holy Office, made at least two visits of investigation to Holland but did not bother to speak to the principal persons involved. Instead the Holy Office in 1956 warned the Dutch hierarchy against erroneous teachings attributed to Dr. Terruwe, without naming her, and then issued an order forbidding seminarians, priests and religious, to consult women psychiatrists. About the same time the Redemptorist Father Duynstee, professor of civil law at the University of Nijmegen and an adviser to Dr. Terruwe, was relieved of his post and ordered to Rome.

The then Archbishop Alfrink and the Dutch bishops demanded the revocation of these measures and the rehabilitation of those whose good names had been impugned by the actions of the Holy Office. One result of Alfrink's intervention was the postponement of his promotion to cardinal until March 1960, after the Dutch papers complained bitterly that he had been passed over twice in the December consistories of 1958 and 1959.

The whole affair became known when the Dutch Catholic progressive journal *De Volkskrant* (October 1964) published a petition which Dr. Terruwe had sent to the Pope, the Dutch bishops, and the Holy Office, demanding that favorable action be taken in her case. Finally, Cardinal Alfrink was able to announce on April 9, 1965, that conversations between himself and the Holy Office had led to the following: "The Holy Office had been concerned from the first with ideas and methods rather than with individuals. If the reputations of any individuals had suffered meanwhile, the Holy Office regretted this very much. In particular it was sorry that any harm had been done to the professional reputation of Dr. Terruwe. It was now completely certain of her Catholic outlook and convinced that her writings, based on sound principles, could be of great help both to priests and to others." One of the things that had apparently shocked the consultors of the Holy Office was her attempt to reconcile the teaching of Thomas Aquinas with Freud, which she had done successfully in the opinion of Dr. Van Loo, a prominent professor and doctor at the University of Nijmegen. Meanwhile, Father Duynstee was quietly allowed to return to his post.

As the French weekly *Informations Catholiques Internationales* pointed out, the case of Dr. Terruwe was probably unique, or nearly so, in the annals of the Holy Office. Individuals had been quietly rehabilitated in the past, condemned works had been withdrawn from the famous *Index of Forbidden Books,* but without publicity. Dr. Terruwe has since published an autobiographical account of the whole affair, pointing out the fact that despite definite Catholic moral teaching regarding the obligation to make restitution in cases of calumny, she has received no such offers from responsible members of the Holy Office.

Another hopeful note was the gathering of Jesuit superiors and delegates in Rome in the Spring of 1965 for the election of a new superior general. The Jesuits form the largest religious Order in the Catholic Church with some thirty thousand members. This meeting proved to be almost a Council in miniature. After some two months of frank discussion, the delegates agreed to adjourn while awaiting the Vatican Council's decisions before drawing up a new look for the Order. The man they selected for their new General (known sometimes as the "Black Pope") was a fifty-nine-year-old former Spanish medical student, Pedro Arrupe, who was in charge of Jesuit novices outside Hiroshima at the time when the first atomic bomb was dropped. When the Jesuit university in Tokyo was restored after the war, he increased its enrollment to several thousand students. In the first press conference ever given by a Jesuit General (June 14, 1965), Father Arrupe commented on the relevancy of the ideas of Teilhard de Chardin. While admitting that there were dubious aspects about Teilhard's thought, his respect for facts in the physical and theological orders, as well as exemplary resignation under implied censure, revealed him as a man of his times and a model Christian. Hidebound Romanists were astonished at this statement, in view of the *monitum* issued by the Holy Office on Teilhard's writings as late as 1962. There was a certain parallel in fact with the case of Thomas Aquinas, whose works were condemned by the thirteenth-century Archbishop of Canterbury, Robert Kilwardby, on a visitation to Oxford. St. Thomas was also looked upon askance by the syndics of the University of Paris, before being universally acknowledged as orthodox.*

The Coordinating Commission met three times to review the agenda of the Fourth Session before its opening, on September 14th: on December 30, 1964, May 11 and September 13, 1965.** At the May meeting it reviewed and approved the revised texts submitted by the various commissions which had held formal meetings for this purpose as follows: Jan. 25–30, Commission for the Apostolate of the Laity; March 29–April 7, Mixed Commission on Doctrine and the Laity; March 29–April 5, Commission for Missions; March 29–April 6, Commission for Discipline of the Clergy and Christian People; April 6–May 4, Commission for Seminaries and Studies and Christian Education; April 27–May 4, Commission for Religious. The Secretariat for Promoting Christian Unity met February 18–March 9 and May 9–15. The Pope approved the texts on May 28, and on June 12 it was announced by the Secretary General that five texts were being sent to the bishops for their examination, viz. Religious Liberty, Schema 13, Missions, Priestly Life and Apostolate of the Laity, the first four of which would be debated at the Fourth Session. The bishops already had the text of Divine Revelation, distributed before the end of the Third Session. In a departure from customary procedure, it was announced at the same time that the revised texts of five other documents,

* Misgivings about Teilhard de Chardin were not likely to be dissipated all at once just because Arrupe had words of cautious praise for him. About the same time the theologian Charles Journet, raised to the cardinalate in January 1965, was writing in an issue of *Studi Cattolici:* "The fault I find in Teilhard is that he has altered—however unwittingly and innocently—not a philosophy, but the very doctrine of the Church." Journet maintains that he has lost sight of the transcendental quality of the Incarnation. *The Catholic Messenger,* June 3, 1965.

** On the latter occasion the meeting was unusually prolonged, lasting from 5 P.M. until 1:10 A.M. The question of a new voting procedure was discussed. *L'Avvenire d'Italia,* Sept. 14, 1965.

viz. Pastoral Office of Bishops, Religious Life, Priestly Formation (Seminaries), Christian Education, and Non-Christians were not being sent to the bishops but would be handed to them after the Session began. The explanation given was that these documents did not have to be discussed, merely voted on, but the real reason seems to have been that the rest were kept back in order to render less conspicuous the retention of the altered text of Non-Christians, so as to control the controversy over this document and avoid a repetition of the previous year's experience.*

The Pope issued an Apostolic Exhortation to the bishops on August 28th, in which he expressed his hope not only that the proceedings would be "orderly and profitable" but that the "hearts of the bishops would remain open to the delicate, powerful, secret and irresistible influence of the Spirit of Truth," while at the same time informing them that in the afternoon of the opening day, September 14th, the Feast of the Exaltation of the Cross, he would lead a penitential procession carrying the relic of the true cross from S. Croce in Gerusalemme to the Lateran Basilica, and calling for a "wave of prayer" for the success of the Council.

The Pope's third encyclical, *Mysterium Fidei* on the eucharist, was published the weekend before the Fourth Session opened. Some of his advisers seem to have persuaded him that there was a threat to the integrity of the Catholic faith in the current controversy among Dutch, Belgian and French theologians over eucharistic theology. Publication of the document, intended for early August, was postponed until just before the Council convened so that it would have maximum impact. It certainly did; it infuriated the Dutch. While there was nothing exceptional in its presentation, by insinuating that the faith was threatened from nameless quarters it put the finger on those countries where everybody knew

* *L'Osservatore Romano,* May 13, 1965 and June 13, 1965.

discussion was going on. One Dutch observer in Rome summed up the effect: "It was like using a sledgehammer to crack a nut." The *Corriere della Sera,* considered liberal, made the outrageous editorial comment that "The Pope has finally and solemnly declared the inviolability of eucharistic dogma and put an end to all symbolic explanations, pernicious Hegelianism, *pastiches à la* Teilhard de Chardin, and all left-leaning reformist tendencies lurking in the Church." One paper ran a banner headline: POPE CONDEMNS HOLLAND. Cardinal Alfrink, of Utrecht, Holland, lost no time in refuting such libellous charges and defending both the good name of Dutch theologians and the orthodoxy of the Dutch Catholic Church, in a press conference in Rome crowded with journalists. His conference inspired a new headline: "CARDINAL ALFRINK'S OFFENSIVE AGAINST ROMAN CURIA." *De Bazuin,* the monthly periodical of the Dutch Dominican Order, seems to have had the last word. It not only questioned both the tone and content of the encyclical because they created the impression that a grave heresy existed in countries like Holland, where there had been controversy over the eucharist, but went on to ask whether the present document was not proof that this type of papal pronouncement is now out of date. The assumption always has been that encyclical letters were equally valid and intelligible everywhere, but it declared flatly that this was clearly not the case.*

* In his somewhat loosely worded *obiter dicta* on the encyclical, Father Gregory Baum, S.A. (*Commonweal,* Oct. 15, 1965) put his finger on a sore point likely to be more and more discussed in the future, the extent to which the relations between the Holy See and the rest of the Church should be reconsidered in the light of the universally applicable principle of dialogue.

II

The Fourth Session Opens;
Creation of the Synod of Bishops;
Debate on Religious Liberty

✠

WHEN THE FOURTH SESSION convened on September 14th, there was little to indicate a change of climate. From the moment he entered the conciliar hall, however, Pope Paul indicated unmistakably his intention to direct the Council's work in his own personal fashion. He walked down the aisle of St. Peter's preceded by the prelates and clergy who were to take part in the opening ceremonies. Gone was the pageantry of red-coated lackeys and aristocratic chamberlains who usually cluttered up papal processions. The mass was con-celebrated by the Pope with 26 other bishops. The practiced eye of professional liturgists detected certain "Dantesque" departures from the established ritual (so-called because they reflected the personal innovations introduced by Archbishop Enrico Dante, for many years papal master of ceremonies before his "elevation" to the cardinalate). However it was made known that the daily masses opening each day's congregation would conform strictly to the norms laid down in the Constitution on the Liturgy (the masses were at first all in the Latin rite, mainly it seems in order to save time, but the custom was later resumed of varying the monotony by celebrating mass occasionally according to one of the colorful Eastern rites).

The Pope's new emphasis on greater simplicity was evident in this opening mass. Paul prefers to enter on foot, vested in a simple cope instead of the elaborate and unwieldy papal mantle, no longer wearing the tiara but only a mitre, like any other bishop. He carried a pastoral staff in the form of a cross which he is said to have designed himself.* An interesting feature was that the Pope chose to enthrone the Gospel himself, instead of delegating this to some other prelate, normally the Secretary General on opening and closing days. (Partly in order to save time and partly to enhance the symbolic significance of the ceremony, it was decided at the Fourth Session to combine the enthronement of the Gospel with the procession of the celebrant of the mass each morning, instead of having it follow the mass.) Another novelty was that the "obedience" of the cardinals and bishops which normally takes place before the enthronement of the Gospel took place after this rite, another example of Paul's eye for the symbolic. As one commentator noted, the whole opening ceremony seemed more like a "family get-together," the impression happily created by the rite of concelebration.

Instead of dealing with dogmatic and disciplinary questions, as had been expected, Paul's opening address began as a mild discourse on charity, the love that the Council should manifest toward God, toward the Church, and toward hu-

---

* For centuries the Popes have traditionally not used a crozier; whether in order to mark the difference between themselves and all other bishops or merely because the custom never took hold in Rome, is not clear. In any case, Pope Paul has decided to abandon a practice at variance with the spirit of the doctrine of collegiality.

manity. It was all the more effective for being unexpected. The Pope carefully refrained from touching on any of the matters before the Council, he said, because he did not want to be accused of compromising the bishops' freedom of discussion. Saving his good news for the last, he first announced that it was his intention to make a personal appeal for peace before the United Nations Assembly in New York in October. This was followed by the warmly applauded disclosure that he intended to establish the long-awaited Synod of Bishops desired by the Council.

The reaction to the Pope's talk was generally favorable. It was noted, for example, that the tone and emphasis of his remarks had been much less sharp than in some recent statements, such as his talk a few days earlier in the Catacombs in which he had compared the present persecution of the Church behind the Iron Curtain to the persecution of the early Church by the Roman emperors. Both in his remarks then and in the address to the Council, however, he insisted that instead of condemning, the Church must be concerned to express only feelings of love. The main theme of his address had obviously been chosen in order to provide a link with his predecessor, Pope John XXIII, who was never more guided by charity than when he was inspired to summon the Council. It also furnished a proper theme on which to end the Council. Far from being the routine affair that observers had predicted, Paul's address was actually one of the most significant pronouncements made at the Fourth Session.

The Synod of Bishops

On the following morning, as the Council Fathers were hurrying to their appointed places for the first business meeting of the session, Archbishop Felici's resonant voice suddenly rang out above all the hubbub announcing the arrival of Pope Paul. The Pope entered the basilica accompanied merely by two secretaries. After assisting at the daily mass, he took his place at the Council Presidents' table in a chair slipped in between those of Cardinals Tisserant and Tappouni. It was made known later that the chair would be left in this position, thus implying that the Pope intended to give effect to his desire to take a more active part in the proceedings. Cardinal Marella, president of the Council commission that had prepared the schema on the Pastoral Office of Bishops, immediately delivered a report in which it was announced that the long-promised Synod of Bishops was about to be promulgated. The Secretary General, Archbishop Felici, read the document, a papal decree or *motu proprio* entitled *Apostolica Sollicitudo*. As he finished there was a hearty round of applause. When on the previous day the Pope had declared his intention to proclaim the Synod "in the near future," almost nobody supposed that it would be done the very next day. After imparting his blessing and with a friendly gesture to the non-Catholic observer delegates, who joined in applauding him, the Pope left the council hall by the same side door by which he had arrived.

The title of the document was well chosen. *Sollicitudo* (care, concern) is a traditional term used by the Popes since at least the fifth century, to describe the collegial relationship between themselves and the rest of the bishops. What the document did was to establish a senate of bishops as papal advisers on a permanent basis, in response to repeated requests from the floor of the Council. Of greatest significance is the provision that the bulk of the membership is to be elected by the national or regional conferences of Catholic bishops throughout the world, for this is a step further in restoring the democratic process of electing bishops that prevailed in the early Church and that is still preserved in principle in the selection of Eastern-rite bishops. The Pope reserved the right to appoint only 15% of the total membership, stipulating that his nominees could be bishops or experts. Ten members are to be elected by the Generals of male religious orders located in Rome to represent their vast constituency; and a sort of preference is given to the Eastern patriarchs and "major archbishops and metropolitans"—at present they number about 12—who are to be *ex officio* members, counterbalancing the cardinal secretaries of Roman congregations—numbering 14—who are also *ex officio* members. The rest of the membership is to be elected according to a rather complicated system designed to effect some kind of balance between the different parts of the world. Conferences are entitled to elect one member for every 25 bishops, with no country (or region) allowed to have more than 4. Thus the United States, with close to 225 bishops, will have as many synod members as Italy, whose total population is approximately the same as the Catholic population of the United States. Moreover the document expressly recommends that bishops be chosen not because of their prestige or prudence but for their familiarity with a particular problem (*cognitio materiae*) in both its theoretical and practical aspects. The assembly's function will be primarily advisory or consultative, but on occasion it can have a deliberative capacity, in which case the Pope must ratify the decisions. As with ecumenical councils, he alone determines the time and place of meeting, and draws up the agenda.

Thus, in a deftly timed move, Pope Paul had acted to redeem part of his pledge to reorganize the central governmental structure of the Church in accordance with the wishes of the Council. (The other half of the pledge related to the reform of the Roman Curia.)

Far from being an innovation in the strict sense of the term, the establishment of the Synod marked a return to an earlier form of church government more in accord with its basic collegial nature as proclaimed in the Constitution on the Church. From the second century until at least the tenth, the principle of synodal government was well recognized in the Western Church. The famous Council of Nicaea (325), which defined the orthodox position in Christology against Arius, laid it down that provincial synods were to be held at stated intervals. The bishop of Rome, for example, frequently consulted with bishops visiting Rome or summoned from Italy and Sicily and deliberated with them about important matters, while at Constantinople from the fifth century onward the so-called *synodos endemousa* or permanent patriarchal synod was convoked at least annually. The system survives today in the permanent synods of the various Orthodox Churches. In the West, on the other hand, for a variety of historical reasons, the synodal principle was allowed to fall into abeyance.

The Curial view of the new organization was presented by Cardinal Marella in a press conference held a week later. He tried to minimize the importance of the term "Synod" as the designation for the new body, claiming that any other term such as "convention," "assembly," or "meeting" would have served as well; nevertheless the choice of this term appears to be highly significant and deliberate. "Synod" means the same thing as "council." It would have been impossible for Pope Paul to choose a more traditional and meaningful designation. "Senate" was ruled out, of course, because of its unsatisfactory secular connotations. The cardinal pooh-poohed the suggestion that there could be any conflict between the new Synod and the Roman Curia as "unthinkable," and his observation that the Curia would be only "too happy" to avail itself of the help of the roughly 160 bishops who would constitute the new Synod sounded too good to be true of that hitherto omnipotent organ of para-papal government. Bishops resent the idea of being treated as underlings by Roman functionaries, some of whom are of not very exalted hierarchical rank, as was repeatedly declared during the debate on the pastoral office of bishops at the Second Session. Although there can be no question of the "subordination" of one to the other—the Curia remains, as Cardinal Marella correctly pointed out, the "Secretary" of the Pope—it seems clear that the Roman congregations are in for a thorough housecleaning, both in function and personnel, now that the Council is over. In the inevitable rivalry between the two, much will depend on the collective or collegial influence which the Synod is able to exert—in the long run this may turn out to be considerable—and the attitude of the Pope himself, whether Paul or his successor.

After the Pope had left the council hall on Wednesday, the proceedings got under way with short speeches by Cardinal Tisserant, head of the Council Presidency, and Cardinal Agagianian, Moderator for the day. The former assured the Fathers that they would be allowed all the time necessary to transact the Council's business and that there would be no interference with freedom of speech. Nothing was said about the duration of the Session. It was noted with relief that the Secretary General limited himself in his various announcements to what was strictly necessary and refrained from indulging in the intimidating tactics of the opening of the Third Session the year before.

The Declaration on Religious Liberty

In accordance with Pope Paul's promise, made during the uproar at the close of the Third Session, the first item of business on the agenda was discussion of the revised text on Religious Liberty.* The version of the document (*Textus Prior*) debated at the Third Session (Sept. 23–25, 1964) had been so thoroughly altered in accordance with a plan suggested by the Pope's personal theologian, Bishop Carlo Colombo, that when the new version (*Textus emendatus*) came up for a preliminary vote, scheduled for November 19, 1964, the minority protested that it had been so changed as

---

* An original version of the document, forming Chap. V of the Decree on Ecumenism (*Textus Prior*), had been scheduled for debate at the Second Session, but formal discussion was postponed at the last minute, the document being considered only in connection with the general discussion of that Decree. The text debated in Sept. 1965 was the *third* version to come before the Fathers for this purpose.

to be no longer a revised text but an essentially new text. Therefore further debate must take place before it could be voted, according to the Rules.* The Council Presidency accepted their petition and the vote was postponed, a decision which Pope Paul refused to reverse. Advantage was taken of the interval between the Third and Fourth Sessions to revise the text still further and it was this latter version (*Textus re-emendatus*) that formed the basis for discussion on September 15, 1965.**

As Bishop De Smedt made clear in his *relatio,* the purpose of the present document was not to deal exhaustively with the whole range of problems that could be subsumed under the broad heading of religious liberty, but only one limited aspect of the problem, the question of civil liberty in religious matters, that is, the extent to which individuals or groups should be free from coercion in religious matters. More than 100 national constitutions now provided for religious liberty, compared with some 50 before 1947. It was therefore clear that modern man was becoming increasingly concerned with the problem of civil liberty in religious matters in keeping with a growing concern in the world over the right to personal freedom and responsibility. The thesis of the schema could be summarized in a series of propositions: 1) every man had a natural right not to be compelled by others to act *against* his conscience in religious matters; 2) he had a right not to be prevented from acting *according to* his conscience, whether in private or in public; 3) this right meant that he should be free to express his religious convictions; 4) this right was also subject to certain limitations. Most of the objections, Bishop De Smedt noted, were

* The booklet dispatched to the bishops in June 1965 contained the *Textus emendatus* and *Textus re-emendatus* printed in parallel columns, together with a *Relatio* listing the changes pro and con suggested by the bishops with respect to the former, and what the Secretariat had done about them in the later; and finally, a highly interesting anonymous *Pars Altera,* defending the schema and rebutting the contentions of the minority.

** The work of redrafting was largely done by Fr. J. C. Murray, S.J.

based on a misunderstanding of the Schema's purpose and scope; they tended to confuse the civil right to freedom in religious matters, with which it was concerned, with other forms of freedom, ontological, moral, psychological, etc., with which it did not attempt to deal.

The text was not divided into chapters but had four distinct parts: an opening section devoted to a Declaration of Principles (a new feature of the *Textus re-emendatus*); this was followed by a section on proofs from reason; a third section came next dealing with the "roots" of the idea in Divine Revelation and emphasizing that religious liberty could not be proved from Scripture, strictly speaking; and finally a concluding section. Bishop De Smedt declared that a number of Fathers had wanted an introductory statement about the broader issue of Catholic doctrine toward freedom *in* the Church, but the feeling of the Secretariat had been that while the suggestion had merit, it was beyond the scope of the limited objective they had set themselves and was beyond the competence of the Secretariat.

Cardinal Spellman, of New York, led off with an emphatic endorsement: "The schema is very pleasing and timely." It was essential for the Council to approve it so that all the world would know that the Catholic Church was in favor of religious liberty, a principle that could "give great impetus to ecumenism," and failure of the Council to approve it would give rise to doubts about the Church's sincerity. Cardinal Cushing, of Boston, not to be outdone by Spellman, was more detailed about the reasons why the document should be adopted and majestically swept aside all objections. Religious liberty was "solidly based on Catholic teaching," not on the subjective order as some had said, but on the objective order of truth. The promulgation of such a doctrine was a pastoral necessity today "of the first order for the whole world." There were dictatorial governments today in many places that restricted human liberty especially in religious matters; where men were denied the right to reli-

gious liberty, they were very often denied other civil liber-
ties as well. With St. Paul and Pope Paul, the Church must
proclaim the "Gospel of freedom." He concluded with a
ringing, "I am not afraid of the gospel of freedom. There are
dangers everywhere but one of the greatest is the denial of
liberty. We must preach the whole Gospel and approval of
this Declaration would be a beginning."

As might be expected, Cardinal Ritter of St. Louis was
also wholeheartedly in favor of approval. "The schema leaves
nothing to be desired except a prompt approbation and promulgation." The eyes of the whole world were turned toward
Rome, he said, and neither charity, nor justice, nor fidelity
would allow of any delay. But he was also, characteristically,
more aware of the shadows on the scene. Approval was a
matter of justice, he explained, because "our separated brothers in Christ" have suffered in certain Catholic countries
owing to disregard for the principles stated in the Declaration. Fidelity to the work of the Council also required the
passage of this document, otherwise the decrees on the
Church and on Ecumenism would remain "worthless and
deprived of any sense."

Approval was also voiced by the two German cardinals,
Frings of Cologne and Jäger of Paderborn, but in a more
nuanced vein. The former felt that the whole section dealing
with the reasons from natural law could be omitted, because
it was not up to the Council but to theologians and philosophers to adduce arguments based on natural law. He also
noted that in Part III No. 9 there seemed to be a confusion
between different concepts of liberty. The freedom we have
from Christ and the freedom given us by the State were not
one and the same thing. And the remarks made about the
doctrine and practice of religious liberty in the history of the
Church were out of place and inexact. He also expressed
puzzlement about the language and style which were not such
as one expected to find in a conciliar document. On the other
hand, Cardinal Jäger found the order in which the argu-

ments were presented good and calculated to appeal to non-Christians. Moreover, by distinguishing between religious liberty in the civil order and moral freedom, the schema avoided the complicated question of the erroneous conscience in bad faith because this problem did not exist in the juridical order: the state could not judge consciences and had to presume that all citizens acted in good faith in religious matters —an important point which the minority continually overlooked or ignored. More enthusiasm was shown by Cardinal Silva Henriquez of Santiago, Chile, who was particularly pleased by the pastoral implications of the treatment of religious liberty in the text. The new spirit of freedom which it breathed would not open the door to relativism, as some had maintained, but would promote a greater sense of responsibility. It offered a clear-cut statement of Catholic teaching on the matter and avoided certain explanations that might raise more questions than they would solve. Care must be taken, however, to see that under the pretext of freedom, no one took advantage of the Declaration to refuse necessary obedience. But we should be more interested in promoting the proper use of liberty than in preventing abuses of liberty.

One of the notable interventions in favor of the document was delivered by Cardinal Heenan two days after the opening of the debate. The cardinal was in good form, wide-ranging, caustic, and slightly inconsistent in the impression he made. The main burden of his talk was the inviolable right of every man to obey his conscience. "This is the whole argument of the Declaration," he asserted. It was absurd to charge that Catholics judged religious liberty and tolerance according to two distinct standards, depending upon whether they were on top or not. It was regrettably true that "in certain places" Protestants had suffered persecution at the hands of Catholics. The ecumenical implications of religious belief were a relatively modern discovery. "Practically nobody ever considered—much less conceded—the right of a man to follow his conscience" in the old days of *cuius regio eius religio.*

"It was the custom of both sides to burn heretics," he noted, and said it would be ironical if the Council did not follow the Pope's lead when he defended the right of every man to follow the dictates of his conscience and practice his religion freely in a recent talk at the Catacombs. "We must back his example and precept because the world is watching us and will judge the fourth and final session of the Council by the way we treat this Declaration." And he reminded the bishops of Cardinal Newman's famous quip when asked about toasting the Pope at dinner. "First I would give a toast to conscience—only then would I toast the Pope," Newman said. It would also be ironical if Catholics did not set an example by helping to banish religious intolerance and hatred, so that people would once again say as they said in the early Church: "See how these Christians love one another!"

Quite a number of speakers while favorable to the schema and desiring its passage were not content merely with praise but launched into a series of modifications they wanted introduced. The effect of some of their interventions, unfortunately, was to create the impression that the text was being more severely criticized than was the case. Cardinal Urbani, Patriarch of Venice, was typical of this group and set the tone for this approach, as it were. His favorable, but critical, speech on the first day was regarded as highly significant coming from one whom the Pope had recently appointed to the board of bishops in temporary charge of the Italian Episcopal Conference in place of the single chairmanship of Cardinal Siri.* Not that the cardinal could claim to speak for the Italian episcopate as such, but he certainly spoke for its *sanior pars*. The text was "substantially satisfactory" because it was both timely and true. The question of religious liberty was "in a sense new, and it cannot be solved by the simple and mere recalling of the past teaching of the Church." He thus disposed of the frequent contention of the minority that it

* *L'Osservatore Romano,* August 20, 1965.

was enough to appeal to the teachings of Gregory XVI or Leo XIII. "The documents of past Popes," Cardinal Urbani went on, "from Gregory XVI to John XXIII show that the doctrine has been progressively enriched. The teaching on civil liberty in religious matters is a part of that progress." It is difficult to see how the cardinal could have expressed himself more clearly on one of the underlying issues, namely whether the present teaching on religious liberty was an instance of real doctrinal progress or development. It was significant also that he saw fit to mention Pope John XXIII. The minority generally preferred to limit their appeals to Pius XII, or even Leo XIII, implying that recent Popes had somehow swerved from the straight and narrow path of orthodoxy. In order to make it perfectly clear that the document had a limited objective, he suggested that the subtitle be changed to read "concerning *civil* liberty in religious matters." He also wanted the distinction between the juridical and moral aspects of religious liberty brought out more clearly, as well as the fact that religious truth is the one possessed and taught by the Catholic Church. The wording of the schema was intentionally low-key here so as not to antagonize non-Catholics or non-Christians. (Schema: "Therefore [religious liberty] leaves untouched Catholic doctrine concerning the one true religion and one Church of Christ.")

Cardinal Meouchi was dissatisfied with the overall approach of the document as too theoretical and abstract. He wanted the presentation to start from concrete considerations first and gradually work up to an exposition of principles. Part III, attempting to justify religious freedom on scriptural or theological grounds, was felt to be awkward and not really necessary by Bishop Elchinger, of Strasbourg, because it would be unintelligible to non-Christians. He also wanted it explicitly said that the right to religious liberty could be predicated analogically of all values that could be called transcendental, otherwise non-Catholics "will doubt our sincerity and believe that when political conditions are favor-

able to her the Church will repudiate this teaching on liberty." Finally he proposed that the Declaration should end
with a fraternal invitation to all men of good will to cooperate in promoting and defending the rights of persons and
communities to religious freedom. An interesting suggestion
was put forward by Bishop Rupp of Monaco which, if it had
been followed, would have greatly simplified the work of the
Secretariat, namely to adopt the seven points of the World
Council of Churches' recent declaration on religious liberty.
In general, many criticized the present schema as too long
and complicated and it would certainly have been a good
idea if a shorter text had been proposed and adopted, but experience showed that such an ideal was probably not attain-
able under the circumstances. The Council had first to thresh
out the theoretical basis for a more simplified statement.

A number of speakers called for greater precision in the
use of language and greater clarity about the limited purpose
of the Declaration, such as Bishop Muldoon, Auxiliary of
Sydney, Australia. Archbishop Kozlowiecki of Lusaka, Zambia called for a revision of the citations from papal documents
in the light of Cardinal Urbani's remarks and wanted greater
emphasis on the rights and authority of God to offset misunderstandings about the nature of religious liberty ("the
Council needs to speak much more clearly about a right conscience, i.e. a conscience formed objectively according to the
will of God"); and Bishop Muñoz Vega, Auxiliary of Quito,
Ecuador, maintained that there was a real danger of confusion in Latin America between freedom of religion and freedom of conscience and pointed to the impact of Protestant
proselytism there. A fundamental objection, not to the idea
of religious liberty as such but to the method of presenting it,
was raised by Bishop Ancel, Auxiliary of Lyons, France,
speaking in the name of more than 100 French bishops. He
wanted the "ontological foundation of religious liberty"
made perfectly clear. "This connection between religious
freedom and the obligation to seek after truth, which is no-

where expressed in a positive manner in the text, should be included in Art. 2, the nucleus of the Declaration, which is the only part that will come to the attention of the ordinary man. Such an addition will give assurance that the schema is not favoring the growing indifference and subjectivism of our day." This touched on one of the principal points that had divided the drafters of the proposal: the French generally being in favor of a more theoretical approach to the problem, Americans and others favoring a more pragmatic line.*

Considerable misgivings were expressed about the paragraph inserted to safeguard the privileged position enjoyed by religious communities in certain countries. Its terms were applicable not only to countries like Spain or Italy with which the Holy See had concordats, but countries like England and Scandinavia where the local Churches were established by law. At the Third Session Cardinal Ottaviani had claimed that the whole concordat system of the Holy See was at stake. Unless the legitimacy of the "confessional state" were recognized, at least in those places where such arrangements were already in effect, the floodgates would be opened to laicism and the ultimate triumph of communism. This point of view ignored what was going on in most of the civilized world as well as the trend, in papal diplomacy, to move away gradually from too close an adherence to the concordat system, nevertheless the Secretariat considered it prudent to leave the provision in. Speaking in the name of the Dutch episcopate, Cardinal Alfrink warned the Council against the danger of speaking in too positive a way about the privileged position enjoyed by any religious community and said that it would be more appropriate to use conditional language. Cardinal Rossi of San Paulo, Brazil seconded this suggestion. Several speakers wanted the provision removed altogether:

* Fr. J. C. Murray, S.J., the chief spokesman for the pragmatic approach and principal drafter of the version of the document before the Council, revealed at the Press Panel (Sept. 20) that he had been in touch with French correspondents during the course of the summer and come to an agreement with them about this particular issue.

Archbishop Lourdusamy of Bangalore, India, Archbishop Ziadé of Beirut, and Bishop Doumith of Sarba, both of Lebanon. The latter in particular noted that the language was equivocal and could open the door to discrimination: "A confessional state among Christians means no more than special honor and privileged status for a particular religion, but in non-Christian areas this idea is used as a means of religious discrimination." Cardinal McCann of Capetown, South Africa wanted the point made clearer that a privileged status did not mean that any special burdens could be placed on those who did not belong to the religion or confession in question. Not with reference to this point specifically but speaking in general, Bishop Lokuang of Tainan, China insisted that the text should contain a clear statement that "a Catholic state is better than an indifferent or neutral state" (though it is difficult to see how such a principle could be made applicable in his homeland), while Cardinal Browne of the Curia was even more emphatic: "In a Catholic state, those in authority must safeguard this [Catholic] faith because in it consists the supreme good of all citizens. The spreading of another religion in a Catholic state is a violation of public morality and harms the right that Catholics enjoy not to have their faith endangered."

Another problem with which both those who were for and those who were against the schema attempted to wrestle was that of the proper limits to religious freedom. It was agreed that it was not the proper function of the state to interfere with or determine religious matters, which were beyond its province, but to protect the right to religious liberty and free expression of religious ideas within certain limits. However, the difficulty was how to define those limits and according to what standard. The vague juridical language of the schema was not likely to have much appeal for those who were accustomed to the precise language of theology, but these critics were at a loss to suggest any better alternative. The schema said that the exercise of religion must be allowed and "not prohibited by any coercive intervention of the civil authority, unless it disturbs the public peace, or public morality, or infringes the rights of others. That is, the legal principle is to be observed, that the freedom of man is to be respected as far as possible and is not to be curtailed except when and in so far as necessary."

This meager definition of the "common good" was a frequent target. Archbishop Hallinan reminded the bishops, however, that it was thoroughly in accord with "the recently evolved doctrine of the Church concerning the constitutional state" on which the principle of religious freedom itself rested. Bishop Añoveros Ataun of Cadiz, Spain held that because the notion of "public order" was so all-embracing, including theological as well as moral and purely juridical elements, the "whole text should be quickly submitted to an appropriate subcommission which could provide a more acceptable schema," particularly as the Secretariat was thought by some of the Fathers to be partial to the separated brethren on whose behalf it had proposed the document for the Council's consideration. This suggestion made on the fourth day of the debate was correctly regarded as a thinly veiled move intended to kill the schema.

There was nothing subtle however about the onslaught directed against the document by those who were its bitterest critics. They could be called the "toleration school," because they were unable to get beyond the thinking of the last century. As Father Murray pointed out, they were not opposed to the institution of religious liberty as such but rather to "the affirmation of progress in doctrine that an affirmation of religious freedom necessarily entails." Their spokesman, Cardinal Siri, put it thus: "The schema affirms religious freedom for all religious communities, and so also for those that deviate from the truth, and even for immoral and sanguinary ones. But God only tolerates and promises to punish such abuses of freedom. We cannot defend what God only tolerates." According to Bishop Gasbarri there was a "true conflict between supporters of this theory of right [expounded in the Declaration] and those who uphold the theory of toleration." He maintained that the question of the rights of an errone- ous conscience did enter into the discussion, because "civil law cannot prescind from considering the truth and error without falling into juridical positivism and existential func- tionalism." The present text would open the door to indif- ferentism. The only solution was to rely on the "traditional doctrine of the Popes" which, in the bishop's estimation, fully supported the theory of toleration. Cardinal Siri was more circumspect in his language regarding this latter point, though he fully agreed with the speaker: "Whether the schema really accords with the teaching on religious freedom found in theological sources and in the Popes should be more deeply explored." He was certain, however, that if the doc- trine of toleration were changed, "we will be undermining theological and our own authority." The opposition had ap- parently not taken the trouble to examine the *Pars Altera* appended to the schema which dealt with most of their objections, for they kept repeating that the schema's intention was to separate religious freedom from truth and this would promote indifferentism. Cardinal Ruffini, for example, as- serted that while the Declaration of Human Rights adopted by the United Nations in 1948 was commendable because it attempted to preserve civil harmony between various re- ligious groups, "it smacked of agnostic indifferentism," a charge that could equally well be levelled against the present schema. He was particularly worried about the possible effects of the Council's Declaration on the concordat between Italy and the Holy See, insisting that both Pius IX and Pius XII had been equally opposed to separation of Church and state, which was not true historically, and vaunting the fact that Catholics enjoyed certain privileges under the concordat which made the latter vulnerable to communist attack.

With a touch of irony in his voice, Bishop Velasco said that "the glorious minority had been over-ridden by the majority" and disregarded because they had remained constant to the teaching of the Church regarding toleration. "We must demand recognition of minority rights," he said, "not only in words but also in deeds. When there is question of a search for truth, it is not the number or quality of the persons involved that counts but the substance of the matter itself." The majority contended that the minority had not understood the text. If this were so, "after long years of study and experience, what chance was there of its being understood by the vast majority of the faithful?" he asked. The broader issue of "the cloven hoof of freedom within the Church" was what worried Archbishop Nicodemo, of Bari.* The text must be amended to show clearly that the Church had authority to "determine for the faithful the purpose and limits of liberty in religious matters." Otherwise there was danger the document might be used to claim a false freedom within the Church. Bishop Carli of Segni fastened on the difficulty of reconciling the notion of religious liberty with some of the evidence from Scripture, claiming that the presentation ignored Tradition, "perhaps because it was sensed that the doctrine proposed was contrary to Tradition." He too purposely ignored what the text itself said, and what the *relator* and other speakers had repeatedly emphasized, with regard to this point.

Contrary to expectations, most of the Spanish bishops who spoke were heavily in opposition. The progress that seemed to have been registered in this quarter since the last session apparently had turned out to be illusory. The danger of proselytism was their main fear, though they felt also that indifferentism would be the end result. It was a mistake to believe that freedom for non-Catholic proselytism would aid the spread of the Gospel, according to Cardinal de Arriba y Castro of Tarragona. "Only the *private* practice of non-Catholic religions could be free; no religion, however, should

* R. Nowell, in *The Tablet*, Sept. 25, 1965.

be forced upon any man." "With the doctrine of the schema," Archbishop Garcia de Sierra y Mendez of Burgos maintained, "it is impossible to defend the purity of the faith and the unity of the Church because the door would be open to the spread of all kinds of error. We cannot, in order to please men, afford to do things that would not please God." He further blamed what he called "the modern itch for all kinds of liberty" and termed the schema "opportunistic" and conducive to "humanism." "Naturalistic humanism" was also one of the faults found in the text by Bishop del Campo y de la Barcena of Calahorra who claimed that "the argumentation of the schema is based on two socio-religious phenomena: religious pluralism and the constitutions of many modern states. But such civil institutions are not worthy to be made the basis of the doctrinal decisions of a Council." It would be the equivalent of proclaiming to the world that the Catholic Church was only one among many, according to Archbishop Alvim Perreira of Lourenço Marques, Mozambique. The entire schema was felt to suffer from a basic weakness, in the opinion of Cardinal Dante of the Curia because it appeared to be based on the nineteenth-century liberalism of Lamennais and Montalembert. If religious liberty were to be restricted only by considerations based on the common good and public order, it would be open to various interpretations of these concepts. In a communist state, for example, ideas like peace and civil rights would be given a completely different meaning from their usual connotations. Archbishop Morcillo of Madrid, and Archbishop Modrego y Casaus of Barcelona, both felt that in places the schema contradicted explicitly or implicitly the teaching of the Popes and this point must be cleared up.

This question of whether the doctrine was or was not in conformity with papal teaching exercised many of the Fathers and became a kind of touchstone by which to separate the sheep from the goats. After launching into a tirade to the effect that "the roots of this doctrine are to be found in such eighteenth-century philosophers as Hobbes, Locke, Rousseau and others," Archbishop Lefebvre concluded: "The text contradicts the teaching of Leo XIII as directed against the above-mentioned philosophers." It was clear to Cardinal Ottaviani that the document must be revised in the light of the teaching of the modern Popes, but he mentioned only Leo XIII and Pius XII. Both Father John Courtney Murray in an exhaustive lecture* treating the whole subject delivered the opening day of the debate, and Cardinal Shehan of Baltimore, speaking in the Council on September 20th, had no difficulty in showing the absurdity of trying to prove anything by appealing to some Popes while ignoring others, and the impossibility of making sense of the present as well as other conciliar documents, unless allowance were made for doctrinal development or progress.

After the first few days of debate the tide of criticism seemed to be running so heavily against Religious Liberty that Bishop Maloney, Auxiliary of Louisville, Kentucky, was persuaded to voice a strong support for the Declaration on the part of the Auditors of the Council and their hopes for its speedy approval and promulgation. Behind the scenes the minority were bending every effort to postpone or prevent a vote altogether, spreading rumors to the effect that since the Council was so hopelessly divided on the issue it would be unwise to have a vote, or there was no need for a vote, depending upon the strategy being pushed at the moment. They were unable to control the imponderables, however. One of these was the strong impression made on the bishops by a number of speakers from behind the Iron Curtain, who stressed the importance of the Declaration in the struggle against communism, a theme broached by Cardinal Heenan. Support for the text by the Polish bishops was voiced by Archbishop Baraniak of Poznan, and Archbishop Wojtyla of Kraków. Cardinal Slipyi, speaking in the name of the Ukrain-

* Murray's lecture at the Dutch Documentation Center, Rome, *The Catholic Messenger*, October 7, 1965.

ian Episcopal Conference, stressed the "opportuneness of the doctrine of religious liberty" in view of present-day religious persecutions in communist countries, while Cardinal Wyszynski declared flatly, "A clear Declaration must come from this Council in the name of the teaching Church," in order to assist the Church in its struggle with communist states. The testimony of the newly created and liberated Cardinal Beran of Prague, in favor of approval, was probably the most decisive of all. "From the very moment when freedom of conscience was radically restricted in my country," he said, "I was witness not only to grave dangers to the faith, but also to serious temptations to hypocrisy and other moral vices that the oppression of conscience brought in its wake." Experience taught that oppression of conscience, even when intended for the good of the true faith, was pernicious. "Thus the Church in my country now seems to be making painful expiation for the sins committed in the past against freedom of conscience in the name of the Church." He cited particularly the burning of the Bohemian reformer John Hus in the fifteenth century by the Council of Constance, and the forcible re-Catholicization of the majority of the Bohemian people in the seventeenth century under the Habsburg rulers. These acts in reality wounded the Church, because the "trauma" hidden in the hearts of the people was a grave impediment to spiritual progress and gave the enemies of the Church plenty of material for agitation. He did not mention, but could have, the wholesale departure from the Catholic Church of over a million Czechs after the dissolution of the Austro-Hungarian Monarchy at the end of the First World War. "History warns us that we must declare the principle of religious liberty and freedom of conscience clearly and without any restrictions."

Another impressive reply to the objectors, based on experience, was delivered by Cardinal Cardijn who spoke in the light of his 60 years among young workers. "This Declaration would arouse great hopes among the younger generation," he declared. "The Church cannot expect religious liberty when she is in a minority unless she practices it when she is in the majority." The charges that it would give rise to indifferentism, amount to a surrender of Catholic teaching regarding the one true Church, and contribute to the spread of error were effectively rebutted in forceful speeches by Cardinal Lefebvre of Bourges, and Cardinal Journet, the latter noting that it was the task of the Church nowadays "to fight error with the arms of light rather than the arms of force."

On Tuesday, September 21, exactly a week after the opening of the Fourth Session, the Council surmounted an important hurdle. At precisely 10:45 on that morning, the presiding Moderator, Cardinal Agagianian, called for a standing vote to close debate on the controversial Religious Liberty schema. While sudden, the Moderator's decision was not altogether unexpected. In four and a half days of debate 62 speeches had been heard. In the judgment of most observers the decision could have come earlier, the prolongation of the debate being due to the Pope's extreme willingness to accommodate the opposition. There was an awkward lapse, for a few minutes, before the *relator* Bishop De Smedt could be found to sum up and assure the Fathers that their suggestions would all be taken into account.* The situation was dramatic because for several days it had been uncertain whether there would actually be a vote or not. The fear was that the document might simply be remanded to committee for amendment, without any preliminary vote guaranteeing that it would not be substantially changed. Opponents of the measure had partially succeeded in creating the impression that it might not win a respectable majority (some reports had it that the *non placets* might be as high as 500). It was said that some of them, including several cardinals, had petitioned

* Bishop Grotti, speaking the next day in the name of 70 Fathers, adjured the bishops to take careful note of what Bishop De Smedt said and see that he lived up to his promise!

the Pope not to allow any vote and that they wanted the document given to a subcommission for rewriting.* This would have meant a signal defeat for the English-speaking bishops in particular, who had to some extent staked the reputation of the Council on passage of the Religious Liberty schema.

It was known that at a joint meeting of the Council leadership (Coordinating Commission, Moderators, Secretary General on the previous evening (Monday, Sept. 20th), a proposal that the schema be presented to the Fathers for a preliminary vote on its merits, in accordance with the usual Council procedure, had lost—some said by a vote of 16 to 9.** Cardinal Spellman, one of the Coordinating Commission members, emerged from the meeting in anger, and Cardinal Shehan was believed to have gone to see the Pope to protest the decision. As night fell it was unknown whether the formula for a vote which Fr. Murray had been working on earlier in the day would become a dead issue or not. All depended on Pope Paul.

A wave of surprise, therefore, swept over the council hall on Tuesday when, halfway through the morning, the voice of the Secretary General, Archbishop Felici, announced over the microphone that, by decision of the Moderators,*** a special secret vote would be taken immediately on Religious

* It was rumored at the beginning of the Session that the *Coetus Internationalis Patrum* had intended to offer their own counter-schema, but they did not go this far. R. Rouquette, writing in *Études* (Nov. 1965), knows of only one petition, signed by about 120 bishops and presented to the Coordinating Commission on Sept. 18th, requesting permission for both the majority and minority to argue their case before a vote, as happened when parts of the schema on the Church were voted (Mary and collegiality). The petition did not ask that the Religious Liberty schema be taken out of the hands of the Secretariat, but it implied this.

** R. Laurentin, in *Figaro* (Sept. 23), says that three proposals were considered by the meeting: 1) to vote according to various formulas; 2) to vote on certain key points; 3) to have no vote at all. The latter carried the day by a majority of 6 votes.

*** Significantly there was no mention of the Council Presidents, usually included in such announcements.

Liberty. He suggested that the bishops take pen in hand and write down the following text, and then in schoolmaster fashion read out in Latin: "Does it please the Fathers that the already amended text on Religious Liberty should be taken as the basis for a definitive declaration, after further amendment in the light of Catholic doctrine on the true religion and amendments proposed by the Fathers in discussion, which will be subsequently approved according to the norms of Council procedure?" The alternatives were *Placet* or *Non placet*. He repeated the formula, then reminded the bishops that they were not to confuse this vote with a ballot already in their hands relating to the text on Divine Revelation. After several minutes of confusion, the latter ballot was disposed of and new ballots were distributed for the vote on Religious Liberty. The outcome was 1,997 in favor as against 224 opposed (with 1 null vote). This amounted to a landslide for the progressives and was greeted with a long round of applause.

Word quickly passed that the vote had been forced by the Pope himself in a dramatic intervention, not unlike Pope John's action in rescuing the schema on Divine Revelation during the First Session. Observant commentators suddenly remembered that Cardinal Tisserant, the Council's President, Cardinal Agagianian, one of the Moderators, and Archbishop Felici, the Secretary General, had all arrived in the council hall tardily that morning, toward the close of the council mass. The secret was soon out. They had been summoned to the Pope's apartment earlier in the morning and informed that, contrary to the recommendation of the Coordinating Commission, Paul wanted a preliminary vote on Religious Liberty. His decision was final. The Pope approved the formula for the vote drawn up by the Secretariat and hastily presented to him, adding the final clause "which will be subsequently approved according to the norms of Council of procedure." This meant that the document would remain under the jurisdiction of the Secretariat and any further changes could not affect its substance.

Some of the 224 *non placet* votes were unquestionably cast by bishops who were in doubt as to what the complicated formula meant and ignorant of how it had been arrived at.

The drama thus resolved had incalculable significance. Pope Paul was scheduled to appear before the United Nations Assembly in New York on October 4th, to plead for peace and respect for human dignity. With all the world aware of Pope John's encyclical *Pacem in terris,* whose principal theme was the dignity of man as the foundation of human liberty, the Pope and his advisers knew he could not effectively face that international body with an ambiguous Council vote on such an important issue as the Catholic Church's stand on religious liberty.

Summary

September 14, 1965, Tuesday—SOLEMN OPENING OF FOURTH SESSION.
—Mass concelebrated by Pope Paul VI.
—Address by Pope Paul.

September 15, 1965, Wednesday—128TH GENERAL CONGREGATION.
MASS: Bishop Cazzaro, Vicar Apostolic of Ayzan, Chile.
MODERATOR: Cardinal Agagianian.
PRESENT: 2,265 Fathers.
ANNOUNCEMENTS: In presence of Pope, Motu Proprio establishing Synod of Bishops introduced by Cardinal Marella and read by SG; words of greeting by Cardinal Tisserant and Moderator, Cardinal Agagianian; telegram from Patriarch Athenagoras I of Constantinople expressing fraternal greetings read by SG.
NEW BUSINESS: Declaration on Religious Liberty.
SPEAKERS: *Relator:* Bishop De Smedt. 1. Cardinal Spellman (New York, N.Y.). 2. Cardinal Frings (Cologne, Germany). 3. Cardi-

nal Ruffini (Palermo, Italy). 4. Cardinal Siri (Genoa, Italy). 5. Cardinal de Arriba y Castro (Tarragona, Spain). 6. Cardinal Urbani (Venice, Italy). 7. Cardinal Cushing (Boston, Massachusetts). 8. Cardinal Alfrink (Utrecht, Holland).

September 16, 1965, Thursday—129TH GENERAL CONGREGATION.
MASS: Bishop Callens, Prelate Nullius of Tunis.
MODERATOR: Cardinal Agagianian.
PRESENT: 2,252 Fathers.
ANNOUNCEMENTS: Names and addresses of presidents of Episcopal Conferences should be submitted to SG; order of schemata to be discussed: Religious Liberty, Church in Modern World (Schema 13), Missionary Activity and Priestly Life and Ministry; order of schemata to be voted: Divine Revelation (Sept. 20), Lay Apostolate, Pastoral Office of Bishops, Religious Life, Christian Education, Priestly Formation, Church and Non-Christians; *modi* should be submitted on durable paper.
PENDING BUSINESS: Declaration on Religious Liberty.
SPEAKERS: 1. Cardinal Ritter (St. Louis, Missouri). 2. Cardinal Silva Henríquez (Santiago de Chile). 3. Cardinal Meouchi (Antioch). 4. Cardinal Slipyi (Lwów, Ukraine). 5. Cardinal Jaeger (Paderborn, Germany). 6. Archbishop Nicodemo (Bari, Italy). 7. Archbishop Morcillo (Madrid, Spain). 8. Bishop Lokuang (Tainan, China). 9. Bishop Velasco (Hsiamen, China). 10. Archbishop Modrego y Casaus (Barcelona, Spain). 11. Archbishop Lourdusamy (Coadjutor, Bangalore, India). 12. Archbishop Aramburu (Tucumán, Argentina). 13. Bishop Carli (Segni, Italy). 14. Bishop Mason (Vicar Apostolic, El Obeid, Sudan). 15. Bishop Marafini (Veroli, Italy). 16. Archbishop Ziadé (Beirut, Lebanon). 17. Archbishop Tagle Covarrubias (Valparaiso, Chile).

September 17, 1965, Friday—130TH GENERAL CONGREGATION.
MASS: Archbishop Aggey of Lagos, Nigeria.
MODERATOR: Cardinal Agagianian.
PRESENT: 2,214 Fathers.
ANNOUNCEMENTS: Today marks 60th anniversary of ordination of Cardinal Maximos IV Saigh (applause); schedule of voting distributed, to begin Sept. 20; discussion of Religious Liberty will continue on Monday.
PENDING BUSINESS: Declaration on Religious Liberty.
SPEAKERS: 1. Cardinal Cooray (Colombo, Ceylon). 2. Cardinal Florit (Florence, Italy). 3. Cardinal Seper (Zagreb, Yugoslavia). 4.

Cardinal Heenan (Westminster, England). 5. Cardinal Conway (Armagh, Ireland). 6. Cardinal Ottaviani (Curia). 7. Archbishop Cantero Cuadrado (Zaragoza, Spain). 8. Archbishop Baraniak (Poznan, Poland). 9. Bishop Sauvage (Annécy, France). 10. Archbishop Baldassari (Ravenna, Italy). 11. Archbishop Elchinger (Coadjutor, Strasbourg, France). 12. Bishop del Campo y de la Barcena (Calahorra, Spain). 13. Bishop Rupp (Monaco). 14. Bishop Maloney (Auxiliary, Louisville, Ky.). 15. Archbishop Alvim Pereira (Lourenco Marques, Mozambique). 16. Bishop Gasbarri (Apostolic Administrator, Grosseto, Italy). 17. Archbishop Hallinan (Atlanta, Ga.). 18. Archbishop García de Sierra y Méndez (Burgos, Spain).

September 20, 1965, Monday—131ST GENERAL CONGREGATION.
MASS: Bishop Torres of Ponce, Puerto Rico.
MODERATOR: Cardinal Agagianian.
PRESENT: 2,204 Fathers.
ANNOUNCEMENTS: SG read letter from Council to Pope thanking him for encyclical *Mysterium fidei*, Motu Proprio on Synod of Bishops, and his proposed visit to UN in New York (applause).
PENDING BUSINESS: Declaration on Religious Liberty.
SPEAKERS: 1. Cardinal Lefebvre (Bourges, France). 2. Cardinal Wyszynski (Warsaw, Poland). 3. Cardinal Santos (Manila, Philippines). 4. Cardinal Beran (Prague, Czechoslovakia). 5. Cardinal McCann (Capetown, South Africa). 6. Cardinal Shehan (Baltimore, Maryland). 7. Cardinal Rossi (São Paulo, Brazil). 8. Cardinal Browne (Curia). 9. Cardinal Cardijn (Belgium). 10. Archbishop Lefebvre, Master General of Holy Ghost Fathers. 11. Bishop Gran (Norway). 12. Bishop Añoveros Ataún (Cadiz y Ceuta, Spain). 13. Bishop Muldoon (Auxiliary, Sydney, Australia).

VOTES: Divine Revelation.

	Total	Placet	Non placet	Placet iuxta modum	Invalid
1–Art. 1-2	2,199	2,175	19	—	5 (1)
2–Art. 3-4	2,183	2,180	—	—	3
3–Art. 5-6	2,071	2,049	20	—	2
4–Chap. I	2,079	1,822	3	248	6
5–Art. 7	2,068	2,049	15	—	4
6–Art. 8	2,122	2,071	49	—	2

September 21, 1965, Tuesday—132ND GENERAL CONGREGATION.

MASS: Father Heiser, Minister General of Conventual Franciscans.

MODERATOR: Cardinals Agagianian and Lercaro.

PRESENT: 2,257 Fathers.

ANNOUNCEMENTS: Cardinals that will accompany Pope to New York; booklet containing members of Council Commissions distributed; English, Spanish, German and Italian translations of Schema 13 will be distributed tomorrow.

PENDING BUSINESS: Declaration on Religious Liberty.

SPEAKERS: 1. Cardinal Dante (Curia). 2. Cardinal Journet (Switzerland). 3. Archbishop Kozlowiecki (Lusaka, Rhodesia). 4. Bishop Muñoz Vega (Ecuador).

NEW BUSINESS: Schema 13, in general.

SPEAKERS: *Relator:* Archbishop Garrone. 5. Cardinal Spellman (New York, N.Y.). 6. Cardinal Landazuri-Ricketts (Lima, Peru). 7. Cardinal Silva Henríquez (Santiago de Chile). 8. Cardinal Jaeger (Paderborn, Germany). 9. Cardinal Bea (Curia).

STANDING VOTE to close debate on Religious Liberty, called for by Cardinal Agagianian at 10:45.

VOTE: To accept Religious Liberty as basis for definitive text.

	Total	*Placet*	*Non placet*	Invalid
Motion	2,222	1,997	224	1

VOTES: Divine Revelation.

	Total	*Placet*	*Non placet*	*Placet iuxta modum*	Invalid
7–Art. 9-10	2,253	2,214	34	—	5 (3)
8–Chap. II	2,246	1,874	9	354	—
9–Art. 11	2,241	2,179	56	—	6 (2)
10–Art. 12-13	2,064	2,029	28	—	7 (4)
11–Chap. III	2,109	1,777	6	324	2

III

The Debate on Schema 13:
The Church in the World of Today;
The Pope's Address at the UN

THE VOTE on Religious Liberty and Pope Paul's announcement of the Synod acted as a kind of tonic. The bishops felt that the shadow of the Pope's nervous and somewhat equivocal attitude had suddenly been banished. It began to seem possible that the Council might finish its work by December.

Schema 13 was an entirely new kind of document for a church council to be concerned with; the time was past when the Church could afford to confine its attention exclusively to itself. Pope John XXIII sensed this. Schema 13, according to Cardinal Suenens who has often been credited with inspiring it, was really suggested by Pope John himself and reflected his whole outlook.

The attitude of the Council toward this novel schema was still hesitant at the Third Session, and it was subjected to scathing criticism. Secretary General Felici tried to maintain that the Appendices (*Adnexa*), which dealt in greater depth with such subjects as human dignity, marriage, culture, economic and social life, were merely "private" and not official Council documents. He had to retract this hastily framed judgment. The substance of the more audacious Appendices was eventually incorporated in the body of the schema, by decision of the Coordinating Commission. This marked an important defeat for the minority.

Pope Paul cut short speculation that Schema 13 would be withdrawn when he remarked, at the end of the Third Session, that it would become the "crown of the Council's work."

Schema 13 had many unique features. Apart from being the third Constitution to be considered by the Council (the other two being the documents on the Liturgy and on the Church), it was the first ever to be addressed "to all mankind." It was the first to be drafted in a modern language, French, because modern thought could only be clearly expressed in a modern language. It was the only conciliar document circulated to the bishops in other modern languages (English, German, Spanish, Italian). Though Archbishop Felici made a great point of emphasizing (in the preface to the English translation, for example) that the Latin version remained the *only* official text, nevertheless the facts speak for themselves.

The text debated in September 1965 was the fourth draft to be produced (the first having been presented to the Coordinating Commission by Cardinal Suenens in 1963). It was based on the third draft debated at the Third Session from October 20th to November 10th, 1964.

The schema was also unique in its subject matter in that it was oriented toward man and was intended to lay the foundations for a Christian anthropology, something never assayed before on the conciliar level. It had much to say about the importance of the community, the socialization and progressive nature of society, the meaning of freedom, respect for human dignity, the necessity of banishing all types of discrimination with regard to sex, race, religion, etc. It stressed the importance of scientific research, admitting that the Church had sometimes erred in its attitude toward science in the past. Above all, it stressed the essential goodness of creation and the central role of Christ in this connection. It called the Church the sacrament of unity of all mankind and Jesus Christ, according to the felicitous phrase of Pope Paul VI, "the focal point of the desires of history and civilization."

Mankind was destined to reform the world. Therefore the Church, to use another Pauline expression, must "historicize itself," insert itself in history, in order to promote the renewal of the world for which it exists.

Speaking in the name of Bishop Guano, who was ill, Archbishop Garrone introduced the debate on Schema 13, on Tuesday, September 21st, immediately after the vote on Religious Liberty. In his *relatio* he pointed out that the new version was both longer and "quite different" from the previous text, because the commission had worked long and hard to do justice to the wishes of the Fathers, by including some of the material in the former *Adnexa* in the body of the schema, and by suppressing some chapters and generally rearranging the whole. The introductory sections (Introduction, Preliminary Statement, Arts. 1-9) were considered of sufficient importance to entrust to a special Subcommission that would report on them separately. The title of "Pastoral Constitution" had been chosen and approved by the Coordinating Commission, Archbishop Garrone explained, because conciliar pronouncements nowadays were either "constitutions" or "decrees," depending upon whether they dealt primarily with matters of faith or practice. Meeting the critics head on, he declared that this designation and the fact that it was addressed to "all mankind" made the schema a document in accordance with "the supreme intention and purpose of the Council, as defined by Pope John XXIII."

The 1964 version came to 27 pages of text and included 24 numbered paragraphs; the 1965 version ran to 80 pages of text and included 106 numbered paragraphs. The 1964 version consisted of an Introduction, 4 Chapters, and a Conclusion; the 1965 version was divided into two Parts, consisting of an Introduction (and Preliminary Statement) and 4 Chapters of Part I, and 5 Chapters of Part II. Chapter IV of the earlier version (dealing with human dignity, marriage, culture, economic and social life, human solidarity, peace) was expanded into separate Chapters in the new version (human dignity being transferred to Part I). This will give the reader some idea of the extent of the changes.*

The discussion opened with consideration of Schema 13 as a whole. While most of the speakers applauded the work of the commission and expressed their approval of the new text, at least in principle, they raised a number of serious objections regarding its tone, emphasis and style. One of the chief difficulties seemed to be that it did not strike a proper balance between naturalism and supernaturalism. According to Bishop D'Avack, "it smacks of naturalism . . . The mystery of the Cross is almost forgotten." While it was of course an exaggeration to maintain with Cardinal Siri that "the dominant spirit of the text is humanistic" and would give the faithful "reason to suspect that we not only would have the Church silent on supernatural matters, but would prefer to limit her concern to the realities of this earth," the schema nevertheless had not been entirely successful in charting a course between this particular Scylla and Charybdis. As Cardinal Shehan pointed out: "An unfortunate separation between the natural and supernatural orders could have been

---

* No useful purpose would be served by listing the paragraphs of the two versions side by side for purposes of comparison, because they differed so considerably; we shall list the titles or headings of the 1965 version debated in September, in order to help orient the reader. The final version, promulgated by the Council on December 7, 1965, while structurally similar to the fourth draft, does not correspond paragraph by paragraph. Only the most important changes have been noted in this chapter and below in Chapter V.

avoided if both had been treated in a more synthetic way." The schema in places suggested that certain truths were mutually exclusive whereas in concrete reality they complemented each other. The truths mentioned in Chaps. 1-3 of Part I were particularly susceptible to this type of treatment. Cardinal Döpfner was of the same opinion.

Another criticism was that the schema was still permeated by a spirit of excessive optimism. It should attempt to "avoid all appearance of the optimism characteristic of the nineteenth century," according to Cardinal Jäger of Paderborn. The same defect was also pointed out by Cardinal Döpfner and by Bishop Renard of Versailles. As usual, Cardinal König was incisive in his analysis: the schema must be purged of its weaknesses. Among these he included a tendency, noticeable particularly in the Introduction, to concentrate on "transitory matters" rather than upon the real problems. The text must avoid the impression of attempting to provide a "panacea" for all the world's ills. It was not always clear who was speaking: the "People of God," the "Sacred Synod," or simply "we." On the other hand, Bishop Jordan of Edmonton, Canada found the schema quite satisfactory in this respect: "The schema dispels the error of those Christians who think that the Church and her ministers have all the answers to all of this century's difficulties; on the contrary it describes the Church as a humble servant sincerely seeking to approach the source of divine and human knowledge and not spurning the aid of others." Speaking in the name of the bishops of Poland, Archbishop Kominek of Wroclaw agreed with Cardinal König that the document must avoid giving the impression that the world could be quickly healed simply "by taking pills"; he found the section on political life and the community of nations inferior to the treatment of these subjects in Pope John's *Pacem in Terris* and suggested that the whole of Part II should be reworked according to a different plan. By contrast, the missionary Vicar Apostolic of El Obeid, Sudan, Bishop Mason, urged that the present text should be

quickly approved; otherwise, if the discussion were dragged
out, "we would end up with a document so long that hardly
anyone will want to read it."

The question of whether or not it should be called a "pastoral constitution" was also debated back and forth. Cardinal
Silva Henriquez was of the opinion that the word "pastoral"
should be eliminated because this was a common trait of all
the Council's pronouncements and would not help to clarify
the status of its authority. Archbishop Morcillo of Madrid
questioned the propriety of calling it a "constitution" because this term was normally reserved for documents that
were addressed to the faithful and suggested instead that it
be designated a "Declaration on a dialogue with the world
of today." The secretary of the *Coetus Internationalis Patrum,* Archbishop de Proença-Sigaud, agreed with Archbishop Morcillo but the main burden of his criticism was
that the schema was too "phenomenological" and not sufficiently scholastic in its approach. Such a method allowed two
propositions to be both true and contradictory at the same
time, the archbishop maintained, thus opening the way for
nominalism and Marxism. The schema's presentation of the
world also smacked too much of Teilhard de Chardin, for his
liking. "The Church can be present to the world either as a
ferment," he said, "while not being 'of' this world. Or the
world can penetrate the Church. In the latter case, which
seems to be the view favored by the schema, there is danger
that the Church will fall into false paganism, as happened to
the promoters of humanism at the time of the Renaissance."
On the other hand, the Ukrainian Archbishop Hermaniuk
of Winnipeg, Canada found that the schema "follows too
slavishly the scholastic method in discussing such questions
as human activity in the world, progress and culture . . ."
The two interventions by bishops of the United States on this
part of the schema were rather unfortunate in the impressions they created. Cardinal Spellman got off to a good start
with wholehearted approval and a warning not to weaken

the text, but then weakened his own case by defining "dialogue," which he declared to be its goal, too much in terms of "obedience towards Church authority." He then compounded the error with a slap at conscientious objection, a subject not slated to come up until later in the debate. The high mark of irrelevance was attained by Bishop McVinney of Providence, Rhode Island, who in criticizing what the schema had to say about concrete solutions launched into a diatribe about "the general breakdown in authority on all levels both in the Church and in the state . . . There is in the Church today a crisis of obedience, not only among the laity but also in the ranks of the clergy, not excluding priests . . ." He was finally reminded by the Moderator that the place for such remarks was later when the schema on Priestly Life and Ministry would be taken up.

One of the chief targets was the style of the Latin into which the document had been "translated" from the original French with which the subcommission members had worked. Some found the language excessively classical in places, and in others almost unintelligible. Cardinal Ruffini: "The Latin leaves much to be desired. Nobody expected it to be Ciceronian but in spots it is hardly even Latin." Cardinal Bea noted that though he had taught in Latin for 50 years, it was sometimes necessary for him to go to the French text to determine what was meant. Various speakers ridiculed such Ciceronianisms as *ludricra certamina* for "sports," *officium conscientiae* for "responsibility," *hominum coniunctio* for "solidarity," *cultus humanus* for "culture." Cardinal Bea asked why not simply use such words as *responsibilitas, solidaritas, cultura,* etc.? Father Tucci, S.J., editor of *La Civiltà Cattolica* and one of the drafters of the text, explained at the Bishops' Press Panel that part of the difficulty was due to the fact that the commission had not been allowed as much time for its work as had been expected in December 1964. Instead of the original deadline of June 1965, the commission had been informed that it must be ready by Easter. The Introduction and Chapter I were the least satisfactory but they were also almost wholly new; Part II was in better shape because less radically changed from the 1964 version.

In spite of the fact that a special subcommission had been appointed to look into the matter, there were still complaints that the presentation was too "western" and unrepresentative of Asian and African thought. Archbishop Lourdusamy, co-adjutor of Bangalore, India, for example, speaking in the name of 6 Indian bishops, said that the description of "man in the modern world" in the text applied mainly to advanced, industrialized regions and would not be recognized by those who constituted the greater part of humanity living in Africa, Asia and Latin America. Unless there were a change of emphasis here, "the people of India would conclude that the Church is not concerned with her problems." The same point was made by Cardinal Rugambwa with respect to Africa and the "viewpoint of peoples who have recently begun to share world government." Like Cardinal Spellman, Bishop de Castro Mayer of Campos, Brazil somewhat anticipated matters by launching into a detailed condemnation of communism before this subject was reached in Part I.

Late Thursday morning, September 23rd, after little more than two days of debate, the Fathers were asked whether they wished to terminate the debate on Schema 13 as a whole by a standing vote and were then polled by secret ballot as to "whether it was pleasing, the debate on the schema as a whole having been terminated, to pass on to an examination of each part?" The results were announced the next day: 2,111 *placet* to 44 *non placet*. However, there was no delay. Bishop McGrath immediately rose on Thursday to give his *relatio* on the Introduction and Part I and the debate continued as if the outcome were already known. Everything proceeded as if the Council had given its preliminary approval to the schema (as it had done in the case of Religious Liberty and other texts at the end of the general discussion). This was declared to be a fact by the press. But such was not the case, technically speaking. Why was the usual question ("Do you approve the present text as the basis for a definitive text . . . ?") not put to the Fathers? Various theories were put forward. One reason may have been a desire on the part of the Council leadership to cover its tracks in case unforeseen difficulties developed preventing promulgation.*

The Debate on Schema 13

INTRODUCTION
1. The Church's solidarity with the whole human family.
2. To whom the Council is speaking.
3. At the service of mankind.

PRELIMINARY STATEMENT
4. Hope and anguish.
5. Deep changes.
6. Changes in the social order.
7. Psychological, moral and religious changes.
8. The imbalances of the modern world.
9. Deep longings and questionings, daily more widespread among mankind.

There were only eight speakers on the Introduction, Preliminary Statement and Part I in general, despite the fact that much care had been given to this part by a special subcommission, probably because most of the bishops wished to save their fire for the detailed discussion of Part I which was to follow.

Although the document was addressed "to all mankind," Cardinal Cardijn did not feel that the Introduction singled out sufficiently three groups in which he had always been particularly interested: youth, the working classes, and the *"tiers monde"*—by which he meant the developing nations. "It would be a great scandal," he maintained, "if the enjoy-

---

* R. Laurentin suggests: 1) fear of upsetting an apparent unanimity; 2) desire not to humiliate the minority; 3) reluctance to bow to democratic procedures. *Le Figaro,* Sept. 25, 1965.

ment of earthly goods were too long confined to the so-called
Christian nations." The Church must avoid any semblance
of adopting a patronizing attitude toward them and be a
strong advocate of sharing the blessings of technical assistance
and education and the banishment of egoism and racial discrimination. Although the treatment of Christian anthropology was not intended to be exhaustive but merely sug-
gestive, Bishop Abasolo y Lecue, of Vijayapuram, India,
expressed astonishment that nothing was said about the im-
mortality of the soul in the section on human dignity.

Cardinal Frings criticized certain ambiguous notions that
seemed to permeate the whole schema: he mentioned specifically the concepts of the People of God and "the world."
Also at fault, in his opinion, was the whole scope of the
schema. He concluded, rather gloomily: "This cannot be
effected by the mere change of a word or a sentence but will
call for far-reaching revision." Bishop Volk of Mainz also
found the Introduction unclear and unsatisfactory from a
theological point of view. One fault was that "sin" was never
treated *ex professo* in the text. The emphasis was upon a
diagnosis of present ills of society without going into such
fundamental questions as sin, sickness, death, and the mystery
of grace and sin. "We must not water down the Gospel for
the sake of dialogue," he warned. "Therefore, I propose that
the description of man in today's world be shortened and that
a more theological outlook be adopted that would include his
relationship to God, his sinfulness and his redemption." The
treatment of the world, sin, and the devil was also considered
inadequate by Bishop Marafini of Frosinone, Italy. It was
while listening to this bishop's long and detailed analysis of
the defects of the schema that one of the experts turned to
his companion and said, "A wave of pessimism seems to be
spreading over the assembly." After three days of debate, the
feeling was that if the text were to be as radically revised as
these speakers were suggesting, the Council could not possibly
promulgate it by December.

The treatment of "the world" also came in for criticism from the coadjutor bishop of Strasbourg, Mgr. Elchinger. "We should be speaking not of 'the world today' but rather of 'the Church in the world today.' " The schema had much to say about what the world was expected to do but not enough about what the Church should do. It should be stated more clearly exactly how the Church intended to realize the legitimate desires of mankind. The Church of course could not expect to have all the answers to every question, but it must at least try to point out a solution. Moreover, the world would pay more attention to what the Church said, if the Church sought effectively to eliminate those things "in herself" that were a cause of disbelief. He was referring specifically to the problem of atheism. While noting that it was "no easy task to propose a definition and description that can satisfy everyone everywhere" Bishop Himmer wanted greater attention paid to the dignity of labor and working men, "who constitute the bulk of the world with which we now begin to be in dialogue." He felt that it would be profitable to follow the lead of *Mater et Magistra* and *Pacem in Terris* by saying something more concrete on this score.

Finally, the Preliminary Statement needed a greater biblical emphasis, according to Bishop Charue of Namur and he too joined the chorus of those complaining about the inconsistency in the use of the term "the world." The drafters should determine the exact sense in which they wanted to use the term and then be consistent with themselves. Ultimately, however, after revision, "the draft should be given enthusiastic approval."

PART I.
  10. Going where the Spirit leads.

CHAPTER I: THE VOCATION OF THE HUMAN PERSON.
  11. Man made to God's image.
  12. The dignity of the human body.

13. The dignity of the soul, and especially of the human intellect.
14. The dignity of man's conscience.
15. The excellence of freedom.
16. The social character of man.
17. The victory over death.
18. Men's knowledge of God.
19. The problem of atheism.
20. Christ, the perfect Man.

CHAPTER II: THE HUMAN COMMUNITY.
21. What the Council has in mind.

Section 1: Basic principles.
22. The interdependence of the human person and human society.
23. The multiplication of social relationships.
24. Affirmation of the rights and duties of the human person.
25. Social order as an essentially evolving process.
26. The universal character of the common good.

Section 2: Practical orientations.
27. Respect for the human person.
28. Respect for adversaries.
29. Love of enemies.
30. The basic equality of all mankind.
31. Social charity.
32. Freedom and human solidarity.
33. The insufficiency of an individualistic moral code.
34. Responsibility and participation.
35. Theological foundations of the life of society.
36. The incarnate Word and human solidarity.

CHAPTER III: THE SIGNIFICANCE OF HUMAN ACTIVITY IN THE WORLD.
37. The terms of the problem.
38. The witness of Holy Scripture.
39. Christian faith and human victories.
40. The autonomy of earthly realities.
41. The relationship between human activity and the Kingdom of God.

42. Man's worth depends on what he "is" rather than on what he "has."
43. The earthly city and the heavenly City.
44. "New heavens" and a new earth.
45. The universal lordship of Christ.
46. God reigned from the cross.
47. Alpha and Omega.

CHAPTER IV: THE ROLE OF THE CHURCH IN THE WORLD OF TODAY.
48. The object of this chapter.
49. The grounds for saying that the Church is present in the world.
50. The order of redemption embraces the order of creation.
51. The Church's universal mission.
52. Unity between faith and concrete existence.
53. The role of the laity.
54. The role of pastors.
55. How the Church is helped by the world of today.
56. The vicissitudes of history.
57. Brotherhood built up in a spirit of poverty.
58. The hope of God's People.

The debate on Part I (which actually covered quite a lot of ground as can be seen from the paragraph headings) soon narrowed down to a discussion of one single item, Article 19, which was only about one page long in the text. An unfortunate tendency was evident to judge the whole schema in the light of its treatment of this one point. The paragraph had been drafted in such a way as to avoid any outright or drastic condemnation of atheism, the emphasis being put on what was lacking in atheistic systems. There was no mention of communism as such.

This was too much for certain prelates from Italy, Spain, and those representing certain ethnic groups who accused the drafters of being "soft" on this issue and wanted the Council to speak out with a resounding condemnation of atheism and communism. The other school, undoubtedly representing the majority of the bishops, was willing to go

along with the schema's moderate approach but wanted certain improvements.

A curious feature of the debate was that the American
contribution was almost nil. The impression given was that
this was an issue of no great concern to the American hierarchy, a contest between European prelates in which African
and Asian bishops occasionally joined in. But a factor may
have been the desire not to "rock the boat," since there are
many vociferous anti-communist groups among the American
Catholic Right.

A number of important observations were made regarding
the relevancy of Part I to the rest of the schema, the order
in which the material was arranged, and the inadequacy of
its approach to a Christian anthropology. Patriarch Meouchi
noted that there was insufficient emphasis on the doctrine of
the resurrection, a central idea in Eastern theology. This historical fact was not merely the end of our redemption, but
the beginning of our sanctification and because this fact had
been lost sight of, the force of the text was greatly weakened.
The same could be said about its emphasis on the role of
the Holy Spirit. Archbishop Ziadé concurred: "The people
of the Orient are so taken up with the place of Christ's resurrection in their lives that a common greeting, even among
ordinary people, is 'Christ is risen,' to which the proper answer is, 'He is risen indeed.' " Meouchi went on to say that
if these points were corrected, the schema would be more
acceptable and not so "western" in tone. The schema's anthropology should be squarely founded on Scripture and
Tradition. Archbishop Garrone found the chief fault of the
treatment to be the unsatisfactory way in which the doctrine
of creation was presented. By reason of this marvelous truth,
all things were related to the Creator. Realizing that God
could bestow material goods as he saw fit should serve as the
basis for a spirituality of poverty. Bishop Schick, the auxiliary
of Fulda, also wanted a clearer emphasis placed on the doctrine of creation.

Archbishop Darmajuwana, in the name of the Indonesian bishops, voiced the opinion that Chapters III and IV of Part I, on which the whole first section of the schema hinged, were weak. There was no dialogue here, merely a monologue. In the opinion of Bishop Romero Menjibar of Jaen, Chapter IV would better be included in the Introduction. Certain details were taken up without a previous consideration of the role of the Church in the world. People were disturbed by the problem of "de-mythologization" today. "Many think the Christian concept of God has been surpassed because it is not based on scientific ideas. Hence it is important for the Church to teach clearly what is substantial in the vision of God and what is attributable to a particular mentality or age." Bishop Corboy of Monze, Zambia, criticized the lack of coordination between the principles enunciated in Part I and the concrete treatment that was supposed to come in Part II, a point frequently mentioned by other speakers such as the Dominican Master General, Father Fernandez, who remarked that in order to "solve the present problems of mankind, theoretical principles are not enough. We must get down to the concrete order, if we wish to bring light and not confusion to these problems."

Cardinal Richaud and Archbishop Guerry both regretted that the document did not have enough to say about the Church's social doctrine, the former suggesting that in Part I and especially in Chapter III of Part I, there should be a reference to Pope John's *Mater et Magistra*. Archbishop Guerry's observation that Part I contained no very specific reference to Pope Paul's Bombay appeal for disarmament in December 1964 seemed more appropriate for Part II than Part I. The attitude of Latin American Spanish-speaking prelates toward the schema was somewhat contradictory. Cardinal Rossi of San Paulo, Brazil, pointed to the particular plight of Latin America and other developing nations and said that it was necessary to bear their problems in mind, though he thought the schema was "very pleasing and worth perfecting." He especially wanted the idea of a "perpetual *aggiornamento*" somehow incorporated in the text. Cardinal Santos of Manila took exception to Article 27, which implied "that there are nations in which men are forced against their will to embrace the Catholic faith," as well as the horrendous thought that nations granting unlimited freedom in religious matters to their citizens were more praiseworthy than those that sought to establish some forms of control over the manifestations of religion. These remarks should be eliminated, he insisted. Bishop Llopis Ivorra of Coria Caceres, Spain, agreed, declaring that "religious liberty should not be regarded as an absolute good, but only as a good for those areas where Catholic unity does not exist," as if the Declaration on Religious Liberty had never been heard of. He felt that "there should be no 'joy' if religious freedom would cause conversion to error." On the other hand, Archbishop Soares de Resende's statement caused something of a sensation in the Portuguese press, particularly his call for the schema "to condemn police state regimes, especially in countries under Soviet domination. Many upright persons, often including priests and bishops, are subjected to so much surveillance merely because they do not belong to the party that their nerves are frayed and their wills subdued. Such violence and harm to the human person should be specifically condemned." (Although the archbishop was referring mainly to Iron Curtain countries, his remarks were interpreted by avant-garde Catholics in Portugal as applicable to the Salazar regime. Only the Catholic newspaper *As Novidades* printed his remarks in full.) Bishop Klepacz of Lodz pointed out that the Council must be doubly clear about its use of such terms as "progress" and "liberty" because these and other words were abused by the communist authorities and used in propaganda against the Church. He also deplored the "principle of state supremacy," insisting that this was still the root of many evils and deserved more outright condemnation. In this connection he called for mention of the Nuremberg trials and the current trials of ex-Nazis in Germany.

Discussion of Article 19 was formally launched by Cardinal Seper of Zagreb who regretted the inadequate treatment of atheism, one of the most serious of present-day problems, because men regard atheism as a mark of true progress and the true humanism. The approach must be not a simple condemnation of atheism or demonstration of the existence of God, but must show how the Church understood atheism and regarded atheists and why faith in God fostered progress, whereas atheism was sterile. "Hence we must admit that Christians who defended the established order and the unchangeableness of social structures too stubbornly, wrongly appealing to God's authority, are partly responsible for modern atheism. We must declare that the notion atheists have of God is false . . ." In fact, God was the true foundation for the promotion of genuine progress.

Cardinal König agreed with Seper that the text failed to distinguish adequately between various forms of atheism, of which the militant was only one type among many. He then briefly went into the historical situation that had resulted in present-day atheism: "Christians have had a large responsibility for the rise and spread of atheism." As for the remedies, Christian cooperation and proper study of the subject were essential: "I propose a theological study of the spread of atheism in the world as well as the axiom 'the soul is naturally Christian' to see how the two principles can be reconciled." Ignorance about atheism among priests and missionaries was a great danger for the Church. As for the present policy: "We must anathematize no one, but the Council must speak out in defense of Christians and seek to establish communication with all men of goodwill. Atheistic governments should be invited to promulgate a doctrine of religious liberty founded on the natural law." A practical suggestion for those living in communist countries would be to "show that on the purely civil level religion makes a more effective contribution to the national welfare than does atheism."

The schema was essentially good, according to Patriarch Maximos IV Saigh, "because it is centered on Christ and shows the world a spirit of love." But its treatment of atheism was faulty. "Rather we must denounce the causes of atheistic communism and above all propose a dynamic mystique and a vigorous social morale, showing workers that Christ is the source of their true liberation." He contrasted the positive attitude of John's *Pacem in Terris* and Paul's *Ecclesiam Suam* with that of the schema which "only deplores and condemns." Many true atheists were really not against the Church; they were seeking, as Pope Paul noted, for a truer presentation of God, an up-to-date religion, and above all a Church in solidarity with the poor. "They are scandalized by a mediocre, selfish Christianity which, relying on riches and arms, defends its own interests. If we had lived and preached the gospel of brotherhood, we would have defeated world atheistic communism." His final paragraph contained a discreet reference to worker priests: "Instead of a banal and repetitious condemnation of atheism, let us send to the working man an increasing number of priests and laymen prepared to take part in their work."

Cardinal Florit, Archbishop of Florence, was particularly disturbed by the "practical atheism" adopted by so many people in Italy and elsewhere these days. While not publicly denying Christianity as such, they lived as if God did not exist. There was also widespread conviction that "the Marxist system can be accepted with regard to economics without accepting its atheistic or materialistic doctrine." The schema should clearly state that such a distinction was impossible. "Dialectical materialism is monistic," according to the archbishop; "economic life, materialistically understood, is considered the only reality, there is thus no room for God." With an eye naturally on the local scene, the Rome daily *Il Tempo* headlined the archbishop's speech: "ARCHBISHOP OF FLORENCE CONDEMNS THOSE WHO WANT TO CARRY ON DIALOGUE."

The views of émigré groups calling for a strong statement condemning communism were perhaps best represented by the auxiliary of Toronto, Bishop Rusnack. Truth and charity demanded that the Council speak out about the perils of atheism, "which stems from a politico-economic system that touches Eastern Catholics very closely." The situation in Czechoslovakia was deplorable. "In one night all the religious communities in Czechoslovakia were suppressed, their members being arrested and herded into concentration camps. Priests were taken out of their parishes . . . To combat this plague, we should add a special Declaration on Communism, in line with the message to all men issued by the Council in 1962. There should be no fear that speaking out will cause reprisals behind the iron curtain. Experience shows that communists will react only to forceful public opinion." According to the Ukrainian Bishop Elko, of Pittsburgh, unless the Council came out with an "explicit condemnation of dialectical materialism as one of the false doctrines against the dignity of the human person, the world will accuse us of fear." In the opinion of the Jesuit Bishop Hnilica, resident in Italy, "To say only what the schema says about atheism is the same as saying nothing at all." On the other hand, Archbishop Wojtyla of Kraków, called for moderation, approving in general what the schema now said: "Atheism can be taken up here only with difficulty because the question is so complex." It was clear from the absence of any enthusiasm on the part of prelates from behind the Iron Curtain that the subject would have to be handled with extreme caution. The Russian Orthodox observer-delegates were weighing every word carefully, for to a certain extent their presence at the Council was conditional on an understanding that there would be no outright condemnation that would place them in a difficult position.

A different line was taken by Archbishop Marty, who

found the present treatment of atheism too abstract. Atheists should be regarded as true humanists who were striving to build a better world, but who saw belief in God as somehow hampering efforts toward improvement. "A revision of the present text might well serve as a plan of action for the Secretariat for Non-Believers," he told the Council. In fact this Secretariat could take the initiative in preparing a statement on this subject for approval by the Council. "Christians would do well to realize that an open dialogue with atheists can eventually bring about a purification of their own faith." Archbishop Bengsch of Berlin also called for revision, particularly with regard to the analysis of atheistic ideology, and suggested that while the commission had done its work well, the existing text was too long and verbose. It would be better to leave details to the Synod of Bishops and episcopal conferences.

The maiden speech of the new General of the Jesuits, Father Pedro Arrupe, created something of a sensation in the world press. The burden of his talk was that Christians were not adequately coping with the task of spreading the gospel and meeting the challenge of the non-believing world. The Church faced this world with her immense treasures, but "we have to admit that she has not yet discovered an effective way of sharing her treasures with the men of our time." He then cited some telling statistics which seemed to prove his point: Catholics formed 18 percent of the 1961 world population; today they formed 16 percent, an appreciably smaller proportion on a world scale. Thus after 2,000 years Catholics were only a small part of the world's population, "and how much of that tiny portion can be said to be really Catholic?" Efforts were too largely "frittered away" owing to bad planning and lack of coordination; the tendency was for the Church to look at things from too theoretical a point of view. A case in point was the treatment of atheism in Article 19. The solutions proposed were too intellectual. This was a mistake that had constantly been made by the

Church in the past. The Church had the truth and the basic
principles, but she did not know how to relate theory to
action. Nobody was likely to disagree with this, but eyebrows were raised when he suggested that not only the mentality and cultural environment found in the modern world
were nourished "at least in practice" by atheism, but that

the world was like the City of Man in St. Augustine; . . . it not
only carries on the struggle against the City of God from outside
the walls, but even crosses the ramparts and enters the very territory of the City of God, insidiously influencing the minds of
believers (including even religious and priests) with its hidden
poison, and producing its natural fruits in the Church: naturalism, distrust, rebellion.

He then went on to state that this godless society operates
in an extremely efficient manner, making use of all scientific,
technical, social and economic knowledge and means, following "a perfectly mapped-out strategy. It holds almost complete sway in international organizations, in financial circles,
in the field of mass communications: the press, cinema, radio
and television." His detailed suggestions on fighting modern
atheism more effectively sounded rather like a page borrowed
from the charter of the controversial activist organization,
largely concentrated in Spain, known as *Opus Dei*. It called
for social action and the widespread penetration of all social,
economic, and political structures in order to spread there
the values of a Christian life and thus combat the influence
of atheism at its source. In order to make progress quickly,
1) it was necessary for specialists to draw up a plan of action
sufficiently flexible to be adaptable to local conditions; 2) to
present this plan to the Pope; 3) for the Pope "to assign
various fields of labor to everyone"; and 4) to invite "all
men who believe in God to this common labor that God may
be the Lord of human society." He then suggested three principles that ought to govern this coordination of effort: a

scientific spirit, animated by faith; "absolute obedience to the Supreme Pontiff"; and all-embracing charity.

It was not so much that Arrupe was recommending a concrete plan for dealing with atheism as the unfortunate fact that he chose to express himself in military terminology (a tradition with the Jesuit Order, or at least some Jesuits, since their founding by Ignatius Loyola, a former soldier). After all, Pope Paul had entrusted the Jesuits with a special role in the struggle against atheism when he received their general chapter in May 1965 before Arrupe's election, but in the Council Arrupe's militant program hardly seemed compatible with the spirit of Schema 13, addressed as it was "to all mankind." He admitted as much in a press interview later, saying: "There have been some misunderstandings and exaggerations. But I don't want to blame the press for this. . . . My remarks were poorly translated into English. I didn't mean that there was a universal atheistic organization." But when *The Tablet* of London printed the Latin text of two paragraphs of his speech alongside the English translation, it was apparent that the translation was accurate and faithful.*

The fate that overtook the Father General was typical of the predicament in which many of the clergy find themselves nowadays, particularly those in authority. Trained in a conservative tradition, accustomed to expressing themselves in outmoded terminology, yet sensitive to the problems facing the Church and desirous of furthering the work of the Council, they may at first fail to make the grade but they persist. Arrupe has granted several interviews, the first General of the Jesuits ever to do so, and not only had a number of "brushes" with the press but—*horribile dictu*—has even been

* *The Tablet*, October 30, 1965. In a provocative article in *L'Osservatore Romano*, Raimondo Matteucci quoted large extracts from Arrupe's speech approvingly, including the unfortunate passages in which he accused international financial circles of being dominated by atheism, implying rather paradoxically that the goal of Marxism was ultimately the same as that of international capitalism.

publicly criticized by one of his provincials.* He seems to be eminently a man of his times.

The Bishop of Cuernavaca made an interesting suggestion that received wide notice in the press, when he regretted that the schema was silent about psychoanalysis "which is a true science today, even if not fully mature, and which is as important as the revolution in technology. The discoveries of Freud are similar to those of Copernicus and Darwin. The subconscious subject is always active and exerts great influence, and its analysis raises questions about man not dreamed of before." The bishop was criticizing the schema's anthropology along the lines suggested by Cardinal Shehan's approach. He continued: "The Church used to assume a position towards psychoanalysis that recalls the history of Galileo. This was due in part to the anti-Christian dogmatism of some psychoanalysts, but because of her distrustful approach, the Church up until now has had no influence on those engaged in this science. Some Catholics have even formed the myth of a 'Christian' psychoanalysis, whereas true science is neither Christian nor anti-Christian. The Church should enter into dialogue with authentic psychoanalysis and the schema should treat the subject at least briefly."

Mendez Arceo's intervention was headlined by *The New York Times:* "MEXICAN BISHOP ENDORSES FREUD." He was referring to an experiment going on in his own diocese. Father Grégoire Lemercier of Louvain, Belgium, who had established a Benedictine monastery there in 1950, decided to see what the results would be if his monks were allowed to submit to psychoanalysis. So with the permission of his superiors this was done. As a result, the monastery of some 50 monks originally, had been reduced to about 20, but Dom Grégoire maintained that these 20, because of the purified nature of their vocation after the experience, were ultimately able to

---

* The Provincial of the Jesuits in Holland issued a statement deploring the harsh tone of Father Arrupe's remarks about criticism of the Church, as reported by the Spanish newspaper *Ya. La Croix,* Nov. 3, 1965.

do the work of the original 50! The misfits apparently left voluntarily, some to marry and others to take up various occupations in the world. Father Lemercier distributed a brochure to the bishops in Rome toward the beginning of the Fourth Session outlining the experience of his monastery with psychoanalysis. While it would be somewhat premature to claim with a writer in the Italian weekly *L'Espresso* (whose article was headlined "FREUD EMPTIES THE MONASTERY"), that the opposition of the Church to psychoanalysis was now over, it was true that some headway had been made in recent years in overcoming conservative opposition to the legitimate use of psychoanalysis and other techniques in the handling of vocations.*

As René Laurentin pointed out, the Cuernavaca experience was not as dramatic or as unique as was sometimes represented. The scandal was not that some monks had left the monastery because psychoanalysis had been applied to vocations, but that the Church, for so long, had adopted an ostrich-like attitude toward the problem of drop-outs and other similar unpleasant facts of life.**

Bishop Kuharic's wish that the Church should "ask pardon for all the scandals committed throughout the centuries and should then exhort all her members to a life that will be holier and more worthy of the Gospel," with reference to Article 56 on "The vicissitudes of history," of course brought forth a rejoinder from the Italian Bishop Ruotolo of Ugento who expressed great misgivings about the language of this article which spoke about the "wrinkles" of the Church in every age and deplored the impression created "in some countries" that the Church was "the friend of the rich and powerful." Such admissions, according to Bishop Ruotolo, "run contrary to the pastoral goal of the Council." Paul VI had reminded the observer delegates that the study of history was "beset with difficulties" and therefore lest the faithful

---

* *L'Espresso*, September 26, 1965.
** *Le Figaro*, November 2, 1965.

be unduly disturbed, it was better to "look to the future, leaving the past to the judgment of God and of history," in the bishop's opinion. Earlier in the debate, Cardinal Ruffini had also expressed displeasure with the attitude that seemed to be calling for the Church to "get down on her knees" and beg pardon for faults at every turn. On the contrary, the Church could be proud of her contribution to progress and civilization . . .

Tired of all the pusillanimity, misgivings, cautiousness, warnings and criticism continually being voiced by the Schema's opponents, Archbishop D'Souza of Bhopal asked ironically whether the Council intended to produce a *Reader's Digest* of modern problems, or prepare the Church for coping with them. If the latter was the case, it was necessary to call a spade a spade and face certain unpalatable facts. In a fine fury he then proceeded to lash out at the hesitant attitude of so many toward adaptation. "How many men were lost to the Church and regarded it as an enemy of human liberty and dignity between the time when the American and French Revolutions clarified the notion of liberty and the time when these rights were first mentioned in a papal document?" It was not until 43 years after the publication of Karl Marx's fundamental work that Leo XIII's *Rerum Novarum* appeared, and in the meantime there had occurred what Pius IX called the scandal of the nineteenth century—the loss of the working man to the Church. "As if the scandal of Galileo was not enough," he went on, "we have since had the cases of Lammenais, Darwin, Marx, Freud, and more recently Teilhard de Chardin. Their works, not without error, were fighting for the very things that our schema recognizes, and yet their works were indiscriminately condemned." History was the teacher of life, Pope John XXIII had said, and past errors should be avoided. Those things should be removed from the Church that prevented it from obeying the voice of God without hesitation. He then proceeded to enumerate a number of such hindrances regarding ecclesiastical organization:

automatic promotions, the administrative or political preoccupations of church leaders, seminary education separated
from the world and conducted according to "obsolete scholasticism," abuse of censorship, insufficient lay participation in
the life of the Church; regarding doctrine: theological texts
so stressed the immobility of God that the political and social
orders seemed to be affected by this immobility too; regarding pastoral life: why was there still so much obsolete pomp
connected with clerical life? Unless the Council was able to
break away from the interminable chain of monologues in
a dead language without open discussion in which they had
been engaging, how could any positive results be expected
to come from their work?

PART II: SOME MORE URGENT PROBLEMS.
   59. Introduction.

CHAPTER I: THE DIGNITY OF MARRIAGE AND THE FAMILY.
   60. Marriage and the family in the world of today.
   61. The sacred character of marriage and the family.
   62. Conjugal love.
   63. The fecundity of marriage.
   64. God, the Master of life.

Introducing Part II, Bishop Hengsbach explained that the
present text was much longer than the previous draft because
many of the points discussed in the former *Adnexa* had been
incorporated here. The reason why the two sections had been
combined was that general principles tend to become too
abstract and vague when treated separately, on the other
hand there was danger that if too many details were mentioned the treatment would become unwieldy. Accordingly
the commission had tried to strike a proper balance. The first
chapter on marriage had been little changed, except that the
text put into clearer light the role of procreation and education as well as the true character of conjugal love. A new
chapter had been added on political life, and the final or

fifth chapter now combined two previously distinct articles in the former draft. The question of giving proper emphasis to the condemnation of war had been a thorny one for the commission. Some wanted an outright condemnation of modern arms and warfare unconditionally. Others felt that distinctions were in order. The commission had followed a middle of the road course that could be formulated as follows: "Any war action that tends indiscriminately to the destruction of entire cities and their inhabitants or, with still greater reason, to the almost total destruction of regions, is of itself and objectively a crime against God and man himself, which must be firmly and unhesitatingly condemned."

On Wednesday, September 29th, after little more than three days of debate on Part I, the Council moved on to the somewhat more colorful theme of marriage, dealt with in the first chapter of Part II of the schema. The text itself skirted the whole issue of birth control, which the Pope had reserved to himself,* stressing the importance of conjugal love as a vital factor in Christian marriage along with the reproductive function. In a significant step forward, it did not repeat the classical contention about primary and secondary ends (found in Pius XI's *Casti connubii* for example), but refused to go into this question, leaving it for discussion among theologians. In itself, of course, this marked an advance over the previous position and one that conservative theologians found very difficult to reconcile with their static view of the non-infallible pronouncements of the teaching Church.

Another advance was the statement that the determination of the number of children must be left to the parents themselves, directly contradicting the assertion of Cardinal Ottaviani at the Third Session that "the freedom granted to couples to determine for themselves the number of their children cannot possibly be approved." On the delicate subject of

* See below, p. 118, for a discussion of birth control policy in connection with Chapter V of Schema 13.

birth control means or methods, the schema contented itself with the very vague statement, "Great reverence must be shown for the human faculty of begetting children, which is wonderfully superior to all that exists in the lower levels of life, and also for the acts proper to conjugal life, when carried out in accordance with true human dignity," in order not to prejudice the work of the special Papal Commission.

Typical of the conservative theology of marriage were the views of the Archbishop of Palermo, Cardinal Ruffini: "The nature and ends of marriage do not stand out in the text with proper clarity . . . Attention could profitably be paid to the traditional distinction between the primary and the secondary ends of marriage." The schema condemned abortion and infanticide, but it was silent about divorce and passed over in silence the vice of "onanism" in all its many forms. "The statements on the fecundity of marriage are obscure," he noted, "and there is no mention of the pill which has been so impudently termed 'Catholic.' " He commented also, "There are times in marriage when chastity is to be observed. This is a difficult requirement but married persons can always count on divine help. Mutual satisfaction is desirable and necessary through marriage, but it is hard to understand what the text intends when it speaks of 'the full perception of the human person.' "

Representative of the new theology of marriage were the sentiments voiced by Cardinal Léger, who began however with a complaint that the treatment of conjugal love "seems to reduce persons to the rank of simple instruments." But he continued, "The text is better in what it has to say about the importance and lawfulness of conjugal love. Its chief defect is that it does not give a proper explanation of the aim of marriage." It was not enough for the faithful to find the text affirming that the purpose of marriage was procreation and the education of children. "We should declare clearly that marriage is not merely a means of procreation, but likewise a community of life and love. We should distinguish between the species and the individual. The text could also be criticized for its order and style. "We must take care," Léger said, "that our Declaration should not turn out to be a diplomatic compromise between various schools of thought. The frequent use of the hortatory tone should be avoided since this gives the impression that the Council is moralizing."

The Polish Bishop Majdanski insisted that the schema must formulate "a clear doctrine on birth control, because of the confusion so widespread in the world today" on this subject. Archbishop Nicodemo regretted the "ambiguous and dangerous use of expressions" and the tendency of the text to indulge in "subjectivism," even to the point of suggesting that praise for large families was insincere. "The text seems to fall into a contradiction," he declared, "when it praises marital fecundity but on the other hand states that married people are free to determine the number of their children according to subjective criteria." He continued: "What is said in Article 101 about conscientious objection is inopportune in a Council document, because it gives the impression that conscientious objectors give a witness to certain principles which is not found in those who answer the call of duty," wandering somewhat from the subject under discussion. Bishop Volk, of Mainz, called for an "explanation of marriage as a state" similar to the explanations of the clerical and religious states.

The debate was clearly bogging down in platitudes and contradictory statements when it was saved from complete dullness by Archbishop Zoghby, Melkite patriarchal vicar for Egypt, who raised the question of what was called in Italy *"il piccolo divorzio,"* the right of the innocent party in cases involving adultery, physical impotence, desertion, etc. to remarry. No such right is recognized under current canon law by the Roman Catholic Church which admits of no exceptions to the indissolubility of a validly performed, consummated and sacramental marriage (between two baptized persons, whether Catholics, Protestants or other). Italian law, tied to Catholic canon law by reason of the Concordat, admits of no such thing either. There has been a certain amount of agitation there however in favor of revising the marriage legislation since a great many Italians, particularly of the upper classes but also among the lower classes are not practicing Catholics and feel unjustly discriminated against because of laws in which they no longer believe. No wonder therefore that the Melkite archbishop's speech aroused considerable interest in the press, particularly since it came at a time when a Socialist deputy was on the point of introducing once again a bill to permit divorce in Italy for those who wanted it.

According to Zoghby, the problem of divorce "constitutes a more serious problem than that of birth control." "What is to be our stand," he asked, "in cases where a marriage has been contracted with great promise but where an innocent spouse has been abandoned and, according to the traditional teaching, must face life in solitude and continence? Another case of the same type," he went on, "would be that of the permanent insanity of one party. The counsel to live a life of solitude . . . calls for heroic virtue which cannot be imposed indiscriminately." He then asked pertinently: "Could not the Church, without prejudice to her doctrine on the indissolubility of marriage, use her authority on behalf of the innocent party in these cases, as has been the case in the Christian East? This practice was also allowed sometimes in the West." Answering in advance the objections of those who maintained that the doctrine and discipline of the Latin Church had always been uniform on this point, he asked: "Did not the Church get from Christ the power to regulate such cases? The Church should decide on the intrinsic force of the passage in Scripture that has been consistently invoked against this practice. The Council of Trent chose a formula that would not offend the orientals . . . This is something that should not be done lightly, of course, because of abuses, nevertheless the problem had to be faced."

The next day the Swiss theologian, Cardinal Journet, rose to repudiate the thought—without mentioning Zoghby—that the Roman Catholic Church was not irrevocably committed to the indissolubility of marriage. "The Catholic Church has always observed and taught the same doctrine revealed by Christ on the indissolubility of sacramental marriage." The passage in Matthew 5:32 where the phrase "except for fornication" occurs, could justify separation in the case of adultery, as modern theologians and canonists hold, but not remarriage. The fact that the practice of divorce was admitted "in some oriental Churches," according to Journet, was due to the influence of the civil law as expressed in Justinian's Code. Other causes were later introduced. "Thus these Churches found themselves following a human policy rather than the Gospel."

Zoghby had little difficulty in showing, at a press conference and later in another intervention, that Journet was wrong about the Orthodox Churches. In allowing divorce, under certain circumstances, they had not bowed to governmental pressure because they had granted divorce and allowed remarriage long before the time of Justinian and some of the Church Fathers countenanced the practice. He explained later, in a second intervention on the floor, that he had not intended to question the doctrine of the indissolubility of marriage. The Orthodox Churches accepted this doctrine also. But there was, or could be, a parallel between the Orthodox practice of allowing the innocent party to remarry according to their doctrine of "economy" and the western practice of dissolving and allowing remarriage in the so-called Petrine cases.* All Zoghby had really wanted to do

* The Pauline Privilege concerns the dissolution of marriages between two unbaptized persons; the Petrine (i.e. papal) Privilege, the dissolution of marriages between an unbaptized and a baptized person. Both marriages are non-sacramental.

was to raise the subject of trying to find some solution for the innocent party other than complete chastity, when this proved impossible. The chief result of his intervention, it seems, was not to suggest that the Roman Catholic Church was about to change its doctrine on marriage, but to set people thinking about ways that could lead to this end. Judging by the comments, he had certainly succeeded in this limited purpose.

A useful suggestion was made by Cardinal Suenens: "It is greatly to be desired that scientific research in the domain of sexual life . . . be directed to man himself, in all his complexity, particularly on the sexual and conjugal level. We must have a better understanding of the laws of human fecundity as well as the psychological laws of self-control . . . The efforts made thus far are insufficient. The few Catholic scientists in this area complain that they are not supported and encouraged. Everyone senses the lack of coordination. Therefore an invitation from the Council for scientific research would be a precious stimulant as well as a proof of our pastoral interest. Our Catholic universities should encourage this research through scholarships . . ." He was careful to note however that "these suggestions do not imply any judgment on the value of any specific method of birth control. They remain purely in the field of science." In a slightly different context, he thought that "it would help married people, to encourage the practice of renewing their marriage vows, as is done for baptismal and religious vows. A particular day could be set aside . . ." The Rome daily *Il Messaggero* apparently deliberately misrepresented what the cardinal had said, for the sake of the publicity, headlining its story: "MARRIAGE SHOULD BE RENEWABLE" and asking whether he had meant to suggest that the marriage contract itself could be renewed. "This would involve a substantial reform," it went on, "because it would amount to establishing a form of divorce, permissible according to certain fixed norms and in a manner acceptable to the Church." Such a preposterous interpretation naturally brought forth a protest from the cardinal, who telegraphed the paper demanding that they print a rectification.*

The speech of Bishop Reuss, auxiliary of Mainz and head of the major seminary there, one of the most advanced in Europe, also member of the Papal Commission on Birth Control, was listened to with particular attention. Chapter I was praiseworthy because it stressed the importance of conjugal love and refrained from becoming involved in questions before the Papal Birth Control Commission. Although "I had no intention of speaking on these problems, yesterday's discussion forces me to do so. If these problems had been so clearly solved already, as Cardinal Ruffini asserted yesterday, the Pope's decision is hard to understand. Cardinal Suenens yesterday made a stirring appeal for further scientific research." The norm for this research and the commission's work must be "the truth, sought with zeal, responsibility before God, and prayer." Love could legitimately be called an end of marriage. "Conjugal love could not be strictly identified with the conjugal act since love extended to the whole married life . . . Hence the truth of the schema, that marriage is not a mere institution for the procreation of children. It is regrettable that the word 'responsibility' is not used in the text, because the responsibility of the spouses determines the whole of married life. By this responsibility, man responds to God's will." Nevertheless, a number of speakers continued to voice regret that the schema had abandoned the classical distinction between the "primary" and "secondary" ends of marriage, notably Cardinal Browne of the Holy Office and Bishop Alonso Munoyerro of Spain, the latter noting that the Holy Office had condemned an erroneous opinion regarding the "primary purpose of procreation."

Several speakers expressed a certain amount of perplexity, perhaps irritation, over the fact that Pope Paul was defer-

* Cf. *L'Osservatore Romano* and *Il Messaggero,* October 1, 1965.

ring his promised statement on birth control methods and their speeches could be viewed as discreet attempts to prod him into action. Cardinal Heenan observed that while "moral principles remain fixed and certain, we still await guidance from doctors, physiologists, and other experts . . . Would it not be better to say nothing at all about marriage in this document rather than discuss it while leaving the really big problem without mention?" He described the present text as "rather tame." The cardinal also said that great care must be exercised in the language of the text. "The Latin text is least important since we are addressing the modern world." Instead of calling it a Constitution, he was in favor of entitling it "Message from the Council to the world today." The document contained "practically nothing that would help married couples in their intimate problems. The difficulties were sketched, but little more. In the name of the Brazilian bishops, Cardinal Rossi agreed with Cardinal Heenan, that unless a decision with regard to birth control means would soon be forthcoming from the Holy See on which the Council could base itself, it was better to remain silent and try and work out a "modus vivendi" for priests and faithful. "Is this not more prudent than running the risk of affirming what might be contradicted tomorrow? . . . The indeterminate and imprecise statements in the schema on this question do not suffice at all."

A notable intervention was that of Cardinal Colombo of Milan, speaking in the name of 32 Italian bishops, who put the seal of his approval on Chapter I which he declared to be both "good in its doctrine and in its pastoral approach" because it "places the foundation of the benefits and aims of marriage in a fully human and personalistic light in order that conjugal life may be declared to be intrinsic and co-essential with the procreational end of marriage." However, he regretted an unfortunate impression in that "the schema does not reaffirm strongly enough the doctrine of the Church and by its timid and reticent tone seems to justify the suspicion that something basic has been changed in Catholic doctrine."*

Bishop De Roo of Victoria, Canada, speaking in "the name of 33 bishops and many married couples of Canada," put in a strong plea for what the schema had to say about conjugal love, which however was not strong enough. *Placet iuxta modum* he said. The laity should be encouraged to progress toward a fuller, more ecclesial married life. Therefore the bishop should set aside preoccupations with the pitfalls of married life and insist rather on the positive vision of the riches of human love and the heights it could reach through grace. The laity appreciated the value of the doctrinal elements, but they knew that "conjugal union cannot really be understood unless it is realized that carnal union gives rise to a communion of the whole persons and lives of the partners. The classical view of procreation as the end of marriage must be perfected, for procreation requires that parents be not only the authors of life, but also an unfailing source of love for the whole family . . . We contradict reality if we consider merely one or another gesture of conjugal love apart from the whole context of daily family life, outside of which they cannot have their full meaning. Christian marriage is a vocation to seek perfection as a team . . . Married couples must never abstain from the daily practice and development of authentic conjugal love. The Council will promote the redemption of all humanity by exalting the positive values of conjugal love." Instead of emphasizing the negative side, the Council should exalt what is positive.**

Cardinals Gracias and Slipyi both regretted the excessively "western" approach to marriage manifested by the schema, as did Archbishop Djajasepoetra who declared: "You West-

---

* This intervention must have made a certain impression on Pope Paul, because he intervened before the end of the Council and ordered the commission to amend the text so as to eliminate any such suspicion. See below, p. 210.

** Fr. Schillebeeckx gave an interesting conference in Rome on "the changing concepts of Christian marriage," on Sept. 29, 1965. Cf. *The Tablet,* October 9, 1965 and *La Croix,* October 1, 1965.

erners always say that people marry because they love each other. In the Orient we say that people get married and then learn to love each other." In his opinion, however, the present text was far superior to the preceding draft. Slipyi went on in a rambling vein about a subject that was not under discussion at all, namely atheism, and insisted that very few speakers had accurately described the situation as it existed in communist countries. Then turning to the subject of marriage, he made his point that East and West looked at marriage from differing points of view: "This could be the most beautiful of conciliar texts. . . ." and on and on until he was finally interrupted by the Moderator, Cardinal Suenens, who begged him to conclude. Instead of doing so, Slipyi quoted the cardinal, who thanked him and once again asked him to conclude. But the Ukrainian was not to be daunted and was about to launch into a quotation from Pope John's *Pacem in Terris* when he was finally stopped.

Harking back to a favorite theme of some Latin American prelates, Bishop De Orbegozo, Prelate Nullius of Peru, insisted once more that the Council must not abandon the teaching on the primary and secondary ends of marriage, and above all must not become an instrument for spreading the birth control propaganda of "certain countries" in Asia, Africa and Latin America. As for what the text said about leaving the number of children to the decision of parents, he hoped that the Council would be more generous. "Soon those who were once considered heroic will have to hide their children if more than two—unless they want to bear public shame for what many think is an irresponsibility and unrestrained lust."

The debate was finally brought to an end by Bishop Hacault of St-Boniface, Canada, who seconded Bishop De Roo's call for a more explicit treatment of the subject of conjugal love. History disclosed many different types of marriage, polygamy, concubinage, bigamy, etc., "The Council should not merely condemn these inferior covenants but show that they culminate in the Christian conception of marriage."

CHAPTER II: THE ADVANCEMENT OF CULTURE.

When Bishop Hacault had finished speaking on Friday, October 1st, Cardinal Suenens asked the Fathers whether they wished to terminate the discussion of the chapter on marriage? The results of a standing vote being affirmative, the Council then passed to consideration of Chapter II on Culture. Since the vote to close the debate on Chapter I had come somewhat earlier than expected, a number of bishops were unable to deliver their scheduled talks, but before taking up the next item the floor was given to Bishop Schmitt of Metz, who in the name of 70 Fathers, had asked to say a few more words about the introduction to Part II of the schema. His point was the rather interesting observation that not enough had been said about the contribution of the world to the Church. As the dogmatic Constitution *Lumen gentium* declared, grace was given to men even outside the boundaries of the Church. In the interests of solidarity therefore it was only fair for the Church to acknowledge its debt to the world. He listed the movement toward socialization, the dignity of the human person, the interdependence of peoples, the distinction between Church and state, etc., as values contributed by the world to which the Church added her own peculiar slant.

The debate on Chapter II was led off by Arthur Elchinger, the Coadjutor-Bishop of Strasbourg. The principal problem of the section was the way the Church ought to conduct herself toward technical civilization. The text was full of many pious exhortations but few practical solutions were offered, he said. The Church must receive the treasures of her own culture, and at the same time convey them to others. "One reason why the Church has lost its influence in the world is that it is expanding now in regions where it had not been previously established. In countries where it had been established, there is a distrust of the Church and it has therefore lost its influence. The Church has not listened to the world as much as it should." Christians must adjust to the cultural pattern of the region where they happen to live and must be in the vanguard of cultural development there.

Elchinger was followed by two other French bishops, Le Couedic and Lebrun. The former insisted that the text should state more clearly that things are not ends in themselves but means for man's betterment and should be used properly with a view to achieving a higher spirituality. The latter stressed the importance of sports and their value from a spiritual point of view, suggesting that certain ideas along this line be incorporated in the schema. The Master General of the Dominicans proposed virtually a new plan for this chapter, maintaining that not enough was said about the contribution of the Church to the development of culture.

One of the more notable interventions of the Session was delivered by the newly appointed Archbishop of Turin, Michele Pellegrino, until recently a professor of ancient

Christian literature in the University of Turin, who spoke on a subject dear to his heart, the right to freedom of research. Chapter II was generally satisfactory, but he called for an explicit mention of the science of history among those disciplines with which the Church should particularly concern itself: "The importance of historical research is evident from its subject matter, which is man himself . . . Moreover, historical study is closely connected with the knowledge of the history of salvation . . . Finally, scholars will welcome such a recognition of their labors, especially those who carry on historical research in the fields (biblical, ecclesiastical, patristic, archeological, etc.) more closely connected with the history of salvation. Commenting on the sentence in Art. 74 which reads, "But, to enable them to carry out their task, the faithful must be allowed the freedom of inquiry and thought which befits a Christian, the freedom also to express their point of view with humility and courage in the fields of their competence," he suggested that after the word "faithful," the words "clerical or lay" should be inserted, to show that this right to freedom of expression applied also to the clergy, and not merely to the laymen mentioned in the previous sentence. As an example of what he meant, he reminded his hearers about certain unsavory aspects of the suppression of the heresy of Modernism earlier in this century, particularly in Italy: "The right and duty of ecclesiastical authority to watch over clerics more closely than over laymen must also be exercised with due reverence for human dignity, which includes freedom of inquiry. We are all grateful to the supreme authority for averting the calamity of Modernism, but who would dare to assert that in that necessary repression the rights and dignity of clerics, whether young priests or bishops or even cardinals, were always duly respected?"

There was inevitably considerable speculation in the corridors as to which cardinals had been hounded in the dark days following Pius X's *Pascendi dominici gregis* (1907), whereas everybody knew about the unfortunate cases of Mon-

signor Louis Duchesne, and Monsignor Pierre Batiffol, the
church historians, and Père F. M. Lagrange, O.P., the biblical
scholar, to mention only a few of those who managed to remain within the Church in spite of the storm. But lest any
of his hearers should get the idea that he was referring to
the distant past, Archbishop Pellegrino went on, "Such things
do not belong only to the past. A few years ago I found a religious living in involuntary exile for having expressed opinions which today we read in papal and conciliar documents.
This was not a unique case." In a strong plea for the rights
of research, he concluded, "Even in the theological sciences,
many things must be subjected to revision with the progress
of research, and the sphere of things susceptible of various
opinions is much broader than is realized by those who have
not experienced the hard and often dangerous work of research. If each one knows that he is permitted to express his
opinion with wholesome freedom, he will act with the
straightforwardness and sincerity that should shine in the
Church; otherwise the abominable plague of dishonesty and
hypocrisy can hardly be avoided."* Obviously these were the
words of one who knew whereof he spoke.**

The fact that an Italian archbishop, a novice—admittedly
a northerner—had dared to be so frank on the floor of the
Council about internal matters that quite a few of his colleagues still feel to be too delicate or painful or embarrassing
ever to be mentioned publicly, was widely hailed as a sign
that progress was being made in updating the Italian Church.
Many of the Italian clergy, particularly the higher and more

* See *Letters from Vatican City* (New York, 1963), p. 18 and Charles Ledré,
Un siècle sous le tiare (Paris, 1955), p. 82–84, for mention of the heresy-
hunting activities of Monsignor Benigni's *Sodalitium pianum*, called "La
Sapinière," which was finally suppressed by Benedict XV shortly before his
death in 1921.

** *The Tablet* (October 9, 1965), printed almost the whole of the archbishop's remarks, whereas the daily press bulletin in English gave only a
six-line summary. The Italian press bulletin did not think it important
enough to mention that he had referred to cardinals, contenting itself with
"*vescovi o gli ecclesiastici.*"

conservative prelates, are curiously under the impression that the Church is still engaged in a life and death struggle with the nineteenth-century Italian *Risorgimento*.

The following speaker, Monsignor Blanchet, rector of the Catholic Institute in Paris, was more critical. He found that there were many "surprising gaps" in Chapter II. The description of modern culture was deficient. Like Pellegrino, he deplored the fact that so little was said about history, "which in a singular way characterizes the modern way of thinking. History is very important because it teaches the change and relativity of things. The study of history has given an impetus to other studies in the Church." He also found the schema weak on the subject of the relations between philosophy and faith. Catholic teachers should stop talking so much about the supposed opposition between science and faith. "Attention was always being called to the fact that the weak must not be scandalized; the Church should begin to think about scandalizing the strong." The text paid insufficient attention to the important matter of environment in the determination of human culture, according to Bishop Padim, Secretary General of Catholic Action in Brazil, while Archbishop Morcillo of Madrid found Chapter II "unworthy of our Council" because it was ambiguous about the relationship between human culture and Christian humanism. God's "role in the progress of culture is very great since the benefits of redemption are extended to *all* creatures. He restores these creatures, as well as the human elements, to his glory and man's salvation." He proposed that the whole of Chapter II be revised in the light of Revelation and history. (The Italian press bulletin had the archbishop calling for the complete suppression of the whole second part of the schema and handing it over to a special post-conciliar commission.) Bishop Frotz, the auxiliary of Cologne, regretted that not enough attention was paid to the separate role of men and women in the evolution of human culture. Both Bishop Spülbeck of Meissen and Archbishop Veuillot, coadjutor of Paris, dealt with the subject of the dialogue between theology and modern science, the former generally approving "the laudable optimism" of the schema with respect to the field of science, the latter certain that "the text, as it stands, will disappoint scientists." The Church should not merely say that she is not opposed to science, according to Veuillot, but declare that she positively fosters it. The tone of the schema does not answer "the growing anguish of modern science in the face of the smallness and fragility of man confronted by the immense and unfriendly universe and in the face of an ever-increasing number of discoveries whose direction and finality are unknown and disputed." The schema should profess the reverence proper for life and exhort scientists to acknowledge the final goal to which science is called, to tell the glory of God.

Science was also the theme of the final speaker on this chapter, Bishop Bettazzi, auxiliary of Bologna, whose point was somewhat different. He recommended that the Council make its own the attitude of Thomas Aquinas to the science of his day. "St. Thomas . . . loved both the Scriptures and the world of his time. The principles of Thomas we have from tradition; but his method applied today would be one of seeking for and adhering to the mentality of our time and place." He then went on to note that this "was the inspiration of Pope John XXIII when he invited the faithful to dialogue. John's name should be mentioned in the text. This question also merits the attention of the new Episcopal Synod." Commentators immediately interpreted this as a discreet reference to a proposal for the spontaneous canonization (or rather beatification) of Pope John XXIII by the Council being advocated on the sidelines by the energetic young bishop and supported by such cardinals as Suenens of Belgium, König of Austria, Alfrink of Holland, Liénart of France, and Lercaro of Bologna. Interesting as the suggestion was, nobody was under any illusions that the move would have much success, unless it suddenly received a nod from on high, in view of the usual reserves expressed by spokesmen for the Congregation of Rites about the desirability of departing from normally accepted procedures in these matters.*

CHAPTER III: ECONOMIC AND SOCIAL LIFE.
75. Some features of economic life at the present day.

Section 1: Economic development.
76. Fundamental law.
77. Must remain under man's control.
78. Grave inequalities must be eliminated.

Section 2: Principles governing economic and social life.
79. Work, working conditions and leisure.
80. Sharing in the enterprise, labor disputes.
81. The goods of this world meant to serve all mankind.
82. Investments and monetary policy.
83. Access to ownership and control of wealth.
84. Relations between rich and poor countries.
85. Economic-social activity and the Kingdom of God.

The debate on Chapter III, Economic and Social Life, was over almost before it began, occupying only part of two successive mornings, October 4th and 5th. The inevitable basis of comparison was recent papal pronouncements in this field, some speakers regretting the fact that the schema was not as explicit, others welcoming its treatment as adequate and satisfactory. The fact that the majority of the bishops had little or nothing to say seemed to indicate that they were in substantial agreement. Actually, so far as a statement of basic principles was concerned, the revised Chapter III was fully as good as, and in some respects surpassed, papal documents on the subject prior to the reign of Pope John XXIII. (In the judgment of experts the final version approved by the Council is fully in accord with the spirit of *Pacem in Terris*. This

* *L'Avvenire d'Italia*, October 5 and October 8, 1965. *Catholic Herald*, October 22, 1965. Certain Italian papers, including the former, kept up a kind of campaign constantly referring to this proposal throughout the months of October and November.

section of the text underwent relatively little revision during the final weeks of the Council.)

Four of the 21 speakers were less concerned with criticizing the text than with using the occasion to propose the formal setting up of a Secretariat to promote Roman Catholic, and inter-Christian, awareness of the problems connected with world poverty and help coordinate activity in this area. Said Bishop Swanstrom, the director of Catholic Relief Services: "There is a great gulf between our accepting the Church's teaching and our putting it into practice. Hence I propose concretely that the Church launch a deep and long-term campaign of education, inspiration and moral influence to promote among Christians and all men of good will a live understanding and concern for world poverty and to promote world justice and development in all their facets." Similar proposals were made by Cardinal de Arriba y Castro of Spain, by Archbishops Thangalathil and Fernandes of India, by Father Mahon, Superior General of the Society of St. Joseph of Mill Hill, and by Bishop Echeverria Ruiz of Chile. Bishop Swanstrom's proposal was actually not new.* Various suggestions along this line had been made by different speakers at the Third Session, notably by the American Lay Auditor active in relief affairs James J. Norris in a speech before the Council on November 5, 1964. The plan now being submitted for formal consideration by the proper authorities called for the establishment of a permanent commission of bishops appointed by the Pope and forming part of the Curia, possibly headed by a cardinal as president, that would have the advice of a "strategy-committee composed of highly competent authorities, technicians and well-known leaders in the field of economics, aid and development, both clergy and lay." The Secretariat was not to become involved in administration but would help lay down the "guidelines" for other

---

* The proposals for a Secretariat at the Fouth Session were inspired by a paper drawn up by Mgr. J. Gremillion, Mgr. L. Ligutti, Fr. A. McCormack, and J. Norris. Cardinal Cushing made a similar suggestion in July 1965.

organizations and bring about a greater public awareness of the need and responsibility for action. Its terms of reference were to be rather broadly defined as relating not only to aid in the largely materialistic sense but to concern for the whole range of problems connected with development and social justice.*

(The draft of Schema 13 debated by the Council contained no specific mention of "organs" either here in Chapter III or later in Chapter V where it might have been expected. Mr. Norris and Bishop Fernandez-Conde were unsuccessful in their attempt to insert the word in Chapter III when the Mixed Commission considered this part of the text on October 28th, but "organs" are expressly mentioned in the revised text of Chapter V, paragraph 90, formerly 103. Pope Paul is known to favor the idea for a Secretariat and has promised to give it his support when those more directly concerned with working out the details have come to some agreement on how it is to function.)

Two conservative prelates who normally could be expected to see eye to eye on most issues took different sides on the subject of the Church's attitude toward private property. Cardinal Siri criticized what Article 81 had to say about the goods of this world being meant for all mankind, especially the words, "Consequently, when man makes use of these goods, he must never regard external possessions as his own but rather as being for common use, intended, that is, not for his own utility alone, but also for the service of others." He held that this was "not exactly what was taught in former papal documents" and wanted the point left out altogether. The cardinal was right in believing that there was a certain discrepancy here, but wrong in thinking that the position taken by the schema did not represent the return to a more ancient and authentic tradition about property, reflected only imperfectly in recent papal statements. The note appended to

* Cf. *St. Louis Review*, October 1, 1965.

this passage made clear that the wording was borrowed from Thomas Aquinas, whereas the only papal authority cited was Pius XII's allocution for Pentecost in 1941. The implication was obvious: the encyclicals of Leo XIII and Pius XI could not be cited because their teaching was obscure and confused regarding the common use of property.* Although in advance of their times in many respects, on this particular point their encyclicals were behind the times. (In the final version of the schema, a reference to Leo XIII's *Rerum Novarum* was worked in and various minor adjustments were made, for the sake of accommodating the sensibilities of people like Cardinal Siri, but the text was not fundamentally altered on this point.) In strange contrast, the generally very conservative Cardinal Bueno y Monreal of Seville felt that the chapter was "too much imbued with a mentality of individualistic liberalism and capitalism" and did not "take sufficient note of the mentality of collectivism existing in a large part of the world." He maintained, correctly, that the doctrine of the absolute inviolability of private property was not identical with Catholic teaching on the subject. "The doctrine on access to ownership, control of wealth, and latifundia should be revised so as to include the possible common ownership of land."

Several speakers, Bishops Hengsbach and Parteli and Archbishop Castellano, wanted more attention paid to the special problems facing agricultural societies. Bishop Höffner, Bishop Franic, and Archbishop Garcia de Sierra y Mendez called for rather drastic revision, Franic proposing that Chapter III and most of the schema be referred to the Synod of Bishops, "which can consider the matters at greater leisure, and, if the Holy Father approves, act on them with conciliar prerogatives." He suggested that a few principles be enunciated in a Synodal Letter now, with the rest being reserved to the Synod. Bishop Coderre of Canada was concerned that the

* See *Third Session*, 1965, p. 175.

chapter was already too dated and hoped that it would be made "more prophetic." In a rambling speech that seemed more intended for consumption in Poland, Cardinal Wyszynski tried to strike a balance between the claims of capitalism and communism and left his hearers in some doubt as to where he stood on the fundamental issues. As might be expected, Cardinal Cardijn spoke on the theme: "Workers of the world, unite!", but in a sense somewhat different from the Communist Manifesto. Finally, Bishop De Vito of India hoped that the position of the Council on economic and social matters would be expressed in language that the poor could understand, not merely experts and theologians, and that the Council would come out strongly against such practices as genocide, the sterilization of women and the vasectomy of men, "which are morally forced on millions of people." Also on the theme of the "Church of the Poor" (Cardinal de Arriba y Castro found the expression objectionable because ambiguous), the Brazilian Archbishop Golland Trindade, in a written intervention, warned the Council: "Pius XI declared that the great tragedy of the Church in the 19th century was that it lost the working class. Let us be careful not to lose the needy, the miserable, the starving who constitute over half of the world's population today!"*

CHAPTER IV: THE LIFE OF THE POLITICAL COMMUNITY.
   86. Public life today.
   87. The nature and end of political society.
   88. The cooperation of all in public life.
   89. The Church and political society.

Briefer still was the discussion of Chapter IV, which consumed only part of one morning, October 5th. There were but four speakers. The only really notable intervention was that of Archbishop Hurley of Durban, who spoke in forthright terms about the need for ridding the Church of out-

* *L'Avvenire d'Italia*, November 3, 1965.

moded forms of expression and thought in the political sphere: "We hope that the traditional reference to the Church as a perfect society (a cliché of scholastic thought) will be dropped. The Church is a society only in an analogical sense. Human activity cannot be divided simply into the temporal order and the spiritual order. In the past, the Church has insisted too much on her own rights. In the future, it is hoped that we will speak with equal concern about the rights of man." (The reference to the Church as a "perfect society" had been dropped in the version debated and was not revived in the final text approved by the Council.) The Polish Archbishop Baraniak, of Poznan, attempted to throw light on the thorny question of the extent to which the faithful living in communist countries should cooperate with communist governments, while the Spanish Bishop Beitia talked about the relations between Church and state as if the Declaration on Religious Liberty had never been heard of and insisted that the confessional state, along Spainsh lines, was the only ideal solution: "No one would dare to defend the essentially lay character of the state, but there are some who do not like the distinction between thesis and hypothesis and propound a diametrically opposite point of view. The contrary, however, has been inculcated by the magisterium. If we look at papal documents from Leo XIII on, we find that the profession of the true religion is required of the state . . ."

The Pope's Visit to the UN

It was not purely coincidental that Pope Paul's visit to the UN was timed to coincide with the opening of debate on the final chapter of Schema 13, on The Community of Nations and the Building Up of Peace. The Pontiff's dramatic gesture was of course intended to convince the world of the Holy See's genuine and sincere desire to do everything possible to promote world peace, but it would also inevitably have the effect of subtly committing the Council to the same cause without of course in any way impinging on its freedom of action. To make sure that this point would be clear to everybody, the Pope deliberately invited a select group of cardinals representative of the different regions of the world and other Council officials to accompany him on his journey.

Early in the year Monsignor Alberto Giovannetti, the emissary of the Holy See at the United Nations headquarters in New York, had handed to Secretary General U Thant a copy of the Pope's disarmament appeal which the Pontiff had made at Bombay on the occasion of his visit to India in December 1964. After nine days the Secretary General replied in a personal letter to the Pope. This correspondence seems to have served as a curtain-raiser for a plan which the Pope had been nurturing for some time.* From the very beginning of his pontificate Pope Paul evinced a marked interest in the UN. It was he who sent Mgr. Giovannetti there as an observer not long after his election. Since January 1965, however, it was noticed that his references to the UN became more frequent in proportion as the state of world peace continued to deteriorate. What was not generally known was that the Pope had been giving serious consideration to a plan for making a personal appearance before the world body to plead for peace, hoping in this way not only to dramatize his efforts but help bolster the waning prestige of that organization. The Holy See has consistently supported the peace efforts of the UN, just as it has faithfully supported every movement tending toward European unity, the Common Market, for example.

During the summer, in a somewhat unprecedented move considering the good relations normally prevailing between them, at least on the surface, differences between the Holy See and French policy came out into the open when the Vatican weekly journal, *L'Osservatore della Domenica,*

* Father Morlion of Assisi, among others, is said to have urged the idea on him.

boldly declared: "French intransigence is endangering the patient work of nearly ten years towards a united Europe." The article viewed the recent impasse at Brussels and withdrawal of the French representative over the failure to reach a common agricultural policy for the Common Market, as well as "the resulting polemics," as a particularly grave development. Vatican authorities were of course unhappy likewise about that part of General De Gaulle's policy that aims at including the satellite countries of Eastern Europe in some kind of European union, if this should mean any weakening of the existing structures as a bulwark against communism.

The first proposal considered was that the Pope would make an appearance before the UN in San Francisco, before the assembly there in June commemorating the 20th anniversary of the UN's foundation. Diplomatic soundings were made. However, it soon developed that this would be impractical for a variety of reasons. The Santo Domingo crisis intervened. An American fundamentalist group threatened to picket Kennedy Airport if the Pope set foot in the U.S. In any case there was scarcely time to prepare for such a momentous event. It was decided therefore to send a papal delegation of lesser note to San Francisco headed by Archbishop O'Connor of the Curia and including Professor Halecki of Fordham University as well as Mgr. Giovannetti. Cardinal Bea had first been slated to head the delegation but this had to be abandoned. Archbishop O'Connor read the papal message before the assembly in San Francisco on June 26, 1965. Shortly before this it became known that the Pope definitely was planning a visit to the UN later this year. Mgr. Giovannetti left for Rome on July 7th, after an interview with U Thant, to work out arrangements for the Pope's appearance.

Papal diplomacy had recently been able to chalk up a success in the way the apostolic delegate in Santo Domingo, Archbishop Clarizio, facilitated the process of getting both sides to discuss their differences. Unlike some members of the

Dominican hierarchy, the Holy See tried to remain strictly neutral in the controversy and thus preserve its effectiveness as a go-between. Ironically some of the communists known to be operating on the island were said to have entered in clerical garb along with the delegates to the Mariological Congress held there in March, before the outbreak of hostilities. Despite the formidable difficulties facing such a visit, the fact that Pope Paul was willing seriously to consider the step was proof of his determination to do all in his power to avert a world catastrophe. Perhaps too one motive was his determination not to allow even the suggestion of an impression to arise that he has been in any way negligent in this regard.

Monsignor Giovannetti was enthusiastic about the papal visit from the first. Since there were no precedents for such an occasion, difficulties arose over the protocol of receiving the Pope. Was the Pope to be received as the head of Vatican City or as the head of the Catholic Church? The Secretary General replied that he intended to receive him as Pope Paul VI, thus brushing aside apparently insoluble dilemmas. There was the question of opposition by members of the Curia, particularly those in the Secretariat of State. It was not so much the old-fashioned view of "It is enough for the Church to speak from Rome and wait for men to come to it," or the belief that it was undignified for the Pope to become involved in the political mêlée, as it was concern that there might be unpredictable consequences. In addition there was a struggle between Monsignor Giovannetti and the Chancery of the Archdiocese of New York over control of the visit. Giovannetti and the UN officials were anxious not to allow the political overtones to get out of hand; the Chancery was understandably desirous that the Archdiocese perform the role of host with regard to the religious aspects of the visit, and that is one of the reasons why the outdoor mass was held at Yankee Stadium rather than outside the Archdiocese. President Johnson was eager to meet the Pope at Kennedy International Airport, but this was ruled out as implying that

the Pope had come to see *him* rather than in response to the
UN invitation. The meeting with the President, though desired, had to be kept as informal and last-minute as possible.
The Pope himself took a personal part in all the planning,
insisting on the long route through Harlem considered dangerous both by his entourage and the New York police. He
wanted to remain in the open car, but was overruled because
of the stiff wind and the fact, not generally known, that he
had started out on the trip with a sore throat from which
some of the other members of his suite were also suffering.
Riding in the bubble-top closed car was therefore a necessary
precaution although it meant that thousands along the route
were able to get only a fleeting glimpse of his white figure.
Typically Pauline also was the desire to underline the journey's ecumenical implications. As he was about to board his
plane in Rome he received a farewell message from the personal representatives of Athenagoras I, Ecumenical Patriarch
of Constantinople. In New York he received Archbishop
Iakovos, local head of the Greek Orthodox Church, in Cardinal Spellman's residence and conferred with him about the
difficulties being faced by Athenagoras under pressure from
the Turkish government. Finally, the Pope met with the UN
representatives of various religious bodies, Protestant, Orthodox, and Jewish, in the Church of the Holy Family on East
47th Street. Two small incidents, noted by those present at
the cathedral were the Pope's gesture of offering Cardinal
Spellman needed support, during their walk around St. Patrick's, by holding out his arm; and his pronunciation of the
name of New York's patron saint, during his brief remarks
inside the cathedral, as "Saint *Pay*trick."

The speech to the UN, broadcast over Italian television,
made a deep impression.* Walter Lippmann's analysis of the
speech was much appreciated and this passage is said to have
pleased the Pope especially: "No one who heard him atten-

---

* See text of the speech, p. 285.

tively, or will read him now, can fail to realize that he was speaking a different language from that which is current and conventional. In fact, the Pope, who is without pride and has nothing to fear, was thinking what is unthinkable for so many, and he was saying it out loud. His conception of the secular world is quite different from the conception which underlies public discussion—be it in Peking or in Washington. The crucial difference is that in the Pope's address the paramount issue is not the cold war or hostile ideologies. Although religion in general and the Roman Church in particular have been treated as the chief enemies of the Communists, the Pope said that the pursuit of peace transcends all other duties, and that the paramount crusade of mankind is the crusade against war and for peace. This is a different set of values than are accepted as righteous in the public life of the warring nations. The Pope was, of course, intending to make this known, and he reached the climax of his message, so it seemed to me, when he declared that the root of evil in this angry, hostile and quarreling world 'is pride, no matter how legitimate it may seem to be' . . . We shall have heard the Pope's message when we have taken those words to heart."

This message was not only "different" and unconventional for statesmen, but for the generality of American Catholics, particularly those clergymen and others who had been expressing scorn for the UN. The moral ratification of the UN by Pope Paul VI, speaking in person from the rostrum of its Assembly, was unquestionably one of the great moments for Roman Catholicism. As Lippmann also said, "This historic act of ratification marks the progress made under the inspiration of John XXIII—the rejuvenation of the Church. The modernizing Church had brought itself into the main stream of human affairs. It has done this by committing itself to the religious reconciliation of mankind." Oddly enough, to the eyes of old Roman hands, this sentiment was echoed in the normally reserved columns of *L'Osservatore Romano.* Not

very long ago it would have been unthinkable for the Vatican
newspaper to print the word "reform" without a whole string
of qualifiers, but the Pope's visit inspired this historic statement: "The trip appears to most people as profoundly connected with the reform of the Church now being carried out
by itself. The *aggiornamento* undertaken . . . has aroused a
great hope in the hearts of mankind. They are convinced that
what has been begun will not go unfinished."*

The Fathers were anxiously awaiting the Pope's return
from New York on Tuesday, October 5, when word reached
the Council floor that his TWA Boeing 707 had touched
down at Fumicino at 12:01. Exactly forty-six minutes later,
the great bells of St. Peter's tolled as his black Mercedes rolled
up to the steps in front of the main door of the basilica in
St. Peter's Square. Smiling and jubilant, as if it were the most
casual thing in the world for a Pope to travel half way round
the globe and back in thirty hours, he alighted from the car.
Then, with a spring in his step, he quickly mounted the red-
carpeted steps to be greeted by the Cardinal Presidents and
Moderators in St. Peter's portico, in a reunion happily devoid
of the usual protocol. Briskly walking up the center aisle, as
the bishops applauded vigorously from their tiered seats on
either side, he took his place at the center of the President's
table. Aware that the morning's session had already been prolonged in order to receive him, he rose at once to give his
address but sat down again when Cardinal Liénart of Lille,
standing beside him in the place of the Cardinal Dean, who
had accompanied the Pope to America, indicated that he
wished to say a few words of greeting. The Pope patiently
heard him out, then delivered his own brief talk in a busi-
ness-like manner, stepped down from the podium, and with a
gesture of greeting to the Protestant and Orthodox observers
in their tribune at the left, and a final lifting of his arms,
hurriedly left the basilica by the side door. The Council

* *L'Osservatore Romano,* October 16, 1965.

ordered the Pope's address to be made part of its official records.

The following day in a general audience Pope Paul explained exactly why he had undertaken such an arduous journey. "There has been much propaganda about peace in recent years, but frequently it has not been very convincing. We felt the need to take up this great theme, to try to get it considered in the light of Christian principles and make everybody more aware of it." Some days before in an interview he had declared, "They asked us to come in connection with the twentieth anniversary of the UN and we said that we would. The Pope could hardly reply, 'Thank you very much for asking us, but we don't have the time.'" He felt that with so many heads of state and statesmen present this was an opportunity that could not be missed, so he had determined, like St. Rocco, Italian patron saint of travelers, to put on his cloak and go. "We wanted to do as the Psalmist says: 'You shall speak in the sight of kings and shall not be confounded.'" Then with a characteristic Pauline gesture of humility he added, "But who knows whether even *we* will carry it off well or badly before so many important people." By common consent he had carried off the business extremely well.

CHAPTER V: THE COMMUNITY OF NATIONS AND THE BUILDING UP OF PEACE.

99. The "balance of terror."
100. International action for avoidance of war.
101. Minor wars and acts related to war.

Section 3: The mission of the Church and of Christians.
102. The Church's presence in the international community.
103. The role of Christians in international institutions.

CONCLUSION
104. The role of each of the faithful and of particular Churches.
105. The dialogue between all men.
106. A world to be built and led to its final destiny.

The Council began to discuss the final and in some ways most crucial chapter of Schema 13 the day the Pope returned from New York. The debate lasted for approximately 3 days.

The section claiming the most attention was of course No. 2, on a stable Peace or the Avoidance of War, which went into the related questions of the horror of modern warfare (98), conventional versus atomic weapons (98), war crimes (98), just and unjust wars (98), the so-called "balance of terror" (99), international action for the avoidance of war (particularly the need for a "public authority wielding effective power at the world level") (100), the possession of nuclear arms not in itself illegitimate (100), the fear of the escalation of war (101), the right to conscientious objection (101), and the need for respecting the "rules of humanity" during wartime (101).* The section began with a ringing Declaration condemning all acts of indiscriminate warfare.** Section 1 dealt with progress and the sharing of wealth (92), development programs (93), the principles governing such programs (94), training and coordination of such work (95), population explosion (96), agriculture and land distribution (96), and controlling population growth (97). The latter paragraph was

* In the final draft of the schema Section 2, considerably rearranged, was placed before Section 1 and combined with Section 3, making for a more logical presentation.
** Quoted by Bishop Hengsbach in his *Relatio*, see p. 226. This Declaration was retained in the final version.

very guarded about public birth control policies, never mentioning the word "birth-control" as such, but instead placed the emphasis on responsible parenthood, education and social improvement, warning against "solutions which completely disregard the moral law and aim at putting a stop to population growth by any available means." It then went on, guardedly, "Where circumstances require it, people are, however, to be informed of the proved findings of scientific progress which present sufficient guarantees from the moral standpoint."*

The majority of the 29 speakers naturally addressed themselves to what might be called the "big issues" in Articles 98–100. About one third also made strong statements on conscientious objection (101); while a somewhat smaller number devoted their attention to Section 1, with a scattering of speakers on various miscellaneous points.

It was fitting that the debate should be led off by Cardinal Alfrink, president of the international Catholic group known as *Pax Christi*. Although the text had been revised in such a way as to emphasize the need for banning all war and to stress the commitment of the Church to this cause, concessions nevertheless had been made to the opposite point of view advocating the "legitimacy," if not the theoretical desirability, of armaments under present world conditions. A crucial passage in Article 100 read:

Nevertheless, as long as international institutions give no adequate guarantee of peace, *the possession of these armaments,* exclusively as a deterrent for an enemy equipped with the same weapons, cannot be said to be in itself illegitimate.

Alfrink commented that the distinction between the possession and use of modern weapons was correct, but the statement about their possession being not illegitimate, "should

---

* This whole paragraph was somewhat expanded in the final version and contained a clearer reference to such approved methods of birth control as the rhythm method.

be dropped from the text because it could serve as an excuse for any nation which wished to participate in the continued equilibrium of terror. The only remedy is the reduction and abolition of modern arms, as Pius XII and John XXIII often said and as our text should declare in place of the last two sentences of Article 100" (which noted that one of the primary concerns of rulers should be "to limit the production and stockpiling of armaments"). In other words, not limited production and stockpiling, but total disarmament should be the goal.

The Dutch cardinal was supported by Abbot Butler: "No one thinks that the great powers merely *possess* such arms. The fact is that, on both sides of the curtain, there is a system of preparation for the use of these arms—and for their illegitimate use in indiscriminate warfare. It might be said: if we think such preparation is legitimate, we had better say so openly, and not hide behind a reference to the mere possession of arms. But then should we not have to go on to say clearly that not only would it be illegitimate to put such preparations into effect in actual war, but the very intention to use them, even a 'conditional intention,' would be gravely immoral? . . . We should do well to avoid such questions. We should not speak about the possession of nuclear arms, because the question is unrealistic and we should also not speak about the legitimacy of preparations for nuclear war. It is obvious enough that the intention of waging war unjustly is itself unjust." Bishop Wheeler, the coadjutor of Middlesborough, concurred in Butler's judgment.

According to Bishop Grant, auxiliary of Northampton, "It is true that the words 'exclusively as a deterrent' could and should be understood, in the sense that all intention to use these arms for the destruction of cities is entirely excluded; but at a cursory glance to the ordinary reader this is by no means clear and most people will understand them as meaning that the retention of these arms destined for the destruction of cities cannot be said of itself to be illegitimate as long as the intention is to use them only for one's own defense and never for the purpose of aggression . . . In order to take away such ambiguity I propose that the words previously cited should be removed from our text; or at least should be so amended that ambiguity is excluded. For example, by adding, after the word 'illegitimate,' the words, 'excluding all intention of ever using them.' " He also suggested that the wording of the previous paragraph should be amended so that it would appear that the Church was not approving the "balance of terror," merely knowledging its existence.

Other speakers were more nuanced in their remarks and did not call for the outright dropping of this passage. For example, Archbishop Beck of Liverpool commented: "It seems clear that a government which possesses nuclear weapons as a deterrent and threatens to use them as such is in a proximate occasion of sin. It may be argued that until our international institutions become effective . . . this proximate occasion of sin is what moralists call a 'necessary occasion' to be accepted as a compromise pending the creation of that balance of trust and discussion which must succeed to the present balance of terror."

The schema practically abandoned the classical distinction between "just" and "unjust" wars in view of the terrible repercussions and potentialities of modern warfare, while at the same time admitting the legitimacy of self-defense:

Consequently it may not be unlawful, when all possibilities of peaceful negotiation have been tried without avail, to use force and coercion against an unjust aggressor in defense of rights that have been unjustly attacked; but it is becoming daily more and more unthinkable that war should be a suitable remedy for the violation of justice.

However, this guarded language was not to the liking of some of the bishops. Cardinal Liénart, for example, said that it was no longer sufficient to talk about the distinction between just and unjust wars, because so much depended on

the means whereby war was waged. Pope John XXIII, in
Pacem in terris, pointed out the way the world should forestall the terrors of war and adjust to the path of peace. The
schema contained a contradiction, according to Cardinal
Léger, in that it tried to show that wars and arms should be
absolutely banned, while at the same time admitting that
wars could be lawful under certain circumstances. "In our
times, the classical theory of the morality of war is unrealistic
and inapplicable." New terms should be found. "The Council should refrain from mentioning 'just' wars and from banning arms in the abstract." Archbishop Martin, of Rouen,
was even more explicit: "The very notion of war must be
banned from our vocabulary and from the field of human
activity, because the world is sitting on a volcano that can
erupt at any time. We cannot talk in the traditional terminology of theology about just and unjust wars because the
total war of today is completely different from war as known
in previous ages . . . According to the expression of Pius XII,
we must wage war on war, and repeat fervently with Paul
VI at the UN the prayer that the world may never again behold the dread spectre of war." The one speaker to put in a
plea for the classical distinction, Bishop Castán Lacoma, of
Siguenza-Guadalajara, Spain, was not able to make much
headway against the overwhelming sentiment that the traditional view was out of date.* As Bishop Rusch of Innsbruck
expressed it: "The Council should solemnly declare that all
aggressive wars are unjust under today's circumstances."

Not that anybody expected one of the bishops to get up
and say that he was actually in favor of war. But about the
same degree of shock and surprise, though in a wholly positive sense, was caused by the totally unexpected support from
Cardinal Ottaviani for the anti-war thesis. The cardinal be-

---

* The final version speaks about the "right to legitimate defense" and
"military action for the *just* defense of the people," but abandons use of the
adjective "unjust" e.g. in the above paragraph, which seemed to imply that,
under certain circumstances, there could be such a thing as "just aggression."

gan by remarking that in his opinion the schema suffered
from a number of defects, one of which was that the "aims of
justice and charity needed to overcome wars" were not sufficiently spelled out, such as civic and religious education, the
fostering of a spirit of fraternity, more use of arbitration,
more respect for the decisions of such international bodies as
the International Court of Justice at the Hague and the
United Nations. It was somewhat unusual for most of his
audience to hear the aged cardinal speaking in this conciliatory and constructive vein, though not for those of course
who knew about his background as a teacher of international
law. Interest picked up when he began to enlarge on the
meaning of war. War must not be understood too narrowly
or conventionally in the sense of military warfare. The concept should be broadened to include such things as armed
revolution, guerrilla activities, and subtle acts of sabotage
and terrorism such as those used by communists to bring
about the subjection of other countries. The schema should
contain "a sharp reproof of war waged to impose a particular
ideology." He then went on to quote a famous passage from
Thomas Aquinas' *Government of Rulers,* to the effect that
when people see their own government inviting ruin by an
aggressive war, they can and must overthrow that government
by just means. The sacred right of rebellion! "War would
only be a memory," according to the cardinal, "if the words
of Pope Paul spoken at the UN were fixed forever in the
hearts of rulers and people alike." In a final burst of fervid
oratory, carried away perhaps by the thought that this would
be his last appearance, he dared to suggest, "The Council
therefore should give its vote to the creation of one world
republic composed of all the nations of the world, in which
there would no longer be strife among nations, but an entire
world living in peace: the peace of Christ in the reign of
Christ!" Such eloquence of course was greeted by tremendous
applause, said to have been one of the longest at the Council,
even from those who on second thought probably had mis-

givings about some of his points. There could be no doubt that the head of the Holy Office was wholeheartedly against war.

None of the other bishops was prepared to go as far as Ottaviani in support of the one-world idea, but many of them gave their enthusiastic endorsement to the more moderate suggestions in the schema for the establishment of a "public authority wielding effective power at the world level" (100), and for various international bodies "to foster and stimulate cooperation between men" (102) as well as the recommendation that the Church should be actively engaged in this lofty work on all levels, "through her official bodies and through a full and sincere cooperation of all Christians" (102). Cardinal Duval, Bishop Rusch, Bishop Brezanoczy, and Bishop Ancel all spoke in this sense, Rusch in particular calling for a "Peace Council at the Holy See, composed of experts in moral, political and military matters."

The text had rather strong language on the necessity of obedience to competent authorities (101): "When God's law is not evidently violated, the competent authority must be presumed to be in the right, and its instructions must be obeyed." On the other hand, its language was rather weak in recognizing a right to conscientious objection:

> Furthermore, under present circumstances, it would seem fitting for legislation to reflect a positive attitude towards those people who, as a witness of Christian meekness, or out of respect for human life or sincere distaste for all use of violence, refuse, in conscience, to do military service or certain actions which, in time of war, lead to barbarous cruelty (101).

However, it was a gain to have this much said. Various suggestions were made for watering down the first statement and strengthening the second. Cardinal Alfrink declared: "The sentence regarding the presumption in favor of competent authority should be omitted, even though true, because it will open the way to abuse, as experience under totalitarian governments has shown. What is said on behalf of conscientious objectors, on the other hand, should be retained, since it is the Church's task to defend the freedom of the human conscience." Cardinal Léger wanted the reference to conscientious objection strengthened, so that the objector's motive would not appear to be mere softness. Dom Butler found objectionable the suggestion, or implication, that objectors were in some way "morally immature." "It would be better to speak simply of objections based on genuinely conscientious grounds (and we might refer to our Declaration on Religious Liberty). Some conscientious objectors may in fact be prophets of a truly Christian morality." According to Bishop Wheeler: "The words describing the conscientious objector are so weak and patronizing as to suggest that he is a milksop. The witness of the conscientious objector is something to be valued and welcomed as a special factor in modern life even by those of us who would not be classed as conscientious objectors. I would like to see these weak descriptions changed to 'as a witness of the Christian vocation to bring about peace.' " Bishop Grant and Archbishop Beck also spoke out in favor of strengthening this passage, the latter in particular expressing the wish "to see stronger emphasis both on what public authority must never do or threaten to do under pain of losing its right to the obedience of its subjects and the rights of conscience of all citizens in certain circumstances . . . We must ask that the rulers of nations should respect the consciences of those of their subjects who look upon certain forms of war as never justifiable even for defensive purposes. This is not a question of Christian meekness or of non-violence."

On the other hand, Bishops Castán Lacoma and Carli were plainly nervous about the whole business of conscientious objection, the former remarking, lamely, that since theologians were not in agreement on the subject, it was a matter best left to the civil authority; the latter urging that this passage should be removed from the schema, because it was

a topic that should either be dealt with consistently or not
at all. Carli's attitude was a reflection of the embarrassment
felt by various members of the Italian hierarchy about the
efforts currently being made to change Italian thinking and
laws on this subject, in conformity with the norms widely
accepted elsewhere, particularly in countries of the English-
speaking world.*

Several speakers availed themselves of the recommendations in Section 1 about aid programs for underdeveloped
countries and the need for international cooperation to raise
living standards as part of a long-range plan for avoiding and
preventing war, to give further endorsement to the idea for
the Secretariat mentioned earlier in connection with the
debate on Chapter III. Again, there was no formal recommendation to this effect in the text, probably because it
would have seemed inappropriate unless other international
organizations were expressly mentioned at the same time.
Archbishop McCann, Bishop Wheeler, and Bishop Grant
spoke on this point. However, the more interesting speeches
related to the demographic problem or population explosion
and several unusually forthright statements were made about
the urgent need for the Church, and responsible authorities,
to begin coping with it, with greater vigor and determination
than the relatively timid language of the schema seemed to
suggest. Bishop Marling of Jefferson City, Missouri felt that
Articles 96–97 did not face up to the basic problem at all,
namely that "capital investment in the poorer nations fails
to keep up with the rate of population growth. Experts say
that to maintain the standard of living in a country with an
annual population growth of 3% (which is typical of Latin

---

* Unfortunately, in the final version of Schema 13, the passage referring
to conscientious objection was somewhat weakened, apparently in deference
to Curial and misguided American sensibilities. Cf. what Cardinal Spellman
had to say when opening the debate on Schema 13, p. 60. Ironically, Archbishop Roberts claimed that there was a conspiracy to keep him from speaking on this subject in the Council, on the grounds that he might damage the
prospects for approval, so he gave his usual press conference. Cf. *Le Monde,*
October 14. 1965 and *Catholic Herald,* October 15, 1965.

America), a 10% increase in investments is required. But this is impossible for poorer countries. It is said that if the agricultural methods used in Holland were applied in India, the latter country could easily feed its multitudes. But to raise India to the standards of Holland would require the annual investment of 12 billion dollars over the next hundred years, even if we pretended that the number of Indian citizens remained constant! As the schema points out, richer nations can give emergency help, but this does not touch the basic question of raising the living standard in the face of a demographic explosion." The bishop went on to ask pointedly, "Is it any wonder that poorer nations turn to what our text calls 'solutions which take no account of the moral law'? The vast difference between rich and poor nations is the basic problem in our economic order and no solution has yet been proposed which is sufficiently daring to be effective. The Council should openly urge public authorities to investigate scientifically those means of family limitation which would be permitted by the moral law." He suggested too that the Church should participate in international congresses exploring this and related problems, such as the Pan-American Assembly on Population that met last year in Colombia.

Bishop Marling's intervention, while strongly advocating investigation of the potentialities of licit birth control methods as a means of controlling the population explosion, was neutral on the subject of which methods might be allowed. Not so Bishop Gaviola, of the Philippines, whose talk was a commentary on the evil being done in various parts of the world by those advocating both licit and illicit methods of birth control. According to the bishop, Pope John, in *Mater et Magistra,* had affirmed that the conclusions of the theory of over-population were too uncertain and changeable to serve as a basis for any such drastic action. "Lest the Council's words be used for their own ends by dishonest advocates of birth control who are often motivated by a desire for profit rather than by a real concern for the common good, the

Council should clearly proclaim the immutable teaching on birth control and the prevention of natural procreation by illicit means.* The Commission should weigh the scientific theories which dismiss the theory of over-population as in no way probable, at least with respect to the entire habitable world. Admission of this theory can lead even believers to question the wisdom of God in creation or can cast doubt on divine Providence, as if God, who gave man the power to multiply life, were failing to provide the means for preserving life." He went on to remark that investigation had shown that a decrease in the population had adverse effects on the economic stability of a country, concluding with the pious exhortation: "Let us not contribute to making the People of God lazy and soft."

If the bishop from the Philippines was opposed to letting down any of the barriers with regard to birth control methods, Bishop Simons of Indore, India, in one of the most outspoken pronouncements on this subject ever made on the floor of the Council, was all for throwing the whole question open to thorough investigation and held out the hope that if the alleged natural law basis for banning the use of artificial contraceptive means was seriously examined, it might not constitute such an obstacle as had been supposed. By a curious irony, the bishop spoke two days after Pope Paul had seemed to many to be reasserting the rigid Catholic position when he told the UN: "You deal here above all with human life; and the life of man is sacred; no one may dare to offend it. Respect for life, even with regard to the great problem of birth, must find here in your assembly its highest affirmation and its most reasoned defense. You must strive to multiply bread so that it suffices for the tables of mankind, and not rather favor an artificial control of birth, which would be irrational, in order to diminish the number of

---

* The bishop's specific recommendations should be compared with the final version of this section of the schema, modified in accordance with Pope Paul's wishes and approved by the Council. See p. 210.

guests at the banquet of life." Some of the delegates found the Pope's words somewhat self-contradictory in that the Catholic Church was known to favor the use of the rhythm method of birth control but seemed to be warning the assembly rather categorically against "artificial control of birth." This may not have been his intention, however. There was nothing ambiguous about Bishop Simons' recommendations. In substance he said: "The demographic explosion is an undeniable fact. Hence, there arises a grave obligation to arrest this growth in population. It is wrong to say that the riches of the world have not yet been completely tapped and that they are inexhaustible. The means used to bring about this check in population growth will depend for their moral aspect upon their effects. Laws, even the natural law, are for men, not men for the laws. Thus, the conclusions of many theologians need to be re-thought. The traditional arguments against birth control based on the frustration of nature are not at all convincing. Since the Church does not condemn the complete non-use of sex, why should it condemn partial use? The moralists of previous generations failed to consider the many aspects of the problem. Not even the precepts of the natural law impose an absolute and never changing obligation. The natural law forbids taking human life but it is lawful to kill in self-defense, to wage war, and to inflict capital punishment. Lastly, in the present state of the question, the sense and binding force of the law prohibiting artificial means of birth control are open to doubt and, according to our basic juridical principles, a law on whose meaning grave doubt exists is not binding."*

Lending poignancy to the scene as the bishops debated the great issues of war and peace, were 20 lay women from various countries, including Dorothy Day of *The Catholic Worker*, who fasted and prayed in a house on the Via dell'Anima calling upon God to enlighten them in their deliberations. The

---

* Summary of English press bulletin.

Fathers were reminded about this by Bishop Boillon, of Verdun, who also recalled for their benefit the fact that he was the bishop of a see that had been the scene of the bloodiest single battle of the First World War.

Archbishop Garrone then rose to sum up the debate, promising that the sharp judgments passed on certain parts of the schema would be taken into account in revising it, the Latin style would be corrected, more care exercised in the use of such terms as "the world," the scriptural references would be checked, the optimistic tone of certain parts would be modified, Parts I and II would be better integrated. He refused to promise any drastic revision of the section dealing with atheism, and said that it was the "mind of the commission" not to effect any change in the title "Pastoral Constitution," but this matter would be carefully weighed. In conclusion he made it clear that a "major revision" would be undertaken, as desired by so many of the speakers.

The Revision of Schema 13

As soon as the Council had finished debating sections of the schema and the oral and written interventions were forwarded to them by Archbishop Felici's office, the various subcommissions (of the Mixed Commission) set to work revising the text. In addition to 9 subcommissions* concerned with the actual drafting of the text, there was also a Central Subcommission, under Archbishop Garrone, which coordinated the work of all the others, acting as a sort of clearinghouse and settling various questions about procedure, order, style, quotations, etc. It consisted of the presidents of the various subcommissions plus seven prelates from outside who

* The 9 working subcommissions were as follows: 1. Signs of the Times, Bishop McGrath president; 2. Human Person, Bishop Wright; 3. Human Activity, Archbishop Garrone; 4. Task of the Church, Bishop Ancel; 5. Marriage and the Family, Archbishop Dearden; 6. Culture, Canon Moeller (replacing Bishop Guano); 7. Economic and Social Life, Bishop Hengsbach; 8. Political Life, Bishop Laszlo; 9. Peace and the International Community, Bishop Schröffer.

were supposed to aid in the achievement of a more balanced view. Unfortunately this body was not able to function as effectively as had been hoped, because of the tremendous pressure involved in producing a text that could be voted and promulgated by December 7th. There was also a small offshoot of this Central Subcommission called the "Small Editorial Subcommission" (*Parva S. Commissio Redactoria*), consisting of Mgr. Philips,* *relator* for the Central Subcommission, and the *periti* Hauptman, Moeller, Tucci and Hirschmann, concerned only with stylistic questions that later went over the drafts produced by subcommissions and gave them final form.

The Mixed Commission was presided over by Cardinals Ottaviani and Cento, the presidents of the two Commissions composing it (Theological and Apostolate of the Laity). The meetings were quite large, consisting of the commission members and as many as 30 or 40 periti and lay auditors (both men and women).

At a meeting of the Central Subcommission, on September 30th, Mgr. Philips summed up the impression of the debate to date, and announced that the section on atheism would be revised by a special subcommission consisting of Cardinal König's Secretariat for Non-Believers and the respective subcommission of the Mixed Commission. Another meeting of the Central Subcommission was held on October 14th. On October 19th the plenary Mixed Commission was able to begin its formal review of the work of the various subcommissions. Mgr. Philips announced that the Commission would meet twice a day every day (except Sunday) until the end of the month and if necessary on November 2, 3 and 4th. A revised text was to be ready for the Fathers by about November 10th. In order to save time, stylistic questions were to be dealt with in writing only. Fifteen minutes had once been spent deciding whether one word should be moved to an-

---

* Mgr. Philips became ill and had to return to Belgium on October 25th. He was replaced by Canon Heylen.

other place in the text. He then said that it would be better for the *relator* to reply to the various points raised at the end of each section, after everybody had been heard. This was agreed, whereupon Cardinal Browne and Bishop Colombo began the discussion of the Introduction.

The Introduction and Chapter I of Part I occupied the Commission during its meetings on October 19, 20, 21, and 22 (Paragraphs 18 and 19 on atheism were discussed on Oct. 21). Chapter II and Chapter III on October 22; Chapter IV on October 23; and Chapter I of of Part II on marriage occupied October 25. Chapter II was discussed on October 26 and 27; Chapter III on October 27 and 28; Chapter IV on October 28 and 29; and Chapter V on October 29 and 30. The Editorial Subcommission worked feverishly on November 2 and 8–9 (on the latter occasion until 5 a.m. the next morning) to get the revised text into final shape. Part II was distributed to the Fathers on November 12th, Part I on November 13th. Because of the unusual length of the booklets (151 pages all told), it was impossible to follow the usual practice of printing the old and new texts side by side.

Summary

September 22, 1965, Wednesday—133RD GENERAL CONGREGATION.
MASS: Bishop Ndong, Auxiliary of Libreville, Gabon.
MODERATOR: Cardinal Lercaro.
PRESENT: 2,260 Fathers.
ANNOUNCEMENTS: Mass tomorrow will be celebrated by Cardinal Cicognani commemorating the 60th anniversary of his ordination (applause); schedule of voting on Apostolate of Laity distributed.
PENDING BUSINESS: Declaration on Religious Liberty.
SPEAKERS (in name of 70 bishops): 1. Archbishop Wojtyla (Kraków, Poland). 2. Bishop Doumith (Sarba, Lebanon). 3. Bishop

Grotti (Tunigaba, Brazil). 4. Bishop Ancel (Auxiliary, Lyons, France).

PENDING BUSINESS: Schema 13, in general.

SPEAKERS: 5. Cardinal Ruffini (Palermo, Italy). 6. Cardinal Siri (Genoa, Italy). 7. Cardinal König (Vienna, Austria). 8. Cardinal Döpfner (Munich, Germany). 9. Archbishop Amici (Modena, Italy). 10. Archbishop Jordan (Edmonton, Alberta, Canada). 11. Archbishop Aramburu (Tucumán, Argentina). 12. Bishop McVinney (Providence, R.I.). 13. Archbishop D'Avack (Italy). 14. Bishop Rusch (Innsbruck, Austria). 15. Archbishop de Proença Sigaud (Diamantina, Brazil). 16. Archbishop Hermaniuk (Winnipeg, Canada).

VOTES: Divine Revelation.

	Total	Placet	Non placet	Placet iuxta modum	Invalid
12–Art. 14-16, Chap. IV	2,233	2,183	—	47	3
13–Art. 17-18	2,230	2,211	15	—	4 (3)
14–Art. 19	2,233	2,162	61	—	10 (7)
15–Art. 20	2,231	2,219	6	—	6 (3)
16–Chap. V	2,170	1,850	4	313	3
17–Art. 21-22	2,040	2,029	8	—	3
18–Art. 23-24	2,012	1,988	21	—	3
19–Art. 25-26	2,057	2,041	9	—	7
20–Chap. VI	2,132	1,915	1	212	—

September 23, 1965, Thursday—134TH GENERAL CONGREGATION.

MASS: Cardinal Cicognani, Secretary of State.

MODERATORS: Cardinals Lercaro and Döpfner.

PRESENT: 2,229 Fathers.

ANNOUNCEMENTS: Revised schema on Priestly Formation distributed.

PENDING BUSINESS: Schema 13, in general.

SPEAKERS: 1. Cardinal Rugambwa (Bukoba, Tanzania). 2. Cardinal Shehan (Baltimore, Md.). 3. Bishop de Castro Mayer (Campos, Brazil). 4. Archbishop Morcillo (Madrid, Spain). 5. Archbishop Lourdusamy (Coadjutor, Bangalore, India). 6. Bishop Renard (Versailles, France). 7. Bishop Mason (Vicar Apostolic, El Obeid, Sudan). 8. Archbishop Kominek (Breslau, Poland). 9. Archbishop Baudoux (Saint Boniface, Canada).

NEW BUSINESS: Schema 13, Introd.
SPEAKERS: *Relator:* Bishop McGrath. 10. Cardinal Cardijn (Belgium). 11. Bishop Abasolo y Lecue (Vijayapuram, India).
STANDING VOTE to close debate on Schema 13 as a whole, at 11:45.

VOTE: Schema 13, whether to proceed to discussion of Part I.

	Total	*Placet*	*Non placet*	Invalid
Motion	2,157	2,111	44	2 (1)

VOTES: Apostolate of the Laity.
Relator: Bishop Hengsbach.

	Total	*Placet*	*Non placet*	*Placet iuxta modum*	Invalid
1–Art. 1	2,224	2,218	5	—	1 (1)
2–Art. 2-3	2,224	2,205	18	—	1 (1)
3–Art. 4	2,206	2,185	19	—	2 (2)
4–Chap. I	2,130	1,904	8	213	5
5–Art. 5-6	2,034	2,025	9	—	—
6–Art. 7	2,077	2,068	8	—	1
7–Art. 8	2,171	2,163	8	—	—

September 24, 1965, Friday—135TH GENERAL CONGREGATION.
MASS: Bishop Franssen, Vicar Apostolic, Gimma, Ethiopia.
MODERATOR: Cardinal Döpfner.
PRESENT: 2,182 Fathers.
ANNOUNCEMENTS: Telegram to Pope congratulating him on his birthday, Sept. 26th.
PENDING BUSINESS: Schema 13, Introd.
SPEAKERS: 1. Cardinal Frings (Cologne, Germany). 2. Bishop Volk (Mainz, Germany). 3. Bishop Marafini (Veroli Frosinone, Italy). 4. Archbishop Elchinger (Coadjutor, Strasbourg, France). 5. Bishop Himmer (Tournai, Belgium). 6. Bishop Charue (Namur, Belgium).
NEW BUSINESS: Schema 13, Part I, Chap. I.
SPEAKERS: 7. Cardinal Meouchi (Antioch). 8. Cardinal Richaud (Bordeaux, France). 9. Cardinal Santos (Manila, Philippines). 10. Cardinal Seper (Zagreb, Yugoslavia). 11. Archbishop Ziadé (Beirut). 12. Archbishop Cantero Cuadrado (Zaragoza, Spain).

VOTES: Apostolate of Laity.

	Total	Placet	Non placet	Placet iuxta modum	Invalid
8–Chap. II	2,167	1,975	2	190	—
9–Art. 9-10	2,172	2,161	8	—	3 (2)
10–Art. 11-12	2,162	2,145	14	—	3 (1)
11–Art. 13-14	2,073	2,065	6	—	1 (1)
12–Chap. III	2,023	1,707	4	313	1
13–Art. 15-17	1,975	1,972	3	—	—
14–Art. 18-19	2,022	2,013	8	—	1

September 27, 1965, Monday—136TH GENERAL CONGREGATION.
MASS: Bishop Loosdregt, Vicar Apostolic, Vientiane, Laos.
MODERATOR: Cardinal Döpfner.
PRESENT: 2,147 Fathers.
ANNOUNCEMENTS: Letter from Pope to Council expressing thanks for telegram read by SG; voting on Pastoral Office of Bishops will begin on Wednesday.
PENDING BUSINESS: Schema 13, Chap. I.
SPEAKERS: 1. Cardinal Maximos IV Saigh (Antioch). 2. Cardinal König (Vienna, Austria). 3. Cardinal Florit (Florence, Italy). 4. Cardinal Rossi (São Paulo, Brazil). 5. Bishop Klepacz (Lodz, Poland). 6. Bishop Ruotolo (Ugento, Italy). 7. Archbishop D'Souza, (Bhopal, India). 8. Bishop Elko (Rutherian Bishop of Pittsburgh). 9. Father Arrupe, Superior General of the Society of Jesus. 10. Archbishop Guerry (Cambrai, France). 11. Bishop Pildain y Zapiáin (Canary Islands, Spain). 12. Bishop Corboy (Monze, Zambia). 13. Father Fernández, Master General of Dominican Order.

VOTES: Apostolate of Laity.

	Total	Placet	Non placet	Placet iuxta modum	Invalid
15–Art. 20-22	2,143	2,104	35	—	4 (3)
16–Chap. IV	2,128	1,834	7	287	—
17–Art. 23-25	2,139	2,123	11	—	5
18–Art. 26-27	2,139	2,121	18	—	—
19–Chap. V	2,140	1,894	9	230	7
20–Art. 28-30	2,080	2,063	17	—	—
21–Art. 31-33	2,020	2,012	5	—	3
22–Chap. VI	2,016	1,865	3	143	5

September 28, 1965, Tuesday—137TH GENERAL CONGREGATION.

MASS: Cardinal Beran of Prague, Czechoslovakia.

MODERATOR: Cardinal Döpfner.

PRESENT: 2,161 Fathers.

ANNOUNCEMENTS: Tomorrow voting on Pastoral Office of Bishops only by *Placet* and *Non placet;* text of an addition to schema distributed, concerning Synod of Bishops; discussion of Part II of Schema 13 will begin tomorrow.

PENDING BUSINESS: Schema 13, Part I.

SPEAKERS: 1. Cardinal Peter Batanian (Cilicia). 2. Bishop Llopis Ivorra (Coria Cáceres, Spain). 3. Bishop Méndez Arceo (Cuernavaca, Mexico). 4. Bishop Hnilica (Czechoslovakia). 5. Archbishop Marty (Rheims, France). 6. Archbishop Garrone (Toulouse, France). 7. Bishop Schick (Auxiliary, Fulda, Germany). 8. Bishop Rusnack (Auxiliary, Ukrainian Eparchate, Toronto). 9. Bishop Soares de Resende (Beira, Mozambique). 10. Bishop Darmajuwana (Semarang, Indonesia). 11. Archbishop Mosquera Corral (Guayaquil, Ecuador). 12. Bishop Kuharic (Auxiliary, Zagreb, Yugoslavia). 13. Archbishop Bengsch (Berlin, Germany). 14. Archbishop Wojtyla (Kraków, Poland). 15. Bishop Romero Menjíbar (Jaén, Spain).

September 29, 1965, Wednesday—138TH GENERAL CONGREGATION.

MASS: Bishop Haller, Abbot Primate of Canons Regular of Lateran.

MODERATOR: Cardinal Suenens.

PRESENT: 2,190 Fathers.

ANNOUNCEMENTS: Letter from Cardinal Cicognani to Cardinal Tisserant, thanking Council in name of Pope for its message regarding the Synod of Bishops, the encyclical, and its hopes for his UN visit.

NEW BUSINESS: Schema 13, Part II, Chap. I on Marriage.

SPEAKERS: *Relator:* Bishop Hengsbach. 1. Cardinal Ruffini (Palermo, Italy). 2. Cardinal Léger (Montreal, Canada). 3. Cardinal Suenens (Brussels-Malines, Belgium). 4. Cardinal Colombo (Milan, Italy). 5. Archbishop Alonso Muñoyerro (Spain). 6. Bishop Taguchi (Osaka, Japan). 7. Bishop Majdanski (Auxiliary, Wroclavek, Poland). 8. Archbishop Zoghby (Patriarchal Vicar for Egypt). 9. Archbishop Nicodemo (Bari, Italy). 10. Bishop Volk (Mainz, Germany).

VOTES: Pastoral Office of Bishops.
Relator: Archbishop Veuillot.

	Total	Placet	Non placet	Invalid
1–Art. 4	2,182	2,160	22	—
2–Art. 5	2,182	2,171	8	3 (2)
3–Art. 8, 1. 13-14	2,162	2,144	18	—
4–Art. 8, 1. 17-22	2,137	2,115	22	—
5–Art. 9	2,122	2,070	51	1
6–Art. 10	2,097	2,041	54	2
7–Rest of Chap. I	2,014	1,999	15	—

September 30, 1965, Thursday—139TH GENERAL CONGREGATION.
MASS: Bishop J. Martin of Bururi, Burundi.
MODERATOR: Cardinal Suenens.
PRESENT: 2,177 Fathers.
ANNOUNCEMENTS: Text of Declaration on Non-Christian Religions
distributed; voting on Religious Life will begin Wed., Oct. 6.
PENDING BUSINESS: Schema 13, Part II, Chap. I.
SPEAKERS: 1. Cardinal Journet (Switzerland). 2. Cardinal Heenan
(Westminster, England). 3. Cardinal Rossi (São Paulo, Brazil).
4. Cardinal Conway (Armagh, Ireland). 5. Cardinal Browne
(Curia). 6. Archbishop Djajasepoetra (Djakarta, Indonesia).
7. Bishop Tomasek (Apostolic Administrator, Prague, Czecho-
slovakia). 8. Archbishop F. da Silva (Braga, Portugal). 9. Bishop
De Roo (Victoria, Canada). 10. Archbishop Urtasun (Avignon,
France). 11. Bishop Reuss (Auxiliary, Mainz, Germany). 12.
Bishop Bednorz (Coadjutor, Katowice, Poland). 13. Bishop Von
Streng (Basel-Lugano, Switzerland). 14. Bishop de Orbegozo
(Prelate Nullius, Yauyosa, Peru).

VOTES: Pastoral Office of Bishops, Chap. II.
Relator: Bishop Jubany.

	Total	Placet	Non placet	Invalid
8–Art. 16	2,178	2,172	5	1 (1)
9–Art. 17	2,175	1,989	185	1 (1)
10–Art. 27	2,176	2,163	13	—
11–Art. 28	2,170	2,137	32	1
12–Art. 29	2,147	2,137	9	1

October 1, 1965, Friday—140TH GENERAL CONGREGATION.

MASS: Archbishop Mar Athanese Jean Bakose, of Baghdad, in Syrian rite.

MODERATOR: Cardinal Suenens.

PRESENT: 2,128 Fathers.

ANNOUNCEMENTS: Mass will be offered for Pope's intention on Monday, when he flies to the UN; on Tuesday bishops will await Pope's return in late morning; schedule of congregations will remain as announced until Oct. 15 to complete discussion of schemata; if necessary congregation will also be held on Sat., Oct. 16; an intersession is foreseen from Oct. 18 to 23; Pope will submit certain questions to Episcopal Conferences; toward end of October it is hoped to hold first Public Session; schedule of voting for remaining texts; message from Pope to UN read by SG; vote on Pastoral Office of Bishops as a whole, next Wednesday.

PENDING BUSINESS: Schema 13, Part II, Chap. I on Marriage.

SPEAKERS: 1. Cardinal Gracias (Bombay, India). 2. Cardinal Slipyi (Lwów, Ukraine). 3. Bishop Ddungu (Masaka, Uganda). 4. Bishop Hacault (Auxiliary, Saint Boniface, Canada). 5. Bishop Schmitt (Metz, France).

NEW BUSINESS: Schema 13, Part II, Chap. II on Culture.

SPEAKERS: 6. Bishop Elchinger (Coadjutor, Strasbourg, France). 7. Bishop Le Couedic (Troyes, Frances). 8. Bishop Lebrun (Autun, France). 9. Father Fernández, Master General of Dominicans. 10. Archbishop Pellegrino (Turin, Italy). 11. Bishop Blanchet (Catholic Institute, Paris). 12. Bishop Padin (Auxiliary, Rio de Janeiro, Brazil).

STANDING VOTE to close debate on Part II, Chapter I of Schema 13.

VOTES: Pastoral Office of Bishops.

	Total	*Placet*	*Non placet*	Invalid
13–Art. 33, 35	2,129	2,093	36	—
14–Art. 35, 1.17ff.	2,125	2,046	76	3
15–Rest of Chap. II	2,118	2,090	26	2
16–Chap. III	2,060	2,039	20	1

October 4, 1965, Monday—141ST GENERAL CONGREGATION.

MASS: Bishop Silvestri, of Foligno, Italy.

MODERATOR: Cardinal Suenens.

PRESENT: 1,944 Fathers.

ANNOUNCEMENTS: Archbishop Krol substituted for Archbishop Felici as SG.

PENDING BUSINESS: Schéma 13, Part II, Chap. II on Culture.

SPEAKERS: 1. Archbishop Morcillo (Madrid, Spain). 2. Bishop Frotz (Auxiliary, Cologne, Germany). 3. Bishop Spülbeck (Meissen, Germany). 4. Archbishop Veuillot (Coadjutor, Paris, France). 5. Archbishop Zoghby (Patriarchal Vicar for Egypt). 6. Bishop Bettazzi (Auxiliary, Bologna, Italy).

NEW BUSINESS: Schema 13, Part II, Chap. III on Economic-Social Life.

SPEAKERS: 7. Cardinal Siri (Genoa, Italy). 8. Cardinal de Arriba y Castro (Tarragona, Spain). 9. Cardinal Bueno y Monreal (Seville, Spain). 10. Bishop Swanstrom (Auxiliary, New York, N.Y.). 11. Bishop Hengsbach (Essen, Germany). 12. Archbishop Thangalathil (Trivandrum, India). 13. Archbishop Fernandes (Coadjutor, New Delhi, India). 14. Bishop Franic (Split, Yugoslavia). 15. Bishop Hoffner (Münster, Germany). 16. Bishop Coderre (St. John, Quebec, Canada). 17. Archbishop García de Sierra y Méndez (Burgos, Spain).

October 5, 1965, Tuesday—142ND GENERAL CONGREGATION.

MASS: Archbishop-Bishop Bengsch, of Berlin, Germany.

MODERATOR: Cardinal Suenens.

PRESENT: 2,174 Fathers.

ANNOUNCEMENTS: End of debate today set for 11:30 to await Pope's return; request made by Cardinal Liénart that Pope's UN address be made part of Council Acts.

RETURN of Pope Paul from UN. Pope reached St. Peter's shortly before 1 P.M. and delivered a brief report on his historic flight.

PENDING BUSINESS: Schema 13, Part II, Chap. III on Economic-Social Life.

SPEAKERS: 1. Cardinal Wyszynski (Warsaw, Poland). 2. Cardinal Cardijn (Belgium). 3. Father Mahon, Superior General of Society of St. Joseph. 4. Bishop Himmer (Tournai, France). 5. Bishop Larrain Errázuriz (Talca, Chile). 6. Bishop Echeverría Ruíz (Ambato, Ecuador). 7. Bishop Añoveros Ataún (Cadiz y Centa, Spain). 8. Bishop Parteli (Tacuarembo, Uruguay). 9. Archbishop I. Castellano (Siena, Italy). 10. Bishop De Vito (Lucknow, India).

NEW BUSINESS: Schema 13, Pt. II, Chap. IV on Political Community.

SPEAKERS: 11. Bishop del Campo y de la Barcena (Calahorra,

Spain). 12. Bishop Beitia (Santander, Spain). 13. Archbishop
Baraniak (Poznan, Poland). 14. Archbishop Hurley (Durban,
South Africa).
NEW BUSINESS: Schema 13, Pt. II, Chap. V on Promoting Peace.
SPEAKERS: 15. Cardinal Alfrink (Utrecht, Holland). 16. Cardinal
McCann (Capetown, South Africa).

October 6, 1965, Wednesday—143RD GENERAL CONGREGATION.
MASS: Archbishop Coucherousset (Bangui, Central African Re-
public).
MODERATOR: Cardinal Suenens.
PRESENT: 2,180 Fathers.
ANNOUNCEMENTS: Distribution of revised text and *modi* of Chris-
tian Education.
PENDING BUSINESS: Schema 13, Chap. V on Promoting Peace.
SPEAKERS: 1. Cardinal Liénart (Lille, France). 2. Cardinal Léger
(Montreal, Canada). 3. Cardinal Duval (Algiers, Algeria). 4.
Archbishop Garrone (Toulouse, France). 5. Bishop Simons (In-
dore, India). 6. Dom Butler (Superior of English Benedictines).
7. Bishop Gordon Wheeler (Auxiliary, Middlesborough, Eng-
land). 8. Bishop Castán Lacoma (Siguenza-Guadalajara, Spain).
9. Bishop Marling (Jefferson City, Mo.). 10. Bishop Grant
(Auxiliary, Northampton, England). 11. Bishop Rusch (Innsbruck, Austria). 12. Bishop Brezanoczy (Ap. Administrator,
Eger, Hungary).

VOTE: Pastoral Office of Bishops.

	Total	*Placet*	*Non placet*
Schema as a whole	2,181	2,167	14

VOTES: Schema on Religious Life. *Relator:* Bishop Compagnone.

	Total	*Placet*	*Non placet*	*Placet iuxta modum*	Invalid
1–Art. 1	2,176	2,163	9	—	4
2–Art. 2	2,124	2,113	9	—	2
3–Art. 3	2,062	2,057	5	—	—
4–Art. 4	2,064	2,057	5	—	2
5–Art. 5	2,057	2,040	15	—	2
6–Art. 6	2,055	2,049	3	—	3

1–Introduction; 2–General principles; 3–Criteria of renovation; 4–Underlying reasons; 5–Common elements; 6–Primacy of spiritual life.

October 7, 1965, Thursday—144TH GENERAL CONGREGATION.
MASS: Bishop Bolatti (Rosario, Argentina).
MODERATOR: Cardinal Suenens.
PRESENT: 2,147 Fathers.
ANNOUNCEMENT: At request of Fathers, further votes will be scheduled on *modi* of Priestly Formation, beginning Monday.
PENDING BUSINESS: Schema, 13, Chap. V on Promoting Peace.
SPEAKERS: 1. Cardinal Martin (Rouen, France). 2. Cardinal Ottaviani (Curia). 3. Bishop Gariola (Cabanatuan, Philippines). 4. Bishop Klepacz (Lódz, Poland). 5. Archbishop Cantero Cuadrado (Zaragoza, Spain). 6. Archbishop Gouyon (Rennes, France). 7. Bishop Carli (Segni, Italy). 8. Archbishop Beck (Liverpool, England).
NEW BUSINESS: Schema on Missionary Activity.
SPEAKERS: *Relatores:* Cardinal Agagianian and Father Schutte, Superior General of Society of Divine Word. 9. Cardinal Meouchi (Maronite Patriarch of Antioch). 10. Cardinal de Barros Camara (Rio de Janeiro, Brazil). 11. Cardinal Santos (Manila, Philippines). 12. Cardinal Jaeger (Paderborn, Germany).
STANDING VOTE at 11:15 to close debate on Schema 13.

VOTES: Schema on Religious Life.

	Total	Placet	Non placet	Placet iuxta modum	Invalid
7–Art. 7	2,140	2,133	4	—	3
8–Art. 8	2,136	2,126	7	—	3
9–Art. 9	2,150	2,142	7	—	1
10–Art. 10	2,148	2,088	57	—	3
11–Art. 11	2,136	2,112	22	—	2
12–Art. 12	2,130	2,126	3	—	1
13–Art. 13	2,097	2,089	7	—	1

7–Renovation of contemplative institutes; 8–Apostolic spirit; 9–Importance of monastic life; 10–Lay religious life; 11–Secular institutes; 12–Chastity; 13–Religious poverty.

IV

The Debates on Missionary Activity
and Priestly Life and Ministry;
The Council Deplores Anti-Semitism

THE SCHEMA on Missionary Activity, which the Council began to debate on October 7th even before the conclusion of the debate on Schema 13, and which occupied four days, is a good example of the type of compromise document for which the Council was obliged to settle in the end. This happened partly because of the lack of time for a thorough reappraisal of the missionary role of the Church in all its aspects, and partly because such a reassessment was blocked by an important Curial office whose effectiveness and relevancy would undoubtedly have been reduced by too drastic a revision. In this case it was the Congregation of Propaganda Fide. No doubt Pope Paul's personal penchant for moderation and middle-of-the-road solutions played its part in helping to convince the Council that this was the wiser course under present circumstances. Not that Propaganda Fide should be thought of as a Curial office dominated by conservative prelates with closed minds who are out of touch with the world and its problems. The struggle here was rather between careerists anxious to maintain control over a highly centralized, bureaucratic and reasonably successful enterprise and those who felt that today it was important for all concerned to have a greater share in the direction of the Church's missionary work, in keeping with the doctrine of collegiality and the renewed emphasis on the Church's awareness of itself as being, by definition, missionary.

As a result of the rather harsh criticism to which the "bare bones" of a missionary schema (in the form of Propositions) was subjected at the Third Session, its commission went to work and produced a much longer, better balanced, and on the whole reasonably satisfactory draft, considering their terms of reference that nothing must be recommended which would be too upsetting to the existing missionary structure. Taking to heart the charges frequently made against the Propositions —that they were lacking in theological perspective, and betrayed a certain unfamiliarity with the problems of modern missiology—the commission consulted a number of theologians and missiologists, such as Yves Congar, O.P., the Jesuits Ratzinger, Grasso and Buijs, André Seumois, O.M.I., and Professor Glaznik of the University of Münster. The new version now opened with an excellent first chapter on theological principles beginning with the Trinity (Will of the Father, Mission of the Son, Mission of the Holy Spirit) and going on to the role of the "Church sent by Christ," a definition of "Missionary Activity," a statement of the "Reasons and Necessity of Missionary Activity," and concluding with some observations about the "Eschatological Nature of Missionary Activity." This made it clear that the missions were not merely an activity which the Church promoted occasionally and, as it were, over and above its normal call of duty. On the contrary they belonged to the essence of the Church and were a goal which the whole Church should at all times be promoting as synonymous with its primary responsibility of spreading the Gospel. When the schema went on to particulars, however, this universalist, all-embracing orientation tended to shift somewhat and the missionary idea became synonymous with a certain type of activity carried on in a definite "territory" under the control of a "Dicastery." The conception of such countries as France, Italy, Germany, Spain, Latin America and even the United States being considered as *pays de mission* just like Africa and Asia, was never completely lost sight of, but the suggestion was not explored. This meant that the schema had little or nothing to say about atheism, de-Christianized urban areas, relations with non-Christian religions, and various sociological problems now widely being discussed within the missionary framework, consideration of which might have been expected in the light of the broadly stated theological principles set forth in Chapter I.*

A welcome feature of the new schema was its recognition of the fact that the missionary idea today was going through a kind of "crisis." As Cardinal Suenens expressed it in an interview, the problem was not only that "the world does not seem prepared to listen to us, but the fact is that we are not prepared to talk to it." The question had been raised, were the missions any longer relevant in the light of increased emphasis on freedom of conscience and a deeper understanding of the religious value and "elements of truth" to be found in all religions? Why disturb people in their beliefs if they could achieve salvation without the Gospel? Perhaps efforts should be directed toward improving their lot socially

* The commission, to its credit, made no bones about trying to hide its motives. It conscientiously endeavored to insert some wording or phrase that would satisfy everybody; with the result that the final draft approved by the Council was something of a mish-mash. However, whenever there was a question of some suggestion that would have broadened the text unduly, the reason for refusing it would be either, "the commission could not become involved in particulars," or "this is a matter that would have to be reserved to the Holy See."

rather than concentrating on the business of evangelization strictly speaking? Was Catholicism in its modern form really a suitable vehicle for conveying to primitive peoples the meaning of the Gospel, loaded as it was with "western" accretions and compromised by too close an association with European civilization? To these difficulties must be added others of a more practical nature caused by the drying up of vocations (not only in the missionary field), the unwillingness of some countries to admit missionaries, differences between missionary institutes and local bishops over the training and control of personnel, the reluctance of ecclesiastical authorities (particularly Propaganda) to condone methods that departed from the usual ways, the time-consuming burden of fund-raising, to mention only some of the problems. The schema proposed few if any radical solutions because of its somewhat restricted outlook, but at least it had the merit of recognizing that problems existed and of attempting to supply answers.

Chapter II dealt with Missionary Work in general, Chapter III with Missionaries, Chapter IV with Planning Missionary Activity (including a recommendation for the reorganization of Propaganda Fide), and Chapter V with Cooperation in support of the missions.*

Most of the speakers were enthusiastic about the revised schema as a whole. Bishop Lamont of Rhodesia, for example, who had characterized it as "bare bones" in 1964, now hailed it as "no longer a naked series of frigid propositions but a solid body of doctrine." In his judgment "missionaries do not want a fine literary document or a text in missiology, but rather something that will make all bishops conscious of their missionary responsibility." One thing the new text certainly did was to stress at every possible turn that support for the missions was essentially a collegial responsibility binding

* In the final version promulgated by the Council, those paragraphs of Chap. II dealing with Particular Churches have been made a separate chapter, Chapter III. Otherwise the two drafts are structurally much the same.

on all the bishops. Famous as an Irish orator of the old school, Bishop Lamont was apt to be carried away by his own rhetoric at times. After delivering himself of the magnificently balanced sentence, "No land is so primitive as to be unfit for the Gospel nor is any so civilized as not to need it," a thought that ranged somewhat beyond the limited horizon of the schema, he concluded with the not altogether felicitous suggestion that there was a parallel between the medieval Crusades and the modern missions when he declared that "Bishops must organize the missions of the Church, as Peter the Hermit had organized the Crusades." Praise for the way in which the document laid the "theological foundations" of the Church's missionary activity was voiced by numerous speakers. Cardinal Frings declared, "In this 'crisis of the missionary conscience' old formulas are not adequate; we need a new basis for our missionary activity, and this is provided by our text." Bishop Velasco, exiled Bishop of Hsiamen, China, was one of the few who begged to differ, "wondering" whether the present version represented much of an improvement over the earlier text and claiming that it was "too heavily weighted with the 'new theology.' "

Concerned lest the relatively liberal imprint which the "new theologians" had succeeded in imposing on the document should give rise to the impression that the Catholic Church was receding from its traditional stand regarding the necessity of the Church, Cardinal Journet plunged headlong into this No. 1 theological problem, by declaring that "the plurality of religions remains a fact, but to suppose that it is intended by God would be a great mistake." He then went on to explain that God did not desert the multitudes to whom the Gospel had not yet been preached. God's grace was present to such people and therefore the Church, although in a rudimentary, abnormal, precarious way. "These beginnings of the Church demand to be set free from internal and external impediments by the preaching of the Gospel. So missionary activity is not merely a matter of advice but rather of

command, not for the *melius esse* but for the *simpliciter esse*
of salvation." He called for a strengthening of the passage
mentioning the necessity of the Church, to make this point
doubly clear. The same thought was echoed by Bishop Geise
of Indonesia, speaking in the name of the Indonesian Episcopal Conference, who declared that "as far as those outside
the Church are concerned, where there is no preaching of the
Gospel or administration of the sacraments, salvation can be
found in an initial way, but not in the proper Christian form
which it requires in order to attain its own perfection."
Bishop Lokuang (Tainan) and Bishop Corboy (Monze, Zambia), the latter speaking in the name of 70 African bishops,
joined in supporting Journet's recommendation.

On the other hand, Cardinal König, president of the Secretariat for Non-Believers, shifting the emphasis, declared
that he was pleased by the schema's recognition of the religious values to be found in the "great religions" and its
recommendation that the work of evangelization should be
begun by establishing a "dialogue" with those who belonged
to such religions as well as others who remained "strangers
to the very knowledge of God." "Since almost all Christians,"
he said, "live in communities with non-Christians, they should
give witness to a truly Christian life. They should look upon
non-Christian religions as ways of seeking God. Even if these
religions are not *the* way to salvation, they nevertheless lead
men toward it. The grace of God is the way to salvation . . .
Even if given outside the Church, it draws men to the
Church." Many younger missionaries were disturbed by a
rumor at the Bombay Eucharistic Congress, according to
Bishop Gay of Basse-Terre, Guadalupe, that the Church
would no longer insist so much upon missionary work and
that the missionary's main task would henceforth be not to
baptize and preach the Gospel, but rather to promote conditions that would help men find Christian values in the non-
Christian religions. As the schema made abundantly clear,
however, the purpose of dialogue with non-Christians was

not merely the discovery of common ground or philosophic contemplation, but the recognition and evaluation of truths that would help people to a better understanding of Christianity.

One point on which there was fairly general agreement was that the schema was inadequate in its approach to the ecumenical problem in the missionary field. Many speakers rose to deplore the "scandal of division among Christians" and to suggest various ways in which this obstacle to the spreading of the Gospel could be overcome, or a least rendered less harmful. Bishop Koppman, Vicar Apostolic of Windhoek, noted that there were some 1,200 separate religious sects operating in Western Africa, his missionary territory, making the problem of collaboration one of vital concern. The often-made charge that cooperation would result in fostering indifferentism was ruled out by Bishop Van Cauwelaert of Congo-Léo, who maintained that if prudently moderated "it would make manifest to all the necessity of unity according to the will of Christ." Others who spoke on this theme were Cardinals Frings and Jäger, Father Degrijse, Archbishop Cordeiro (Karachi), and Cardinal de Barros Camara (Rio de Janeiro). The common view was probably expressed by Father Degrijse (Superior General of the Immaculate Heart of Mary) who suggested various practical ways in which the cooperation of "Christ's disciples" in the missionary field could be obtained, through a more accurate knowledge of each other, the common use of external means such as the radio, television, newspapers, hospitals and schools, more emphasis on united Christian social action, for example against such evils as racism, and even a certain collaboration in the business of evangelization. "I am well aware," he said, "of the immense difficulties confronting those who seek to collaborate in this field, and certainly faithfulness to Catholicity must not suffer any harm. Nevertheless the ecumenical movement progresses not only through theological dialogue, but also and even especially through concrete action, as we can see from the examples of Pope John XXIII and Pope Paul VI. Such acts have their best and least-harmful place in the field of pre-evangelization. Experience in various parts of the world, especially with the Taizé community, has shown that common action can produce results. Such cooperation, far from diminishing efforts, tends to increase the zeal for bearing Christian witness."* Not all were equally enthusiastic about opening the doors too widely however. Cardinal de Barros Camara, speaking in the name of 57 Latin American bishops, read a statement said to have been signed by 316 bishops warning against the dangers of proselytism: "(The undersigned) desire that this Council explicitly make it known that it is useful for the progress of real ecumenism to present clearly to the faithful the Catholic doctrine in regard to the proselytism undertaken among Catholics by certain denominations of the separated brethren . . . and that it would be very useful to include standards and norms about this in the ecumenical directory that the Secretariat for Promoting Christian Unity intends to draw up and publish."

Father Arrupe, General of the Jesuits, began by launching into a scathing denunciation of the inadequacies of the whole western approach to the missionary problem, dominated as it was by a romantic and infantile outlook. Missionaries who returned to the West were often appalled by the defects discernible in those who were supposedly responsible for the destinies of missionary work, namely their infantile attitude toward the importance of accurate information; their sentimentalism in distributing funds to favored projects rather than where they were most needed; their sense of superiority, so typical of "Westerners"; their myopia, in thinking of the missions only when they had taken care of the needs of their

---

* The final version of the schema was appropriately revised to bring out more clearly the close connection between missionary activity and the ecumenical movement. Specifically, a new paragraph was added to No. 29 calling for collaboration between Propaganda and the Secretariat for Promoting Christian Unity.

own dioceses; and finally the "mendicity" which required too much time to be spent on collecting funds that should be spent preaching the Gospel. He proposed that the text should be amended to provide for a greater flow of information to and from the field and for more cooperation in the selection and training of missionaries. Cardinal Suenens also touched on the matter of better training, recommending that special centers be established in every important missionary area affiliated, if possible, with outstanding universities. As the exiled Archbishop of Nanking, Yu-Pin, rather plaintively expressed it: "Christ became man. Why can missionaries today not become Chinamen? China also forms part of mankind."

Though the schema had the advantage of being revised after the Constitution on the Church had been passed, which made clear the significant role the laity were expected to play in the People of God, Cardinal Alfrink and a number of other speakers still felt that the document was too hierarchical in its outlook. Missionary work actually belonged to the whole People of God, whereas the schema still occasionally suggested that only the hierarchy were really involved. Bishop McGrath of Santiago Veraguas, Panama agreed and called for a strengthening of Chapter V in this sense. Fortunately the Council was able to hear the case for the laity put by one of the lay auditors, M. Eusèbe Adjakpley, a Negro from Togo, who was invited to address the assembly on October 13th, the last day of the debate. The point of his talk was that the missionary situation today was very different from what it had been when missionaries first went out to areas like Africa and Asia to lay the foundations of new Churches. The world today was fast becoming one "in which all men are becoming increasingly aware of their dignity and less willing to tolerate inequality and injustice." Consequently the missions were everywhere. "All groups comprising the Church must be missionaries; all can and must cooperate.

The laity desires to place their witness and their skills at the service of the Church's mission to evangelize the world." The implication of his speech was that Africa now had something that it could perhaps teach Europe or America.*

Of immediate concern to quite a few prelates nullius in South America and other bishops throughout the world was the rather limited way in which the term "missionary territory" was defined, whereas, as Bishop Gazza of Brazil pointed out, there were some 130 ecclesiastical territories in Latin America where missionary activity was being carried on as described in the schema but which were not entitled to the benefits of such territories because they did not fall under the official designation. In its final revision of the text the commission admitted the justice of this claim to a certain extent and redefined the concept of "missionary territory" in a sense acceptable to these prelates. A similar proposal that formal recognition should be given to the practice of assigning definite missionary territories to certain dioceses, in the way that such territories were assigned to various missionary religious institutes, was received with more reserve. 120 Fathers, including 7 cardinals, actually submitted a request to the commission along this line, but the reply was that the practice of "commissioning" territories was now on the decline and that in any case there could be no question of approving a custom "not proven by experience," however there was no objection to the establishment of such relations on an informal basis.

It had long been the custom of the Holy See (Propaganda) to assign certain missionary territories to religious institutes (or religious orders) which then assumed the responsibility for providing missionaries and supporting the missions established there. However, in the course of time these missions

* A new paragraph, No. 21, on Promoting the Apostolate of the Laity, was added to the final text, and minor changes were made in Chapter V, No. 41, on the Missionary Task of the Laity.

developed into full-fledged Churches, with their own native hierarchies and diocesan organizations like other Churches. The resulting conflict of jurisdictions gave rise to endless bickering and controversy, aggravated by the fact that the missionary societies were themselves going through something of a "crisis" owing to a variety of causes, the shortage of vocations, the difficulty of adjusting to new situations, their inflexibility, rigidity, etc. As Bishop Ntuyahaga (Burundi) explained the situation: "Relations between the ordinaries of new dioceses and the heads of missionary orders are still theoretically ruled by the law according to which areas are entrusted to institutes, but practically this law has become antiquated. From this discrepancy, confusion and unpleasantness have arisen. The schema states that it would be good to enter into agreements to regulate these relations, but nothing further . . . We ask the Council not merely to recommend particular agreements between ordinaries and generals, but also to lay down detailed norms and guidelines for these agreements. The norms thus worked out by Propaganda should be incorporated in the Code of Canon Law." A number of prelates, particularly Father Quéguiner (Superior General of the Missions Society, Paris) and Cardinal Zoungrana (Upper Volta) suggested various concrete ways in which these difficulties could be overcome. (The final text of the schema represented a compromise, endeavoring to do justice to both sides, without proposing any radical solutions.) Many of the African bishops who spoke on this theme, such as Bishop Sibomana (Rwanda) and Bishop Gahamanyi (Rwanda), were firm in their assertion that control of the local Church must be in the hands of the bishop, but they also paid tribute to the debt of gratitude those Churches owe the institutes, and generally minimized the conflicts.

There were few references to the matter of funds for the missions. Bishop De Reeper of Kenya declared that when the bishops returned to their homes, they would not be asked what the Council had done about defining the concept of a mission, but rather how much cooperation and support they could expect from the dioceses in Christian lands which supplied the funds and personnel. The schema had largely settled this matter by incorporating in Chapter VI, No. 38 (in the final version) the provision that episcopal conferences were to "decide what definite offering each diocese should be obliged to set aside annually for the work of the missions, in proportion to its own budget; they should [also] consider how to direct and control the ways and means by which the missions receive direct help; they should deal with assisting and if need be, founding, missionary institutes and seminaries for diocesan missionary clergy, and the promoting of closer relations between such institutes and the dioceses." This was done in response to repeated requests made at the Third Session. A plea for more explicit recognition of the vital work performed by the Pontifical Missionary Societies in various countries collecting funds for the missions was lodged by Bishop Poletti, director of the Pontifical Missionary Societies in Italy.* Finally, to satisfy the persistent demands of those Fathers who at the Third Session had called for a "reorganization" of Propaganda Fide and a greater participation by the episcopate in its work, Chapter IV of the revised schema provided that "all those who take part in missionary work, namely cardinals, patriarchs and bishops of the whole world, regardless of rite, as well as the directors of pontifical institutes and works" should be "members" of this Roman Congregation and should "exercise the supreme government of all missionary work under the authority of the Roman Pontiff."

At the last minute, there was substituted for this rather strongly worded text that seemed to meet the essential objections of the critics of Propaganda, a weaker text (printed at the end of Father Schütte's *relatio*) watering down its effectiveness to a considerable extent. However, either because the

---

* Paragraph No. 38 was strengthened in this sense.

bishops were unaware of its existence or failed to assess its importance, there was no appreciable discussion of this point on the floor. Nor were there any significant repercussions when the Council voted to accept the schema as the basis for a final text on October 12th by an overwhelming 2,070 *placet* to 15 *non placet*. Shortly after this vote, however, it became known that a group of 60 Indian, 11 Divine Word, and 20 African bishops had presented a petition to the Council Secretariat, expressing their "amazement" that the schema had been revised by certain authorities (Propaganda) without consulting the other members of the missionary commission, along lines suggested, it was said, by the Papal Commission for the Reform of the Roman Curia, headed by Cardinal Roberti.* The two most important of the proposed changes were that, instead of being "members" of Propaganda Fide, the delegates were merely to "have an active and decisive role" (*partem actuosam et decisivam*) in that congregation; and instead of exercising "supreme government" (*supremam gubernationem*) over all missionary work, they were to exercise merely "supreme control" (*supremam ordinationem*) of such work. If finally accepted, the modifications would largely leave intact the essential structure and present freedom of action of Propaganda which the critics were trying to alter in a collegial sense. Accordingly the petitioners requested a return to the original text and put forth certain counter proposals of their own: the episcopal delegates forming part of the central organism should be elected by their respective episcopal conferences; they should be summoned to meet at fixed times; and their term of office should probably be limited in order to avoid the risk of careerism. If the number of delegates turned out to be too large, it could be limited provided their distribution were still representative.**

---

* It is said that the petition of the African bishops became lost while being circulated and was never presented to the Secretariat. Cf. *Le Monde*, October 14 and 15, 1965; *L'Avvenire d'Italia*, October 22 and 23, 1965.

** See below, p. 202, for the outcome of this move.

The Schema on Priestly Life and Ministry

At 11:40 Monday morning, October 11th, while the Council was still discussing the schema on Missionary Activity, Cardinal Tisserant stopped the debate and announced that Archbishop Felici would read a letter which he had just received from Pope Paul. The letter said:

We have learned that certain Fathers intend to discuss the law of ecclesiastical celibacy in the Council as it is observed in the Latin Church. Therefore, without infringing in any way on the right of the Fathers to express themselves, we make known to you our personal opinion, which is, that it is not opportune to have a public discussion of this topic, which demands so much prudence and is so important. We not only intend to maintain this ancient, holy and providential law to the extent of our ability, but also to reinforce its observance, calling on all priests of the Latin Church to recognize anew the causes and reasons why this law must be considered most appropriate today, especially today, in helping priests to consecrate all their love completely and generously to Christ in the service of the Church and of souls (applause). If any Father wishes to speak about this matter, he may do so in writing by submitting his observations to the Council Presidency which will transmit them to us (applause).

For several days the press had been printing sensational reports about the number of requests before the Holy Office from priests desiring to be released from their vow of celibacy. Some said there were as many as 10,000, others more. It was known that several bishops did in fact intend to bring the matter up, especially certain Latin American prelates. Afraid of the consequences of a public debate and knowing that the hierarchy was divided on the question, a number of Latin American Fathers, including Cardinal de Barros Camara of Rio de Janeiro, talked to Cardinal Tisserant and begged him to intervene with the Holy Father to prevent a discussion. The result was the Pope's letter.

However, the announcement was made too late to prevent

the printing of one of the intended interventions, by the Dutch Bishop Koop of Lins, Brazil.* The bishop explained later that he had not intended his speech for publication but had distributed it to some of the bishops and it inadvertently got into the hands of the press. Whatever the facts regarding its disclosure, the speech showed that what the bishop wanted, and presumably also the others who intended to speak, was not an abolition of the law of celibacy but a modification of the existing legislation that would permit a married clergy to operate alongside a celibate clergy in areas like Latin America, where the pastoral needs were so immense and the possibility of meeting them with the existing personnel almost nil. According to René Laurentin, the problem of a married clergy for Latin America and other areas, along the lines of the Eastern discipline, had been before the Holy See ever since the days of Pope Pius X, but the Roman authorities had always felt that any concession here would inevitably lead to reconsideration of the status of those living in clerical concubinage in Italy and other countries, estimated variously in the thousands, and this they were not prepared to face.**

The Pope's letter to Cardinal Tisserant was not read until after the seventh vote on the schema dealing with Priestly Formation (Seminaries) which concerned the question of maintaining the law of celibacy in the Latin Church. The results (1,971 for to 16 against) were then cited as evidence of the overwhelming support among the bishops for celibacy. somewhat too hastily and naïvely it would seem. The bishops were not aware that their vote would be regarded as a test case. If the question had been put to them whether they would approve some relaxation of the existing legislation along the lines suggested by Bishop Koop, the outcome might have shown that the Council was more divided on the issue than was generally supposed. It is not unreasonable to assume

---

* Printed in *Le Monde,* October 12, 1965, which was on the newsstands the previous day.
** *Le Figaro,* October 13, 1965.

that the Council might have divided roughly the same way it did over the question of a married diaconate.

But it was precisely this nearly fifty-fifty split that Pope Paul was anxious to avoid, the fruitless and embarrassing revelation that the bishops were hopelessly divided on a subject that could not possibly be debated and resolved if the Council were to complete its work on time. Few commentators felt that the Pope had acted unwisely or arbitrarily. While there was some regret that more attention had not been paid to the matter earlier when there was still time, it was considered significant that the Pope had not closed the door on revision of the existing legislation at a later date, but had merely reserved the question to himself in order to remain the master of a controversial issue.*

Pope Paul's action ruled out any possibility that celibacy would be openly discussed on the floor. Cardinal Ruffini, however, could not resist the temptation to gloat that the rule of celibacy had been saved not only in the Western Church but "in no small part of the Oriental Church" as well, thus implying rather insultingly that the whole Eastern Church ought to follow the discipline of the West. Cardinal Bea set the record straight in an important intervention on Saturday, October 16th. "Celibacy is not required by the nature of the priesthood," he said. "The schema makes this clear, but it then goes on to insist on the Latin discipline in a way that is too exclusive. It gives the impression that the married clergy of the East are second-class priests, not fully priests. But they are very deserving. Our Council is an ecumenical council. It must speak to the East also. Therefore the schema should refer to two types of priesthood, the celibate and married. This is of the greatest importance (*summi momenti*) for the East. Each clergy should be trained with a view to its special role."**

* Cf. Gary McEoin, in the *St. Louis Review* (October 29, 1965): "I believe it was a good decision . . . Better to consolidate the advances and pray for the success of Vatican III."

** This recommendation, slightly altered, was incorporated in the final text.

The day before the discussion of the important schema on Priestly Life and Ministry began, on October 14th, Archbishop Marty, *relator* for the commission, read a detailed report explaining that the document attempted to describe the pastoral mission of the priest and to show how this mission was, or should be, the focal point for his whole life and ministry. "The priest is never an isolated individual," the archbishop said; "with other priests he forms the *presbyterium* of the bishop. He carries on his work in constant contact with the laity. The foundation of priestly holiness and the food of his spiritual life are in his pastoral mission which he exercises in the person of Christ and the Church." The ideal inspiring the commission's work had plainly been that of the *Mission de France,* founded by Cardinal Suhard, which attempted to strike a balance between the excessive otherworldly spirituality expected of priests in former days and excessive immersion in the affairs of the world to the disadvantage of their spiritual ministry. Many of the bishops had requested a more detailed treatment of certain points, but the commission deliberately refrained from this, preferring to leave such questions to the national or regional episcopal conferences while laying down universal norms.

In spite of the archbishop's moderate and conciliatory tone, a large number of the speakers preferred to judge the schema rather severely giving the impression that it would have to be subjected to a drastic revision. However, a closer look at their remarks revealed that many, if not all, were in substantial agreement about the general acceptability of the present text and merely wanted this or that aspect brought out more clearly. There was such widespread agreement among them, as a matter of fact, that this was probably the most prolix and repetitious of all the debates held in the council hall. Instead of reaching an end with the 43rd speaker after three full days of debate, the Council was obliged to sit through two more mornings of 12 speakers, on October 25th and 26th, with part of another morning being devoted to a speech by Monsignor Thomas Falls, a pastor from Philadelphia. Many of the speakers, obviously, were airing their views for the benefit of the record, because this was the final debate, or in order to impress the clergy back home because of a certain feeling that the Council had tended to concentrate its attention too much on bishops to the exclusion of mere priests.

The critics of the schema tended to fall into two categories: those who felt that it did not emphasize sufficiently the cultic or sacramental role of the priest; and those who wanted more attention paid to practical matters and the role of the priest in today's world. The former was represented for the most part by prelates steeped in the "Latin" tradition such as Archbishop D'Avack, Archbishop Fares, Cardinals Florit, Landázuri-Ricketts, Richaud and De Arriba y Castro, Bishops Segedi, Garcia Lahiguera and Compagnone. Among their various suggestions: the title of the schema should be changed to "Priestly Holiness" (De Arriba y Castro); not enough was said about the individual devotion of priests and in particular their devotion to the Holy Spirit (D'Avack); there was too much emphasis on the ministry of priests and not enough on the development of their spiritual life (Richaud and many others); the schema should say more about the central place which the eucharistic sacrifice should occupy in priestly life (Landázuri-Ricketts); more should be said about the grave obligation to priestly poverty (Florit and Zak); in order to promote the spirituality of priests, a group of "holy priests" should be formed in each diocese to give retreats and set an example (Garcia Lahiguera); not enough was said about the role of the priest in administering the sacrament of penance (Fares). Finally, priests were letting slip a golden opportunity of preaching to the faithful at funerals (Segedi)!

A number voiced criticisms of a general nature. Cardinals Tatsuo Doi and Meouchi both found the text too "western," the former noting that it had little to say about the clergy in missionary lands because its remarks were directed almost exclusively to the relations between priests and the Catholic faithful, the latter complaining that it was too juridical and had nothing useful to say about the Eastern clergy, particularly those who were married. In Cardinal Döpfner's opinion, the schema read more like a "spiritual lecture" than a conciliar document. What was needed was a plainer style in keeping with today's mentality. Priests would be annoyed, he said, if they found themselves being called "a precious spiritual crown of their bishops." A religious motive seemed to be attributed to everything, even the most trivial of everyday happenings in a priest's life. The schema unfortunately repeated many things that were known to everybody. Its theological terminology might be suitable for a book of devotional reading but was hardly good enough for a conciliar document. "I propose that the style be improved and that the schema stress more the problems of today's priests."

Quite a few speakers had remarks to make about the way in which the schema dealt with the theology of the priesthood. As Bishop Soares de Resende said, the theology of the priesthood was not yet sufficiently mature for a definitive statement, however it was possible to make certain assertions more confidently. According to Bishop Henriquez Jimenez, auxiliary of Caracas, a firmer theological emphasis would help many priests, especially the younger ones, "resolve the crisis of hope and cheerful acceptance of their state" in which many found themselves. Cardinal Colombo summed up fairly well the point that most speakers were trying to make when he said: "The ministry of the priest should be portrayed in close communion with the mystery of the Church, because thus he would be in close communion with Christ. It can never be sufficiently stressed that the fullness of the priesthood can be achieved only in the mission and mystery of the God-Man. The text should delete any remark that makes it seem impossible for a secular priest to be said to be living in a state of perfection. This is an open question which should not be prejudiced by any conciliar statement." Other pertinent observations: the schema should bring out clearly that the priesthood was a sharing in the priesthood of Christ and the priestly obligation to holiness stemmed from this (Flores Martin); the Holy Spirit rendered the priest fit to act in the person of Christ (Cardinal Jäger); the text neglected the spiritual fatherhood of priests, whose proper role was to generate the life of Christ (Cardinal Lefebvre); the evangelical counsels were not handled properly (Bishop Charue); the two aspects of priestly life and ministry should be better integrated theologically (De Roo); not enough attention was paid to Mary's relationship to the priesthood (Pechuan, Barela). When Bishop Ndongmo of Cameroun, after a long speech on the nature of the priesthood, somewhat pompously said: "I ask the Moderators for an exhaustive discussion of this schema," he was abruptly cut short by the presiding Moderator of the day.

A leading spokesman for a more activist or pastoral approach to the priesthood was Cardinal Alfrink who found the presentation too sacral: "You would think that the priest never left the sacristy or church." The text should stress the importance of carrying on a dialogue with those Catholics who were such in name only as well as with other Christians and even atheists, as one of the daily duties of priests. Unfortunately almost nothing was said about the attitude of the clergy toward social and economic matters. Article 5 called for priests to have a profound knowledge of the encyclicals of the Popes, but nothing, strangely, was said about their knowing the documents and spirit of the Second Vatican Council. Many of the Fathers, Cardinal Alfrink noted, had asked for a treatment of the problems that were causing uncertainty and anxiety in the priesthood today, but these topics were barely mentioned. The doctrinal revision of the text gave the impression that "everything is calm and clear concerning the life and ministry of priests."

Cardinal Suenens charged that while the doctrine of the

schema was solid enough and an attempt had been made to coordinate the schema with *Lumen Gentium,* the statements were too conceptual or related to an age that was now past. They were too remote from the questions being asked by priests today. Priests today were having a difficult time finding their place in a world that regarded them as alien and in a Church that seemed to regard them as mainly useful for the sacramental ministry only. The schema offered the elements of a solution, but in a somewhat haphazard way. He suggested that more attention should be paid to the relationship of priests to Jesus Christ, the episcopal college, and the laity. According to Cardinal Léger too, the presentation of priestly holiness was too otherworldly and unrealistic. The type of sanctity offered was not one suitable for priests today. The schema should avoid any notion of priestly holiness founded on the opposition between the exterior and the interior life. The difficulties which priests today had to face must indeed be mentioned, but as realities of human life which could and should bring them closer to God. "Christ and his grace were found in the men whom the priest meets every day." Instead of defining the priestly life in terms of the religious vows of obedience, chastity and poverty, more emphasis should be put on such virtues as zeal, apostolic concern for all men, universal love, especially for children, the poor and sinners, and the desire for apostolic work and perseverance in the midst of difficulties, as Monsignor Falls brought out in his final talk on October 27th. On the other hand, Archbishop Santin of Trieste warned the Fathers against making too many concessions to the laity; he objected in particular to what the schema said about "charisms of the laity" as being liable to false interpretation: "We don't want to increase the number of those who think that they are specially inspired."

The last speech by a conciliar Father, the newly appointed Archbishop of Turin, Michele Pellegrino, was a moving plea for a more open attitude on the part of the bishops toward the intellectual life of their priests. It was significant that he spoke in the name of 158 Council Fathers including 12 cardinals.

In our day, in some regions at least, a kind of pragmatism is widespread which almost exclusively esteems external works to the neglect of the importance of studies. Thus it happens that clerics seriously engaged in theological studies are considered to be on a lower level than those engaged in strictly pastoral work or even in temporal administration. Why must professors in seminaries often teach for a very poor salary? Why do not a few ecclesiastical libraries suffer from a lack of necessary funds? Why are assistants lacking in some faculties who, while engaging in scientific work in their own fields, help the professors with their work and instruct the students in methods of critical investigation? Why are so few monographs published? Certainly the Church always suffers from poverty, but even in regions where money is said to be lacking for the promotion of theological studies, we see sumptuous new buildings daily rising up for various uses and immense projects being carried out. No less care should be taken to foster intellectual work. Unfortunately there are depressed areas also as regards intellectual activity in the theological field, and the principal reason for this, in my opinion, is not so much a lack of funds, as an insufficient appreciation of the importance of these studies. In the post-conciliar period there will be two dangers: that of watering-down the norms of the Council which change old customs, and that of passing over everything that is old and of undertaking whatever is new only because it is new. To avoid these pitfalls, priests will need not only humble obedience and a vigorous interior life, but also a clear view of problems and the historical reality within which these problems are to be solved. For this reason the Church needs many clerics to indicate ways of both preserving the essentials of tradition and of accommodating this tradition to our times.

The archbishop was immediately surrounded by well-wishers congratulating and praising him for the forthright remarks with which he had brought the Council's discussions to a close.

The archbishop of Turin was not the only Father to speak out boldly on a number of specific problems relating to the schema. A few days earlier Cardinal Heenan had some rather pointed remarks to make about a generally taboo subject, the question of "fallen" priests: "When a wretched man has made shipwreck of his priestly life, it is not at all uncommon for his closest associates to express no surprise. It is easy to be wise after the event . . . Every language has some version of the saying: 'A stitch in time saves nine.' Priests unhappily, rarely speak up in time. In this matter they are inclined to behave like schoolboys. At all costs they do not want to be regarded as sneaks or informers. So they remain silent while a brother priest rushes to his ruin." It was therefore important for the schema to say something about a priest's responsibility for his fellow priests. Having got this off his chest, the cardinal then went on to recommend the virtues of golf: "It is by no means a waste of time for priests to play a round of golf together. Priestly company brings a kind of blessing in itself." He deplored the standoffishness of the clergy in certain countries: "In countries where the Church has not lost touch with the working-class, the priest spends a great deal of time with the laity . . . Where the clergy visit their flocks anti-clericalism does not exist." (He did not say that in Italy the parish clergy are expected to be locked in by nine o'clock in the evening, for fear of "scandal.") He concluded with some facetious remarks about monks who "stay at home to write books and articles about the People of God, while bishops are hard put to it to find enough priests to go out into the missions." Bishop Brzana, auxiliary of Buffalo, also pleaded for a more humane treatment of fallen priests: "I have never heard of a priest being scandalized because of mercy shown to a repentent brother."

Many of the speeches dealt with specific problems or aspects of the pastoral ministry: the need for allowing priests to engage in manual work, provided this did not interfere with their spiritual duties, and the importance of paying them a suitable salary (Argaya Goicoechea, Nabaa); the possibility of reviving the worker-priest movement (Guyot *pro*, Tomé *contra*); the clergy should always wear some kind of distinctive dress (Foley); the unfortunate lot of parish assistant priests (Leven); improving the level of sermons by providing better training (Bank, Herrera y Oria); legislation for diocesan associations of priests (Jubany); new methods with "priest-teams" in certain areas where there was a shortage of priests (Miranda y Gomez); more respect for diocesan priests who were not strictly parish clergy (Roy); the deplorable state of affairs in Latin America where "shepherds are dying without sheep in some areas, while in others sheep are dying without shepherds and are left victims to the ravening wolves of ignorance, superstition and injustice (Arrieta Villalobos).

Nine or more of the Fathers dealt more or less explicitly with the knotty question of priestly obedience and the proper relations that should obtain between a bishop and his clergy. According to Cardinal Shehan, the schema was not clear about the foundation of these relations. It was essential to adhere to the guidelines laid down by *Lumen Gentium* and for bishops to avoid a false "episcopalism" that made them seem more like overbearing masters than true collaborators in the ministry. The document on the Church specified that the bond which priests and bishops shared in common was the priesthood of Christ. The schema gave the impression of reversing the order by implying that the priest participated in the priesthood of Christ because he partook of the episcopal mission; this should be corrected. Cardinal Quiroga y Palacios was afraid that too much emphasis was being put on the dependence of priests on their bishops and that this might stifle their individual initiative; Bishop Renard called for clarification of what the text meant by describing the bishops as the "perfector" of priests; Bishop Mancini, auxiliary of Porto-Santa Rufina, wanted priests "neither to have complete freedom to undertake rash projects, nor to be reduced to the level of mere record keepers"; Bishop Franic thought that if priests and bishops could be persuaded to lead a common life together this would help to conquer Marxism. "What is deplorable today," said Bishop Charbonneau of Hull, Canada, "is not so much the crisis of submission on the part of the clergy as the crisis of responsibility about which the schema does not speak." This was plainly not the view of Archbishop Connolly of Seattle for whom the blame was almost entirely on the side of the rebellious clergy: "A crisis of obedience seems to have developed here and there owing to a false notion of freedom and independence, of a new atmosphere generated by this Council. Some priests, pseudo-existentialists, denigrate authority as such; each one wants to be a law unto himself. Even the *aggiornamento* of the Church can make it more difficult for a priest today to obey an order whose wisdom for the apostolate he does not personally see, and in these days of ferment, priests are more apt to have their own opinions on many important matters. Obedience has its ultimate root in the divine will . . ." Fortunately for the archbishop, the bishops were by then so benumbed by rhetoric that his slur on the Council passed virtually unnoticed.

Pope Paul VI unquestionably has an eye on the symbolic and the timing of important announcements. Shortly before the end of the debate on Priestly Life and Ministry, late Saturday afternoon, October 23rd, the French hierarchy suddenly announced at the conclusion of their meeting in Rome that the Holy See had agreed to a revival of the worker-priest movement that had been so popular in France with the working classes during the period 1943–54. Suppressed by Pius XII in the latter year at the insistence of the Holy Office and other Curial bodies because some of the priests had drifted into communism, members of the French hierarchy had never ceased to hope that the experiment, properly overhauled and with adequate safeguards, could be revived as part of a long-range program to help win back many of the French people to the Church. In many audiences with members of the French hierarchy, Pope Paul lent a sympathetic ear to their plea and finally asked the Holy Office to reconsider its ban, making possible the above announcement.

Among the changes insisted on were that the experiment was to last for three years initially; the priests chosen were not to be called *prêtres-ouvriers* but *prêtres au travail,* a subtle distinction safeguarding their sacerdotal status as apostles among the working class rather than workers pure and simple; and they were to maintain close contact with their ecclesiastical superiors and live in community with other priests instead of on their own.*

The schema was accepted as the basis for a final text with a vote of 1,507 *placet,* 12 *non placet,* and 2 invalid votes.

The Council Deplores Anti-Semitism

Few Council documents aroused as much controversy, or were followed with such close interest, as the famous Declaration on the Jews later incorporated in a more broadly conceived Declaration on Relations with Non-Christians (including Hindus, Buddhists, Moslems as well as Jews). Although the expanded Declaration was destined to become the *magna carta* of the newly formed Secretariat for Relations with Non-Christian Religions, under Cardinal Marella (announced in the spring of 1965), it was on the Jewish portion that public attention was almost exclusively focused, largely because of the intense interest in it shown by a few Jewish groups, notably the American Jewish Committee.** As a result of this campaign, the Council found itself in the rather anomalous position of dealing with a subject that seemed at times to be of greater moment to Jews than to Christians for whom its statement was primarily intended. In essence, the Jewish sec-

* Cf. *Le Monde,* October 26, 1965; *Le Figaro,* October 24, 1965.
** See Joseph Roddy, *Look,* January 25, 1966.

tion tried to do three things: stress the close ties that bound Jews and Christians together; kill the old charge of deicide which intemperate Christians frequently hurled against the entire Jewish people; and finally extinguish once and for all the flames of Christian Anti-Semitism.

The history of the Jewish section had been stormy. It originated as an idea of Pope John XXIII in 1960 after he met and talked to the French historian and scholar, Jules Isaac. In the later spirit of *Pacem in Terris,* John expressed the opinion that since it was high time to mend fences, the subject of Jewish-Christian relations was one fence that needed mending most of all. The Secretariat for Promoting Christian Unity, presided over by Cardinal Bea, was entrusted with the task of drawing up a suitable text in 1961, and in May of the following year a first draft was presented to the Central Commission which was passing on the suitability of texts for discussion in the Council due to open in September. Bowing to pressure from Arab states and conservative forces within the Church, the Commission refused to accept the draft. So nothing was done about the question during the First Session.

In December 1962, after the Pope recovered from his illness, he asked Bea to revise the document and gave it his approval. To get around any objections from the Coordinating Commission (which had taken over from the Central Commission), it was decided to annex the document to the schema on Ecumenism as Chapter IV. When Ecumenism came up for discussion in the Second Session in 1963, after Bea's official report had already been distributed and as the cardinal was preparing to introduce the text, it was suddenly announced that because of "lack of time" the discussion would have to be postponed until the next session. Pressure had again been brought to bear by the usual quarters. When the text actually reached the floor of the Council in the Third Session, it had been so altered meanwhile that Archbishop Heenan of Westminster, one of the Secretariat mem-

SACROSANCTUM OECUMENICUM CONCILIUM
VATICANUM SECUNDUM

DECLARATIO

DE ECCLESIAE HABITUDINE
AD RELIGIONES NON-CHRISTIANAS

de qua agetur in Sessione publica
diei 28 octobris 1965

(*Sub secreto*)

TYPIS POLYGLOTTIS VATICANIS
MCMLXV

Title-page of Declaration on Non-Christian Religions, promulgated October 28, 1965 bers, declared that it was virtually unrecognizable. Mention of the word deicide had been dropped and other changes made along conservative lines. The sponsoring of this bastardized text was probably Pope Paul's single greatest mistake and gave rise to more misgivings about his intentions than anything else.* After two days of debate, it became clear that the previous text would have to be restored.

The May 1965 version represented a compromise with the restored version approved by the Council on November 20, 1964. Though the passage rejecting the charge of deicide had been strengthened, the word itself was omitted. The wording of the previous version, "deplores, indeed condemns" hatred and persecution of Jews, was changed in the new version merely to "deplores" but added the words, "displays of Anti-Semitism directed against Jews." The old version warned Christians not to teach anything that could give rise to hatred and persecution of Jews, the new version less explicitly urged them not to teach "anything inconsistent with the truth of the Gospel and with the spirit of Christ." As one of the experts involved in the drafting of the text put the matter: "If it had not been for the publicity surrounding the previous versions, the present text offered to the Council in 1965 would probably be regarded as excellent."

The contention of the Arab states that the document tended to favor recognition of the state of Israel, or the political aspirations of Zionism, was denied by a clause specifying that the Council had been "moved not by any political considerations, but by the Gospel's spiritual love," and by a series of diplomatic trips to the Near East by members of Bea's staff

---

* The Pope's apparently casual remark in the course of a Passion Sunday sermon on April 4, 1965 also caused something of a furor: "That people [the Jews], predestined to receive the Messiah, who had been awaiting him for thousands of years . . . when Christ comes . . . not only does not recognize him, but opposes him, slanders him and finally kills him." The charitable explanation was that owing to a "slip" the Pope had fallen into the centuries-old habit of attributing the death of Jesus to the whole Jewish people without making the necessary distinctions.

to assuage these misgivings and obtain suggestions for the
text on the Arab Christians.*

It was a foregone conclusion that the document would win
a majority when it was put to a vote on October 14th and
15th, the only question being whether those disappointed
over the omission of the word deicide, Bishop Carli's *Coetus
Internationalis Patrum* who opposed it on theological
grounds, and those who felt that there were still political
objections, would be able to register enough *non placet* votes
(two-thirds) to bring about rejection or seriously impair the
unanimity with which Council documents were supposed to
be approved.** One estimate was that the opponents might
be able to muster as many as 500 votes but hardly more. As
usual the Fathers were deluged with literature beforehand.
Bishop Carli's group urged *non placet* votes on most counts
(there were 8 votes on various paragraphs of the text and 1
vote on the document as a whole) on the grounds that it
favored indifferentism by tending to regard all religions as
on the same level, would retard the "conversion of the Gentiles," and would "put an end" to missionary work. The specifically Jewish portion was objectionable because "many
Biblical scholars hold that it can be proved from Scripture
that the Jewish religion is reprobated and accursed." One of
the most violent pamphlets was a four-page affair signed
allegedly by 31 so-called "Catholic organizations" which

---

* A statement issued by Patriarch Maximos IV on his return from the
Third Session showed that considerable assuaging was called for: "If the
great majority of the Council, and namely the American prelates, voted for
the Declaration, it is for personal reasons and interests. The personal reasons
are dictated by sentiments of pity due to the massacre of millions of Jews by
Nazism, and the interest is due to the fact that the great number of Americans have commercial interests with Jews. Such is the truth and whoever dis-
torts it promotes demagoguery. In addition one cannot defeat Israel by becoming the enemy of the Holy See because everyone knows the strength of
the Vatican's power in the balance of the forces of this world." *The Pilot*,
Jan. 9, 1965.

** Bishop Carli published an important article condemning the theological
basis of the Declaration in *Palestra del Clero*, 44 (1965) 185–203 (February
1965) to which Cardinal Bea replied, refuting his contentions point by point,
in *La Civiltà Cattolica*, Nov. 6, 1965.

trumpeted: "No Council, no Pope, can condemn Jesus, the Catholic Apostolic and Roman Church, its Popes (naming several from Nicholas I to Leo XIII) and the most illustrious Councils. But the Declaration on the Jews explicitly involves such a condemnation, therefore it should be rejected . . ." It went on to accuse the Jews of trying to compel the Church to disgrace and disavow itself before the world and described the Declaration as being worthy of "an antipope or a schismatic council." Most of the signatories promptly disavowed any connection with the manifesto, which turned out to be largely a hoax concocted by some crank. Father DePauw, for example, publicly stated in Rome that his Traditionalist Movement in the United States had had nothing to do with it and that their name had been used without authorization. Several French organizations issued similar statements.

So much tension had been generated, however, that the authorities naturally took seriously an anonymous letter received by Cardinal Marella, Archpriest of St. Peter's, from a person threatening, half in French and half in German, to blow up the basilica and the whole Council if the Jewish document were voted, and extra police were detailed to guard the building. Except for a resounding crash when some workmen's scaffolding collapsed, the voting proceeded smoothly on October 14–15th. The results: 1,763 for and 250 against on the motion approving the document as a whole. This ensured that it would be promulgated. Pope Paul lost no time in confirming the Council's action and announced on Monday, October 18th that it would be added to the list of four texts already scheduled for solemn voting and promulgation on October 28th.

A minor crisis occurred Friday, October 15th as the Council was preparing to complete its voting on the document. It had been decided earlier to postpone two final votes to Saturday morning's congregation, when Archbishop Krol, one of the Council's undersecretaries, suddenly remembered that many of the bishops would be absent on a pilgrimage to the

Holy Land because of the holiday the following week. It would have been disastrous, and something that could probably never be explained satisfactorily, if a sizeable majority had not been reached because of these absences, so he hurriedly consulted Cardinal Cicognani and the entire voting was completed that day. As things turned out, some 700 bishops were absent the following morning.

World opinion, on the whole, hailed the passage of the Declaration as marking an important turning point in the relations of the Catholic Church with other religions, though regret was freely expressed about its shortcomings.

Few would have concurred in the judgment of one rabbi who is supposed to have said, "If the document is approved in its final form, any real dialogue between Catholics and Jews will be impossible for decades."[*] And those writers and commentators who mistakenly seized on words like "pardon" and "forgive" in expressing their outrage over the Church's "absolving and forgiving" the Jews, were guilty of misplaced indignation, for these words do not occur in the text of the Declaration. The document is addressed not to Jews but to Christians, teaching them that anti-Semitism is wrong. One writer[**] has called the Declaration "the most astonishing bureaucratic impertinence of all times." It is, of course, exactly the opposite—the fruit of Pope John's love of all men, and of his determination to do what Jules Isaac had asked, that is, reverse past Catholic teaching that approved of anti-Semitism. To label as an "impertinence" the years of effort on the part of Cardinal Bea and his Secretariat, and the Council's final endorsement of this historic Declaration, is mischievously to misread history. Many of the bishops who wanted a stronger text nevertheless voted for this one for fear that if there were too large a negative vote the document might be withdrawn. The adverse vote on the schema as a whole (250),

[*] Roddy, *Look*, op. cit.
[**] William Jovanovich, *Stations of Our Life*, 1965, Harcourt, Brace & World, p. 25.

though disgraceful, was offset by 1,763 affirmative votes. All attempts by either side to force last-minute modifications failed, and thus the document was at long last scheduled for promulgation.

Summary

October 8, 1965, Friday—145TH GENERAL CONGREGATION.
MASS: Archbishop Ghattas of Thebes, Egypt, in Coptic rite.
MODERATOR: Cardinal Agagianian.
PRESENT: 2,143 Fathers.
ANNOUNCEMENTS: Written observations on Schema 13 will be accepted until tomorrow; new schedule of votes on Priestly Formation distributed; after debate on Missions and Priestly Life there will be preliminary votes, as in case of Religious Liberty, according to decision of Moderators; reminder that circulation of notes and other documents prohibited except with permission of Secretary General; will be vote on Religious Life as whole on Monday.
PENDING BUSINESS: Further discussion of Schema 13, Chap. V (in name of 70 Fathers).
SPEAKERS: 1. Bishop Ancel (Lyons, France). 2. Bishop Rupp (Monaco). 3. Bishop Faveri (Tivoli, Italy). 4. Bishop Philbin (Down and Connor, Ireland). 5. Bishop Boillon (Verdun, France).
PENDING BUSINESS: Missionary Activity cont'd.
SPEAKERS: 6. Cardinal Frings (Cologne, Germany). 7. Cardinal Alfrink (Utrecht, Holland). 8. Cardinal Journet (Switzerland). 9. Father Legarra Tellechea (Prelate Nullius, Bocas del Toro, Panama). 10. Bishop Mazzoldi (Vicar Apostolic, Juba, Sudan). 11. Bishop McCauley (Fort Portal, Uganda). 12. Bishop Koppmann (Vicar Apostolic, Windhoek, Southwest Africa).

VOTES: Schema on Religious Life.

	Total	Placet	Non placet	Placet iuxta modum	Invalid
14–Art. 14	2,150	2,122	27	—	1
15–Art. 15	2,152	2,134	16	—	2
16–Art. 16	2,141	2,127	12	—	2
17–Art. 17	2,132	2,110	20	—	2
18–Art. 25	2,112	2,109	2	—	1
19–Art. 18-24	2,082	2,071	9	—	2

14–Religious obedience; 15–Community life; 16–Enclosure; 17–Adaptation of religious habits; 18–Training of religious; 19–New institutes; 20–Modifications; 21–Institutes without vocations; 22–Cooperation; 23–Conference of Superiors; 24–Vocations; 25–Conclusion.

October 11, 1965, Monday—146TH GENERAL CONGREGATION.
MASS: Abbot Gillet, Abbot General of the Trappist Order.
MODERATOR: Cardinal Agagianian.
PRESENT: 2,128 Fathers.
ANNOUNCEMENTS: Distribution of *relationes* on Priestly Life and Ministry and Relations of Church with Non-Christian Religions; new schedule of voting on Christian Education, on Wednesday; letter from Pope to Cardinal Tisserant about avoiding public discussion of celibacy read by SG.
PENDING BUSINESS: Schema on Missionary Activity cont'd.
SPEAKERS: 1. Cardinal Ruffini (Palermo, Italy). 2. Cardinal König (Vienna, Austria). 3. Father Quéguiner, Superior General of Foreign Missionary Society of Paris. 4. Bishop Sapelak (Apostolic Visitor for Ukrainians, Argentina). 5. Bishop Gonçalves da Costa (Inhambane, Mozambique). 6. Archbishop Cordeiro (Karachi, Pakistan). 7. Bishop McGrath (Santiago de Veraguas, Panama). 8. Bishop Lokuang (Tainan, China). 9. Bishop Geise (Bogor, Indonesia). 10. Archbishop Corboy (Monze, Zambia). 11. Archbishop Attipetty (Verapoly, India).

VOTE: Religious Life.

	Total	Placet	Non placet	Invalid
Schema as a whole	2,142	2,126	13	3 (2)

votes: Priestly Formation (Seminaries). *Relator:* Bishop Carraro.

	Total	*Placet*	*Non placet*	Invalid
1–Intr.	2,138	2,125	11	2
2–Art. 2	2,139	2,119	119	1
3–Art. 3	2,141	2,046	95	—
4–Art. 4	2,127	2,038	88	1
5–Art. 5	2,057	2,054	3	—
6–Art. 9	2,024	2,020	3	1
7–Art. 10	1,989	1,971	16	2
8–Art. 11	1,981	1,975	6	—
9–Art. 12	2,022	2,011	11	—

2–Priestly vocations; 3–Minor seminaries; 4–Major seminaries; 5–Seminary faculties; 9–Seminary spiritual life; 10–Positive approach to celibacy; 11–Training in human virtues; 12–Age for ordination and active diaconate.

October 12, 1965, Tuesday—147TH GENERAL CONGREGATION.
MASS: Bishop Liston, of Port Louis, Mauritian Islands.
MODERATOR: Cardinal Agagianian.
PRESENT: 2,126 Fathers.
ANNOUNCEMENTS: Letter of Cardinal Tisserant to Pope replying to Pope's letter about celibacy (applause); new list of votes on Christian Education distributed; sets of commemorative stamps distributed; Public Session will be held on Oct. 28 in memory of election of John XXIII (applause).
PENDING BUSINESS: Missionary Activity.
SPEAKERS: 1. Cardinal Rugambwa (Bukoba, Tanzania). 2. Cardinal Suenens (Malines-Brussels, Belgium). 3. Cardinal Zoungrana (Ouagadougou, Upper Volta). 4. Archbishop D'Souza (Bhopal, India). 5. Bishop Guffens (Belgium). 6. Bishop Garaygordobil (Prelate Nullius, Los Rios, Ecuador). 7. Bishop Sibomana (Ruhengeri, Ruanda). 8. Bishop J. Martin (Bururi, Burundi). 9. Bishop Gahamanyi (Butare, Ruanda). 10. Bishop Ntuyahaga (Bujumbura, Burundi). 11. Father Grotti (Prelate Nullius, Acre e Purus, Brazil). 12. Father Arrupe, Superior General of the Society of Jesus. 13. Bishop Poletti (Italy). 14. Archbishop Yu-Pin (China). 15. Bishop Soares de Resende (Beira, Mozambique). 16. Archbishop Kinan Ro (Seoul, Korea). 17. Bishop Lamont (Umtali, Rhodesia, in name of 70 Fathers).
STANDING VOTE to close debate on Missionary Activity.

VOTE: To accept Missionary Activity as basis for final text.

	Total	Placet	Non placet	Invalid
Motion	2,085	2,070	15	—

VOTES: Priestly Formation (Seminaries).

	Total	Placet	Non placet	Invalid
10–Art. 13	2,179	2,164	14	1
11–Art. 15	2,185	2,127	58	—
12–Art. 16	2,189	2,170	16	3
13–Art. 19	2,186	2,180	6	—
14–Concl.	2,174	2,166	6	2
15–Other articles	2,135	2,120	13	2

13–Studies; 15–Philosophy; 16–Theology; 19–Training in spiritual guidance; Conclusion (new).

October 13, 1965, Wednesday—148TH GENERAL CONGREGATION.
MASS: Bishop Schmitt, of Bulawajo, Rhodesia.
MODERATOR: Cardinal Lercaro.
PRESENT: 2,210 Fathers.
ANNOUNCEMENTS: Congregation on Saturday, and also on Monday, if necessary; *relatio* on Christian Education distributed.
PENDING BUSINESS: Schema on Missionary Activity (in name of 70 Fathers).
SPEAKERS: 1. Archbishop Heerey (Onitsha, Nigeria). 2. Father Degrijse, Superior General of Congr. of Immaculate Heart of Mary. 3. Bishop Gazza (Prelate Nullius, Abaete de T., Brazil). 4. Bishop Van Cauwelaert (Inongo, Congo). 5. Bishop Gay (Basse-Terre, Guadalupe). 6. Bishop Nagae (Urawa, Japan). 7. Bishop Velasco (Hsiamen, China). 8. Bishop Pirovano, head of Pont. Institute for Foreign Missions. 9. Bishop Han Kongryel (Jeon Ju, Korea). 10. Bishop De Reeper (Kisumu, Kenya). Lay Auditor: M. Eusèbe Adjakpley, Togoland. *Relator:* Father Schütte.
NEW BUSINESS: Schema on Priestly Life and Ministry.
Relator: Archbishop Marty (only the *relator* spoke today).

VOTES: Priestly Formation (Seminaries).

	Total	*Placet*	*Non placet*	Invalid
Schema as a whole	2,212	2,196	15	1

VOTES: Christian Education. *Relator:* Bishop Daem.

	Total	*Placet*	*Non placet*	Invalid
1–Intr.	2,202	2,117	85	—
2–Art. 1	2,194	2,098	96	—
3–Art. 2	2,181	2,105	76	—
4–Art. 3	2,120	2,007	111	2
5–Art. 3 bis	2,108	2,020	85	3
6–Art. 4	2,088	2,000	83	5
7–Art. 5	2,063	1,961	99	3
8–Art. 6	2,040	1,956	79	5
9–Art. 7	2,083	1,977	102	4

1–Right to education; 2–Christian education; 3–Responsibility of parents; 3 bis–Methods; 4–Schools; 5–Rights and duties of parents; 6–Religious education in schools; 7–Catholic schools.

October 14, 1965, Thursday—149TH GENERAL CONGREGATION.
MASS: Bishop Maze, Vicar Apostolic of the Tahiti Islands.
MODERATOR: Cardinal Lercaro.
PRESENT: 2,189 Fathers.
ANNOUNCEMENTS: If results of voting on Christian Education are favorable, there will be vote on schema as a whole.
PENDING BUSINESS: Priestly Life and Ministry.
SPEAKERS: 1. Cardinal Meouchi (Antioch). 2. Cardinal Ruffini (Palermo, Italy). 3. Cardinal de Arriba y Castro (Tarragona, Spain). 4. Cardinal Quiroga y Palacios (Santiago de Compostela, Spain). 5. Cardinal Léger (Montreal, Canada). 6. Cardinal Richaud (Bordeaux, France). 7. Cardinal Colombo (Milan, Italy). 8. Bishop Argaya Goicoechea (Mondonedo-Ferrol, Spain). 9. Bishop Guyot (Coutances, France). 10. Bishop Henríquez Jiménez (Auxiliary, Caracas, Venezuela). 11. Archbishop Santin (Trieste, Italy). 12. Bishop Jubany (Gerona, Spain).

VOTES: Christian Education.

	Total	Placet	Non placet	Invalid
10–Art. 8	2,187	2,068	116	3 (1)
11–Art. 9	2,180	2,043	132	5 (1)
12–Art. 10	2,184	2,095	87	2 (1)
13–Art. 11	2,181	2,079	100	2 (1)

8–Kinds of Catholic schools; 9–Catholic faculties and universities; 10–Faculties of sacred sciences; 11–Coordination and conclusion.

VOTE: Christian Education.

	Total	Placet	Non placet	Invalid
Schema as a whole	2,096	1,912	183	1

VOTES: Declaration on Relations with Non-Christian Religions.
Relator: Cardinal Bea.

	Total	Placet	Non placet	Invalid
1–Art. 1	2,185	2,071	110	4
2–Art. 2	2,143	1,953	184	6 (2)
3–Art. 3	2,105	1,910	189	6
4–Art. 4	2,099	1,937	153	9 (2)
5–Art. 4	2,072	1,875	188	9 (1)
6–Art. 4	2,080	1,821	245	14 (4)

1–Introd.; 2–Non-Christian religions in general; 3–Islamic religion; 4–Jews and People of New Testament; 5–Responsibility for death of Christ cannot be attributed to all Jews; 6–Jews not reprobated or accursed by God.

October 15, 1965, Friday—150TH GENERAL CONGREGATION.
MASS: Archbishop Ayoub, of Aleppo, Syria, in Maronite rite.
MODERATOR: Cardinal Lercaro.
PRESENT: 2,122 Fathers.
ANNOUNCEMENTS: Will be general congregation tomorrow; general congregations will resume on Oct. 25, with voting on handling of modi for Religious Liberty, Divine Revelation, Apostolate of Laity, and any remaining discussion (in name of 70 Fathers); at Public Session on Oct. 28, Pastoral Office of

Bishops, Religious Life, Priestly Formation (Seminaries) and Christian Education will be promulgated; change in ceremonial for public sessions; may be general congregation on Oct. 29; suspension of general congregations between Oct. 30 and Nov. 8; general congregations will resume on Nov. 9; possibly another Public Session on Nov. 18.

PENDING BUSINESS: Schema on Priestly Life and Ministry.

SPEAKERS: 1. Cardinal Döpfner (Munich, Germany). 2. Cardinal Tatsuo Doi (Tokyo, Japan). 3. Cardinal Alfrink (Utrecht, Holland). 4. Cardinal Landázuri Ricketts (Lima, Peru). 5. Cardinal Suenens (Malines-Brussels, Belgium). 6. Cardinal Jaeger (Paderborn, Germany). 7. Cardinal Herrera y Oria (Málaga, Spain). 8. Archbishop Miranda y Gómez (Mexico City, Mexico). 9. Archbishop Franic (Split, Yugoslavia). 10. Archbishop D'Avack (Italy). 11. Archbishop Nabaa (Beirut, Lebanon). 12. Bishop Charue (Namur, Belgium). 13. Bishop Brzana (Auxiliary, Buffalo, N.Y.). 14. Bishop Renard (Versailles, France). 15. Bishop Mancini (Auxiliary, Porto and Santa Rufina, Italy). 16. Bishop Tomé (Mercedes, Argentina).

VOTES: Declaration on Non-Christian Religions.

	Total	*Placet*	*Non placet*	Invalid
7–Art. 4	2,118	1,905	199	14 (3)
8–Art. 5	2,128	2,064	58	6
9–*Modi* as whole	2,108	1,856	243	9 (2)

7–Anti-Semitism reprobated; 8–Universal brotherhood; 9–Handling of *modi* in general.

VOTE: Declaration on Non-Christian Religions.

	Total	*Placet*	*Non placet*	Invalid
Schema as a whole	2,023	1,763	250	10 (1)

October 16, 1965, Saturday—151ST GENERAL CONGREGATION.

MASS: Father Pedro Arrupe, Superior General of the Society of Jesus.

MODERATOR: Cardinal Lercaro.

PRESENT: 1,694 Fathers.

ANNOUNCEMENTS: Fathers invited to be present at beatification of Bl. Jacques Berthieu, of Society of Jesus, tomorrow; Fathers still desiring to speak on Priestly Ministry on Oct. 25 must submit complete texts by Oct. 18; amended texts of Divine Revelation and probably also Religious Liberty will be distributed during coming week; general congregations will be held on Oct. 25, 26, 27 and 29, with Public Session on Oct. 28 at which four documents will be promulgated.

PENDING BUSINESS: Schema on Priestly Ministry and Life.
SPEAKERS: 1. Cardinal Lefebvre (Bourges, France). 2. Cardinal Rugambwa (Bukoba, Tanzania). 3. Cardinal Roy (Quebec, Canada). 4. Cardinal Florit (Florence, Italy). 5. Cardinal Heenan (Westminster, England). 6. Cardinal Shehan (Baltimore, Maryland). 7. Cardinal Rossi (São Paulo, Brazil). 8. Cardinal Bea (Curia). 9. Bishop Klooster (Surabaja, Indonesia). 10. Bishop Bank (Auxiliary, Györ, Hungary). 11. Bishop Leven (Auxiliary, San Antonio, Texas). 12. Bishop Zak (Sankt Pölten, Austria). 13. Bishop Fernández Conde (Córdoba, Spain). 14. Bishop Barela (Czestochowa, Poland). 15. Bishop Soares de Resende (Beira, Mozambique). 16. Bishop Ndongmo (Nkongsamba, Cameroun).
STANDING VOTE to close debate on Priestly Life and Ministry.

VOTE: Priestly Life and Ministry.
Relator: Archbishop Marty.

	Total	*Placet*	*Non placet*	Invalid
Schema as a whole	1,521	1,507	12	2

October 25, 1965, Monday—152ND GENERAL CONGREGATION.
MASS: Bishop Suhr, O.S.B., former Bishop of Copenhagen.
MODERATOR: Cardinal Döpfner.
PRESENT: 2,028 Fathers.
ANNOUNCEMENTS: *Modi* on Religious Liberty may be submitted until Oct. 29; brochure containing *modi* on Divine Revelation distributed, voting on Oct. 29; definitive texts of Pastoral Duties of Bishops, Religious Life and Non-Christian Religions distributed; letter from Cardinal Cicognani to Cardinal Liénart read, granting request that Pope's talk before UN be included in Council Acts.
PENDING BUSINESS: Priestly Life and Ministry.
SPEAKERS (in name of at least 70 bishops): 1. Bishop Arrieta Villalobos (Tilaran, Costa Rica). 2. Bishop De Roo (Victoria,

British Colombia). 3. Bishop Charbonneau (Hull, Quebec). 4. Bishop Flores Martín (Barbastro, Spain). 5. Bishop Segedi (Auxiliary of Apost. Administrator, Krizevci, Yugoslavia). 6. Archbishop Connolly (Seattle, Wash.). 7. Bishop García Lahiguera (Huelva, Spain).

VOTE: Declaration on Religious Liberty. *Relator:* Bishop De Smedt (only the *relatio* read today).

October 26, 1965, Tuesday—153RD GENERAL CONGREGATION.
MASS concelebrated by Bishop De Zanche (Concordia, Italy), Bishop Gavilanes Chamorro (Portoviejo, Ecuador), Bishop Grimley (Vicar Apostolic, Cape Palmas, Liberia), Bishop Gassongo (Auxiliary, Fort Rousset, Republic of the Congo), Abbot Kleiner (Abbot General of Cistercian Order).
MODERATOR: Cardinal Suenens.
PRESENT: 2,220 Fathers.
ANNOUNCEMENTS: Definitive texts of Christian Education and Priestly Formation distributed; bishops reminded of their duty to attend congregations and vote, apropos voting on Divine Revelation; brochure containing *modi* to Apostolate of Laity will be distributed on Oct. 29, voting to begin on Nov. 9.
PENDING BUSINESS: Priestly Life and Ministry.
SPEAKERS (in name of 70 bishops): 1. Bishop Foley (Lancaster, England). 2. Archbishop Fares (Catanzaro, Italy). 3. Bishop Pechuán Marín (Cruz del Eje, Argentina). 4. Bishop Compagnone (Anagni, Italy). 5. Archbishop Pellegrino (Turin, Italy).

VOTES: Declaration on Religious Liberty.

	Total	Placet	Non placet	Placet iuxta modum	Invalid
1–Art. 1	2,232	2,031	193	—	8 (2)
2–Art. 2-3	2,234	2,000	228	—	6 (2)
3–Art. 4-5	2,236	2,026	206	—	4 (1)
4–Art. 6-8	2,223	2,034	186	—	3 (2)
5–Art. 1-5	2,161	1,539	65	543	14
6–Art. 6-8	2,161	1,715	68	373	5

1–Consciousness of human dignity, man's duties to true faith and Church; 2-3–General notion of religious liberty; 4-5–Freedom of religious groups; 6-8–Concern for religious liberty, duties of civil authorities, limitations of religious liberty, education in exercise of r.l.

October 27, 1965, Wednesday—154TH GENERAL CONGREGATION.

MASS: Father Ireland, Prefect Apostolic of Falkland Islands.

MODERATOR: Cardinal Agagianian.

PRESENT: 2,240 Fathers.

ANNOUNCEMENTS: Statement of SG about voting and *iuxta modum* votes; omission, through error, of reference to Secular Institutes in text of Religious Life to be voted tomorrow.

PENDING BUSINESS: Priestly Life and Ministry.

SPEAKER: Monsignor Thomas Falls (Pastor of Sacred Heart Church, Philadelphia).

VOTES: Declaration on Religious Liberty.

	Total	Placet	Non placet	Placet iuxta modum	Invalid
7–Art. 9-10	2,238	2,087	146	—	5 (1)
8–Art. 11-12	2,238	1,979	524	—	5 (1)
9–Art. 13-15	2,239	2,107	127	—	5 (1)
10–Art. 9-12	2,236	1,751	60	417	8
11–Art. 13-15	2,202	1,843	47	307	5

9–Doctrine of religious liberty founded in revelation; 10–Freedom of act of faith; 11–Conduct of Christ and Apostles; 12–Church imitates it; 13–Freedom required for Church; 14–Role of Church; 15–Conclusion.

V

The Final Weeks of the Council;
Closing Ceremonies

✠

THE FORMAL DEBATING of conciliar texts ended technically on October 16th but actually on October 27th, after a number of additional speakers were heard who requested to speak in the name of sizeable groups of bishops. The remaining congregations would be devoted almost exclusively to voting and, as Archbishop Felici put it, "gathering the fruits of their labors," with a number of weekly interruptions during which only the various commissions preparing the texts for final voting and approval would be at work. The first intermission lasted from October 17th to October 24th.

Already the Council could rack up an impressive list of accomplishments. Archbishop Felici was able to announce, in the session on October 15th, that four documents would be promulgated by the Pope in a first Public Session on October 28th, namely the texts on the Pastoral Office of Bishops, the Renovation of Religious Life, Seminaries and Christian Education. Three other texts, the Declaration on Religious Liberty and the schemata on Divine Revelation and the Apostolate of the Laity were already sufficiently advanced so that final voting could begin on October 25th, with the possibility of a second Public Session on November 18 at which time some or all of these texts could be proclaimed. This left only 4 texts out of the original 11 before the Council at the beginning of the Fourth Session on September 14th, still to be acted on, namely Schema 13, Missionary Activity, Priestly Life and Ministry, and the Declaration on Relations with Non-Christian Religions. The overwhelming approval accorded the latter in an historic vote on Friday, October 15th, before the close of the debates, ensured that this too would be promulgated on October 28th.

Gone was the mood of uncertainty and pessimism prevailing at the beginning of the Fourth Session. It was now clear that real progress was being made and the end of the Council's work was in sight—barring some upset over a failure to reach agreement on the controversial Schema 13 or renewed efforts on the part of the Pope to pacify the minority that might result in a crisis similar to the one that accompanied the close of the Third Session. Both eventualities now tended to be discounted.

The mood of the Council Fathers at this point could be called one of resigned euphoria. They were resigned because of the realization that more acceptable texts could not be achieved under present circumstances and it was better to be grateful for the great progress already accomplished than mourn over unattainable ideals. The important thing, as Cardinal Suenens noted, was not whether *aggiornamento* had been achieved, but whether the groundwork had been laid for future action. "Perhaps we can say," he declared, "that we have not yet reached May but are only in April when night frosts still occur, nevertheless there can be no doubt

that spring has come and no question of a return to winter."
When the first fruits were garnered in the Public Session
on October 28th, statistical evidence seemed to prove what
most observers had been predicting for weeks, that all the
conciliar documents were going to be voted through with a
minimum of stir.

Texts promulgated	Previous Non Placet votes	Final Non Placet votes
Bishops	14	2
Religious	13	4
Seminaries	15	3
Christian Education	183	35
Non-Christians	250	88

The second and fourth were probably the least successful
documents of the lot. That the Decree on Renewal of the
Religious Life did not arouse more determined opposition
at this late date could be explained by its limited interest and
the fact that those who hoped for a more vigorous approach
to the problem had lost the battle much earlier. The Commission on Religious, dominated by the ultra-conservative
Curial Congregation on Religious under Cardinal Antoniutti, consistently refused to allow women religious, for example, to have any deliberative part in their discussions despite
the fact that well over half the number of religious in the
Church are women (nuns and sisters). Although there are
abundant signs that dissatisfaction with the traditional ordering of religious life in convents and monasteries has now
reached the boiling point, the Congregation has persistently
ignored the real causes of this *malaise* and insisted on regarding all instances of disquiet as rebellion against authority.
Antoniutti himself has set a fine example of insubordination,
continually accosting the Pope's ears with complaints about
the rebelliousness of nuns while refusing himself to comply
with the spirit of the Pope's directives. The tragedy is that the
Decree would do so little for those, namely the religious themselves, for whom it was primarily intended. While ordering a

reform of the religious life, it was clear that in the mind of the drafters this reform was to be largely confined to the tidying up of externals such as the updating of religious garb with a minimum of attention being paid to underlying theological issues. Significantly, the section on obedience was five times longer in the finally approved text. However, the difficulty here is that the process of reform, once unleashed, may be impossible to keep under control.

More encouraging was the situation with regard to the Decree on Priestly Formation (Seminaries) and the Declaration on Christian Education, voted by the Council on October 11–12 and 13 respectively, because the commissions preparing them had managed more or less successfully to escape from the control of the equally conservative Roman Congregation for Seminaries and Universities, nominally governed by the senile Cardinal Pizzardo, actually run by the energetic but hopelessly *intégriste* Archbishop Dino Staffa. Distribution of the second text was delayed by the archbishop's efforts to insert wording that would strongly commend Thomas Aquinas, and scholasticism generally, as a unique model to be followed by the Church, as opposed to the more scientific attitude advocated for example by Cardinal Léger at the Third Session and presently reflected by the text.* The archbishop also tried to strengthen paragraphs 13 and 16 of the Decree on Seminaries dealing with philosophical and theological studies in the same sense. Both moves failed completely. The commissions preferred to heed the example of Pope Paul VI who in an important address before the Thomistic Congress on September 10, 1965 just before the opening of the Fourth Session, and again in an audience granted to

* The Decree on Priestly Formation (Seminaries) recommends in art. 16: ". . . students should learn to penetrate [the mysteries of salvation] more deeply with the help of speculation, *under the guidance of St. Thomas (S. Thoma magistro)*"; the Declaration on Christian Education, art. 10, speaks of "investigations carefully made according to the example of the doctors of the Church and *especially of St. Thomas Aquinas (praesertim S. Thomae Aquinatis vestigia premendo)*."

COETUS INTERNATIONALIS PATRUM

Eccellenza Reverendissima,

un gruppo di Padri Conciliari, desiderosi di contribuire ad un maggior esito del Concilio, ha organizzato qualche riunione de studio sugli Schemi del Concilio, e preparato alcuni "modi" per le votazioni.

Lo scopo delle Riunione di studio e chiarire i problemi e risolvere le difficolta.

Lo scopo dei "modi" e dare una formulazione piu o meno simile alle simili opinioni dei Vescovi, perche sia facile alle Commissioni raggrupare i voti secondo il loro contenuto.

Siccome non tutti i Padri Conciliari sono interessati a tali Riunioni, Conferenze e "Modi", domandiamo a Vostra Eccellenza Reverendissima di communicarci se caso mai desidera essere invitato alle Riunioni, o se desidera ricevere gli studi, i "modi" ed altre informazioni che possiamo inviarla, sempre seguendo come criterio la dottrina tradizionale della Chiesa.

Caso lo desideri, La preghiamo di rinviarci la schedola che trovera in clusa.

Con la espressione della nostra fraterna devozione

in Gesu Cristo

+ Geraldo da Proença Sigaud,
Arciv. di Diamantina (Brasile)

+ Marcel Lefebvre
Arciv. tit. di Sinnata di Frigia

+ Luigi Maria Carli
Vesc. di Segni

Letter of the conservative *Coetus Internationalis Patrum* inviting the bishops to receive their literature.

Exc.me Domine,

cum plures Patres a nobis petierint ut opinionem nostram de singulis Schematibus huius quartae Sessionis patefaceremus, desiderio moti ut conciliaria documenta quam perfectissime conficiantur, audemus Tibi reverenter communicare quid de Schemate "DE ECCLESIAE HABITUDINE AD RELIGIONES NON CHRISTIANAS" sentimus.

Observanter in Domino,

+ Geraldo de Proença Sigaud
+ Marcel Lefebvre
+ Aloysius Maria Carli

Ad quaesitum I - NON PLACET, ut postea explicatur.
Ad quaesitum II - NON PLACET, ut postea explicatur.
Ad quaesitum III - NON PLACET, ut postea explicatur.
Ad quaesitum IV - Totum placet exceptis lin. 26-32, propter rationes postea allatas.
Ad quaesitum V - Placeret, quia vox "Iudaei" sumitur aequivoce, ut postea dicetur.
Ad quaesitum VI - NON PLACET, ut postea explicatur.
Ad quaesitum VII - Placerent omnia, cum aliqua clausula, quae postea explicatur.
Ad quaesitum VIII - In dubio sumus.
Ad quaesitum generale: NON PLACET ob rationes allatas.

Rationes horum votorum inveniri possunt in subsequentibus paginis.

Voting on Non-Christian Religions, suggested by *Coetus*.

the Canadian Thomas Aquinas Foundation on October 8th, adopted a sensible approach to the whole problem, referring to Aquinas on the latter occasion as "a sure norm for the teaching of the sacred sciences" but not as a master to be followed exclusively or in a formalistic way.*

The most interesting feature about the Decree on Seminaries was the provision in the very first paragraph for greater autonomy: "Since only general laws can be made where there exists a wide variety of nations and regions, a special program of priestly training is to be undertaken by each country or rite. It must be set up by the episcopal conferences, revised from time to time and approved by the Apostolic See." The initiative for reorganizing and modernizing seminaries was thus clearly handed over to the local hierarchy which, to an extent as yet undetermined, were to be freed from excessive control by the Roman Congregation of Seminaries and Universities. Another progressive feature was that students were to be "brought to a fuller understanding of the Churches and ecclesial communities separated from the Apostolic See of Rome, so that they may be able to contribute to the work of re-establishing unity among all Christians according to the prescriptions of this holy synod." Such a ruling would have been unthinkable, had it not been for the Council. There was considerable dissatisfaction with the Declaration on Christian Education on the part of some of those most directly concerned both bishops and priests, as reflected in the rather high number of *non placet* votes: 183. One commentator described it as "probably the most inferior document produced by the Council," others preferred to reserve this accolade for the Decree on the Apostolate of the Laity, the Decree on the Religious Life, or the Decree on Communications. The state-aid-to-education clause in particular was a disappointment to many of the American bishops, including Cardinal Spellman, who wanted a clearer

* *L'Osservatore Romano,* October 10, 1965.

statement of the obligation of the state to support religious education, whereas the compromise text was more in accordance with world thinking because conditions varied so from country to country (Par. 6: ". . . the public power, which has the obligation to protect and defend the rights of citizens, must see to it, in its concern for distributive justice, that public subsidies are paid out in such a way that parents are truly free to choose according to their consciences the schools they want for their children"). The obligation of parents to send their children to Catholic schools was somewhat mitigated again owing to different world conditions. The Americans saw this too as a possible threat to their extensive and expensive parochial school system. The principles enunciated by the schema were to be "developed" at greater length by a Post-Conciliar Commission and "applied" by the various episcopal conferences according to varying local conditions. Perhaps another reason why the Americans were dissatisfied was the knowledge of how weak their own episcopal conference traditionally was when it came to carrying out any concerted action. After the high *non placet* vote on October 13th there was talk of appealing to the Administrative Tribunal to get a new discussion of the text which had been rather thoroughly revised by the commission, but nothing came of this move.* One tired bishop summed up his thoughts as follows: "Last year I would have voted *non placet* because the text is so bad that it deserves to be turned down. But this year we all know that the possibility of getting anything better is nil. The Pope wants the Council to end. The bishops are all anxious to go home. Negative votes would only complicate matters. Therefore I voted *placet,* even though I have grave misgivings about the value of the present text."

The Decree on the Pastoral Office of Bishops which went through without a ripple when voted on September 29 and

---

* In the booklet distributed before the vote on Oct. 13th, the new material was printed in roman and the old in italics, contrary to the usual practice.

30, October 1 and 6, was not a revolutionary document in any sense of the word, but its provision calling for the establishment and strengthening of episcopal conferences was bound eventually to alter the traditional pattern of church government. No surprise was caused by the fact that the Declaration on Non-Christian Religions registered a total *non placet* vote of 88. There was merely relief that the figure was not higher.

The Revision of Divine Revelation

There can be little doubt that the Constitution on Divine Revelation will be regarded as the most important document promulgated by the Council after the Constitution on the Church. Together with *Lumen Gentium,* it enshrined and consecrated the new biblical approach to theology which has become one of the hallmarks of Vatican II. But this victory was not achieved without a struggle. An original draft entitled "The Sources of Revelation" *(De Fontibus Revelationis),* prepared by the ultra-conservative pre-conciliar theological commission, after being subjected to a gruelling debate during the First Session (Nov. 14–21, 1962) on its general merits, was withdrawn by Pope John XXIII when a crucial vote showed that 1,368 of the Fathers, as opposed to 822, were not in favor of going on to a discussion of the individual chapters. Revision of the text was entrusted to a Mixed Commission headed by Cardinal Ottaviani (of the Theological Commission) and Cardinal Bea (of the Secretariat for Promoting Christian Unity). This Mixed Commission produced a more liberal version *De divina revelatione* that was approved by Pope John on April 23, 1963 and debated by the Council at its Third Session, Sept. 30–Oct. 6, 1964. On the basis of the debate a *textus emendatus* was prepared, but this was readied too late to be submitted to the Fathers for a vote before the end of that session. The revised text was therefore voted at the Fourth Session, Sept. 20–22, 1965.

The schema was approved with a comfortable margin, however there were a rather large number of *iuxta modum* votes for each of the six chapters, indicating that a substantial agreement had not yet been reached on several controversial points.* An examination of the *modi* revealed that these points were mainly the three on which concord had always been difficult from the very beginning, namely 1) the relation of Scripture to Tradition; 2) the question of the inerrancy of the Bible or "truth" of Scripture; and 3) the historical nature of the Gospels. The Council's progressive majority was generally satisfied with the highly skillful and balanced way in which the revised text dealt with these problems, in a sense that would not close any doors but leave the way open to future speculation. The minority, on the other hand, felt that the text was too "liberal," abandoned essential Catholic positions, and opened the way to heresy. The *iuxta modum* votes of course were not all offered by the minority. Some of the majority felt that various improvements should be made before the document could be finally promulgated, however it is clear from what follows that the minority were the prime movers in the attempt to change the schema on these three fundamental counts.**

Pope Paul followed the revision of this document with very close attention. Although the Secretariat for Promoting Unity had had nothing to do with the work after the presen-

---

* Chapter I—Divine Revelation Itself (Arts. 1–6)—248 *iuxta modum* votes; Chapter II—Transmission of Divine Revelation (Arts. 7–10)—354 *iuxta modum* votes; Chapter III—Divine Inspiration of Scripture and its Interpretation (Arts. 11–13)—324 *iuxta modum* votes; Chapter IV—Old Testament (Arts. 14–16)—47 *iuxta modum* votes; Chapter V—New Testament (Arts. 17–20)—313 *iuxta modum* votes; Chapter VI—Scripture in the Life of the Church (Arts. 21–26)—212 *iuxta modum* votes.

** Pope Paul obviously authorized Fr. G. Caprile, S.J., to publish a full account of the maneuvering relative to this schema in order to forestall erroneous interpretations of his own actions and set the record straight. Caprile's article, *"Tre emendamenti allo schema sulla Rivelazione,"* was published in *La Civiltà Cattolica,* February 5, 1966. (A similarly revealing article was published by the Jesuit editor in February 1965, throwing light on Paul's actions during the controversial closing days of the Third Session.) Our account is based on Caprile's article.

tation of the first revised draft, the Pope was anxious that
Cardinal Bea should be associated with its closing stages,
probably in order to make clear some kind of continuity with
Pope John's Mixed Commission and for the effect that Bea's
presence would have in helping the commission to reach
agreement on a satisfactory text. (When Father Daniélou
declared that the Secretariat had been represented at the final
commission discussions, thus implying that the Mixed Commission had in a certain sense been revived, Cardinal Bea
publicly denied this, maintaining that he had been present
in a personal capacity and had given his views without consulting the members of his Secretariat, however it seems that
the Pope's view was as stated above.)

The Theological Commission proceeded to examine the
modi submitted by the Fathers and in a series of plenary
meetings, on October 1, 4 and 6, decided what attitude to
adopt with regard to them, on the basis of the recommendations of the special Subcommission headed by Cardinal Florit
charged with preparing the text. Approximately about this
time the Pope began to be besieged by various Fathers complaining that the Subcommission and the Commission had
not paid sufficient attention to their opinions. Accordingly,
after consulting a large number of people during the first
two weeks of October, Paul had Cardinal Cicognani, Secretary of State, send a letter to the Theological Commission on
October 17th (dated the 18th) requesting a reconsideration
of the revised text with a view to reaching a better consensus
of opinion particularly on the three above mentioned points.
It was also his wish that Cardinal Bea should take part in the
discussions. The plenary Theological Commission met on the
afternoon of Tuesday October 19th to consider the Pope's
proposals and vote on a final text. This *textus re-emendatus*
was then voted by the Council on October 29th.

It is convenient in what follows to discuss separately the
three points raised in the Pope's letter, though they were of
course dealt with in the same communication.

1. Paragraph 9, of Chapter II, dealing with the relation between Scripture and Tradition, read in part as follows in the version of the text voted by the Council in Sept. 1965:

. . . Sacra Scriptura est locutio Dei, quatenus divino afflante Spiritu scripto consignata, sacra autem traditio verbum Dei, a Christo Domino et a Spiritu Sancto apostolis concreditum, successoribus eorum integre transmittit, ut illud, praelucente Spiritu veritatis, praeconio suo fideliter servent, exponant atque diffundant. Quapropter utraque pari pietatis affectu ac reverentia suscipienda et veneranda est.

. . . Sacred Scripture is the word of God inasmuch as it is consigned to writing under the inspiration of the divine Spirit, while sacred tradition takes the word of God entrusted by Christ the Lord and the Holy Spirit to the apostles, and hands it on to their successors in its full purity, so that led by the light of the Spirit of truth, they may in proclaiming it preserve this word of God faithfully, explain it, and make it more widely known. Therefore both sacred tradition and Sacred Scripture are to be accepted and venerated with the same sense of loyalty and reverence.

In the final version, voted on October 29th and promulgated by the Council December 7th, this read as follows:

. . . Sacra Scriptura est locutio Dei . . . diffundant; *quo fit ut Ecclesia certitudinem suam de omnibus revelatis non per solam* Sacram Scripturam *hauriat.* Quapropter . . .

. . . Sacred Scripture is the word of God . . . more widely known; *consequently it is not from Scripture alone that the Church draws her certainty about everything which has been revealed.* Therefore . . .

Among the 354 *iuxta modum* votes on Chapter II, 111 demanded that the following clause (or a variation of it) be added after *diffundant:* "*quo fit ut non omnis doctrina catholica ex sola Scriptura directe probari queat*" ("therefore not every Catholic doctrine can be directly proved by Scripture alone"). Three *modi* asked that a similar clause be inserted in the following paragraph 10 (on the relation of Scripture and Tradition to the Magisterium). The Subcommission revising the text at first agreed to accept this latter suggestion, then changed its mind and opted for the first alternative. However, when the proposed amendments were voted by the plenary Commission on Oct. 1, 4 and 6, the full Commission rejected the Subcommission's rceommendation for an addition to Par. 9, and also a suggestion for amending Par. 10, after having momentarily accepted the latter. In the course of the heated discussion of these points, one of the experts (Fr. Tromp?) suggested that since the Commission was so hopelessly divided on the question of how to express the relationship of Scripture to Tradition, it would be best to return to the old idea of "two sources" and insert a statement to this effect in Par. 9. This naturally caused the majority in the Commission to freeze in their opposition to any change and matters stood at this point when the Pope intervened.

The minority was determined to effect some change in the language of the text that would permit the "constitutive" role of Tradition to be brought out more clearly, even if there was no hope of going back to the old view of "two sources" of divine Revelation. Pope Paul was not averse to trying to satisfy their desires, provided this could be done without upsetting the delicate balance of the existing text. On September 24th he had transmitted to the Commission a text from St. Augustine's *De Baptismo contra Donatistas* (V, 23, 31) which suggested a possible alternative wording, but for some mysterious reason his communication never reached its destination.

Members of the minority were not the only ones to make their views known to the Pope. Others assured him that the text as drafted was perfectly acceptable. One cardinal suggested that while the text seemed to be satisfactory as it stood, a way out might be for the Commission to introduce the clause *quo fit . . .* which it had first accepted then rejected, because this still left open the question of whether some truths were to be found in Tradition which were not found in Scripture, a point that the text was not intended to settle. Pope Paul kept on consulting various people and had a meeting with the Moderators on October 12th. Two days later one of the Moderators submitted a written memorandum in which he proposed a solution similar to that of the above cardinal, recommending the insertion of another *modus, "quo fit ut Ecclesia certitudinem suam de omnibus revelatis . . ."* shifting the emphasis from "doctrine" to "certainty regarding doctrine."

This seemed to be the best solution, so on October 17th the Pope had Cardinal Cicognani write to the Theological Commission and suggested that the latter should consider 7 possible alternative readings, all approximately with the same meaning, and choose the one that seemed to be the best. Cardinal Bea was asked for his opinion first and chose No. 3, the wording suggested by the Moderator. There were 28 members of the Commission present. The first ballot was indecisive because the necessary two-thirds majority was not reached. However the second ballot produced the required majority and so the Commission ordered this clause inserted in Par. 9.

2. Par. 11 of Chapter III, dealing with the inspiration of Scripture, read in part as follows, in the version voted by the Council in Sept. 1965:

. . . Cum ergo omne id, quod auctor inspiratus seu hagiographus asserit, retineri debeat assertum a Spiritu Sancto, inde Scripturae libri integri cum omnibus suis partibus *veritatem salutarem* inconcusse et fideliter, integre et sine errore docere profitendi sunt.

. . . Therefore since everything asserted by the inspired author or sacred writer must be held to be asserted by the Holy Spirit, it follows that the books of Scripture completely and in all their parts must be acknowledged as teaching solidly and faithfully, fully and without error *the truth of salvation.*

The final text as amended and promulgated by the Council read:

. . . Cum ergo omne id, quod auctores inspirati seu hagiographi asserunt, retineri debeat assertum a Spiritu Sancto, inde Scripturae libri *veritatem, quam Deus nostrae salutis causa litteris sacris consignari voluit,* firmiter, fideliter et sine errore docere profitendi sunt.

. . . Therefore since everything asserted by the inspired authors or sacred writers must be held to be asserted by the Holy Spirit, it follows that the books of Scripture must be acknowledged as teaching solidly, faithfully and without error *that truth which God wanted put into the sacred writings for the sake of our salvation.*

Of the 324 *iuxta modum* votes on Chapter III, about 200 dealt with the expression *veritatem salutarem*. 184 of these wanted to eliminate the word *salutarem;* 76 wanted to substitute other wording because the present language seemed to restrict the inerrancy of Scripture to matters of faith and morals. Others approved of the expression, but wanted it more fully explained in a note, with references to St. Augustine (*De Gen. ad litt.* 2, 9) and papal documents. The Commission had made it clear in its commentary on the revised text that *"salutaris* had been added to cover the *facts* mentioned in Scripture in connection with the history of salvation" and that it was not being used in an unduly restrictive sense, but this did not satisfy the minority.

The various alternative suggestions proposed by the bishops were all rejected both by the Subcommission and by the plenary Commission, which insisted that "the word *salutaris* did not imply that Scripture was not wholly inspired and the word of God." The proofs of the Commission's *expensio modorum* were sent to the Pope on October 14th. But before they reached him, a group of the minority had made known their objections through one of the cardinals, probably the same group that had voted the 184 *modi* mentioned above, asking that the word *salutaris* be deleted and complaining about the way in which the Commission had disregarded the objections of so many Fathers. They were afraid that the Commission was restricting the inerrancy of Scripture merely to supernatural matters affecting faith and morals (ignoring the explanations offered by the Commission), that the text would give dangerous leeway to exegetes, would deal a severe blow to the Church, etc. In the following days other views were made known to the Pope, pro and con. Some held that the formula should not be dropped but explained, all the more so since it had been introduced into the text by the Commission after the debate in 1964 and not adequately discussed by all the bishops.

After reflecting on all these various conflicting views, the

Pope proposed, in the letter of Cardinal Cicognani, that the Theological Commission should "consider whether the expression *veritas salutaris* might be omitted. The perplexity of the Holy Father is greater with regard to this point because it is a question of a doctrine not yet commonly taught in biblical theology, and because it does not seem that the formula has been sufficiently discussed in the aula, and finally in the judgment of competent persons, because this formula is not without the risk of misinterpretation. It seems premature for the Council to pronounce on a problem that is so delicate. The Fathers are perhaps not in a position to judge of its importance or whether it could be misinterpreted. Omitting it would not preclude future study of the question."

The Commission was left free to consider any possible alternative wording. In the meeting on October 19th Cardinal Bea was again asked for his opinion first. He opted for dropping the expression *veritatem salutarem* pointing out that it was liable to misinterpretation and that in any case it had been added to the text after the first revised draft had been prepared by the Mixed Commission.

The voting on the proposition "whether the formula should be omitted or retained" was very sticky. There were three ballots, none of which produced the required two-thirds majority. A dispute then arose over whether the Commission should be guided by canon law or the Rules of the Council in determining what constituted a majority. It was finally decided that the Rules alone were normative. An alternative wording was then sought that would be acceptable to both sides. This was found in the clause *"veritatem, quam Deus nostrae salutis causa litteris sacris consignari voluit"* suggested by 73 of the Fathers among the *modi*. A fourth ballot succeeded in garnering a two-thirds majority for this wording. At this point, in a last desperate move, the minority again raised the question of what constituted a majority. If the Commission took its stand on canon law, then the first vote had been valid and the phrase would have been rejected.

Consideration was given to referring this point to the Administrative Tribunal, but this idea was dropped and the Commission stood by its fourth ballot.

The wording adopted had the advantage of spelling out what was meant by *salutaris* without in the slightest departing from the stand that the Commission had adopted on this point.

3. Par. 19, of Chapter V, dealing with the "Historical Nature of the Gospel," read in part as follows, in the version voted by the Council in September 1965:

. . . Sancta Mater Ecclesia firmiter et constantissime tenuit ac tenet quattuor recensita Evangelia vere tradere quae Iesus, Dei Filius, vitam inter homines degens, ad aeternam eorum salutem reapse et fecit et docuit . . . Auctores autem sacri quattuor Evangelia conscripserunt... ita semper *ut vera et sincera* de Iesu nobis communicarent.

. . . Holy Mother the Church has firmly and with absolute constancy held, and continues to hold, that the four Gospels just named, truly hand on what Jesus, the Son of God, while living among men, really did and taught for their eternal salvation . . . The sacred authors wrote the four Gospels . . . in such fashion that they told us *the honest truth* about Jesus.

The final version of the text as amended and promulgated by the Council read:

. . . Sancta Mater Ecclesia firmiter et constantissime tenuit ac tenet quattuor recensita Evangelia, *quorum historicitatem incunctanter affirmat,* fideliter tradere quae Iesus, Dei Filius, vitam inter homines degens, ad aeternam eorum salutem reapse fecit et docuit, usque in diem qua assumptus est . . . Auctores autem sacri quattuor Evangelia conscripserunt... ita semper ut vera et sincera de Iesu nobis communicarent.

. . . Holy Mother the Church has firmly and with absolute constancy held, and continues to hold, that the four Gospels just named, *whose historical character the Church unhesitatingly asserts,* faithfully hand on what Jesus, the Son of God, while living among men, really did and taught for their eternal salvation until the day he was taken up into heaven . . . The sacred writers wrote the four Gospels . . . always in such fashion that they told us the honest truth about Jesus.

Among the 313 *iuxta modum* votes on Chapter V, the majority had to do with the words *ut sincera et vera,* claiming that this expression did not assert unequivocally the historical character of the Gospels. Various suggestions were put forth designed to remove the alleged ambiguity.

In this case too the Theological Commission rejected all their suggestions, maintaining that the addition of the word "historical," for example, would not solve the problem because of its ambiguous meaning. The use of the word *sincera* was not intended to imply that the Commission thought there was anything "fraudulent" about the Gospels. It was merely intended as a complement to *vera*.

This decision caused the minority to appeal to the Pope, who had already come to the conclusion that the Commission must be asked to clarify its use of the word *sincera*. Accordingly, in his letter of October 17th, the Secretary of State asked that the historicity of the Gospels should be better defended by the insertion of the following phrase instead of *sincera et vera:* "*vera seu historica fide digna.*" "It seems," the papal letter went on, "that the former expression does not guarantee the historical nature of the Gospels; therefore, on this point, it is obvious that the Holy Father could not approve a formula that left in doubt the historical nature of these holy books."

Cardinal Bea, again asked at the meeting on October 19th to state his opinion first, said that the wording *vera et sincera* was ambiguous and opted for the papal amendment. Other speakers brought out, however, that the new formula would not accomplish its purpose because the Bultmannian and other Protestant schools understood *fides historica* in a purely subjective sense. Therefore in order to make this point perfectly clear, it would be necessary to retain *vera et sincera* and insert above a clearer explanation of what was meant. The wording eventually chosen and inserted in the text was adopted by a vote of 26 to 2.

It is clear from the Pope's letter that his one concern was to find some formula that would enable the largest number of Fathers to agree on a final text, without doing violence to what had already been accepted by the Council, much less compromising any essential position. About his sincerity here there can be no doubt. It is obvious also that he was at great pains not to give the impression that he was in any way trying to "impose" his will on the Commission ("The Holy Father regards it as opportune . . ." "The Holy Father hopes that the Commission will attach the same importance to his suggestion that it attaches to that of any other father . . ." "The Commission is invited to reconsider the text because he considers this the clearest and best way for the Commission itself to take into account all the elements useful for the task assigned to it . . .").

It is clear also, from the outcome, that the Commission did not slavishly bow to the papal wishes or accept all of his suggestions at least in the form in which they were communicated to them.

What is disturbing about the Pope's (Cicognani's) letter is that the language seems to go beyond what might have been expected of an impartial arbiter recommending the views of the minority to the favorable consideration of the Commission. To a certain extent it seems to identify the Pope with those opinions. What if the Theological Commission had not had the force of character to "turn" the papal requests to its own advantage?

In the course of these maneuverings one of the Council Fathers (possibly a cardinal) wrote to the Pope expressing his alarm at the bad impression being created in certain countries, England or the United States, by these papal interventions, at the last minute, designed to alter texts on which the Council had already agreed with sizeable majorities. In his reply the Pope defended his right to work for the improvement of all documents like any Council Father and maintained that his interventions had all been "perfectly regular." He then went on, "Finally, regarding the point you make concerning respect for the Council and observance of the customary procedures, nothing gives us more pleasure than to have these principles recalled that are dear not only to

Anglo-Saxons but also to Romans. I can assure you that they have been scrupulously observed throughout the Council."*

In his *relatio,* before the final voting on October 29th, Cardinal Florit disclosed that the Commission had also rejected another move of the minority designed to limit the meaning of doctrinal progress. The *modus* in question wanted the text to speak only of "progress in the understanding of Tradition," not of "any objective progress of Tradition." But this would have been inconsistent with the Church's teaching according to Florit. There was progress in Tradition in the sense in which every living thing changed, while remaining substantially the same. "The clearer perception of both things and words in Tradition does not remain extraneous to them but freely becomes one of their proper elements. Thence it follows that the Church is really tending to the fullness of Revealed Truth itself and achieves this to the degree that Tradition realizes its internal progress." This was obvious from the fact that the Church did not arrive abruptly at the fullness of truth. She could not express and proclaim all at once the entire deposit of Revelation, "as is proved and always will be proved by the history of dogma."

The Commission's handling of the *modi* was overwhelmingly approved by the Council on October 29th. It was later announced that the schema on Divine Revelation would be voted and promulgated by the Council at its next Public Session on November 18th.

That the minority would stop at nothing to prevent itself from being completely worsted on all major issues became evident when an American professor at the Biblical Institute was carefully scrutinizing the Italian translation of the Constitution on Divine Revelation and discovered that a principal passage has been astutely mistranslated. The translator made the clause *quam Deus nostrae salutis causa litteris sacris consignari* read: "God, the author of our salvation, had de-

* G. Caprile, *La Civiltà Cattolica,* February 5, 1966, p. 231.

sired to confide truth to the sacred books." This could be interpreted to mean that every syllable of the Bible was unerring, as Cardinal Newman had once been assured in Rome was the case by the Jesuit theologian Perrone, who told him that even the phrase in the Book of Tobias stating that "the dog wagged its tail" was infallibly true.

Taxed with this literary trickery, the translator, Monsignor Garofalo, said that he had consulted members of the Sub-commission and been assured that this was a good translation, though as any Latinist knows, the use of the word *causa* after a phrase in the genitive case can only mean "for the sake of." Abbot Butler had the final say on the matter. He brought up the question of the translation at a meeting of the Theological Commission and offered four reasons why the translation "God the cause of our salvation" was untenable theologically. Father Tromp observed that his reasons were only probable; whereupon Butler retorted, "I take it then that Father Tromp does not believe in the law of probabilities." Butler's view of course prevailed; but theologians and *periti* were properly warned that such attempts to doctor the texts of conciliar documents must be expected. Vigilance was more than ever the order of the day if the work of the Council was to remain intact.*

The Discussion of Indulgences

Toward the middle of October it became known that the Pope intended to consult the various episcopal conferences about a number of documents that he was thinking of issu-

* Father Tromp's account of this incident is somewhat different, and does not mention the exchange with Abbot Butler: "On November 20–21 the Secretary (Tromp) met with Mgr. Garofalo and Frs. Betti and Castellino in the hospice of S. Marta to go over the Italian translation of the constitution on Divine Revelation which Mgr. Garofalo had prepared. Three of the revisers had failed to note a mistranslation in paragraph 11 which had the text say that the Scriptures '*insegnano con certezza fedelmente e senza errore la verità che Dio, causa della nostra salvezza, volle fosse consegnata.*' A literal translation, but not in accordance with the mind of the Commission. *Honni soyt qui mal y pense.*"

ing.* The presence of so many members of these conferences in Rome was said to have suggested to him the desirability of finding out how the proposed Synod of Bishops might be expected to work, while at the same time the consultation would prove that he was serious about his intention to put teeth into the principle of collegiality. The presidents of the various conferences were requested to poll their members about a proposed reform of the penitential discipline of the Church and meet with him in the Vatican Palace on October 21st to report their findings. After delivering a short discourse the Pope departed, turning the meeting over to Cardinal Ciriaci, Prefect of the Congregation of the Council, who presided while Monsignor Palazzini read a report on the draft of a Motu Proprio reforming the discipline governing fasting and abstinence and each of the conference presidents rose to make known the views of their respective bodies. The whole dossier was then turned over to the Pope to serve as the basis for a final decree.

A second meeting was tentatively scheduled for November 11th on the subject of a reform of the discipline regarding indulgences.** The document under consideration was a draft or Schema for the Revision of the Discipline regarding Indulgences, prepared by one of the Curial offices, the Tribunal of the Sacred Apostolic Penitentiary which customarily handled all matters relating to the granting of indulgences and had worked up a similar draft during the pre-conciliar stage that had never been used. In the mind of the canonists of the Apostolic Penitentiary, one of the conservative strongholds of the Curia, what was called for was not a thoroughgoing theological review of the whole question of indulgences but a limited overhauling of the existing practices that would leave theological presuppositions untouched. The plan was

---

* *Il Tempo,* October 13, 1965.

** There were many rumors about other subjects (mixed marriages, regulations for the Synod of Bishops, birth control, the diaconate, emigration, etc.) the Pope was said to be considering laying before the bishops, but he was known to have submitted only these two.

to issue their document eventually as a papal decree without any reference to the Council. However, when Pope Paul read the document and learned of their plan, it is said, he insisted that the bishops be consulted. Whatever the facts, the meeting scheduled for November 11th was cancelled and the conference presidents were invited to deliver their reports in the council aula when the general congregations resumed on November 9th. The Apostolic Penitentiary tried to exercise some control over the scope of the "debate" by limiting copies of the schema at first to the conference heads, compelling the bishops to give their opinions on the basis of mere summaries. But this move too was ultimately defeated. Information soon spread about the true nature of their proposal.

Cardinal Cento, Grand Penitentiary, rose to deliver his formal *relatio* on the schema on Tuesday, November 9th. In a series of forthright statements alternating with others of a more timid nature on the following three days, the point was made that the present text was wholly inadequate and superficial and that if the question of reforming indulgences was raised at all it was necessary to go into the theological background thoroughly. Strong speeches in this sense were delivered by Cardinals Maximos IV, Alfrink, König and Döpfner. The latter suggested that since the present text had been prepared largely by canonists, it was advisable to consult theologians also. A new document should be prepared taking into account recent theological thought and a series of papal directives issued to facilitate the transition from the old to the new discipline. Maximos IV let it be known that Archbishop Felici had asked him to suppress certain passages in his talk, which the patriarch immediately gave to the press. Also suppressed was any indication in the daily press bulletins of what the various speakers had said.

Two days after the Dutch Dominican theologian Father Schillebeeckx delivered a lecture on the encyclical *Mysterium fidei* at the Domus Mariae, a hotel for conventions on the Via Aurelia, as part of a series being sponsored by the Brazilian

SACRA PAENITENTIARIA APOSTOLICA

Prot. N. 2633/65

POSITIO
DE SACRARUM INDULGENTIARUM
RECOGNITIONE

(Sub secreto)

TYPIS POLYGLOTTIS VATICANIS
A. MDCCCCLXV

Title-page of Proposal for Reform of Indulgences

bishops, Archbishop Felici startled the Fathers by announcing that many requests had been received by the already over-
worked Secretary General's office whether these lectures were
official or had been cleared with the Council authorities, to
which he replied with a resounding "OMNINO NEGA-
TIVE"—Absolutely not! The next day in the course of his
announcements the archbishop remarked rather cryptically
that his office was the object of considerable criticism; but
since he was functioning under orders from higher authority,
he preferred to remain silent about such calumny, observing
piously, "In silence one remains close to God." The Council
Fathers were all set for an apology for his attack on the Domus
Mariae lectures. No such gesture was forthcoming. Instead
the Secretary General insisted that the reports on indulgences
during the past week had come in for considerable criticism
themselves. He reminded the Fathers that the Apostolic Penitentiary had deliberately approached the subject of indulgences from a canonical rather than a theological standpoint
because it had been asked to do so by "higher authority."
However some of the Fathers had disregarded this fact and
raised theological issues anyway, "to which certain exceptions
would have to be taken." Consequently there would be no
more public reading of reports. The Fathers were invited to
submit their comments to the Secretariat in writing.

A second Public Session was held on November 18th at
which two more documents were voted and promulgated, the
Constitution on Divine Revelation and the Decree on the
Apostolate of the Laity. Approval of the latter had been voted

	Previous	Final
	Non Placet	Non Placet
Texts promulgated	votes	votes
Divine Revelation	27	6
Apostolate of the Laity	2	2

almost unanimously when the Council voted on the commission's handling of the *modi* on November 10th and there was
curiously no change in the final balloting. However, the ab-

sence of any appreciable opposition was somewhat deceptive. While the document was intended to foster the apostolate of the laity and presumably represented the thinking of the Church on that subject, it had been compiled without much regard for the views of laymen themselves and remained until the end an essentially clerical text. Nevertheless, with this schema and the important Constitution on the Church, the groundwork had been laid for a more balanced statement in the future. The most important result of Apostolate of the Laity would be the Secretariat which the text called for, provided this were properly staffed and allowed to function in the intended way.

Pope Paul's speech on this occasion was notable not only for the number of his announcements, interesting in themselves, about his intention to facilitate the eventual canonization of his two predecessors, Popes Pius XII and John XXIII, to build a church in Rome in honor of Mary commemorating Vatican II, to proclaim a special jubilee for six months following the end of the Council, and to inaugurate the reform of the Curia by "publishing soon a new statute governing the Holy Office," but even more for the concern which he was beginning to express about the post-conciliar period, the way in which the Council would be received, the significance that would be attributed to the work of *aggiornamento* in the years to come. In a Hortatory Letter issued somewhat earlier (November 6th), he had urged the bishops to prepare for the close of the Council by ordering a triduum of prayers to mark the occasion and suggesting that they take advantage of the enthusiasm generated by the Council's activities, by capitalizing on the excellent press which had been accorded to church affairs during the past four years, to bring home to their faithful the essential message which the Council had been attempting to convey. Any delay in complying with the Council's directives could spell disaster, he maintained. Success was not to be expected from a multiplicity of laws but from a determination to make the Council's decisions effective. The faithful must be prepared to accept the new norms and those who refused to conform must be jolted in their complacency; "those who indulge in too many personal initiatives" must be restrained otherwise harm might come to "the healthy renewal already undertaken." The Pope's words were the first indication in many months that he was giving serious attention to the possibility of real resistance to the work of the Council.

The Schema on Missionary Activity

On November 10th and 11th the Council voted on the commission's handling of the *modi* on Missionary Activity. Father Schütte explained the principal changes in his *relatio:* the theology of the missionary idea had been somewhat developed; the definition of "missionary area" had been expanded to include various parts of Latin America that were theoretically Christian, but actually *pays de mission* and therefore ought to be treated as such; the inhabitants of missionary areas were to be regarded henceforth not merely as "objects" but as "subjects" of missionary activity, capable of making a contribution on their own; the role of the laity was brought out more clearly; the problem of the relations between missionary and ecumenical activity was more thoroughly stressed; and the right of ordinaries to control all activities within their jurisdictions was made clear, while religious orders could still be exempt so far as internal matters affecting their institutes and orders were concerned. However, on the important matter of the reorganization of Propaganda Fide, the commission rejected the petition of the Indian bishops and stood by the revision that would have watered this down in the sense desired by Propaganda. It was explained that the suggestion for having the delegates elected by the various episcopal conferences could not be accepted, because this would make Propaganda too large and unwieldy. When the votes were counted, it was seen that all the other amendments proposed by the commission went through smoothly enough, but Chapter V containing this provision about the reorganization of Propaganda Fide failed to receive the required two-thirds majority (1,428 *placet,* 9 *non placet,* 712 *placet iuxta modum*). The commission was therefore bound to revise it and would have to make some concessions to the minority.

Before the final vote on this schema on November 30th, Father Schütte again read a long *relatio* explaining what the commission had done about the *modi.* It developed that 461 Fathers had again requested a strengthening of that section of Chapter V dealing with the reorganization of Propaganda Fide along the lines suggested earlier by the Indian bishops: they now asked that the missionary delegates be given a "deliberative vote," that they be elected by the episcopal conferences, and for limited terms of office. The commission granted the first request, but in effect rejected the other two as limiting the "freedom of the Pope" unduly. The delegates were to be chosen by the Holy See, "after hearing the episcopal conferences," a vague phrase that could mean anything; and the questions of when they were to meet and how long they should serve were reserved for the decision of the Pope. 265 Fathers had requested that the text provide for a closer relationship between Propaganda Fide and those dioceses desiring this for missionary reasons. It was merely proposed that Propaganda would endeavor to work out suitable arrangements with the Roman Congregations in charge of such areas with a view to facilitating missionary work. 74 Fathers wanted all missionary work to depend directly on the new Synod of Bishops. The commission rejected this suggestion on the grounds that the relationship between the Synod and missionary work was already clearly enough brought out in the text. Approximately 100 Fathers demanded that the agreements between local ordinaries and missionary institutes should be expressly approved by the Holy See (Propaganda). The reply was that the Holy See would lay down norms and guidelines, but not require the submission of each agreement. This

marked an important step in the direction of decentraliza-
tion. 58 Fathers asked for the removal of the paragraph relating to ecumenical cooperation. This was rejected on the
grounds that the Decree on Ecumenism was now binding on
the Church. The final text was overwhelmingly approved in
a series of 10 votes all taken the same day Nov. 30th, only
Article 29 dealing with the reorganization of Propaganda
Fide registering as many as 54 *non placets*.

The Final Revision of Schema 13

The Council had voted on November 15–17th to accept
the Commission's revision of the text on the basis of the oral
and written interventions, but a rather large number of *modi*
were handed in on each chapter. (The figures of those voting
placet iuxta modum only indicate the persons who voted, not
the number of *modi* actually submitted. Father Tromp*
points out, curiously, that on investigation it was found that
not all those who had voted *iuxta modum* actually submitted
a *modus,* while some of those who had voted *placet* handed
in a *modus* anyway. The latter *modi* were of course ignored
by the subcommissions. Nevertheless the number of *modi*
which had to be considered was very high and the subcommissions were able to get through the mountain of work only
by pushing themselves to the utmost.)

The Mixed Commission began its review of the work of
the subcommissions on November 22nd, Monday, and continued to meet throughout the week, mornings and evenings.
In order to expedite matters, it was agreed on the 23rd that
only those *modi* would be considered which the subcommission thought ought to be taken up. The subject of whether

---

* What follows is based on Father Tromp's official *Relatio* or Report of
the Mixed Commission's proceedings from Sept. 14–Dec. 1965, dated Feb. 8,
1966, which will form part of the Council's *Acta*. Father Tromp was Secretary
of the Theological Commission. There will undoubtedly be Reports covering
the proceedings of each of the other Commissions and they will presumably
be published.

the title of Schema 13 should be changed was disposed of in the Commission's meeting on November 27th:

ARCHBISHOP GARRONE (*relator* for the Central Subcommission): "The voting in the aula has indicated that 541 Fathers desires a change, most of them preferring the terms 'Declaration' or 'Letter.' On the other hand it is clear that more than 1,500 do not want any change. The Central Subcommission proposes that a Note be inserted either at the beginning of the schema or the beginning of Part II, stating that Part I is doctrinal and that Part II is concerned with applications."

BISHOP QUADRI: "I see nothing objectionable to the use of the term 'Constitution.' However, the Note should say that Part II is *particularly (praesertim)* concerned with applications, because it also discusses principles."

ABBOT BUTLER: "Many want a new title in order to lessen the importance of the document."

ARCHBISHOP GARRONE: "This would certainly be the case if we were to add *praesertim* with reference to Part II."

FATHER ANASTASIUS OF THE HOLY ROSARY: "I suggest that the Note be placed at the beginning of the schema. This would make it clear at once what kind of document it is intended to be."

ARCHBISHOP WOJTYLA: "A Note is definitely necessary. The document is really a 'Constitution' but one that is 'pastoral.' This latter term should be carefully explained. It is much more concerned with life than with doctrine. Moreover, I think that Part I is also very pastoral in places, especially where it discusses the human person. Both parts must be seen in a pastoral light."

BISHOP ARANGO HENAO: "I think that the question of what the title should be ought to be decided by the Fathers themselves in a special vote."

ABBOT BUTLER: "It is possible that many of the Fathers who did not vote were actually in sympathy with those who wanted a new title."

BISHOP MCGRATH: "I agree with the Abbot, because it was not really a proper vote."

ARCHBISHOP GARRONE: "He who remains silent is assumed to agree."

BISHOP CHARUE: "I agree with Archbishop Wojtyla that the document is really a Constitution, but a pastoral one. The title should not be changed unless the matter is put to a special vote in the aula."

FATHER ANASTASIUS OF THE HOLY ROSARY: "I propose that the Fathers be asked to vote on the following proposition: 'Is the handling of the *modi* with regard to the title pleasing?' "

BISHOP POMA: "I think there should be an explanation in the aula of the title and why we are retaining it."

The upshot was that the Commission decided to accept the proposal of the Central Subcommission. Consideration of Chapter V was begun the same day and concluded on Monday, November 29th. Bishop Schröffer, president of the Subcommission, and Father Dubarle as *relator*, led off with some preliminary remarks.

BISHOP SCHRÖFFER: "The revision of the *modi* of this chapter had to be done with particular care because one of the Fathers (Cardinal Heenan) said in the aula that the chapter 'was teeming with errors.' The *modi* were concerned with four points primarily: 1. non-violence; 2. conscientious objection; 3. total warfare; 4. balance of terror. I think the members will agree that the revised text is more nuanced than the original *(minus apodictice sonari)*."

There was a long discussion about the *modi* relating to conscientious objection, lasting a full hour (paragraph 79, formerly 83). The Subcommission produced a new text containing the clauses "frequently led by religious motives" *(frequenter religiosis motivis ducti)* and "led by patriotism" *(amore patriae ducti)*. Among the speakers were Canon Moeller, Archbishop Fernandes, Abbot Butler, Cardinal Ottaviani, Father Fernandez O.P., Bishop Charue, Bishop Heuschen, Cardinal Browne, Cardinal Cento and Bishop Henriquez. Abbot Butler and Bishop Fernandez-Conde kept

---

Text as finally approved by the Council:

Insuper aequum videtur ut leges humaniter provideant pro casu illorum qui ex motivo conscientiae arma adhibere recusant, dum tamen aliam formam communitati hominum serviendi acceptant.

Moreover, it seems right that laws make humane provisions for the case of those who for reasons of conscience refuse to bear arms, provided however, that they agree to serve the human community in some other way.

---

making the point that a distinction must be made between "right conscience" and a "false conscience." The use of the word *frequenter* was displeasing to many. Bishop Charue suggested *forsan*, Bishop Heuschen *etiam*, and Cardinal Browne *interdum*.

CANON MOELLER: "The phrase *amore patriae ducti* does not seem suitable, because there may be other motives for conscientious objection."

ARCHBISHOP DEARDEN: "I suggest that the matter be put hypothetically: *qui vero amore patriae ducti*."

CARDINAL BROWNE: "The new text of the subcommission seems to be an improvement, but I question whether this is what we ought to say at this particular point."

A vote was then taken and it was decided by a two-thirds majority not to accept the new text.

BISHOPS GONZALEZ MORALEJO AND HENRIQUEZ: "I propose that we now amend the old text."

BISHOP CHARUE: "The new text was rejected too hastily, because we now have to deal with the old text which many of those who voted against the new text will find even more displeasing, because harsher."

ABBOT BUTLER: "Nevertheless we are bound by the rules.

Perhaps some of those to whom the idea of conscientious objection is objectionable voted for the new text because it seemed to be the less undesirable."

Votes were then taken. Whether the old text should stand? *Placet.* Whether it should remain where it was? On the second ballot, *placet.* Whether it should be modified by the clause "laws should *humanely* provide" (*leges humaniter provident*), as suggested by Bishop Doumith? *Placet.*

The Mixed Commission concluded its revision of the *modi* on Monday, November 29th, at about 11:15 A.M. The grave doubts whether it would be able to complete its work on time were then dispelled. The text went to the printers and was distributed to the Fathers in two brochures on December 2nd and 3rd, for the final voting on December 4th and 6th.

The Attempts to Condemn Communism

The final three weeks were as filled with maneuvering and surprises as any period in the Council's six years. Except for the voting on texts on days when general congregations were held, the main activity took place in commissions which worked feverishly revising documents so that they would be ready in time for promulgation at the closing Public Session set for December 7th.

Meanwhile, the opposition armed itself for a final skirmish. The attack came on four vital points. The *Coetus Internationalis Patrum,* under the leadership of Bishop Carli of Segni, kept up an incessant campaign throughout the Fourth Session in favor of an outright condemnation of communism, thus showing their contempt for the injunction of Pope John that the Council was not to engage in sterile condemnations. Pope Paul VI had also on numerous occasions made it abundantly clear that he was opposed to this fierce desire for vindictive name-calling. Leaders of the Christian Democratic Party in Italy, on the other hand, pointed out that the absence of such a condemnation would play into the hands of the Italian communists who could claim that, as the Council had not condemned communism explicitly, Italians could continue to vote for the PCI with good conscience. At one point, toward the end, the *Carlifato* managed to enlist the sympathy of a number of Eastern-rite bishops, particularly Ukrainians living outside Iron Curtain countries. When one of the latter circulated a letter appealing for a strong condemnation of communism (characteristically *not* signed by Cardinal Slipyi), he was personally rebuked by the Secretariat of State and told that the Church behind the Iron Curtain was being endangered by such action.

Both the subcommission and the Mixed Commission were required to display a certain amount of skill in dealing with Carli's various moves and petitions. When the revised text of Schema 13 was distributed on November 13th (which the Council was to vote on November 15–17th), it became obvious that the subcommission had not been swayed by Carli's last-minute *modi* submitted on October 9th, or by his petition signed by 450 bishops (out of some 800 circulated) of October 19th, all designed to produce a stronger text on communism, in the sense desired by Carli and his supporters. The most that the subcommission was prepared to concede to their point of view was a footnote in the section on atheism referring to the papal encyclicals that condemned totalitarianism of all types. Although Bishop Carli claimed that some two hundred *modi* had been submitted by him on October 9th, only two were acknowledged and dealt with by the subcommission in its report. The indignation of the Carli group can easily be imagined! It seems that Monsignor Glorieux, secretary of the subcommission, receiving from Archbishop Felici the Carli *modi* submitted at the last minute, hurriedly glanced over them, found that they were all identical and related to a point already disposed of by the subcommission, and therefore failed to submit them for the subcommission's consideration as he undoubtedly should have. The Fathers were again circularized with a new *modus* from Bishop Carli on November 15th, prior to the crucial vote that day on the revised text of Chapter I. The voting on this occasion produced 453 *non placets* for Chapter I as a whole, approximately half of which were thought to be inspired by Carli. At the same time the bishop wrote an indignant letter to Cardinal Tisserant (and possibly also to the Secretary General) complaining about the subcommission's neglect of his petition of 450 names and the way in which Monsignor Glorieux had cavalierly dismissed his earlier *modi*.

While engaged in the work of revising Schema 13 in the light of the November 15–17th voting, the Mixed Commission, on November 27th, received a letter from Cardinal Tisserant forwarding the complaint of Bishop Carli that the subcommission had not paid any attention to "the *modus* submitted by about 340 Fathers who had asked for the condemnation of communism." The subcommission's reply, according to Father Tromp, was that "this particular request had already been dealt with in the reply to a similar *modus* submitted by 220 Fathers. However, in the printed text of the handling of the *modi* a note would be inserted to the effect that the *modus* of the 340 Fathers had been overlooked through error, although the matter had been sufficiently dealt with elsewhere." The Commission's reply to Tisserant was read by Archbishop Garrone in its meeting on November 29th. Although the responsible officials admitted that the subcommission had technically been at fault in not acknowledging Carli's original *modi,* Father Ralph Wiltgen, director of the Divine Word Press Service, which had been used to air the whole matter of the mix-up, would not be appeased and declared so flatly before the American Bishops' Press Panel on November 23rd.

The Papal Modi on Marriage

While difficulties were also being encountered by the commissions revising the documents on Missions and Priestly Life, the main attack seemed to be centered on the Declaration on Religious Liberty where a final attempt was made to strip it of its full significance. Despite the addition earlier of a sentence affirming that the Catholic Church was the one true Church which all were obliged to seek and embrace (a truth constantly taught by the Catholic Church), the revised text repudiated the thesis that error had no rights, insisted on human dignity as the basis for men's liberty in accordance with Pope John's formula, and said explicitly that the Catholic Church must assist society in vindicating a man's right to freedom even when he was wrong in his beliefs and assertions. These three truths were anathema to the conservatives and they did their best by way of final *modi* to eviscerate them; to no avail.

Their efforts here, however, proved to be a mere distraction. On Wednesday afternoon, November 24th, a mortar shell was catapulted into the Mixed Commission revising Schema 13. Cardinal Ottaviani was in the chair. The meeting was convened at 4:30 P.M. Before finishing the discussion of the amendments to Part I and going on to the crucial Chapter I of Part II (dealing with marriage and family life), the cardinal reminded the prelates and periti of their oath of secrecy and then asked the Secretary, Father Tromp, to read two communications. The first was a message from Archbishop Felici stating that the *expensio modorum* had to be ready for the printers by November 29th. The second was a letter from the Secretary of State requesting the Commission, in the name of 'higher authority,' to make explicit mention in the chapter on marriage of Pius XI's *Casti connubii* and Pius XII's Allocution to Italian Midwives. Attached to the letter were four *modi* which, the Secretary observed, "seem to have to be included in the text." The words 'higher authority' of course could only mean the Pope.* When the *modi*

---

* The question of the submission of the *modi* seems to have been decided upon, or at least discussed, at a meeting of the Pope, Bishop Colombo, and Father De Riedmatten, secretary of the Special Papal Commission on birth control, earlier the same day, November 24th, according to *Il Messaggero*, Nov. 27, 1965. The object of this meeting according to the paper was "to harmonize, if possible, the doctrine of the conciliar text with the results of the Special Commission's labors."

were read, to the consternation of the Subcommission members, there was a look of triumph on the faces of the American Jesuit Father John Ford and the Franciscan Father Ermenegildo Lio, advocates of an intransigent position on the subject of birth control, while Cardinal Browne is alleged to have said, "*Christus ipse locutus est*—Christ Himself has spoken."

The move had been perfectly timed and planned. The four *modi* were to be inserted in the text at specific crucial points with a view to exploding the idea that conjugal love enjoyed equal status with procreation as one of the ends of marriage and reasserting Pius XI's doctrine of *Casti connubii* banning all and every type of artificial contraception unequivocally.* At one fell swoop not only would the work of the Council so far be compromised, but the Special Papal Commission entrusted with the whole matter of demographic study and family planning by the Pope himself would have been rendered useless. The stunned Mixed Commission would hardly have time to work out a compromise. Consideration of the *modi* was reserved for the following day.

It was quickly surmised that Father Lio himself and the

* The *modi* read as follows (references are to the text of Schema 13 which the Commission was considering): Modi missi ab Em.mo Secretario Status. Caput I. 1) Pag. 5, lin. 22: ARTES ANTICONCEPTIONALES debent habere mentionem simul cum referentia ad Casti Connubii, ita ut textus iam legatur: "siquidem polygamia, divortii lue, amore sic dicto libero *artibus* anticonceptionalibus, aliisve *deformationibus* obscuratur." Cfr. Pius XI, Litt. Encycl. *Casti Connubii:* AAS 22 (1930) p. 559 et 560. Denz. 2239-2240 (3716-3717).

2) Pag. 8, lin. 11: Omittatur verbum "etiam," atque brevis haec enuntiatio in extremam periodum addatur, ad lin. 13: "Filii sunt praestantissimum matrimonii donum et ad ipsorum parentum bonum maxime conferunt."

3) Pag. 9, lin. 28-29: Haec dicantur: "Quibus principiis *innixi*, (*docemus*) filiis Ecclesiae in procreatione regulanda vias inire *non licere*, quae a Magisterio *improbatae sunt vel improbentur*"; vel: "Quibus principiis *innixis*, filiis Ecclesiae in procreatione regulanda vias inire *non licet*, quae a Magisterio *improbatae sunt vel improbentur*." Praeterea in adnotatione de duobus praestantissimis de hac materia documentis mentio fiat, scilicet: de Encyclicis Litteris "Casti Connubii," AAS 22 (1930): cfr. locos in Denz.-Schon. 3716-3718; ac de oratione a Pio XII ad obstetrices habita: AAS 43 (1951).

4) Pag. 9, lin. 15: Haec addantur: ". . . non posse, sed ad difficultates superandas omnino requiri ut coniuges castitatem coniugalem sincero animo colant."

Dominican canonist Father R. Gagnebet were the probable authors of the papal *modi*. The previous spring Lio had been expressly excluded from the Subcommission on Family Life headed by Archbishop Dearden, much to the annoyance of Cardinal Ottaviani; but he had now been brought in as that cardinal's personal theologian along with the clerical members of the Special Papal Commission on birth control. The presence of the American Father Ford at the Mixed Commission meetings was a considerable surprise. As a matter of fact, his activities proved harmful to the intransigent cause when it became apparent how obstructionist his views really were. Several of the periti suspected that he had been summoned to Rome at the suggestion of the Apostolic Delegate to the United States, Archbishop Vagnozzi, who brought him to the Secretariat of State in the hopes that he would be able to convince both the Council and the Pope that the Church simply had to re-affirm its old position on marriage and birth control or the integrity of its moral theologians would be called in question. Seemingly the rights and perplexities of millions of wives and husbands faced with an intolerable burden had nothing to do with the matter. While it was perfectly proper to hold them to impossible moral obligations, it was outrageously wrong to ask moral theologians to reconsider their teaching in the light of new facts.*

However, when the Mixed Commission reconvened Thursday morning, it was evident that the attack would be met head-on. After disposing of some preliminary matters relating to Part I, the Commission got down to the business of the *modi* on marriage at 10:05 A.M. The chairman of the Subcommission that had drafted the text, Archbishop Dearden, was the first to speak. He was followed by Canon Heylen and Father De Riedmatten as *relatores*. The archbishop began by questioning the authenticity of the papal *modi*. In the en-

---

* Canon Heylen is reported to have said of Father Ford and other conservative theologians: "They obey the Pope when the Pope obeys them." Cf. Lois Chevalier, *Ladies Home Journal*, March 1966, p. 89.

suing discussion he was backed up to a man by the members
of his own Subcommission and even by some of the Commission bishops who were critical of the revised text but resented
the way in which their body was being "bulldozed" into acceptance of the papal *modi*. As Chapter I had received an
absolute majority in the previous voting on November 16th,
its text could not be substantially changed according to the
Council rules. But the insertion of the papal *modi* would involve such substantial changes. Canon Heylen observed that
since the matter of birth control had been withdrawn from
discussion in the Council, it would perhaps be a good idea to
stress the point by adding a sentence at the end of the introductory paragraph, stating "The Holy Synod leaves other
matters . . . to the Special Papal Commission." It was decided
to take up this matter after all the *modi* had been considered.

When Canon Heylen raised the question of what to do
about the first papal *modus* at 10:45, the Commission immediately became bogged down in a heated, prolonged discussion about the meaning of terms (*artes anticonceptionales*,
abusus conceptionales) and the importance to be attached to
the papal *modi* as well as the method of dealing with them.
The Secretary was again obliged to read Cicognani's letter.
Bishop Henriquez felt that it was perfectly proper for the
Mixed Commission to consider the *modi*. Bishop Charue, on
the other hand, thought there was some doubt about the
jurisdiction of the Mixed Commission because it was a matter
that had not been discussed in the Council and was up in the
air, so to speak, until the Special Papal Commission had given
its reply. The Mixed Commission should be able to discuss
the matter freely, without any strings, if it took up the question at all. Father Tromp said that according to Cicognani's
letter it was "the wish of the Pope that the Commission
should follow the doctrine of the Encyclical *Casti Connubii*
and the allocution of Pius XII to midwives, and therefore
there could be no question of freedom with regard to doctrine, but only with regard formulation."

At this point, Cardinal Léger read a strong statement. He

deplored the tenor of the proposed amendments and maintained that, if adopted as they stood, the prestige and reputation of the Holy See might be irreparably damaged. Father Anastasius of the Holy Rosary asked that the text of Cicognani's letter and the accompanying *modi* be distributed to the Commission periti. Bishop Colombo and Cardinal Browne thought that it was a matter that concerned only the prelate members. At this point something like pandemonium broke out and the meeting was adjourned for a coffee-break. Cardinal Léger left at 11:37, apparently to go and see the Pope. The Commission's afternoon session was devoted to the Subcommission's handling on the *modi* on Chapter I and the first paragraphs of Chapter II on Culture.

Despite Cardinal Ottaviani's reminder about the oath of secrecy binding the Commission members and periti, news of the morning's proceedings spread like wildfire throughout Rome and the substance of the story was leaked to the press. The next morning *L'Avvenire d'Italia* ran an account of what had taken place.

Bishop Colombo, the Pope's personal theologian, also hurried to the Pope's apartments after the morning's meeting on Thursday, to explain the situation to him. Representations were also made to the pontiff by the Lay Auditors. Both sides were girding for a showdown struggle when Cardinal Ottaviani reconvened the Commission on Friday morning, November 26th.

He began with a rather severe statement deploring the fact that information about the four *modi* had become public knowledge, then declared that the Pope had decided that the periti were not to be excluded from discussion of the *modi*. However, there could be no question of discussing doctrine, it was merely allowed to discuss the way in which they were to be formulated. The Secretary, Father Tromp, then read a second letter from the Secretary of State which specified that 1) the Pope considered the *modi* to be of great importance; 2) the method of formulation was not obligatory; 3) certain things could be added, provided the sense was retained; 4) the Pope himself would later decide whether the Commission's decisions were acceptable. After the reading of the Pope's letter, Cardinal Léger was seen to fold a paper he had in his hand and slump back in his chair. He had made an agreement with the Subcommission to speak only if necessary. While some of the Mixed Commission members felt that the second papal letter was even stronger than the first in tying their hands, the majority seized upon point 3 and set to work to deal with the papal *modi—secundum spiritum,* according to their obvious meaning and the rules of the Council.

MODUS I.—The first papal *modus* called for mention of the phrase "contraceptive practices" (*artes anticonceptionales*) in Paragraph 47 (formerly 51) after the words "so-called free love" and an explicit reference to Pius XI's encyclical *Casti connubii* condemning artificial contraception in a footnote. Canon Heylen was the first speaker.

Text as proposed by Commission:

47 (51). (Marriage and the Family Today) . . . Yet the excellence of this institution is not everywhere reflected with equal brilliance, since polygamy, the plague of divorce, so-called free love and other disfigurements have an obscuring effect. In addition, married love is too often profaned by an excessive self-love and worship of pleasure.

Text as finally amended and approved:

47. (Marriage and the Family Today) . . . Yet the excellence of this institution is not everywhere reflected with equal brilliance, since polygamy, the plague of divorce, so-called free love and other disfigurements have an obscuring effect. In addition, married love is too often profaned by excessive self-love, the worship of pleasure, *and illicit practices against human generation* (*illicitis usibus contra generationem*).

CANON HEYLEN: "I wish to make three points: 1) The term 'practices' (*artes*) is not good. I propose instead that we say 'abuses' (*abusus*). 2) The term 'anticonceptional' is not good either. An abortion is not contraceptive, although it is an evil; on the other hand, periodic continence may be called contraceptive, although it is not an evil, as Father De Riedmatten has stated. 3) It would perhaps be better to place the *modus* a little later, after mention of 'self-love and worship of pleasure,' and phrase it as follows: 'and by the perversion of love and the sources of life' (*et perversione amoris fontiumque vitae*)."

In the general discussion that followed, Archbishop Castellano, Cardinal Browne and Father Anastasius of the Holy Rosary agreed with Heylen that the *modus* should be placed later. Cardinal Browne thought that it would be better to say "uses" rather than "abuses." Father Anastasius suggested the phrase "illicit uses against generation." Bishop Poma preferred "illicit means for preventing conception." Bishop Colombo: "illicit uses against conception." Bishop Doumith observed that a single expression would not do, the word "illicit practices" itself needed explanation.

Cardinal Ottaviani proposed that the question first be settled where the *modus* was to go and it was decided to insert it after the words "worship of pleasure."

CANON HEYLEN: "If we wish to avoid the use of the words 'abuses' and 'anti-conceptional,' practically speaking the choice will have to be between the two phrases 'illicit practices preventing generation' and 'perversion of love and the sources of life.' The Subcommission recommends that the Commission adopt the second phrase."

Bishop Charue also thought that these words were better because more in harmony with what was said before. When Canon Heylen and Archbishop Dearden noted that this phrasing was better because "more general," Bishop Colombo remarked: "And therefore weaker." Father Anastasius thought that it was illogical to say that love was profaned by the perversion of love. Bishop McGrath agreed with Bishop Doumith that the Commission must not be too vague and misleading.

When Bishop Henriquez proposed: "Let the Pope himself

decide which wording he prefers," many of the members shouted, "Only after we have voted!" Whereupon Cardinal Ottaviani put the matter to a vote and it was decided to adopt the first formula suggested by Canon Heylen, by a vote of 22 to 13, with 2 blank ballots.

ABBOT BUTLER: "We must now decide where the reference to *Casti connubii* is to go in the footnotes. It seems to me that it would be better to place it in the text of Paragraph 47 (51) itself, because that would make it clearer that it had not been added as a result of discussion in the aula (by the extraordinary magisterium) but at the specific request of the Pope (by the ordinary magisterium)."

BISHOP FRANIC: "I do not agree at all. There has often been discussion of *Casti connubii* in the Council."

BISHOP COLOMBO: "Nor do I, because the Pope makes a text conciliar by his approval and corrections. It is up to the Mixed Commission to decide where it thinks the reference should go. The Pope himself will decide whether the Council has acted wisely or not."

CARDINAL BROWNE: "There is no reason why the encyclical should not be cited since it has already been mentioned elsewhere."

CARDINAL OTTAVIANI: "The Pope has already decided that the encyclical should be cited. There can be no discussion of this."

BISHOP POMA: "It seems to me that we are confronted by two difficulties here: 1) Paragraph 47 (51) is largely descriptive in nature, whereas the encyclical should be cited at a place where the discussion is more doctrinal; 2) the reference to *Casti connubii* is to a specific point, whereas the language of Paragraph 47 (51) is much more general in nature."

ARCHBISHOP GARRONE: "I suggest that we add, to the two references called for in the papal *modus,* a reference to Pope Paul's Allocution to the Cardinals, of June 1964, in which he said that the doctrine of *Casti connubii* is binding as of now (*fin'ora*)."

The pertinent passage of the Pope's allocution was accordingly read.

BISHOP CHARUE: "The Pope clearly says that the matter is an object of study and that is why it has not been discussed by the Fathers in the Council."

CARDINAL OTTAVIANI: "The Pope also says that it is an object of study for the ordinary magisterium (Pope)."

BISHOP CHARUE: "Of course, it is *now*."

ARCHBISHOP DEARDEN: "I do not see any reason why there cannot be a reference to the Pope's Special Commission in a footnote, but I do not think this would be proper in the text."

The upshot was that the majority of Commission members agreed that *Casti connubii* should be cited at some other point in the schema. There was no consensus as yet about citing Paul's Allocution to the Cardinals.

MODUS II.—The second papal *modus* required the omission of the word *"etiam"* and the introduction of the sentence "Children are the supreme gift of marriage and contribute very substantially to the welfare of their parents" (*Filii sunt praestantissimum matrimonii donum et ad ipsorum parentum bonum maxime conferunt*) in Paragraph 50 (54), which would have had the effect of reasserting procreation as the primary end of marriage.

Text as proposed by Commission:

50 (54). (The Fecundity of Marriage). Marriage and conjugal love are by their nature ordained toward the begetting and educating of children. The God himself who said, "it is not good for man to be alone" and "who made man from the beginning male and female," wishing to share with man a certain special participation in his own creative work, blessed male and female, saying "Increase and multiply." Hence, the true practice of conjugal love and the whole meaning of family life which results from it, also (*etiam*) have this aim: that the couple be ready with

stout hearts to cooperate with the love of the Creator and the
Savior, who through them will enlarge and enrich his own family day by day.

Text as amended and approved by the Council:

50. (The Fecundity of Marriage). Marriage and conjugal love
are by their nature ordained toward the begetting and educating
of children. *Children are really the supreme gift of marriage and
contribute very substantially to the welfare of their parents.* The
God himself who said . . . and multiply." Hence, *while not
making the other purposes of matrimony of less account,* the
true practice of conjugal love and the whole meaning of the
family life which results from it, have this aim: that the couple
. . . day by day.

CANON HEYLEN: "The use of the word *etiam* was not meant
to imply that procreation was of a secondary nature compared
to conjugal love, but was intended to express the doctrine
that procreation was not the only end of marriage. I propose
that the word *etiam* be deleted and that the sentence *Filii . . .
ad ipsorum parentum bonum maxime conferunt* be placed
at the beginning of the paragraph, omitting the first sentence
now there "Marriage and conjugal love . . . educating of
children."

When Father Anastasius of the Holy Rosary objected to
the proposed omission, Canon Heylen and Archbishop Dearden pointed out that a similar phrase occurred earlier in
Paragraph 48 (52). Archbishop Castellano also felt that such
an omission would not be permissible. Accordingly Canon
Heylen suggested that the sentence *Filii . . . ad ipsorum parentum maxime conferunt* be inserted immediately after the
first sentence and the particle *vero* used to connect the two
[changed to *sane* in the final draft]. The insertion of the
clause "while not making the other purposes of matrimony of
less account" not only robbed the papal *modus* of its last
sting, but made the text much clearer than it was before on
this matter of the ends of marriage.

MODUS IV.*—At 11:55 it was decided to omit consideration of *Modus* III for the time being, and go on to the fourth *Modus* which called for insertion of the words "but if spouses are to overcome their difficulties, it is altogether necessary for them to practice the virtue of conjugal chastity sincerely" (*sed ad difficultates superandas omnino requiri ut conjuges castitatem coniugalem sincero animo colant*) at the end of the sentence which says that there cannot be a contradiction between the divine laws pertaining to the transmission of life and those pertaining to authentic conjugal love, in Paragraph 51 (55).

CANON HEYLEN: "It seems that the best place for a reference to conjugal chastity would be at the end of Paragraph 49 (53). A second alternative would be to combine Modus III with Modus IV and make the end of the third sub-paragraph of Paragraph 51 (55) read as follows: 'Relying on these principles, sons of the Church, *who must sincerely cultivate the virtue of conjugal chastity,* may not undertake methods of birth control which have been or shall be found blameworthy by the magisterium.'" Archbishop Castellano objected that this reading did not do justice to the implication in the Pope's words, *"ad difficultates superandas."* Bishop Colombo agreed and suggested the wording, "Such a goal cannot be achieved unless the virtue of conjugal chastity is sincerely practiced."

After various alternate proposals had been considered, Archbishop Dearden and Canon Heylen rallied to Colombo's suggestion and this was carried by an almost unanimous vote.

MODUS III.—The third papal *modus* had specified that, in Paragraph 51 (55), at the end of the third sub-paragraph, the words "Relying on these principles, sons of the Church may not undertake methods of birth control which have been or may be found blameworthy by the magisterium" (*improbatae sunt vel improbentur*) were to be inserted, and there should be a reference in a footnote to the two important

* This is the order in which they were discussed by the Commission.

papal documents on the subject, Pius XI's *Casti connubii* and Pius XII's Allocution to Italian Midwives. The text proposed by the Commission spoke of "methods of birth control considered blameworthy" (*improbandas*) but there were no references to the papal documents.

CANON HEYLEN: "The words are clear enough with regard to the past, but can we bind consciences in the future?"

BISHOP DOUMITH: "The Church must always have the same teaching whether as regards the past, present or future."

BISHOP HENGSBACH: "The words *filiis Ecclesiae* mean that the phrase is intended to have reference only to the faithful."

Bishop Colombo proposed that the present tense *"improbantur"* be substituted for the past and apparent future tenses of the *modus,* and suggested that the words be explained in a footnote with reference to the papal documents. This was agreed.

The Secretary, Father Tromp, noted that the form *improbentur* seemed to be a grammatical error for the future *improbabuntur,* required by the context.

A proposal of Bishop Gonzalez Moralejo to insert the words "interpreted with the help of the magisterium" (*ope magisterii explicanda*) after "divine law" was rejected by Archbishop Garrone as implying that the magisterium was confined to interpreting the divine law.

Archbishop Dearden moved that mention be made in the footnote of Paul VI's Allocution to the Cardinals, of June 1964, and this was agreed. He also moved that the note should state that while the Special Papal Commission was at work, the Council did not wish to propose any final solutions. This motion was seconded by Bishops Colombo and Ancel, the latter declaring that the facts required such a statement.

Once again, using an opening, the Subcommission had strengthened the schema in an open-door sense.

Text as amended and approved by Council (additions in italics):

51. (Conjugal Love). . . . Hence when there is question of harmonizing conjugal love with the responsible transmission of life,

the moral aspect of any procedure does not depend solely on sincere intentions or on an evaluation of motives, but must be determined by objective standards. These, based on the nature of the human person and his acts, preserve the full sense of mutual self-giving and human procreation in the context of true love. *Such a goal cannot be achieved unless the virtue of conjugal is sincerely practiced. Relying on these principles, sons of the Church may not undertake methods of birth control which are* found blameworthy by the the teaching authority of the Church in its unfolding of the divine law.

Footnote 14 appended to this last sentence reads: Cf. Pius XI, encyclical letter Casti Connubii: AAS 22 (1930); Denz-Schoen. 3716–3718; Pius XII, Allocutio Conventui Unionis Italicae inter Obstetrices, Oct. 29, 1951: AAS 43 (1951), pp. 835–854; Paul VI, address to a group of cardinals, June 23, 1964: AAS 56 (1964), pp. 581–589. Certain questions which need further and more careful investigation have been handed over, at the command of the supreme pontiff, to a commission for the study of population, family, and births, in order that, after it fulfills its function, the supreme pontiff may pass judgment. With the doctrine of the magisterium in this state, this holy synod does not intend to propose immediately concrete solutions.

The work of revising the text was completed over the weekend and shown to the Pope who gave his approval to the Commission's new version.

It appears that one reason for the ease with which the subcommission finally won its points was the fact that it had suddenly occurred to Bishop Colombo that while he was a theologian, his field was doctrinal and not moral theology and he might be swimming in water over his head. He seems to have conveyed this feeling to the Pope, for when Father Ford on Monday morning presented the Pope with the arguments of the intransigents, the Pope was said to have replied: "You, as a moral theologian, tell me there is only one way to look at this matter. On the other hand, Bishop Reuss is also a moral theologian and he tells me just the opposite. Go to him and argue the matter out. When you two moralists reach an agreement, come back to me with an answer."*

The Pope's acceptance of the wording of the commission seemed to indicate that the twice-promised papal statement on birth control was still far from being settled in his mind, and was probably not to be expected in the near future. Actually, the Special Papal Commission on birth control was scheduled to hold an early spring meeting. It was most unlikely that Pope Paul would jump the gun on so delicate an issue. The judgment as to the means for family limitation, at least in principle, according to the new Pastoral Constitution, was left up to the conscience of a married couple, although for the time being they were to follow the norms laid down by Pius XII in 1958. These were strict directives ruling out artificial means, but the open end achieved in the conciliar document left a final decision as to the licitness of various means up to the study of theologians and scientists, and more pertinently, to the couple concerned.

That crisis had hardly passed when new threats momentarily endangered Chapter III on economic and social life and Chapter IV on political life. Throwing caution to the winds, the *Coetus* sent out copies of *modi* demanding a strictly *non placet* vote on the fourth chapter, alleging as reasons that it was shot through with modernism, relativism, evolutionism, and could only lead to abandonment of the doctrine that the Catholic Church was the one true Church. However, little attention was paid to their assertions, for the majority of bishops had by now grown tired of their tirades. About the same time, while the Mixed Commission was rushing to complete work on Chapter V on November 29th, it received a communication from the Franco Government of Spain, forwarded by Archbishop Dell'Acqua of the Secre-

---

* Lois R. Chevalier has Cardinal Ottaviani writing to the Pope at this point and saying, "I did all possible to have the commission accept the modifications of Your Holiness, but I was always in the minority . . ." *Ladies Home Journal*, March 1966, p. 89 and 173.

tariat of State, requesting certain changes in Chapters III and IV. The archbishop had not even bothered to translate the communication into Latin. The first *modus* asked that the fundamental right to form labor unions be modified by the clause "according to forms recognized by law"; the second asked that mention of "political parties" be qualified by "where they are lawful." Most of the members were indignant at this last-minute attempt to influence the course of events and rejected the suggestions out of hand. Bishop Gonzalez Moralejo was particularly outraged, claiming that the proposed modifications were injurious to Spain and an insult to the Spanish bishops who had already approved the text.

Nuclear Warfare and the Reform of the Holy Office

Meanwhile, the newly appointed Archbishop of New Orleans, Philip Hannan, a former paratroop chaplain, had taken a dim view of Chapter V (on peace and the elimination of war). He thought the statement referring to the have and have-not nations and particularly the condemnation of the use of nuclear arms was palpably disparaging to the United States. He had said this in a speech on the council floor, toward the close of the Third Session. However his contention had been rejected by the American *periti* and most bishops on the grounds that his point of view would give a handle to communist charges that the U.S., and now the Council, was guilty of war-mongering. Despite these remonstrances, however, Hannan began to agitate for his point toward the close of the final session, even though the subcommission in question had all but eviscerated the text of Schema 13 in an attempt to meet this objection.

The amended text insisted that under modern conditions war was all but unthinkable. Actually it was merely reflecting the minds of Pius XII, John XXIII, and most particularly Pope Paul himself in his address before the UN assembly. The document likewise stated that the possession of nuclear

arms could give rise to war. Finally, great care was taken not
to give the impression that limited defensive warfare was unlawful. Despite these precautions, the archbishop was seen in
earnest conversation with Cardinal Spellman and Archbishop
Vagnozzi after the meeting of the Council on Thursday, December 2nd and was overheard talking about the matter with
greater agitation each time. Several friends and acquaintances
among the bishops and *periti* tried to assure him that his
criticism of the document was unjustified. Brushing their
arguments aside, he went ahead with his plans, prepared
three *modi,* and had them translated into 6 languages to be
distributed to the Council Fathers. To compound the mis-
chief, he persuaded 10 bishops to sign his petition, including
Cardinals Spellman and Shehan, Archbishop O'Boyle of
Washington and Denis Hurley of Durban, South Africa.

The U.S. *periti* were particularly upset as copies of this
letter made the rounds. All during the final session their
bishops had been severely criticized by the press and most of
the European bishops and theologians for their complete
lack of interest in the most important conciliar document—
Schema 13—dealing with practical problems; this despite the
fact that they had always prided themselves on being such
eminently practical churchmen. Only a handful of Americans had raised their voices during the final weeks of debate;
and the only American bishops who showed any real interest
in what was going on were those on commissions and subcommissions who gave a good accounting of themselves.

When approached about his signature on Hannan's letter,
Cardinal Shehan authorized Father McCool to declare before
the Bishops' Press Panel (Dec. 4th) that he had withdrawn
his name from the letter after reflecting on the matter.
Archbishop O'Boyle claimed that he had signed because he
felt that he should, out of loyalty to his former auxiliary
bishop. Just why Cardinal Spellman allowed his name to be
used was not clear. In any case, the move served to confuse a
large number of non-American bishops. Hannan's *modi* in

le 2 décembre 1965

Votre Excellence,

On suggère respectueusement que le chapître V, De Bello Vitando, reçoive un vote <u>Non Placet</u>. On suggère également que si les erreurs décrites ci-dessous ne sont pas corrigées, le Schéma entier reçoive un <u>Non Placet</u>. (Le Schéma pourrait être laissé au Synodus Episcoporum pour d'autres études et corrections).

1) La possession des armes nucléaires (arma scientifica) est condamnée comme immorale au N.80 ("Singulare belli hodierni periculum in hoc consistit quod illis <u>qui recentiora arma possident quasi occasionem praebet</u> <u>talia scelera perpetrandi</u> et, connexione quadam inexorabili, hominum voluntates ad atrocissima consilia impellere potest".) et aussi au N.81 ("Belli exinde causae quin eliminentur, potius paulatim aggravari minantur...Potius quam dissensiones inter nationes vere ac funditus sanentur, iisdem aliae partes inficiuntur".)
Ces affirmations ignorent le fait que la possession des arma scientifica a préservé la liberté dans une grande partie du monde. La défense d'une grande partie du monde contre l'aggression n'est pas un crime, mais un grand service.
Ces affirmations ignorent aussi le fait que la guerre et les dissensions entre les peuples sont provoquées par l'injustice et non par la possession des arma scientifica (p.ex. la cause de la seconde guerre mondiale n'était pas la possession d'armes par certaines nations, mais l'injustice). Prétendre que les <u>arma scientifica</u> sont la cause des guerres et des dissensions est aussi illogique que d'affirmer que la loi et la police d'une ville sont la cause des crimes et des désordres commis dans cette ville.
L'inclusion de pareils textes dans le Schéma porteront certainement dommage à la cause de la liberté dans le monde.
Ces textes contredisent aussi la sentence du N.79 (comme aussi une part de l'adresse du Pape Paul VI aux N.U. en septembre) affirmant le droit d'une nation à sa propre défense. Dans le monde d'aujourd'hui il n'y a pas de défense adéquate pour les nations les plus grandes sans la possession <u>d'arma scientifica</u>.

2) Nous dénions également que "les Papes récents" aient condamné la guerre totale d'une manière aussi catégorique qu'elle est condamnée dans cette section:"His attentis, haec Sacrosancta Synodus, suas faciens condemnationes belli totalis iam a recentibus Summis Pontificibus enuntiatas, declarat".(N.80). Où sont les références pour appuyer cette affirmation ?

3) Le Concile ne devrait pas prendre une décision dans cette matière dans laquelle il n'y a pas encore un consensus d'opinions parmi les théologiens les plus spécialisés en cette matière.

+ Francis Card.Spellman, New York
+ Patrick L.O'Boyle, Washington
+ Miguel D.Miranda, Mexico
+ Denis E.Hurley, Durban
+ Joseph Khoury, Tyr Maronitarum

+ Lawrence Card. Shehan, Baltimore
+ Philip M.Hannan, New Orleans
+ Guilford Clyde Young, Hobart
+ Adolfo Servando Tortolo, Paraná
+ Felipe Cueto González,Tlalnepantla

Letter composed by Archbishop Hannan, urging a *Non Placet* vote on Chapter V of Schema 13.

Excellentissime Domine,

In aliquo folio, subscripto ab Em.mo Card. Spellman et 9 aliis Patribus Conciliaribus, ultimis his diebus divulgato, suggeritur ut Patres ad Caput V "De bello vitando" votum dent "Non placet".

Attamen rationes pro hac suggestione allatae admitti nequeunt, propter erroneam interpretationem textus quam continent.

1º- Nullibi in nn. 80 et 81 possessio armorum nuclearium condemnatur ut immoralis. Attendenda sunt accurate verba textus de consulto selecta: "periculum consistit" - "quasi occasionem praebet" - "impellere potest" - "aggravari minantur".

Neque negatur possessione et accumulatione talium armorum ad tempus servari posse libertatem. Negatur tantum cursum ad arma "securam esse viam ad pacem firmiter servandam", quod correspondet doctrinae Pontificum.

Neque dicitur arma scientifica esse causas bellorum; dicitur tantum: "ex cursu ad arma causae belli aggravari minantur".

Textus praefati neque contradicunt iuri, in contextu affirmato, defensionis violentae alicuius nationis contra iniustas aggressiones. Contrarium continetur in contextu.

2º- Referentiae ad documenta Pontificia, quibus bellum totale condemnatur, exhibentur in Nota 2 huius Capitis. Specialem attentionem meretur textus Pii XII d.d. 30.9.1954, qui in antecedenti redactione in Nota ad verbum citatus erat: "Ici (i.e. in casu destructionum indiscriminatarum) il ne s'agit pas de la défense contre l'injustice et de la sauvegarde nécessaire de possessions légitimes, mais de l'annihilation pure et simple de toute vie humaine à l'intérieur du rayon d'action. Cela n'est permis à aucun titre": (AAS 46, p. 1589).

3º- De textu, prouti post diligentissimum examen nunc iacet, non exsistit diversitas opinionum inter theologos; indiscriminatam enim destructionem, qualis hic intelligitur, nullus theologus catholicus moraliter licitam esse admittit vel admittere potest.

+ Josephus Schröffer
ep.pus Eystettensis
Praeses Subcommissionis de
Capite V

+ Gabriel Marie Garrone
archiepiscopus Tolosanus
Relator Generalis

Romae, 5. XII. 1965.

Refutation of Hannan's letter by
Bishop Schröffer and Archbishop Garrone.

themselves were obviously erroneous. Where the document stated that the indiscriminate use of atomic warfare could easily "go beyond the norms of legitimate defense," the *modus* said that the document outlawed defense. Where the text claimed that the possession of nuclear weapons could easily be a quasi-occasion for the outbreak of war, Hannan read it to mean a cause of war, and launched into a tirade about hunger and injustice being the true causes of war, as the document itself declared very clearly. Finally, Hannan urged that if there were insufficient votes against Chapter V to kill it or bring about its revision, all the bishops should vote *non placet* on the schema as a whole and thus force Pope Paul to withdraw it entirely. Before the crucial voting on Saturday morning, December 4th, Hannan was seen approaching Archbishop Felici in the company of Vagnozzi, apparently in order to persuade the Secretary General to make some announcement about their move; but all that he got from Felici was a waving of his two arms in a gesture that said, "Impossible, absurd!"

At the press panel that afternoon Father McCool rose to answer the first question and stated, as we have said, that Cardinal Shehan had withdrawn his signature from Archbishop's Hannan's letter. Unfortunately Chapter V had been voted that morning, although the results were not announced until Monday. The auxiliary Bishop of Philadelphia, Gerald McDevitt, then assured the reporters that the majority of American bishops did not agree with Archbishop Hannan's position and his statement was concurred in by the other bishops present as well as the *periti*. Monsignor Higgins, in particular, pointed out the absurdity of the *modi* when compared with what the text actually said.

Over the weekend Bishop Schröffer, the subcommission chairman, and Archbishop Garrone, prepared a point-by-point rebuttal of the Hannan thesis, which was accepted by Cardinal Spellman, who suddenly realized that he had been unfairly used in the matter (the cardinal had been suffering

from a cold and the inclemency of the Roman weather and on
at least two occasions had been seen to leave the Council hall
early, giving rise to false rumors that he had gone to see the
Pope). The Schröffer rebuttal was gladly endorsed by the
bulk of the American bishops, and it was even suggested that
mention of it should be made in an announcement before the
final vote on Schema 13 as a whole, on Monday morning.
After a hurried conference, Cardinal Tisserant telephoned
the Pope to ask whether the vote should be postponed because of the large vote (483) against Chapter V on Saturday,
and received the reply that the voting was to proceed according to the rules.

That morning (Monday) when the papal document proclaiming a special jubilee from January 6th to June 29th, 1966
was read in the aula, reporters pounced on its ridiculously
outmoded formulas granting confessors powers to absolve
penitents from censures incurred for reading forbidden
books, or belonging to the Masonic Order or secret or forbidden societies. The panel canonist Father McManus walked
a tightrope trying to explain why such a worthy exhortation
asking bishops and faithful to meditate on the implementation of the Council should be larded with medieval formulas.

While the Hannan *modi* helped swell the *non placets* on
Chapter V to 483 on Saturday, the opposition shrank to 251
votes on Monday when Schema 13 was approved as a whole.
It is uncertain just what part the Apostolic Delegate Archbishop Vagnozzi played in all this, but his actions revived
murmuring among the American bishops about meddling in
U.S. diocesan affairs.

On Monday, before the voting began, Pope Paul's long-
awaited Motu Proprio inaugurating the reform of the Curia
was read by Archbishop Felici. As announced earlier by the
Pope himself, the Supreme Congregation of the Holy Office
was given a new designation and statute. The former name,
recalling unpleasant memories of the "Holy Inquisition"

which it had once been called, was now dropped in favor of the less alarming "Congregation for the Doctrine of the Faith." More important, if it could be made to stick, was the stipulation that the new office was to be more concerned with promoting theological investigation than with heresy hunting. Like the old organization, the new would have the Pope as its head and a cardinal as Secretary,* and its functions would continue to be both administrative and judicial. The Index of Prohibited Books would remain under its jurisdiction. However, there was an important change both with respect to authors and persons who might be denounced for heterodoxy. Instead of being condemned in silence and very often without being able to offer any defense, such persons were henceforth to have the right to defend themselves according to accepted and published norms and no action was to be taken against anybody without informing the local bishop. In short, the charges raised by Cardinal Frings in his famous speech on the council floor denouncing the Holy Office—an attack bitterly resented by the secretary of that body, Cardinal Ottaviani—were accepted virtually *in toto* and became the basis of the new regulation. The tribunal still retained jurisdiction over marriage cases involving Catholics and non-Catholics, an area in which it had generally functioned more or less commendably. Observers were pleased by the Pope's announcement, but much would necessarily depend on whether there were to be any corresponding changes in personnel. There had been strong rumors for several weeks that the Pope had Cardinal Ottaviani's resignation on his desk. This was denied by members of the Holy Office staff, but when the Vatican paper *L'Osservatore Romano* failed to publish an official denial, old Roman hands saw this as a sign that the rumors were probably true. The cardinal described himself as just "an old *carabiniere*" in an interview granted to Alberto Cavallari.

* Called Pro-Secretary, as of February 1966.

The Concluding Ceremonies

Since both previous sessions of the Council held under Pope Paul VI had ended under a cloud, the common assumption was that the Fourth Session too would probably end badly or at least in a draw. Contrary to expectations, however, Vatican II came to a close on December 7th and 8th in something like a blaze of glory. The chief credit for this happy turn of events belonged to Pope Paul who has an eye for the symbolic and eloquent gesture, as the world now knows. While the Council itself was feverishly locked in battle over the wording of the remaining documents, the Pope was carefully planning the strategy of the closing days. Pope John had declared that the twofold purpose of the Council was to be the *aggiornamento* or renewal of the Roman Catholic Church and the promotion of Christian unity. The sixteen decrees promulgated by the Council would be eloquent evidence of the seriousness with which the first purpose had been met. But what about the prospects for Christian reunion?

On Saturday, December 4th, four days before the Council was scheduled to close, Pope Paul took part with the non-Catholic observer delegates and the Council Fathers in an unprecedented interdenominational "Liturgy of the Word" in the historic basilica of St. Paul's without the Walls, where Pope John had first announced his intention to summon the Council over six years earlier. The service was unprecedented because it marked the first time that any Pope had ever taken part in a similar ceremony. It consisted, appropriately, of prayers, psalms, lessons from Scripture, and hymns, the heritage of one or more of the Catholic, Protestant and Orthodox traditions. The lessons were read respectively in English, French and Greek by the Methodist observer Dr. A. C. Outler, the French Catholic priest Pierre Michalon, and the Orthodox observer and rector of the Orthodox parish church in Rome, Archimandrite Maximos Aghiorgoussis. The hymn

"Now thank we all our God" in which all joined in English was written by the seventeenth-century Lutheran composer Johann Crüger.

Two hours before the ceremony several members of the Secretariat for Promoting Christian Unity, the American Paulist Father Stransky and the Jesuit Father Long, raced out to the basilica to check on the final arrangements. They found that the good Benedictine monks had erected a papal throne of magnificent, medieval proportions, and had considerable difficulty in persuading the abbot that such a display of pomp was contrary to the Pope's own wishes. Finally a straight-backed only slightly ornamented chair was substituted for the elaborate throne. When the Pope arrived he seated himself in it, or stood in front of it, as the service proceeded, with the utmost simplicity. There had been no time to bind the booklet containing the service in buckram with the papal arms, so the Pope was handed a simple pamphlet like the rest. He joined in the singing of the hymns and canticles as if this type of service was for him the most natural thing in the world.

In the course of his moving talk the Pope declared, "We would like to have you with us always." The departure of the observers would not mean the end of the ecumenical dialogue, which had been so fortunately begun "in silence." The Council had shown that reunion could eventually be achieved, "slowly, gradually, loyally and generously" the Pope emphasized. In a passage that particularly impressed his hearers, the Pope acknowledged that there had been "failures" on the part of Catholics and others in the past with regard to reunion, but such things were the result of un-Christian influences which every effort would be made to transform into sentiments "worthy of the school of Christ." He was referring specifically to the now outmoded polemical approach to reunion and insistence on matters of prestige. Henceforth the Roman Catholic Church would be guided by the spirit of charity so eloquently proclaimed by St. Paul, he assured them. As a sign he pointed to the fact that the Council had not issued any "anathemas, but only invitations." He concluded his remarks, "May this ray of divine light, beloved brethren, cause us all to recognize the blessed door of truth."

Each of the non-Catholic observers was afterward presented to the Pope by Cardinal Bea in the same adjoining Benedictine monastery where Pope John had first announced the Council to the cardinals in January 1959. Each was given a special gift of a bronze clock with the emblems of the four Evangelists around the base and the monogram of Christ on top. As one of the Protestant observers commented later, "It was one of the most impressive moments of the whole Council." Some of them were moved to tears by the solemnity of the occasion and the place.

The thousand or more bishops present who sat in the nave were greatly edified by this unprecedented gesture on the Pope's part. Not so, however, a number of those who did not attend. Professing to be scandalized, a select group of bishops apparently under the guidance of Archbishops Staffa and Vagnozzi (the latter acting as spokesman for a number of easily persuaded American bishops) sent a message to the Pope the following morning, Sunday, expressing their amazement at the encouragement he had given to what they had been taught to believe was a *communicatio in sacris* with heretics. As one of them put it, "It may be all right for the Pope to do this, but half our people would walk out on us if we tried the same thing," thus betraying their abysmal ignorance of what the Council had decreed. The Pope was somewhat shocked himself by their reaction. After communicating his opinion to Archbishop Dell'Acqua, the latter passed the word and telegrams began arriving in droves from the bishops stating how pleased they were.

During the final week of the Council the Pope managed to see an extraordinary number of people in private audiences. On Tuesday evening, December 7th, he gave audiences to at least 5 separate groups of people connected with the Council, including the Council Auditors, chauffeurs and handymen, and finally, at 7:30, the Council *periti,* in the Sala Clementina. On the latter occasion, while reading a short formal paper in French, the Pope suddenly dropped the paper and spoke to his hearers directly from the heart. He was obviously greatly moved as he thanked the *periti* for all that they had done and their courage and long-suffering throughout the Council. He acknowledged frankly that it was their efforts, as well as those of the bishops, that had made the Council such a great success. Urging them to continue to love the Church and preserve it from "capricious innovation or exaggeration in doctrine," he suggested slyly that since they had now learned how to talk to bishops, they should go on doing so in the post-conciliar period. As a souvenir he gave each one a pocket-sized copy of the Latin New Testament.

Earlier, at 6 P.M., he had received the Italian bishops. His talk was an intimate, heart-to-heart sharing of confidences and dealt principally with the attitude they would be expected to adopt after the Council was over. "Now that the Council is finished," the Pope asked, "will everything go back as it was before? Appearances and custom say Yes. But the spirit of the Council says No. Some things, many things, will be new for us all. Is it merely a question of external changes? In a sense yes, but we are not thinking of these things right now. It is a question of the way we look at the Church. The period following the Council cannot be one of back-to-normal or the good-old-days. It must be a period of immense labor. We must be convinced that pastoral effectiveness will come not so much from the wisdom and authority of what the Council has decreed, as from the docility and alacrity with which its laws are put into practice."

The personal reaction to this speech of the two Italian cardinals so doggedly opposed to the process of conciliar reform was not known; but the two cardinals in question, Siri of Genoa and Ruffini of Palermo, were seated beside the Pope directly on his right and it was obvious from the Pope's tone that he expected compliance from them too. Cardinal Siri's domination of the Italian Episcopal Conference had been ended in August, but he retains the support of powerful right-wing elements and wealthy industrialists and could still cause trouble. The attitude of this group may be illustrated by an incident involving the indomitable Bishop Carli of Segni. On November 18th, during the promulgation of the document on Divine Revelation, Cardinal Ottaviani's former spokesman was seen squirming with excitement at his seat. After the end of the session, Father Balic, a Holy Office consultor, rushed up to him and said: "Calm yourself, *Eccellenza, non sono definizioni*—these texts are not technically definitions of the faith." He was echoing a statement attributed to Cardinal Siri the week before when after a conference criticizing the work of the Council, he was asked by a priest about the value to be attributed to conciliar decisions and replied: *"Non sono definizioni; non ci obblighino mai—* they are not definitions; they will never bind us." On December 7th, by contrast, Bishop Carli had full control of himself and between the final votes joked with the French bishops about De Gaulle's discomfiture. Whereupon a South African bishop asked him whether he had heard the most recent Carli joke. *"No; ne ditemi,"* said Carli. The story was that after the Council's close Carli was going to immolate himself on the Piazza S. Pietro, like a Buddhist monk, in protest against the Council's work, when some bishops offered to chip in for the gasoline. "Don't bother," Carli had told them. "I can buy Vatican gasoline at a much cheaper price, and maybe it won't burn!"

If it was the Protestants who were primarily moved by the significance of the service in St. Paul's, three days later it was the turn of the Orthodox to be gratified. In the course of the final public session in St. Peter's on Tuesday, December 7th, a joint declaration of the Pope and the Orthodox Patriarch of Constantinople Athenagoras I was read out in which both Churches removed from memory and "consigned to oblivion" the centuries' old mutual excommunications which had poisoned relations between them and declared that their gesture was to be seen as an "invitation" to the entire Christian world to seek the ultimate unity commanded by Christ when He said, That they may be one. When Metropolitan Meliton of Heliopolis, Patriarch Athenagoras' representative, knelt to kiss the Pope's ring after receiving the papal brief formally annulling the papal sentence of excommunication against the eleventh century Patriarch Michael Caerularius, he was graciously raised up by the Pope and embraced in a kiss of peace. Turning to go back to his place, the Metropolitan was greeted by a thunderous burst of applause as the Council Fathers put the seal of their approval on this act of reconciliation. At the same time the aged Melkite Patriarch Maximos IV of Antioch rose from his place at the patriarchal table and went over to the Orthodox observers to give them all the kiss of peace. A similar ceremony took place simultaneously in the patriarchal cathedral in Istanbul, where Atheganoras I read the above mentioned declaration from his throne in the presence of a papal delegation headed by Cardinal Lawrence Shehan of Baltimore. As one Protestant observer delegate commented later: "If the Church is able to express its regret for the past with such ease and humility, anything is possible."

The concluding ceremony the following day in the open air in front of the basilica of St. Peter's was somewhat overly pompous and anti-climactic by comparison. After the Pope's discourse a slight confusion occurred while he was distributing the sum of $90,000 to cardinals and bishops from needy countries for specific pastoral projects. Cardinals Spellman and Heenan, it seems, were to have flanked him at this moment, but instead they found themselves among the recipients and stood there looking somewhat perplexed. A series of "conciliar messages to the world," read in French, were intended to embrace all categories of the human family whom the Council had tried to reach: rulers, scholars,* artists, women, workingmen, the poor and sick, and youth. After the reading of the papal brief closing the Council (it was read by Secretary General Archbishop Felici as his last official act), six bishops representing different parts of the world and supported by the expert voices of the Sistine Choir, chanted the Acclamations or Litany, traditional at ecumenical councils since the fifth century, for the Pope, the soul of Pope John XXIII, the Moderators, the bishops, the observer delegates, the heads of governments, the people of God and all men of good will. The Pope dismissed the assembly with a final blessing, *"Ite in pace*—Go in peace."

Summary

October 28, 1965, Thursday—PUBLIC SESSION.
MASS concelebrated by Pope and 24 bishops.

VOTING AND PROMULGATION OF DECREES

	Total	*Placet*	*Non placet*	Invalid
Pastoral Office of Bishops*	2,322	2,319	2	1
Priestly Formation*	2,321	2,318	3	—
Religious Life*	2,325	2,321	4	—
Christian Education*	2,325	2,290	35	—
Non-Christian Religions	2,312	2,221	88	3

* It was announced that the first four would not be legally binding (*vacatio legis*) until after June 29, 1966.

ADDRESS by Pope Paul.

* Represented by his old friend, Jacques Maritain, reminding commentators of the irony of this honor. Not many years ago no U.S. Catholic university would employ this scholar because of his opposition to Franco, until a secular institution (Princeton) accepted him.

October 29, 1965, Friday—155TH GENERAL CONGREGATION.
MASS: Archbishop Tayroyan, of Baghdad, in Armenian rite.
MODERATOR: Cardinal Lercaro.
PRESENT: 2,240 Fathers.
ANNOUNCEMENTS: Schedule for November; will be Public Session on Nov. 18, to be followed by another intersession; presidents of Episcopal Conferences should have reports on indulgences ready for reading in aula on Nov. 9; file of documents on indulgences will be distributed to bishops on Nov. 9, when congregations resume; medal struck to commemorate fourth session distributed today.

VOTES: Divine Revelation.
Relatores: Archbishop Florit and
Bishop Charue (for Bishop Van Dodewaard).

	Total	*Placet*	*Non placet*	Invalid
Introd. & Chap. I	2,194	2,169	23	2 (1)
Chap. II	2,185	2,123	55	7 (1)
Chap. III	2,189	2,154	31	4 (2)
Chap. IV	2,188	2,178	8	2
Chap. V	2,139	2,115	19	5
Chap. VI	2,146	2,126	14	6 (2)
Schema as a whole	2,115	2,081	27	7 (1)

November 9, 1965, Tuesday—156TH GENERAL CONGREGATION.
MASS: Bishop Youakim, of Zahleh, Lebanon, in Melkite rite.
MODERATOR: Cardinal Döpfner.
PRESENT: 2,152 Fathers.
ANNOUNCEMENTS: Documents on indulgences distributed today, by directive of Pope, not Council documents; brochure containing *modi* to Missionary Activity distributed, voting on text tomorrow; revised text of Priestly Life and Ministry distributed, voting following Missionary Activity; certain changes in Apostolate of Laity made by commission read before voting on this began; will be general congregation Saturday of this week and on Nov. 19; Pope, in letter to Cardinal Tisserant, has fixed final Public Session for December 7, with closing ceremony on December 8, feast of the Immaculate Conception.

NEW BUSINESS: Proposed reform of discipline relating to Indulgences.

SPEAKERS: *Relatores:* Cardinal Cento, Grand Penitentiary, and Monsignor Sessolo, Regent of Apostolic Penitentiary.

VOTES: Schema on Apostolate of the Laity.
Relator: Bishop Hengsbach.

	Total	*Placet*	*Non placet*	Invalid
1–Introd. & Chap. I	2,127	2,117	10	—
2–Chap. II	2,116	2,099	16	1 (1)
3–Chap. III	2,087	2,075	12	—
4–Chap. IV	2,076	2,061	14	1
5–Chap. V	2,097	2,089	8	—
6–Chap. VI	2,109	2,100	6	3

I–Vocation of laity; II–Goals; III–Fields of activity; IV–Various forms; V–Role of clergy; VI–Formation.

November 10, 1965, Wednesday—157TH GENERAL CONGREGATION.
MASS: Cardinal Cicognani, in presence of Holy Father, for Council Fathers deceased in last year.
MODERATOR: Cardinal Suenens.
PRESENT: 2,224 Fathers.
ANNOUNCEMENTS: Schedule for remainder of Council; no congregations from Nov. 21 to 28, but they will resume Nov. 29; Schema 13 will be distributed in two parts, on Friday and Saturday of this week, voting the following week; voting on *modi* to Religious Liberty foreseen for Nov. 19; Divine Revelation will be voted and promulgated on Nov. 18; bishops reminded that subject of indulgences is not a conciliar matter.
PENDING BUSINESS: Indulgences.
SPEAKERS (reading reports of respective Episcopal Conferences): 1. Cardinal Tappouni (Patriarchal Synod of Antioch, Syrian rite, declined to speak). 2. Cardinal Maximos IV Saigh (Melkite Episcopal Conference). 3. Cardinal Meouchi (Maronite Episcopal Conference, declined to speak). 4. Cardinal Stephanos I Sidarouss (Coptic Episcopal Conference). 5. Cardinal Gonçalves Cerejeira (Portuguese Episcopal Conference). 6. Cardinal Gilroy (Australian Episcopal Conference). 7. Cardinal Shehan (United States Episcopal Conference).

VOTE: Apostolate of the Laity.

	Total	Placet	Non placet	Invalid
Schema as a whole	2,208	2,201	2	5

VOTES: Missionary Activity of the Church.
Relator: Bishop Schütte.

	Total	Placet	Non placet	Placet iuxta modum	Invalid
1–Art. 1-4	2,207	2,183	21	—	3
2–Art. 5-6	2,135	2,012	117	—	6
3–Art. 7	2,114	2,106	5	—	3
4–Art. 8-9	2,128	2,083	11	—	34 (27)
5–Chap. I as whole*	2,142	1,858	7	272	5
6–Art. 10-12	2,161	2,154	7	—	—
7–Art. 13-14	2,175	2,165	9	—	1
8–Art. 15-18	2,182	2,138	37	—	7
9–Chap. II as whole*	2,116	1,982	13	118	3
10–Art. 19-20	2,166	2,160	4	—	2
11–Art. 21-22	2,109	2,106	2	—	1

* I–Doctrinal principles; II–Missionary work.

November 11, 1965, Thursday—158TH GENERAL CONGREGATION.
MASS: Bishop Blanchet, Rector of Catholic Institute, Paris.
MODERATOR: Cardinal Agagianian.
PRESENT: 2,204 Fathers.
ANNOUNCEMENTS: Volume containing decrees promulgated Oct. 28 distributed and a definitive edition of all the conciliar decrees being prepared; SG defines meaning of term "Session" and gives list of those regarded as Public Sessions.
PENDING BUSINESS: Indulgences.
SPEAKERS: 1. Cardinal Wyszynski (Polish Episcopal Conference). 2. Cardinal Alfrink (Dutch Episcopal Conference). 3. Cardinal Arriba y Castro (Spanish Episcopal Conference). 4. Cardinal Urbani (Italian Episcopal Conference). 5. Cardinal König (Austrian Episcopal Conference). 6. Cardinal Döpfner (German Episcopal Conference).

VOTES: Missionary Activity of the Church.

	Total	Placet	Non placet	Placet iuxta modum	Invalid
12–Chap. III as whole	2,209	2,066	10	131	2
13–Art. 23-26	2,165	2,138	18	—	9
14–Art. 27	2,151	2,117	4	—	30
15–Chap. IV as whole	2,138	1,816	11	309	2
16–Art. 28-29	2,131	2,064	53	—	14
17–Art. 30-31	2,125	2,105	16	—	4
18–Art. 32-34	2,142	2,101	37	—	4
19—Chap. V as whole	2,153	1,428	9	712*	4
20–Chap. VI as whole	2,171	2,006	6	158	1

* This chapter did not receive required two-thirds majority.
III–Local Churches; IV–Missionaries; V–Coordination of missionary activity; VI–Cooperation.

November 12, 1965, Friday—159TH GENERAL CONGREGATION.
MASS concelebrated by Cardinal Slipyi and Ukrainian bishops, in Ukrainian rite.
MODERATOR: Cardinal Lercaro.
PRESENT: 2,174 Fathers.
ANNOUNCEMENTS: Second half of revised Schema 13 distributed; *modi* should be submitted with vote or by Nov. 17 at latest; SG emphatically denied that conferences at Domus Mariae were held under auspices of the Secretariat General, in reply to a question put to him; *modi* to Priestly Life must be submitted by tomorrow at latest.
PENDING BUSINESS: Indulgences.
SPEAKERS (the following scheduled to speak submitted only written interventions owing to lateness of the hour): 1. Cardinal Pizzardo (Curia). 2. Cardinal Masella (Curia). 3. Cardinal Silva Henríquez (Chile). 4. Archbishop Olçomendy (Singapore). 5. Archbishop Mosquera Corral (Ecuador). 6. Archbishop Kozlowiecki (Zambia). 7. Archbishop Amissah (Ghana). 8. Archbishop Rodríguez Quirós (Costa Rica). 9. Archbishop Gantin (Dahomey). 10. Archbishop Santos Hernández (Honduras). 11. Archbishop Varthalitis (Greece). 12. Bishop Jelmini (Switzer-

land). 13. Bishop Larrain Errázuriz (Chile). 14. Bishop Bayet (Thailand). 15. Bishop Baroni (Sudan).

VOTES: Priestly Life and Ministry.
Relator: Archbishop Marty.

	Total	Placet	Non placet	Placet iuxta modum	Invalid
1–Chap. I as whole	2,154	1,772	16	361	5
2–Art. 4-5	2,118	2,073	20	—	25
3–Art. 6	2,118	2,095	16	—	1
4–Art. 7	2,114	2,073	35	—	6
5–Art. 8-9	2,120	2,016	84	—	20 (17)
6–Art. 10	2,125	2,107	16	—	2 (1)
7–Art. 11	2,142	2,131	8	—	3 (3)
8–Chap. II as whole	2,129	1,548	9	568	4
9–Art. 12-14*	2,134	2,037	2	95	—

* On vocation to holiness, greatly revised.

November 13, 1965, Saturday—160TH GENERAL CONGREGATION.
MASS: Bishop Phakoe, of Leribe, Basutoland.
MODERATOR: Cardinal Döpfner.
PRESENT: 2,090 Fathers.
ANNOUNCEMENTS: Apostolate of Laity will be voted and promulgated on Nov. 18; definitive text of Divine Revelation distributed; also first part of revised Schema 13; and Apostolic Exhortation of Pope urging prayers for close of Council; Pope will concelebrate with *periti* on Nov. 18; exhibition of photographs of Council will be inaugurated on Monday; reports of Episcopal Conferences on Indulgences cannot be read today owing to shortness of time, and bishops are reminded that some have gone beyond the limits by commenting on theological aspects.
PENDING BUSINESS: Indulgences.
SPEAKERS (only submitted written interventions): 1. Cardinal Tatsuo Doi (Japan). 2. Slipyi (Ukraine). 3. Archbishop Gori (Latin Patriarchate of Jerusalem). 4. Archbishop Nguyen Van Binh (Vietnam). 5. Archbishop Muñoz Duque (Colombia). 6. Archbishop Perraudin (Ruanda-Burundi). 7. Archbishop Mihayo (Tanzania). 8. Archbishop Alvim Pereira (Mozambique). 9. Archbishop Sacariego (Guatemala). 10. Archbishop Darmajuwana (Indonesia). 11. Archbishop Clavel Méndez (Panama).

12. Bishop Sosa Goana (Paraguay). 13. Bishop Peiris (Ceylon). 14. Bishop Necsey (Czechoslovakia). 15. Bishop Noser (New Guinea). 16. Bishop McEleney (Antilles). 17. Bishop Loosdregt (Laos-Cambodia). 18. Cardinal Antoniutti (Curia).

VOTES: Priestly Life and Ministry.

	Total	Placet	Non placet	Placet iuxta modum	Invalid
10–Art. 15-16*	2,091	2,005	65	—	21 (17)
11–Art. 17	2,097	2,070	6	—	21
12–Art. 15-17*	2,076	1,434	11	630	1
13–Art. 18-19	2,075	2,023	45	—	7
14–Art. 20-22	2,073	1,059	9	—	5
15–Art. 18-22	2,058	1,510	4	544	—

* 15–Humility and obedience; 16–Acceptance and esteem for celibacy.

November 15, 1965, Monday—161ST GENERAL CONGREGATION.
MASS: Bishop Schröffer, of Eichstatt, Germany.
MODERATOR: Cardinal Suenens.
PRESENT: 2,199 Fathers.
ANNOUNCEMENTS: Status of Constitution on Divine Revelation as a conciliar document; *modi* to Schema 13 must be submitted by Wed., Nov. 17, at latest.

VOTES: Schema 13, Church in the Modern World.
Relator: Archbishop Garrone.

	Total	Placet	Non placet	Placet iuxta modum	Invalid
1–Art. 1-10	2,187	2,009	41	134	3
2–Art. 11	2,113	2,074	27	—	12
3–Art. 12-18	2,133	2,088	35	—	10 (8)
4–Art. 19-22*	2,144	2,057	74	—	13 (11)
5–Chap. I as whole	2,149	1,672	18	453	6
6–Art. 23-26	2,115	2,074	34	—	7 (3)
7–Art. 27-32	2,155	2,115	35	—	5 (3)

* 19-21–On Atheism.

November 16, 1965, Tuesday—162ND GENERAL CONGREGATION.
MASS: Bishop Jubany Arnau, of Gerona, Spain.
MODERATOR: Cardinal Agagianian.

PRESENT: 2,210 Fathers.

ANNOUNCEMENTS: Definitive text of Apostolate of Laity distributed; declaration of Theological Commission on status of Divine Revelation distributed; bishops are reminded that they must "hurry" if Council is to end on time.

VOTES: Schema 13, Church in the Modern World.
Relator (for Part II): Bishop Hengsbach.

	Total	Placet	Non placet	Placet iuxta modum	Invalid
8–Chap. II as whole	2,212	1,801	18	388	5
9–Art. 33-36	2,216	2,173	33	—	10 (8)
10–Art. 37-39	2,227	2,169	45	—	13 (9)
11–Chap. III as whole	2,223	1,727	25	467	4
12–Art. 40-42	2,227	2,107	13	—	7 (3)
13–Art. 43-45	2,222	2,095	112	—	15 (11)
14–Chap. IV as whole	2,202	1,817	99	284	2
15–Art. 50,* Part II	2,149	2,106	39	—	4
16–Art. 51-53**	2,150	2,052	91	—	7 (4)
17–Art. 54-56**	2,163	2,011	140	—	12 (10)
18–Chap. I as whole	2,157	1,596	77	484	5
19–Art. 57-63	2,158	2,102	52	—	4 (2)
20–Art. 64-66	2,125	2,058	51	—	6 (2)
21–Chap. II as whole***	2,146	1,909	44	185	8
22–Art. 67-70	2,162	2,115	40	—	7

* Paragraph numbering changed in final version promulgated by Council, Art. 46ff.

** 51-56–Marriage and Conjugal Love = Chap. I.

*** II–Promotion of Culture.

November 17, 1965, Wednesday—163RD GENERAL CONGREGATION.
MASS: Father Tomzinski, Superior General of Monks of St. Paul the Hermit, Czestochowa, Poland.
MODERATOR: Cardinal Lercaro.
PRESENT: 2,261 Fathers.
ANNOUNCEMENTS: Revised text of Religious Liberty distributed, voting on *modi* Friday, Nov. 19; concelebrants tomorrow will be representatives of superiors general, *periti* and pastors; dead-

line for *modi* to Schema 13 is midnight tonight; written recommendations regarding qualification of Schema 13 as Constitution can be submitted until end of congregation on Friday.

VOTES: Schema 13, Church in the Modern World.

	Total	Placet	Non placet	Placet iuxta modum	Invalid
23–Art. 71-72	2,260	2,182	68	—	10 (4)
24–Art. 73-76	2,233	2,182	68	—	8 (3)
25–Chap. III* as whole	2,253	1,740	41	469	3
26–Art. 77-78	2,261	2,188	70	—	3 (5)
27–Art. 79-80	2,217	2,145	66	—	6 (5)
28–Chap. IV as whole*	2,241	1,970	54	210	7
29–Art. 81-86	2,242	2,081	144	—	17
30–Art. 87-90	2,170	2,122	43	—	5
31–Art. 91-94	2,200	2,126	65	—	9
32–Art. 95-97	2,218	2,165	33	—	20
33–Chap. V as whole*	2,227	1,656	45	523	3

* III–Economic-Social Life; IV–Political Community; V–Promoting Peace.

November 18, 1965, Thursday—PUBLIC SESSION.
MASS concelebrated by Pope with 23 heads of religious orders, *periti* and pastors.

VOTING AND PROMULGATION OF DECREES.

	Total	Placet	Non placet	Invalid
Constitution on Divine Revelation	2,350	2,344	6	—
Decree on Apostolate of Laity*	2,342	2,340	6	—

* It was announced that decrees would not go into effect until after June 29, 1966.

ADDRESS by Pope Paul.

November 19, 1965, Friday—164TH GENERAL CONGREGATION.
MASS: Bishop Dudas, of Hajdudorog, Hungary, in Byzantine Hungarian rite.
MODERATOR: Cardinal Döpfner.
PRESENT: 2,268 Fathers.
ANNOUNCEMENTS: Schedule for final days of Council; next general congregation on Nov. 30; revised text of Missionary Activity will be distributed Nov. 26, voted on the 30th; general congregation on Dec. 2; Priestly Life and Ministry will be distributed Nov. 30, voted Dec. 2; general congregations on Dec. 4 and 6 when Schema 13 will be voted, text will be distributed Dec. 2; text of encyclical *Mysterium fidei* distributed to bishops only, as well as special edition of Dante's *Divine Comedy*; also volume on Pope's trip to India.

VOTES: Declaration on Religious Liberty.
Relator: Bishop De Smedt.

	Total	*Placet*	*Non placet*	Invalid
1–Art. 1-5	2,242	1,989	246	7 (3)
2–Art. 6-8	2,200	1,957	237	6 (2)
3–Art. 9-12	2,210	1,989	217	4 (2)
4–Art. 13-15	2,228	2,033	190	5 (1)
5–Schema as whole	2,216	1,954	249	13 (7)

November 30, 1965, Tuesday—165TH GENERAL CONGREGATION.
MASS concelebrated by Cardinal Meouchi, in Maronite rite.
MODERATOR: Cardinal Agagianian.
PRESENT: 1,922 Fathers.
ANNOUNCEMENTS: Mass on Thurs. in honor of St. Joseph, for Church unity, and mass on Sat. in honor of St. John the Baptist, for those subject to persecution; correction in final vote on Apostolate of Laity on Nov. 18 owing to failure of computer; special service for unity will be held Sat. at St. Paul's without the Walls in which Pope will take part.

VOTES: Missionary Activity of the Church.
Relator: Bishop Schütte.

	Total	*Placet*	*Non placet*	Invalid
1–Art. 6	2,229	2,209	20	—
2–Chap. I as whole	2,210	2,189	18	3
3–Chap. II as whole	2,162	2,133	26	3
4–Chap. III as whole	2,161	2,142	16	3
5–Chap. IV as whole	2,169	2,147	22	—
6–Art. 29*	2,169	2,112	54	3
7–Art. 32**	2,168	2,152	14	2
8–Rest of Chap. V	2,195	2,175	18	2
9–Chap. VI as whole	2,186	2,159	24	3
10–Schema as whole	2,182	2,162	18	2

* 29–Reorganization of Propaganda Fide.
** 32–Coordination of work of Institutes.

December 2, 1965, Thursday—166TH GENERAL CONGREGATION.
MASS concelebrated by Archbishop Neto, of Brazil, and six other bishops.
MODERATOR: Cardinal Lercaro.
PRESENT: 2,280 Fathers.
ANNOUNCEMENTS: Definitive text of Schema 13 distributed, brochure containing *expensio modorum* for Part II will be distributed tomorrow; beatification of Maronite monk Charbel Maklouf on Sunday.

VOTES: Priestly Life and Ministry.
Relator: Archbishop Marty.

	Total	*Placet*	*Non placet*	Invalid
1–Intr. & Chap. I	2,298	2,291	5	2
2–Chap. II	2,301	2,262	38	1
3–Art. 12-14, Chap. III	2,278	2,261	15	2
4–Art. 15-17, Chap. III	2,271	2,243	27	1
5–Art. 18-21, Chap. III	2,268	2,254	11	3
6–Schema as whole	2,257	2,243	11	3

VOTES: Schema 13, Church in Modern World. *Relator:* Archbishop Garrone (only the *relatio* read today).

December 4, 1965, Saturday—167TH GENERAL CONGREGATION.

MASS: Bishop Dud, Vicar Apostolic of Wau, Sudan.

MODERATOR: Cardinal Döpfner.

PRESENT: 2,250 Fathers.

ANNOUNCEMENTS: Gold rings and diplomas will be distributed to the bishops Monday, the gift of the Pope; SG read Message of the Observer-Delegates to the Council Fathers (applause); also, at request of Cardinal Wyszynski, asked Council prayers for 1000th anniversary of establishment of Christianity in Poland to be celebrated next year, Fathers given picture of Mary venerated at shrine of Czestochowa; special prayer service at St. Paul's this afternoon only for Observer-Delegates and Council Fathers, brochure containing *ordo* distributed; bishops will be given silver medals as gift from mayor and city of Rome on Monday.

VOTES: Schema 13, Church in Modern World.

	Total	*Placet*	*Non placet*	Invalid
1–Introd.	2,230	2,153	72	5 (1)
2–Chap. I, Part I*	2,238	2,103	131	4 (3)
3–Chap. II	2,236	2,166	68	2 (1)
4–Chap. III	2,230	2,165	62	3 (1)
5–Chap. IV	2,228	2,149	75	4
6–Chap. I, Part II**	2,209	2,047	155	7 (1)
7–Chap. II	2,206	2,137	81	8
8–Chap. III	2,212	2,110	98	4 (1)
9–Chap. IV	2,214	2,086	121	7
10–Chap. V***	2,201	1,710	483	8 (2)
11–Conclusion	2,174	2,039	128	7
12–Title of Schema	2,174	1,873	293	8 (1)

* On Atheism.
** On Marriage.
*** On Promoting Peace.

December 6, 1965, Monday—168TH GENERAL CONGREGATION.

MASS: Bishop Elko, of Pittsburgh, in Byzantine Ruthenian rite.

MODERATOR: Cardinal Suenens.

PRESENT: 2,392 Fathers.

ANNOUNCEMENTS: Definitive texts of Priestly Life and Ministry and ceremonial for Public Session tomorrow distributed; bull for indiction of extraordinary Jubilee to last until end of Pentecost 1966 read by SG; medals from city of Rome distributed to bishops, and later, the gold rings and diplomas from the Pope; dispensation from fast and abstinence tomorrow, the vigil of feast of Immaculate Conception; SG expressed his thanks to the bishops in Latin verse, while Moderator expressed thanks to all officials responsible for general congregations and other Council meetings; Council adjourned at 12:15 P.M.

VOTE: Schema 13, Church in the Modern World.

	Total	Placet	Non placet	Invalid
13–Schema as a whole	2,373	2,111	251	11 (1)

December 7, 1965, Tuesday—PUBLIC SESSION.
MASS concelebrated by Pope and 24 Presidents of Episcopal Conferences.

VOTING AND PROMULGATION OF DECREES.

	Total	Placet	Non placet	Invalid
Religious Liberty	2,386	2,308	70	8
Missionary Activity*	2,399	2,394	5	—
Priestly Life and Ministry*	2,394	2,390	4	—
Church in Modern World	2,391	2,309	75	7

*Announced that decrees would not be legally binding until after June 29, 1966.

SPECIAL CEREMONY: Formal Annulling of Excommunications of A.D. 1054.
ADDRESS by Pope Paul.

December 8, 1965, Wednesday—SOLEMN CLOSING CEREMONY (in St. Peter's Square).
ADDRESS by Pope Paul.

VI

Toward Vatican Council III

In 1961 the distinguished German theologian Father Hans Küng asked, "Can the Council Fail?" The question was not altogether beside the point. Exhilarating as the announcement of the Council was, the full import of what came to be known as "Pope John's revolution," could only be vaguely discerned. The preparations for the Council were firmly in the hands of Curial bodies bent on rigidly controlling the papal initiative, while the experiment of the Roman diocesan synod which was intended as a sort of dress rehearsal for the Council itself, was frankly discouraging. The first bombshell was Pope John's opening address in which he made clear that he had no sympathy with those "prophets of doom" who were opposing the Church's renewal and that the Council was to have a pastoral rather than a dogmatic orientation, since it was to confront the world with charity and understanding rather than with definitions and the anathematizing of errors. As one of the theologians commented afterward, "In the light of the Pope's remarks, we have to do our work all over again." A second bombshell was dropped when the Pope withdrew the pitifully inadequate draft schema on Divine Revelation and entrusted it to a mixed commission more representative of the Council for redrafting, after a crucial vote of no-confidence disclosed that this was the only possible course. The era of *aggiornamento* really dates from that memorable November 21, 1962 which first disclosed the real strength of the progressive majority among the Council Fathers. All at once, as one observer noted, "there was let loose a whole batch of movements that had been simmering in the Church for many years," the biblical, liturgical, ecumenical, and 'new theology' movements, as well as countless trends and tendencies aimed at bridging the gap between the Church and the world in the moral, scientific, social and economic spheres. All acquired a kind of *droit de cité* from that moment which could not be gainsaid, despite the continuing frowns and threats of the Holy Office.

Four years later, on November 3, 1965, Hans Küng emerged from a 40-minute audience with Pope Paul VI in which he gave the Pontiff a positive and on the whole quite optimistic appraisal of the work of the Council. The Pope, for his part, was pleased that this most outspoken critic of the Curia was now inclined to view events as a step in the right direction.

There could be no doubt that the Council had brought about a fundamental change, both as regards the Catholic Church's attitude toward itself and its outlook on the world, though there was naturally less agreement about the extent and meaning of the change. As Cardinal Heenan put it, "No one can doubt that a beginning of far-reaching importance has been made and that the Church will never retrace the path it has chosen . . . People without sealed minds could not fail to recognize the changes. They would be blind." In another article the cardinal spoke of the "depressing" atmosphere at the beginning of the Council and contrasted this with the "uplifting" atmosphere at the end. Cardinal Bea hailed the Council as marking the "end of the Counter-Reformation." Archbishop Pellegrino condemned the "myopia of those who still refuse to admit there is any need for *aggiornamento* or renewal of the Church, so often asserted by Popes John XXIII and Paul VI." The mood of change, or at least a popular version of it, seems to have been captured by two Roman artists, Ettore De Concilis and Rosso Falciano, who felt justified in adorning the walls of a new Roman church dedicated to St. Francis of Assisi in pell-mell fashion with the profiles of Pope John, Castro, Kosygin, Mao Tse Tung, Bertrand Russell, Giorgio La Pira, Togliatti, Sophia Loren, and Jacqueline Kennedy.

It has become something of a commonplace to say of the Council, "Nothing has changed, even though things will never be the same again." Taking the work of the Council as a whole and considering it from a purely superficial point of view, it is not difficult to make out that there have been few radical changes and to put the stress on continuity. Almost every conciliar statement has its counterpart in the theological literature of the recent past (though what the shortsighted fail to point out is that many of these statements occur in the writings of those formerly considered "heretics"). Though all the documents bear the mark of compromise, when the successive versions of the documents are placed side by side one can really see what tremendous strides have been made.

What the Council has really done is to lay the groundwork for a thorough "reappraisal" of Catholicism, appearances to the contrary notwithstanding. More important than the documents themselves, the Council has consecrated a new spirit destined in the course of time to remake the face of Catholicism. More important than the specific provisions of this or that decree, are the truly revolutionary, biblically-oriented principles found scattered throughout the Council's work, which in time will bring about the necessary transformation and lead ultimately to the desired goal of reunion.

For example, in the Pastoral Constitution on the Church in the Modern World, it is said that "The Church guards the heritage of God's word and draws from it moral and religious principles *without always having at hand the solution to particular problems"* (Part I, Chap. III, par. 33). A similar statement occurs in the Declaration on Religious Liberty: "(The Council) searches into the sacred tradition and doctrine of the Church—the treasury out of which the Church continually brings forth new things that are in harmony with the things that are old." At stake is the whole question of doctrinal development, called the No. 1 theological problem of Vatican II, the process by which the Church passes from a less complete to a more complete understanding of the word of God without ever being able to understand fully what it possesses. While not new, this acknowledgment of the limitations of its knowledge is a healthy sign that the Church is turning more and more from the triumphalism and dogmatism of the past to a more plausible explanation of its message in terms which the modern world can understand. The humility which this approach implies is also consistent with the pastoral purpose of the Council and its refusal to characterize any of its pronouncements as infallible statements. This "downgrading" as it were of the whole problem of infallibility (notwithstanding the reaffirmation of papal infallibility in terms identical with those of 1870) marks one of the important steps forward taken by the Council.

The Decree on Ecumenism boldly states: ". . . in Catholic doctrine *there exists a 'hierarchy' of truths,* since they vary in their relation to the fundamental Christian faith" (Chap. II, par. 11). This means that while no part of Christian revelation is unimportant, some elements are more important than others; for example, the doctrines of the Trinity and the Incarnation are more important than papal infallibility. Together with the correlative principles—"From time to time one tradition has come nearer to a full appreciation of some aspects of a mystery of revelation than the other" (par. 17), and "All who have been justified by faith in baptism are members of Christ's body . . . and are correctly accepted as brothers by the children of the Catholic Church" (par. 3)— these liberating truths not only constitute the firm basis for a fruitful ecumenical dialogue among Christians, but imply a new attitude toward itself on the part of the Catholic Church. Henceforth Catholic theology will be less dominated by juridicism and conceptualism than by biblical and historical research, less concerned with what divides than with what unites, everything implied by the French word *ressourcement,* going back to the biblical and patristic sources of the undivided Church.* Many parts of the Constitution on the Church, the Constitution on Divine Revelation, the Decree on Ecumenism, and the Declarations on Non-Christians and Religious Liberty, already strongly reflect this new biblical emphasis. Another lesson here has been recognition of the fact that a certain amount of pluralism, both in theology and discipline, is not only inevitable but positively desirable, and contributes to a deeper understanding of the Christian message. The kiss of peace exchanged between Pope Paul VI and Patriarch Athenagoras I in Jerusalem, as well as subsequent ecumenical developments, seem to suggest that an eventually re-united Church will emerge from the gradual coalescing of different bodies, namely the present large-scale denominations including the Roman Catholic communion, which will probably be very different from what they are now, while retaining essential continuity with the past and their own individuality. When receiving the non-Catholic observer-delegates in 1962, Pope John quoted the words of the Psalmist:

---

* As Y. Congar says: "True reform implies an appeal from a less perfect to a more perfect tradition, a going back to the sources," *Informations catholiques internationales,* January 1, 1966, p. 5.

"May God be blessed every day!"* In their final message to
the Council, read by Archbishop Felici on December 4, 1965,
the observer-delegates enlarged on this theme: "Blessed be
God for all that he has given us so far through the Holy
Spirit, and for all that he will give us in the future." Oscar
Cullmann, the noted Swiss theologian, summed up their
thoughts when he declared: "The hopes of Protestants for
Vatican II have not only been fulfilled, but the Council's
achievements have gone far beyond what was believed possible."

It would be difficult to overemphasize the importance of
the definition of the Church in terms of the biblical concept
of the *People of God,* which finds such a magnificent expression in the Constitution on the Church. Suffice it to say that
the older ecclesiologists accustomed to thinking of membership in the Church in terms of data that could be processed
in an IBM machine are bound to feel uncomfortable in the
new atmosphere which prefers to look upon the Church as
a mystery, in the Pauline sense, and to think of it as embrac-
ing not three sharply divided groups, clergy, religious and
laity, but as a single large community made up of many
smaller communities. Laity, religious and clergy are all
equally important as members of Christ's Body, they simply
have different functions or callings to perform with respect
to the whole. Unfortunately there was not time for a thorough redrafting of all the Council documents so that they
would reflect the renewed theology of the lay apostolate.
Even if there had been time, it is not likely that the resistance
of conservative theologians could have been overcome. Cardinal Ottaviani, in a recent interview, has declared that he is
concerned about "overboldness on the part of the laity" and
expressed the opinion that "some of them might overreach

---

* In an audience the Methodist observer Bishop Corson once asked Pope
John: "How long do you think it will be before Christian unity is realized,
perhaps 200 years?" The Pope replied: "My dear Bishop Corson, you and I
have achieved it already."

themselves and try to dominate the clergy, judging from what they were already saying."* But, on the whole, the idea of the Church as a living community and the enhanced role of the laity come through with remarkable clearness and seem bound to have a great influence on future thinking. While not granted a deliberative vote or any real voice in the proceedings, a number of Lay Auditors, both men and women, by their presence at the Council, did exercise a considerable influence on the course of events.

The most striking accomplishment of the Council has unquestionably been the proclamation of *episcopal collegiality,* the principle that the bishops form a college and govern the Church together with the Pope who is their head. Although every precaution was taken to ensure that the Pope's special authority would not suffer any infringement, the fact nevertheless remains that the new doctrine is bound to influence the exercise of that authority *in practice,* particularly if Pope Paul's plans for the reform of the Roman Curia and the establishment of the Synod of Bishops are fully carried out. While the Pope would become more responsive to the wishes of the world episcopate, the bishops themselves would become more responsive to the wishes of each other through the institution of episcopal conferences, while the individual bishops in turn have been advised by the Council to consult the wishes of their clergy and faithful. Thus collegiality, if carried out to its logical conclusion, could mean that the whole clergy, not merely the higher echelons, were becoming more responsive to the claims of public opinion, in keeping with the idea of ecclesiastical authority as service, *diakonia.*

With typical conscientiousness Pope Paul began to worry in public about the way in which the Council would be received even before the end. In an Exhortation issued shortly after the end of the debates, on November 6th, he urged the bishops to be "vigilant" about carrying out its decrees,

* Interview with Monsignor Adamo, *The Catholic Transcript,* December 24, 1965.

persuading the faithful to accept them, restraining the un-
seasonable zeal of some and prodding others into action. The
text was given to the press on Saturday. The following
day he complained, at the Angelus, that the newspapers
had not paid sufficient attention to his exhortation which
was, on the contrary, he maintained, of considerable importance! Some idea about the Pope's own attitude toward the
Council can be gathered from a study of the words he frequently uses when referring to it. The favorite word by far
these days is *rinnovamento*—renewal. The Johannine word
aggiornamento, updating, was never a favorite with him and
is now used less than ever, and the word *riforma* hardly ever,
probably because these words imply too radical a departure
which is not congenial to his way of thinking. To the Italian
mind the word *riforma* means either the reform of a religious
order or the Protestant Reformation, the latter meaning of
course being enough to ruin it for general use without plenty
of qualifying phrases. *Aggiornamento* has the disadvantage
of implying "conformity with the world" against which Paul
is always warning. On the other hand, *rinnovamento* has an
element of spirituality about it which particularly recommends it to a person of Paul's spiritual sensitivity. In fact, he
told the various diplomatic missions present for the concluding ceremonies of the Council, in a farewell audience granted
to them on December 7th: "The primary purpose of these
great assemblies is always inner renewal of each Catholic and
the renewal of the whole social body which the Church is.
But there is also an influence on the whole human family . . ."
Later in the same address he speaks of "renewal of life and a
new ardor to put into practice the message of the Gospel."
Earlier he stated: "The Church meditates, consults, examines
itself; it concentrates its energies, purifies its manner of thinking and acting, proceeds to a 'renewal,' but to a renewal that
is primarily interior, which concerns the relations between
the Christian and his God." The same thought occurs in his

talk to the diplomatic corps (January 8, 1966): "Councils are by definition religious events and concern first of all the internal renewal of the Church's life."

Another favorite word of his to describe the Council is "fervor." In his talk to the Curia on December 23, 1965: "The Council has not inaugurated a period of dogmatic and moral uncertainty . . . On the contrary, it has sought to initiate a period of greater fervor, greater cohesion, greater faithfulness to the Gospel, greater pastoral charity and a greater ecclesial spirituality." Elsewhere he refers to the Council as inaugurating "a spring season," "a rebirth," and of the Church as having been "reborn."

Like everybody else the Pope is not entirely consistent in the use of language and too much importance should not be attributed to his use of this or that term in an informal context. For example, in the above talk to the cardinals on December 23rd, he acknowledged that the Council was an "innovating Council." On the other hand in general audiences the word "innovators" is generally reserved for those who are prepared to go too far in introducing changes in contrast to those, like himself, who prefer to do things gradually and prudently. This has been a frequent theme as, for example, in a general audience on October 13, 1965. *Il Tempo* headlined this talk: "SEVERE PAPAL WARNING TO IMPRUDENT INNOVATORS," ignoring the fact that the Pope went on to say that there was good in both approaches and they should be regarded as complementary.

Again, exaggerating of course in order to make his point clearer, he contrasts those who want to return everything to the way it was before the Council and those who would call everything into doubt. The proper attitude for the faithful now, in the post-conciliar period, is "not to put in doubt and subject to inquiry all that the Council has taught us, but that of putting this into practice, of studying, understanding and applying the lessons of the Council in Christian life" (Decem-

ber 15, 1965, general audience). In a general audience on
January 12, 1966, the same point was made even clearer with
respect to the maintenance of doctrinal continuity: "It would
be wrong to think that the Council represents a break or as
some believe, a liberation, from the traditional doctrine of
the Church. They also would be wrong who would promote
a facile conformity to the mentality of our times in its ephem-
eral and negative aspects rather than those that are certain
and scientific, or would allow each individual to attach whatever value he thinks best to the truths of the faith." The
teachings of the Council must not be severed from the doctrinal heritage of the Church, but we must see how they are
consistent with it and give witness to it. When seen in this
light, the "novelties of the Council" do not imply that the
Church has been unfaithful to its teaching, but make that
teaching appear in a clearer light. He went on to explain that
this was so even though the Council made no infallible pronouncements. Its teachings carried the weight of the "ordinary magisterium."

The Fourth Session did see some improvement in the overall picture of the Pope's relations with the world press. At
least it was something that there were no awkward scenes
between Council press officials and the working press similar
to those that marred the Third Session. The Pope made a
personal visit to the large *Sala Stampa* on the Via della Con-
ciliazione, where journalists normally gathered to be briefed
and to send their dispatches, shortly before the end of the
Council (November 26th) and made an address in which he
told them: "You have fulfilled a role that we do not hesitate
to call providential." He went on to remind his audience
about the difficulties of reporting Vatican news because of
the need to avoid anything "sensational" and criticized them
for trying to dramatize the news of the Council by speaking
about it in terms appropriate to "civil society," whereas the
life of the Church was "entirely spiritual and interior." He
concluded on a friendly note, speaking vaguely about "a fra-

ternal, prudent and sincere exchange" and promising to keep the news flowing to them after the Council.

The wall of secrecy normally surrounding the Pope and his immediate advisers seems to have been partially breached. Disturbed by the adverse publicity resulting from the Third Session, the Pope decided to grant an interview to the journalist Alberto Cavallari, which was printed in the Milanese daily *Corriere della Sera,* the day before the Pope's departure for the UN in New York. During the following month the same paper published an unprecedented series of interviews with a good many of the top advisers of the Pope, such as Cardinals Ottaviani, Roberti, Bea, Colombo, König, Archbishops Dell'-Acqua and Samoré. More to the point perhaps was the Pope's recent decision to allow Father G. Caprile, one of the editors of the Jesuit monthly *La Civiltà Cattolica,* to publish a factual, highly revealing account of the Pope's intervention in the handling of the *modi* on Divine Revelation, intended to dissipate the impression that Paul had been acting in violation of the rules of the Council and he had taken sides with the minority against the majority. (The previous year Caprile had published a similar article intended to throw light on the Pope's motives during the final "dark days" of the Third Session, but without the detail and clearness of the papal point of view achieved in the second article.) Pope Paul has let it be known, privately, that he does not object to what journalists say about him personally, his only concern is that "the truth" be made known. His determination to publish the wartime correspondence of Pius XII, contrary to Vatican rules which preclude publicity until at least a hundred years or more after the death of a Pope, seems to be a step in this direction. Apparently the usual Vatican attitude of disdain and hauteur for the calumnies of Hochhuth is not considered good enough by the present Pope. There is reason to believe also that the full official record of the Council will be published as soon as possible and that those parts not suitable for publication will be made available to scholars much earlier than was the case with Vatican I.*

As the world has had ample occasion to learn by now, a man of Paul's temperament cannot be judged by his words alone. Words must be linked to actions. Judged by this standard, he appears to be moving slowly but surely in the direction of implementing the Council's decisions as a "bridge-builder," to use an expression of the Methodist observer Bishop F. P. Corson. Claiming that Paul was "acting for the solidarity of the future and not for the popularity of the hour." Corson was impatient with those critics who found him "a conservative man, fearful of change, suspicious of liberty, myopic on certain areas of modern life." A *Motu Proprio* issued January 1, 1966 continued the Council's Coordinating Commission as a Central Commission, presided over by Cardinals Tisserant and Cicognani, to supervise the work of five subordinate Commissions for Bishops, Religious, Missions, Education and the Lay Apostolate, charged with responsibility for drafting the instructions that have to be issued following the promulgation of the respective conciliar decrees, after which, when their work is completed, all these organs are to go out of existence. The same *Motu Proprio* also provided for the publication of the Council's Acts, entrusting this task to the former Secretary General Archbishop Felici who becomes secretary general of the new Central Commission, and gave Cardinal Bea's Secretariat for Promoting Christian Unity a permanent status in the Curia. Since the above instructions must be published by June 29, 1966, the date on which the various conciliar decrees are to go into effect, no attempt was made to bring in new men. The same officials on the former conciliar commissions were simply continued in the new organs, to provide continuity.

It has long been contended that nothing would come of the proposed reform of the Roman Curia unless new men

---

* Several highly prejudicial accounts of that Council were published and widely circulated before the Vatican moved to allow scholars to dip into the records and produce a more balanced account.

were brought in to replace those who found it impossible to accept the Council's new spirit. Pope Paul had shown by his decree reforming the Holy Office, published December 6th, two days before the final close of the Council, that he intended to give substance to his often repeated promises to bring about an effective reform. Early in February 1966 he appointed two new men to important posts in two offices: Archbishop Garrone of Toulouse, as permanent head (with the title of Pro-Secretary, the aged Cardinal Pizzardo remaining as Secretary) of the Congregation of Seminaries and Universities, and Canon C. Moeller, of the University of Louvain, to the number three post in the Congregation for the Doctrine of the Faith (Holy Office) as undersecretary. Both promptly issued statements making clear the fact that a new era had arrived so far as the past policies of both offices were concerned. The appointment of Garrone was all the more significant because he had been one of the most determined critics of Seminaries and Universities and had called for its thorough overhauling at the Third Session. A curious "incident" shortly before Garrone's appointment may, or may not, have had something to do with the timing of the announcement of his appointment. Toward the middle of January the Congregation of Seminaries published a decree requiring the use of Latin as a liturgical language in all seminaries of the Latin rite. Although the language was technically consistent with the Constitution on the Liturgy which provided for extensive use of the vernacular, many seminaries, for example, those in the United States, had already been using English in the liturgy for some time and the new decree seemed to be a backward step. An instruction published several days later made it plain that exceptions could be made depending upon local circumstances. It is doubtful whether the decree would have been drawn up in the same language (it was actually drafted before the end of the Council) if Archbishop Garrone had been the congregation's head at the time. Soon after Moeller's appointment, it became

known that new procedures would be followed in the future
with regard to the censoring of books and while the Index
was not formally abolished, it was clear that a new regime
had arrived here too. The Pope's appointment of Cardinal
Ottaviani as head of the new episcopal commission to advise
him on birth control (to which the already existing Papal
Commission of Experts would become advisory) may have
been dismaying to some, but a look at the membership of
the new commission should have been enough to dissipate
any undue alarm. The names of Cardinals Suenens, Döpfner,
Lefebvre and Shehan, and Bishop Reuss, were enough
to ensure that no mere rubber-stamping of the past was
contemplated, since they were among the strongest critics of the existing legislation regarding birth control in the
Council. It is curious that this episcopal commission was
actually called for by several Council Fathers during the
Third Session, but since the Pope had removed the question
of birth control from the jurisdiction of the Council, it was
not expedient to set it up then. The appointments are still
another sign that Pope Paul has every intention of consulting
his "brothers" the bishops more frequently in the future in
accordance with the doctrine of episcopal collegiality, as he
has so often proclaimed.

The return of the Roman Church to a spirit of poverty,
the elimination of an alien spirit of triumphalism, and the
ideal of a continual revitalization expressed in the maxim
"Ecclesia semper reformanda" all require time. The world
is no longer asking whether Pope Paul will emulate his mentor, Pope Pius XII, who once said with respect to liturgical
renewal, "I will move so far with the reform that a return
will be made impossible." It is now clear that he intends to
go farther and that the Council has merely laid the groundwork for more extensive long-range changes than the prophets
even dreamed of in 1959. But the important thing for him

and for the Church if this ideal is to be realized, is to keep doors open. Christ Himself, as we are told in the third chapter of the Book of the Apocalypse, laid down an eternal law: "Behold, I have caused doors to be opened before thee, which no one can shut."

Appendices

Opening Address of Pope Paul VI

SEPTEMBER 14, 1965

Venerable brothers, in the name of the Lord we are happy to proclaim the opening of the fourth session of the Second Vatican Council.

Let us give praise and thanks to God our Father Almighty, through Jesus Christ His Son and our Savior, in the Holy Spirit the Paraclete who animates and guides the Holy Church, for having happily brought us to the present final session of this Sacred Ecumenical Council. We come to it with a strong and common determination of loyalty to the Word of God, in a deep brotherly adhesion to the Catholic Faith. We meet for a free and fervent study of the manifold problems regarding our religion and particularly the nature and the mission of the Church of God. We unanimously desire to forge stronger bonds of union with those Christian brethren who are still separated from us. We mean to address to the world a heartfelt message of friendship and salvation. With humble and firm confidence we expect from the divine mercy all the graces which, though undeserved, are necessary to us for fulfilling our pastoral mission with loving and generous dedication.

This Council is indeed a great event. We are filled with joy by so solemn a celebration of the unity of the visible Church—a unity which we have experienced and professed in the sessions not only exteriorly but even more within our hearts, coming to know one another and carrying on an intense dialogue in prayer, reflection, discussion and final agreement. We are desirous and happy to reflect and promote that mystical unity which Christ left to His Apostles as the most precious and authentic heritage and as His supreme exhortation.

In this unique celebration—which evolves with a regular annual rhythm in this basilica consecrated to St. Peter, the visible foundation of the Church of Christ—the Catholic hierarchy has expressed, strengthened and illustrated the bonds which unite it in a loyal and unambiguous communion. Such a communion might seem impossible in view of the manifold diversity of our human origins and the implacable divisions which separate men from one another. Yet before our eyes and through our persons it is a happy reality, the mysterious actual Catholic reality.

We are reminded of the words of that eminent doctor, our ancient and holy predecessor, Leo the Great:

"When I see this distinguished gathering of so many of my fellow-priests, I have the impression that with so many saints we are in an assembly of angels."

Let the whole Church rejoice with us, her pastors and representatives, in the knowledge that by her assent she is gathered with us in a kind of spiritual harmony that not only pervades the entire Church, but even enraptures her, if only she be alert to such inspiration.

This Council is indeed a great event. The regular repetition of its sessions may weaken the sense of novelty in this historic meeting; yet we should not therefore be less aware of its extraordinary character. Rather the habituation produced by the succession of meetings should enable us better to explore its great, complex and mysterious significance. Let not this solemn hour pass by almost unnoticed, lost among the many ordinary events which constitute the warp and woof of our normal lives. This is a unique experience. Let us remember that we are not alone to meet here: with us is Christ in Whose name we are gathered (cf. Matt. 18, 20) and Whose assistance always accompanies us on our journey through time (cf. Matt. 28, 20).

The obligation of living this final phase of the Council with full application constitutes a responsibility which each one must weigh in his own conscience and which demands of each one certain moral and spiritual attitudes. It should not be irksome, venerable brothers, before entering upon the manifold and absorbing work that awaits us, to set aside a moment for reflection and to put ourselves in the dispositions most favorable for that mysterious conjunction of the divine and the human action which is necessary in a council. This conjunction is indeed always operative in the domain of grace, but it is so in a special form and measure when the future of the Church is being decided, as happens in the holding of a council. Here we can fully apply to ourselves the words of St. Paul: "For we are God's helpers" (1 Cor. 3, 9)— not indeed because we can presume to give efficacy to the work of God, but because we hope that our humble and willing effort may draw vigor and merit from the divine action.

This assembly, as we know, will have the privilege to use for its decisions the sacred and formidable formula used by the Apostles: "It has seemed good to the Holy Spirit and to us" (Acts 15, 28). We must therefore endeavor earnestly to bring it about that the action of the Holy Spirit may unite itself with ours, pervade, illumine, strengthen and sanctify it. And what kind of endeavor is called for, we also know. Seven times in the book of the Apocalypse (1, 7–3, 22) the message of the Apostle is enjoined on the pastors—called angels—of the primitive churches: "He who has ears to hear, let him hear what the Spirit says to the churches."

To listen, to hearken to the mysterious voice of the Paraclete, this must be our first duty during the coming days of the final session of the Council; to let the Holy Spirit infuse into our hearts that charity which expresses itself in wisdom, that is, in rectitude of judgment according to the highest norms of knowledge. By this wisdom the human mind reascends to God from Whom it has received this ineffable gift. Every one of its thoughts, every one of its actions becomes love, becomes charity. The charity that comes down from God becomes charity that rises up to God, and tends to return from man to God.

This development in charity ought to characterize the conclusion of our Ecumenical Council. Now more than ever before, we should be enabled to complete within ourselves this process of growth in charity in order to manifest the full meaning and importance of this juncture fraught with vital consequences for the life of the Church. From charity we should derive inspiration and orientation toward those truths which we intend here to clarify and toward those proposals which we wish here to set forth, truths and proposals which not only cannot fail to be expressions of charity, but which have already been proclaimed by this Council, the instrument of supreme pastoral authority which is exercised in the spirit of the deepest love. Therefore, in our search for truth, whether doctrinal or disciplinary, let love guide us and let us always remember the brilliant statement of St. Augustine: "Nothing good is perfectly known without being perfectly loved" (*De diversis quaest.*, 83).

It does not seem difficult to signalize our Ecumenical Council with the characteristics of an act of love, of a great threefold act of love for God, for the Church and for humanity.

1) Venerable brothers, let us first look at ourselves. How can one de-

scribe the situation in which we have been placed by the convocation of the Council? Is not that situation to be termed a state of tension, of spiritual struggle? The summoning of the Council has dislodged us from the torpor of ordinary life. It has reawakened in us the full consciousness of our vocation and of our mission. It has stirred hidden powers within us. It has kindled in our souls the spirit of prophecy which is proper to the Church of God. It has aroused in us a realization of our need, yes, of our duty to proclaim our Faith, to sing the praises of God, to bind ourselves to Christ, to announce to the world the mystery of revelation and of redemption.

Is this renewal anything less than love? Summoned to this Council, where one contemplates the contemporary world shrouded with the mists of doubt and with the shadows of irreligion, we seem to have stepped forth into the realm of the light of God. It seems that we, who are no more than the companions and brothers of the people among whom we live, have mounted to this spiritual vantage point, risen above the earth with its involvements and ruins, and attained a view of the clear warm light of the sun of life—and that life was the light of men (John 1, 4)—and even that we speak in spirit and in truth to God our Father with words that spring from a humble, filial and joyous soul, and that through our songs and tears we tell Him our praise of the greatness of His glory which has today become more evident to us because of advances in our knowledge of His cosmos. It seems that we thank Him for our good fortune in that He had revealed to us His name, His kingdom, and His will, and finally that we express to Him the world's burden of sorrow, of toil, of miseries and of spreading errors. But here more than ever we feel ourselves strengthened in the certainty which makes our hearts beat with peculiar strength, and which reminds us that we are the defenders of spiritual values, the guides of human destiny, the interpreters of genuine hopes. Is not this true love, which Sacred Scripture expresses so magnificently and so vividly: "We have believed in the love which God brings us" (I John 4, 16)?

In fact, this Council is being written into the history of the modern world as the most lofty, most illuminating and most humane affirmation of a religion which is ennobling, which was not invented by men but rather revealed by God, and which consists of the elevating relationship of love which our indescribable Father, through the mediation of His Son and our Brother, has established with the human race through the life-giving action of the Holy Spirit.

2) We come now to the second object of the love which should characterize the Council. From what has just been said, we must realize that we are not alone, that we are a people, the people of God, the Catholic Church, a unique society which is visible and spiritual at the same time. The Council makes us realize more clearly that our Church is society founded on the unity of Faith and on the universality of love.

The search for a perfect and higher form of social living constitutes the fundamental and seemingly insoluble problems of society, even if we consider merely the never-ending vicissitudes of Babylonia which are being so tragically repeated in our own times. But at least in its basic principles, this search has ended for us, even though, in point of fact, the search has been only virtually completed. We know that the solution which we possess cannot be proven false. That solution is the unity which binds us together and which we are proclaiming. It cannot be proven false, because it is based not on any norms that imply the deification either of the individual or of society, but rather on the unassailable religious principle of love, a love for men which is rooted not in their merits or our interests, but in the love of God.

Never before, from the earliest days when the Church "was of one mind and one heart" (Acts 4, 32), has the Church to the same degree affirmed, lived and enjoyed, prayed for and desired that real and spiritual unity which is given to her by Christ as in the holding of this present-day Council. In the confusion of contemporary events, in anticipation of more upheavals to come, in the midst of the repeated experience of disillusionment which follows upon never ending strife among men, caught up in the irresistible movement of all men toward unification, we had a need to verify experimentally the unity which makes of us all the family and temple of God, the Mystical Body of Christ. We needed to meet and know each other really as brothers, to exchange the kiss of peace, to love one another, in a word, as Christ loved us.

And our love here has already been and will be expressed in ways which characterize this Council in the history of today and of the future. These expressions will one day give an answer to the questions of whoever will try to define the Church in this decisive and critical moment of her existence. He will ask: What was the Catholic Church doing at that moment? The answer will be: She loved! She loved with a pastoral heart, as everyone knows, even if it is quite difficult to fully understand the depths and the riches of this love, a love which Christ called forth three times from the repentant and ardent heart of Simon Peter. (Do you remember? "Jesus said to Simon Peter: 'Simon, son of John, do you love me more than these?' He said to Him: 'Yes, Lord, you know that I love you.' He (Jesus) said to him: 'Feed my lambs' " (John 21, 15). Yes, the mandate, flowing from the love of Christ, to feed His flock still continues to exist and is the basis for the existence of this See, just as it continues through time and is the basis, venerable brothers, for the existence of each of your Sees. And today this mandate is affirmed with full awareness and new power. This is what the Council says: the Church is a society founded on love and governed by love. What they will say of the Church, of the Second Vatican Council is that she loved, loved with a heart filled with missionary zeal.

All know that this Holy Synod has summoned every good Catholic to be an apostle and has emphasized the universality of apostolic zeal, stressing that it must embrace all men, all races, all nations and all classes. Whenever universal love conquers the forces which persecute it or demands of a Catholic complete and heroic dedication, such love by this very reason has received its solemn expression. And may this always happen!

Yes, and the Church of the Second Vatican Council loved with an ecumenical heart, that is to say, with open liberality, humility and affection toward all Christian brothers who are still outside the perfect communion with our Holy, Catholic and Apostolic Church. If there has been a recurring and moving note in the deliberations of this Council, it is certainly the one regarding the great problem of reintegrating all Christians in the unity willed by Christ with all its difficulties and hopes. Is not this, venerable brothers and reverend and dear observers, a mark of charity?

3) Nor can this conciliar assembly, concentrated as it is on the name of Christ and of His Church and having therefore well-defined characteristics and objectives, be described as complacent, closed in, ignorant or unconcerned about the interests of others, of those innumerable masses of men who do not share our good fortune of being welcomed as we are, without any merit on our part, in this blessed kingdom of God which is the Church.

No, not at all. The love that animates our communion does not isolate us from men. It does not make us exclusivists or egotists. On the contrary, since love which comes from God gives men the sense of universal brotherhood, our truth urges us toward charity. Remember the warning of the Apostle: "Practicing the truth in love," we move on in our practice of the truth toward charity (Eph. 4, 15). And here in this assembly the expression of such a law of love has a sacred and serious name: responsibility. St. Paul would speak of urgency: "The love of Christ urges us" (2 Cor. 5, 14). We feel ourselves responsible toward the entire human family. We are under obligation to all (cf. Rom. 1, 14). The Church in this world is not an end in herself. She is at the service of all men. She must make Christ present to all, both to individuals and to peoples, as widely and as generously as possible. This is her mission. She is the bearer of love, the messenger of true peace. She re-echoes the words of Christ: "I came to cast fire upon the earth" (Luke 12, 49). This is something else the Church needed to become aware of and to declare. And the Council gave her the occasion to do so.

Can we indeed forget that here passes the centuries-long flow of salvation history, the earthly history of heavenly love? Shall we pass over the fact that this Council has given to the Church herself a fuller and deeper awareness of the reasons for her existence, the mysterious reasons of God "who loved the world" (John 3, 16), and of the reasons for her mission, a mission always rich and productive of the ferments of renewal and life for humanity?

The Council offers to the Church, especially to us, a panoramic view of the world. Can the Church, can we ourselves, do anything but look upon it and love it? (cf. Mark 10, 21). Such a contemplation will be one of the chief activities of the present session of the Council. Again, and above all, love; love toward all men of today whoever they are or wherever they are. While other currents of thought and action proclaim other principles for building up human civilization, such as power, wealth, science, struggle, self-interest and the like, the Church proclaims love. The Council is a solemn act of love for humanity. Christ is helping it in order that this may really be so.

At this point we are struck by a thought that seems to go counter to this gentle yet forceful expression of Christian and human sympathy of ours toward all persons and all people on earth. We know very well by bitter and ever recurrent experience that even love, and perhaps especially love, meets with and provokes indifference, opposition, contempt and hostility. There is no drama, no tragedy, comparable to the sacrifice of Christ who precisely because of His love and because of the hostility of others had to suffer the cross. The art of loving often transforms itself into the art of suffering. Will the Church, then, withdraw from her mission of love because of the risks and the difficulties involved?

Listen once more to the words of St. Paul: "Who then shall ever separate us from the love of Christ?" (Rom. 8, 35). Ponder the list of afflictions that he defiantly sets down to remind us that nothing can, that nothing should separate us from the love of God. And so this Council humbly begs of our Lord the grace to rejoice in being accounted worthy, like the first Apostles (cf. Acts 5, 41), to suffer reproach for the name of Jesus. And the Council begs this grace because although filled with goodwill toward all, it has to bear with grievous wrongs.

Not a few of those who ought to have taken their places with you, venerable brothers, have been unable to accept our invitation, because unjustly prevented from coming. This is an indication of the dire oppression which in not a few countries weighs upon the Catholic Church and with cold calculation aims at stifling and suppressing her. Our heart is grieved at the thought, for it reveals how far the world still remains from justice, liberty and love—that is to say, how far removed from true peace, to use the words of our venerated predecessor, John XXIII (cf. Encycl. *Pacem in terris*).

Faithful, however, to the spirit of this Council, our answer will be a twofold one of love. Our love goes out first of all to our brothers in their affliction. Oh, may the angels of God be the bearers of our greeting, of our remembrance and our affection. May the knowledge that their sufferings and their example bring honor to the Church of God be their consolation. Instead of giving way to grief, may they draw renewed hope from the common bonds of charity that unite her to them.

Toward those also who oppose Christ and His Church, who intimidate and restrict the liberty of those who believe in God, we wish to testify our love, that humble and unrivaled love taught us by the Divine Master: "Love your enemies and pray for those who persecute you" (Matt. 5, 44). This Council will indeed remain firm and unambiguous in matters dealing with right doctrine. Toward those, however, who by blind antireligious prejudice and unjustified opposition, cause her so much suffering, the Church, instead of condemning, will entertain feelings only of love. For them she will pray. Yes, and inspired with love, we will all pray that God show them that same mercy which we implore for ourselves.

For all of us, may it be love alone that prevails.

May peace among men triumph—that peace which is in these very days being wounded and is bleeding between peoples so sorely in need of peace! We cannot, not even in this moment, hide our most fervent wish that war may end, that mutual respect and concord may return among men and that peace may soon prevail and triumph always.

We have come now to the end of our address. The only purpose of our remarks has been to point out the significance of this last session of the Council and to give it renewed energy. As you see, venerable brothers, we have not touched on any of the themes that will be submitted to the examination of this assembly. Our silence has been deliberate. It is to be interpreted as a sign of our unwillingness to compromise by any words of ours your freedom of opinion with regard to the matters to be presented to you.

Nonetheless there are some matters we cannot pass over in silence.

The first is our gratitude toward all who have worked so assiduously on the commissions and subcommissions to improve the composition of the schemas soon to be discussed. Whatever be your final judgment on these schemas, the study, time and labor that have gone into their preparation deserve our admiration and grateful recognition.

In the second place, there is the announcement that we are happy to make to you of the setting up, in accordance with the wishes of the Council, of an episcopal synod composed of bishops to be chosen for the greater part by the episcopal conferences and approved by us, which will be convened, according to the needs of the Church, by the Roman pontiff, for consultation and collaboration when for the general good of the Church this will seem opportune to us. We consider it superfluous to add that this collaboration of the episcopate is meant to be of the greatest help to the Holy See and to the whole Church. And in a special way it can be of use in the day-to-day work of the Roman Curia to which we owe so much gratitude for its effective help. Just as the bishops in their dioceses, so we too always need a Curia for carrying out our apostolic responsibilities. Further details will be brought to the notice of this assembly as soon as possible. We did not wish to deprive ourselves of the honor and pleasure of making this announcement to you, in order to give you a further proof of our confidence and brotherly esteem. We are placing under the protection of Mary Most Holy this new proposal, which is full of such splendid possibilities.

The third matter is one of which you are already aware, namely the decision to accept the invitation extended to us to visit the New York headquarters of the United Nations Organization on the occasion of the 20th anniversary of the establishment of that worldwide body. And this we shall do, please God, during the present session of the Council, absenting ourselves briefly in order to bring with respectful homage to the representatives of the nations there assembled a message of peace. We should like to believe that our message will have your unanimous support. For our only intention is that through us may be heard your voices, which in obedience to and by virtue of the apostolic mission entrusted by Christ to you as well as to us, are raised in a plea for harmony, justice, brotherhood and peace among men of good will, among men beloved of God.

We desire to avail ourselves of this opportunity of extending to all of you who are gathered together from the East and from the West, the Fathers of this Council and our brothers, our respectful and heartfelt greetings. We wish to welcome the members of the diplomatic corps with particular sentiments of pleasure and esteem. We extend our welcome likewise to each of the observers, happy and honored at having them with us. We greet also our dear auditors, ladies as well as gentlemen, the periti and all those whose assistance contributes to the successful progress of the Council, with a special word for the press, radio and television. To all, our apostolic benediction.

Motu Proprio of Pope Paul VI Establishing a Synod of Bishops for the Universal Church

SEPTEMBER 15, 1965

Our apostolic concern whereby, carefully searching the signs of the times, we endeavor to adapt the principles and the methods of the sacred apostolate to the growing needs of the times and the changed conditions of society, impels Us to tighten the bonds of our union with the Bishops "whom the Holy Ghost has placed . . . to rule the Church of God" (Acts, 20, 28). To this we are inspired, not only by the reverence, esteem and gratitude which we rightly nurture for all our venerable brothers in the episcopate, but also by the very heavy charge of universal shepherd which has been laid upon us and whereby we have the duty to lead the People of God to everlasting pastures. In this day and age, disturbed and filled as it is with dangers and yet so open to the salutary inspirations of heavenly grace, we have learned from daily experience how helpful for our apostolic office is this union with the shepherds of the Church, a union which it is our intention to promote and encourage in every way lest, as we declared on another occasion "we be deprived of the consolation of their presence, the help of their prudence and their experience, the safeguard of their counsel and the assistance of their authority" (AAS, 1964, p. 1011).

Wherefore it was most fitting, especially during the sessions of the II Ecumenical Vatican Council, that we should be profoundly convinced of the importance and the necessity of a broader use of the assistance of the bishops for the welfare of the universal Church. Still more, the ecumenical Council provided us with the occasion for the project of setting up permanently a special body of bishops, to the end that, also after the end of the Council, there would continue to flow out upon the Christian people that vast abundance of benefits which happily resulted from our close collaboration with the bishops during the Council.

But now, with the II Ecumenical Vatican Council drawing to a close, we feel that the opportune moment has come to finally implement a new plan which has long been in mind, and this we do all the more willingly because we know that the bishops of the Catholic world are favorable to this plan, as is clear from the desires expressed by many bishops during the Council.

Therefore, after careful consideration, as an expression of our esteem and respect for all Catholic bishops, and in order to provide them with a clearer and more effective means of sharing in our solicitude for the universal Church, on our own initiative and by our apostolic authority, we erect and constitute in this city of Rome a body for the universal Church, directly and immediately subject to our authority to which we give the special name of synod of bishops.

This synod which, like all human institutions, can be still more perfected with the passage of time, will be governed by the following general norms:

I

The synod of bishops, whereby bishops chosen from various parts of the world lend their valuable assistance to the supreme pastor of the Church, is so constituted as to be: a) a central ecclesiastical institution; b) representing the complete Catholic episcopate; c) by its nature perpetual; d) as for its structure, performing its duties for a time and when called upon.

II

By its very nature it is the task of the synod of bishops to inform and give advice. It may also have deliberative power, when such power is conferred on it by the sovereign pontiff, who will in such cases confirm the decisions of the synod.

1. The general aims of the synod of bishops are: a) To encourage close union and valued assistance between the sovereign pontiff and the bishops of the entire world, b) To insure that direct and real information is provided on questions and situations touching upon the internal action of the Church and its necessary activity in the world of today,

c) To facilitate agreement on essential points of doctrine and on methods of procedure in the life of the Church.

2. The special and proximate ends of the synod of bishops are: a) To communicate useful information, b) To proffer advice on the topics proposed for discussion in the individual meetings of the synod.

III

The synod of bishops is directly and immediately subject to the authority of the Roman pontiff, to whom it consequently pertains:

1. To convoke the synod as often as he may deem it advisable, designating also the place of meeting.

2. To confirm the election of the members mentioned in articles VII and VIII.

3. To determine topics for discussion at least six months, if possible, before the date for the convening of the synod.

4. To decide on the dispatching of material to those who are to take part in the discussion.

5. To determine the agenda.

6. To preside over the synod either personally or through a representative.

IV

The synod of bishops can be convoked in general, extraordinary, or special meeting.

V

The synod of bishops convoked in general meeting consists first and per se of the following:

1. a) Patriarchs, major archbishops and metropolitans outside the patriarchates of the Catholic Churches of the Eastern rites; b) bishops elected by the individual national episcopal conferences, according to the provisions of article VIII; c) bishops elected by the national episcopal conferences of several nations, for those nations which do not have their own national conference, according to the provisions of article VIII; d) ten religious to represent clerical religious institutes, elected by the Roman Union of Superiors General.

2. The cardinals in charge of the dicasteries of the Roman Curia take part in the general meetings of the synod of bishops.

VI

The synod of bishops convoked in extraordinary session is composed of the following:

1. a) Patriarchs, major archbishops and metropolitans outside the

patriarchates of the Catholic Churches of the Eastern rites; b) The presidents of the national episcopal conferences; c) The presidents of the episcopal conferences of several nations which do not have their own individual conferences; d) Three religious representing clerical religious institutes, elected by the Roman Union of Superiors General.

2. The cardinals in charge of the dicasteries of the Roman Curia take part in the extraordinary meetings of the synod of bishops.

VII

The synod of bishops assembled in special meeting includes patriarchs, major archbishops and metropolitans outside the patriarchates of the Catholic Churches of the Eastern rites, as also the representatives both of the episcopal conferences of individual nations or of several nations, as well as the representatives of religious institutes, as stated in Nos. V and VIII. All these members, however, must belong to the regions for which the special meeting of the synod was convoked.

VIII

The bishops representing the national episcopal conferences are elected on the following basis: a) one for each national conference having no more than 25 members, b) two for each national episcopal conference having no more than 50 members, c) three for each national episcopal conference having no more than 100 members, d) four for each national episcopal conference having more than 100 members.

The episcopal conferences of several nations elect their representatives conformably to these same norms.

IX

In the election of those who will represent the episcopal conference of one or several nations and clerical religious institutes in the synod of bishops, special attention shall be paid not only to their learning and prudence in general, but also to their theoretical and especially their practical knowledge of the matters to be discussed in the synod.

X

If he so wishes, the sovereign pontiff may add to the members of the synod of bishops, adding either bishops or religious, to represent religious institutes, or, finally, ecclesiastical experts, up to 15% of the total membership mentioned in Nos. V and VIII.

XI

The conclusion of the session for which the synod of bishops was convoked entails the automatic cessation of both the personal membership of the synod and of the offices and functions filled by the individual members as such.

XII

The synod of bishops has a permanent or general secretary, who will be provided with an appropriate number of assistants. Besides, each individual synod of bishops has its own special secretary, who remains in office until the end of the said session.

Both the general secretary and the special secretaries are appointed by the sovereign pontiff.

These things we decree and establish, anything to the contrary notwithstanding.

Given at Rome, in St. Peter's, on the 15th day of September, in the year 1965, the third of our pontificate.

PAULUS PP. VI

Address of Pope Paul VI
To the United Nations General Assembly

OCTOBER 4, 1965

As we commence our address to this unique world audience, we wish to thank your Secretary General, U Thant, for the invitation that he extended to us to visit the United Nations, on the occasion of the 20th anniversary of the foundation of this world institution for peace and for collaboration between the peoples of the entire earth.

Our thanks also to the President of the General Assembly, Mr. Amintore Fanfani, who used such kind language in our regard from the very day of his election.

We thank all of you here present for your kind welcome, and we present to each one of you our deferential and sincere salutation. In friendship you have invited us and admitted us to this meeting; and it is as a friend that we are here today.

We express to you our cordial personal homage, and we bring you that of the entire Second Vatican Ecumenical Council now meeting in Rome and represented here by the eminent Cardinals who accompany us for this purpose.

In their name and in our own, to each and every one of you, honor and greeting!

This encounter, as you all understand, marks a simple and at the same time a great moment. It is simple, because you have before you a humble man, your brother; and among you all, representatives of sovereign states, the least-invested, if you wish to think of him thus, with a miniscule, as it were symbolic, temporal sovereignty, only as much as is necessary to be free to exercise his spiritual mission, and to assure all those who deal with him that he is independent of every other sovereignty of this world.

But he, who now addresses you, has no temporal power, nor any ambition to compete with you. In fact, we have nothing to ask for, no question to raise; we have only a desire to express and a permission to request: namely, that of serving you in so far as we can, with disinterest, with humility and love.

This is our first declaration. As you can see, it is so simple as to seem insignificant to this assembly, which always treats of most important and most difficult matters.

We said also, however, and all here today feel it, that this moment is also a great one. Great for us, great for you.

For us: you know well who we are. Whatever may be the opinion you have of the Pontiff of Rome, you know our mission. We are the bearer of a message for all mankind. And this we are, not only in our own personal name and in the name of the great Catholic family; but also in that of those Christian brethren who share the same sentiments that we express here, particularly of those who so kindly charged us explicitly to be their spokesman here. Like a messenger who, after a long journey, finally succeeds in delivering the letter that has been entrusted to him, we appreciate the good fortune of this moment, however brief, which fulfills a desire nourished in the heart for nearly 20 centuries.

For, as you will remember, we are very ancient; we here represent a long history; we here celebrate the epilogue of a wearying pilgrimage in search of a conversation with the entire world, ever since the command was given to us: go and bring the good news to all peoples. Now, you here represent all peoples. Allow us to tell you that we have a message, a happy message, to deliver to each one of you and to all.

1. We might call our message a ratification, a solemn moral ratification of this lofty institution. This message comes from our historical experience. As "an expert in humanity," we bring to this organization the suffrage of our recent predecessors, that of the entire Catholic Episcopate and our own, convinced as we are that this organization represents the obligatory path of modern civilization and of world peace. In saying this, we feel we are making our own the voice of the dead and of the living; of the dead, who fell in the terrible wars of the past; of the living who survived those wars, bearing in their hearts a condemnation of those who would try to renew wars; and also of those living who rise

up fresh and confident, the youth of the present generation, who legitimately dream of a better human race.

And we also make our own the voice of the poor, the disinherited, the suffering, of those who hunger and thirst for justice, for the dignity of life, for freedom, for well-being and progress. The peoples of the earth turn to the United Nations as the last hope of concord and peace; we presume to present here, with their tribute of honor and of hope, our own tribute also.

That is why this moment is great for you, also.

2. We feel that you are already aware of this. Hearken now to the continuation of our message. It becomes a message of good wishes for the future. The edifice that you have constructed must never fall; it must be perfected, and made equal to the needs that world history will present. You mark a stage in the development of mankind, from which retreat must never be admitted but, from which it is necessary that advance be made.

To the pluralism of states, which can no longer ignore one another, you offer an extremely simple and fruitful formula of coexistence. First of all, you recognize and distinguish the ones and the others. You do not confer existence upon states; but you qualify each single nation as fit to sit in the orderly congress of peoples.

That is, you grant recognition, of the highest ethical and juridical value, to each single sovereign national community, guaranteeing it an honoured international citizenship. This in itself is a great service to the cause of humanity, namely, to define clearly and to honour the national subjects of the world community, and to classify them in a juridical condition, worthy thereby of being recognized and respected by all, and from which there may derive an orderly and stable system of international life.

You give sanction to the great principle that the relations between peoples should be regulated by reason, by justice, by law, by negotiation; not by force, nor by violence, not by war, not by fear or by deceit. Thus it must be. Allow us to congratulate you for having had the wisdom to open this hall to the younger peoples, to those states that have recently attained independence and national freedom. This presence is the proof of the universality and magnanimity that inspire the principles of this institution.

Thus it must be. This is our praise and our good wish; and, as you can see, we do not attribute these as from outside; we derive them from inside, from the very genius of your institution.

3. Your Charter goes further than this, and our message advances with it. You exist and operate to unite the nations, to bind states together. Let us use this second formula: to bring the ones together with the others. You are an association. You are a bridge between peoples. You are a network of relations between states. We would almost say that your chief

characteristic is a reflection, as it were, in the temporal field, of what our Catholic Church aspires to be in the spiritual field: unique and universal. In the ideological construction of mankind, there is on the natural level nothing superior to this. Your vocation is to make brothers not only of some, but of all peoples. A difficult undertaking, indeed; but this is your most noble undertaking. Is there any one who does not see the necessity of coming thus progressively to the establishment of a world authority, able to act efficaciously on the juridical and political levels?

Once more we reiterate our good wish: advance always! We will go further, and say: strive to bring back among you any who have separated themselves, and study the right method of uniting to your pact of brotherhood, in honour and loyalty, those who do not yet share in it. Act so that those still outside will desire and merit the confidence of all; and then be generous in granting such confidence. You have the good fortune and the honour of sitting in this assembly of peaceful community; hear us as we say: ensure that the reciprocal trust that here unites you, and enables you to do good and great things, may never be undermined or betrayed.

4. The inherent logic of this wish, which might be considered to pertain to the very structure of your organization, leads us to complete it with other formulas. Thus, let no one, inasmuch as he is a member of your union, be superior to the others: never one above the other. This is the formula of equality. We are well aware that it must be completed by the evaluation of other factors besides simple membership in this institution; but equality, too, belong to its constitution. You are not equal, but here you make yourselves equal. For several among you, this may be an act of high virtue; allow us to say this to you, as the representative of a religion that accomplishes salvation through the humility of its divine founder. Men cannot be brothers if they are not humble. It is pride, no matter how legitimate it may seem to be, that provokes tension and struggles for prestige, for predominance, colonialism, egoism; that is, pride disrupts brotherhood.

5. And now our message reaches its highest point, which is, at first, a negative point. You are expecting us to utter this sentence, and we are well aware of its gravity and solemnity: not the ones against the others, never again, never more! It was principally for this purpose that the organization of the United Nations arose: against war, in favour of peace! Listen to the lucid words of the great departed John Kennedy, who proclaimed, four years ago: "Mankind must put an end to war, or war will put an end to mankind." Many words are not needed to proclaim this loftiest aim of your institution. It suffices to remember that the blood of millions of men, that numberless and unheard of sufferings, useless slaughter and frightful ruin, are the sanction of the pact that unites you, with an oath that must change the future history of the

world: no more war, war never again! Peace, it is peace that must guide the destinies of peoples and of all mankind.

Gratitude to you, glory to you, who for 20 years have laboured for peace, gratitude and glory to you for the conflicts that you have prevented or have brought to an end. The results of your efforts in recent days in favour of peace even if not yet proved decisive, are such as to deserve that we, presuming to interpret the sentiments of the whole world, express to you both praise and thanks.

Gentlemen, you have performed and you continue to perform a great work: the education of mankind in the ways of peace. The UN is the great school where that education is imparted, and we are today in the Assembly Hall of that school. Everyone taking his place here becomes a pupil and also a teacher in the art of building peace. When you leave this hall, the world looks upon you as the architects and constructors of peace.

Peace, as you know, is not built up only by means of politics, by the balance of forces and of interests. It is constructed with the mind, with ideas, with works of peace. You labor in this great construction. But you are still at the beginnings. Will the world ever succeed in changing that selfish and bellicose mentality which, up to now, has been interwoven in so much of its history? It is hard to foresee; but it is easy to affirm that it is toward that new history, a peaceful, truly human, history, as promised by God to men of good will, that we must resolutely march. The roads thereto are already well marked out for you; and the first is that of disarmament.

If you wish to be brothers, let the arms fall from your hands. One cannot love while holding offensive arms. Those armaments, especially those terrible arms, which modern science has given you, long before they produce victims and ruins, nourish bad feelings, create nightmares, distrust and sombre resolutions; they demand enormous expenditures; they obstruct projects of union and useful collaboration; they falsify the psychology of peoples. As long as man remains that weak, changeable and even wicked being that he often shows himself to be, defensive arms will, unfortunately, be necessary.

You, however, in your courage and valiance, are studying the ways of guaranteeing the security of international life, without having recourse to arms. This is a most noble aim, this the peoples expect of you, this must be obtained! Let unanimous trust in this institution grow, let its authority increase; and this aim, we believe, will be secured. Gratitude will be expressed to you by all peoples, relieved as they will then be from the crushing expenses of armaments and freed from the nightmare of an ever-imminent war.

We rejoice in the knowledge that many of you have considered favourably our invitation, addressed to all states in the cause of peace from Bombay, last December, to divert to the benefit of the developing countries at least a part of the savings that could be realized by reducing armaments. We here renew that invitation, trusting in your sentiments of humanity and generosity.

6. In so doing, we become aware that we are echoing another principle that is structural to the United Nations, which is its positive and affirmative high point; namely, that you work here not only to avert conflicts between states, but also to make them capable of working the ones for the others. You are not satisfied with facilitating mere coexistence between nations; you take a much greater step forward, one deserving of our praise and our support—you organize the brotherly collaboration of peoples. In this way a system of solidarity is set up, and its lofty civilized aims win the orderly and unanimous support of all the family of peoples for the common good and for the good of each individual. This aspect of the organization of the United Nations is the most beautiful; it is its most truly human visage; it is the ideal of which mankind dreams on its pilgrimage through time; it is the world's greatest hope; it is, we presume to say, the reflection of the loving and transcendent design of God for the progress of the human family on earth—a reflection in which we see the message of the gospel that is heavenly become earthly. Indeed, it seems to us that here we hear the echo of the voice of our predecessors, and particularly of that of Pope John XXIII, whose message of "Pacem in Terris" was so honourably and significantly received among you.

You proclaim here the fundamental rights and duties of man, his dignity, his freedom—and above all his religious freedom. We feel that you thus interpret the highest sphere of human wisdom and, we might add, its sacred character. For you deal here above all with human life; and the life of man is sacred; no one may dare offend it. Respect for life, even with regard to the great problem of birth, must find here in your assembly its highest affirmation and its most reasoned defense. You must strive to multiply bread so that it suffices for the tables of mankind, and not rather favour an artificial control of birth, which would be irrational, in order to diminish the number of guests at the banquet of life.

It does not suffice, however, to feed the hungry; it is necessary also to assure to each man a life confirmed to this dignity. This, too, you strive to perform. We may consider this the fulfillment before our very eyes, and by your efforts, of that prophetical announcement so applicable to your institution: "They will melt down their swords into ploughshares, their spears into pruning-forks" [IS. II, 4]. Are you not using the prodigious energies of the earth and the magnificent inventions of science, no longer as instruments of death but as tools of life for humanity's new era?

We know how intense and ever more efficacious are the efforts of the United Nations and its dependent world agencies to assist those governments who need help to hasten their economic and social progress.

We know how ardently you labor to overcome illiteracy and to spread good culture throughout the world; to give men adequate modern medical assistance; to employ in man's service the marvelous resources of science, of technique and of organization—all of this is magnificent, and merits the praise and support of all, including our own.

We ourself wish to give the good example, even though the smallness of our means is inadequate to the practical and quantitative needs. We intend to intensify the development of our charitable institutions to combat world hunger and fulfill world needs. It is thus, and in no other way, that peace can be built up.

7. One more word, gentlemen, our final word: this edifice that you are constructing does not rest upon merely material and earthly foundations, for thus it would be a house built upon sand; above all, it is based on our own consciences. The hour has struck for our "conversion," for personal transformation, for interior renewal. We must get used to thinking of man in a new way; and in a new way also of man's life in common; with a new manner, too, of conceiving the paths of history and the destiny of the world, according to the words of Saint Paul: "You must be clothed in the new self, which is created in God's image, justified and sanctified through the truth" (Eph. 4, 23). The hour has struck for a halt, a moment of recollection, of reflection, almost of prayer. A moment to think anew of our common origin, our history, our common destiny. Today as never before, in our era so marked by human progress, there is need for an appeal to the moral conscience of man. For the danger comes, not from progress, nor from science—indeed, if properly utilized, these could rather resolve many of the grave problems that assail mankind. No, real danger comes from man himself, wielding ever more powerful arms, which can be employed equally well for destruction or for the loftiest conquests.

In a word, then, the edifice of modern civilization must be built upon spiritual principles, which alone can not only support it but even illuminate and animate it. To do this, such indispensable principles of superior wisdom cannot but be founded so, as you are aware, we believe upon faith in God. That unknown God of whom Saint Paul spoke to the Athenians in the Aeropagus. Unknown by them, although without realizing it they sought Him and He was close to them, as happens also to many men of our times. To us, in any case, and to all those who accept the ineffable revelation that Christ has given us of Him. He is the living God, the Father of all men.

Address of the Pope

You have just heard, venerable brothers and very dear sons, the words of the Apostle treating of the work of Christ our Lord who, from the heights of heaven continues His work in the Church, a work which is not merely one of the preservation of what He Himself accomplished during His temporal life on earth, but is also one of building up, that is to say of progress and of growth. This He proclaimed Himself in a well-known incident in the Gospel when He described Himself as the artisan of the organic and consistent development of the edifice founded by Himself on the rock which He had chosen and made capable of holding up such a great weight: "I shall build my Church" (Mt. 16, 18). In fact, in the passage to the Ephesians which has just been read for our meditation, St. Paul expresses himself thus: "To some Christ has granted to be apostles, to others to be prophets, to still others to announce the Gospel, to others to be shepherds and teachers; and all this in view of the building up of Christians and the good fulfilment of the ministry. Thus the building up of the Pod of Christ will continue unto the day when we shall all reach the age of perfect men, unto the measure of the fullness of the age of Christ" (Eph. 4, 11-13). This reality, divine in its source and human in its historic and experimental nature, can still be attained with our spiritual senses today, provided that they be open to such a prodigy. We can make our own the messianic words spoken by Jesus: "Today is this Scripture accomplished in your ears" (Luke 4, 21).

In fact, what is taking place here today in this basilica? You already know. In the course of this holy Council, which is a guide and synthesis of the holy Church of God, after careful examination and with the assistance of unceasing prayer, there will be promulgated four decrees touching on the life of the Church itself, namely, the pastoral ministry of bishops, the religious life, priestly formation, and Christian education. To these solemn laws will be added a declaration which is no less solemn, on the relationships between the Catholic Church and those who profess other religions. There is no need for us to explain to you the content of these documents—with which you are all already acquainted—nor to stress the importance and the repercussions which they will have throughout the world and for the future, nor the consequences which we hope will be salutary for souls and for the life of the Church of tomorrow, because each one of you has already been able to appreciate the admirable aspects of these acts. We shall say only that it will be extremely profitable for our ministry if we will, even after their promulgation, consider anew and with calm these decisions which in the highest and most responsible exercise of its authority and certainly under the inspiration of the Holy Spirit it draws from the bosom of its interior wisdom, sets before itself as conquests of its loving and laborious concern and determines for itself as a new obligation, which does not place upon it a new burden but which rather supports it, elevates it and confers upon it that fullness, that certainty and that joy to which we can give no other name than that of life.

The Church lives! And here is the proof: here we have its breath, its breath, its song. The Church lives!

Is it not for this, venerable brothers, that you have come in answer to the convocation of this ecumenical Council? To feel the life of the Church or, still more appropriately, to make it live more intensely, to discover, not the years of its old age, but rather the youthful energy if its lasting vitality, to establish a new relationship between time which passes—and which today carries everything along with it in the changes which it provokes and presents—and the work of Christ, the Church. There is no question of proceeding to a historical re-constitution, nor to a reduction to the metamorphoses of profane culture, of the nature of the Church which is always the same and faithful to itself, such as Christ wanted it and as authentic tradition perfects it. The question is rather to enable the Church more capable of developing its mission of good in the renewed conditions of human society. This is why you have come, and these concluding acts of the Council are providing you with an experience of this: the Church lives. The Church is thinking, the Church is speaking, the Church is growing, the Church is building itself up.

We must enjoy this astonishing phenomenon. We must experience its messianic aspect. It is from Christ that the Church comes and to Christ that it goes, and here are its steps, that is to say, the acts whereby it perfects itself, and strengthens, develops, renews and sanctifies itself. If we look at it carefully, all this effort at perfecting the Church is nothing else but an expression of love for Christ our Lord, that Christ who arouses within the Church the exigency to feel itself faithful, to keep itself authentic and coherent, living and fruitful, the Christ who calls it and guides it toward Himself, its Divine Spouse. This movement has its cause precisely in the apostolic character of the Church: that function with which Christ endowed His mystical and social body and which brings into evidence and effectiveness an apostolic and pastoral hierarchy, which draws its words, its grace and its power from the Lord Himself, preserves, perpetuates, transmits, exercises and develops them, thus rendering the People of God internally living and holy and externally visible, that is to say social and historical.

We are engaged in celebrating one of the fullest and most significant moments of this apostolicity. We must feel ourselves clothed with it, certainly not in order to attribute the merit of it to our persons, but in order to make the glory of these acts redound toward Christ, for it is in His Name and in the power of the Holy Spirit which He infuses into us that we accomplish what we are doing so that, as humble ministers and mediators that we are, we may cause to descend upon the great family of God and the Holy Church, the constructive growth prepared for its building-up which is a constant reality.

It is a pleasure for us that this is taking place on the feast of the Holy Apostles Simon and Jude, those apostles to whom the Lord did the honor of consecrating one of the words which we have just heard in the reading of the Gospel. This is not a word which promises happiness and satisfaction in the apostolic mission but which announces rather the difficulties and the sufferings of those who live it.

We are also pleased that this should be happening on the anniversary day of the election of our venerated predecessor, Pope John XXIII, to whose inspiration is due the convocation of the Council.

Lastly, we are happy to have around us, concelebrating at this apostolic altar, bishops who are dear to us and who represents countries where liberty—to which the Gospel has a supreme right—is restricted, if not refused, and where certain of their number are witnesses of the sufferings which Christ foretold to His Apostles. To these bishops, to the Churches whose passion they recall, to the countries which their presence makes us love all the more, we send the expression of our solidarity, our charity, and our prayers for better days.

We likewise address an affectionate greeting to our brothers the bishops who are assisting us and who come from nations where peace is troubled by so many tears, by blood and by ruins, and where there is the threat of new sufferings. We pray that order and justice, concord and veritable peace may be happily restored in their countries.

In the same way, to all of you, very dear brothers in Christ, apostles and shepherds in His name, heralds of the Gospel and builders of His Church, who are assisting at this concelebration or taking part in it, there is added the assurance of our charity and an invitation to persevere with us with one sole heart and soul, encouraged by the new conciliar decrees to build up the Church of God.

May the Lord deign—the Lord who is mystically present in our midst and who before long will be sacramentally present—to grant strength and holiness to our apostolic and pastoral charge, for the welfare and happiness of the universal community of the clergy, of religious and of the faithful, as a new manifestation of charity, for this is in fact the goal set by Christ for the hierarchical ministry.

May our Christian brethren, still separated from the full communion of the Catholic Church, wish to contemplate this new manifestation of its renovated face. May such contemplation come also from the followers of other religions and, among them, those whom one same relationship in Abraham unites, especially the Israelites, objects certainly not of reprobation or distrust, but of respect, love and hope.

The Church is progressing in fact in the firmness of truth and faith, in the development of justice and charity. Such is the very life of the Church.

Apostolic Exhortation of the Pope

NOVEMBER 4, 1965

✠

The final Session of the Second Ecumenical Vatican Council is now drawing to a close. This vast assembly, brought together four years ago at the tomb of St. Peter the Apostle to find an answer to the expectations, the desires and the more serious and urgent needs of the Christian people, will shortly be dispersed. You the, venerable brethren, will be returning to your sees after your long and fruitful labors, with hearts filled with justifiable satisfaction at having prepared the providential instruments for the true renewal of the Church, for Christian unity and the pacification and elevation of the temporal order.

While the Ecumenical Council which has already completed its task seems about to release a new and abundant outpouring of spiritual life within the Church and in the world, We cannot fail to address a paternal appeal to the faithful to raise up their voices to God in more frequent and fervent prayers. We desire, venerable brethren, that the fervor of prayer to which we have exhorted the sons of the Church on several occasions during the conciliar proceedings should not diminish after the end of the Council itself, but that it be further intensified, so that the entire Church at this time and in every part of the world may be united in fervent prayer with the successors of Peter and the Apostles, as were the first Apostles gathered around Mary the mother of Jesus and of all men in the Cenacle, to implore a new Pentecost which, by virtue of the Holy Ghost, may renew the face of Christ's bride and of society.

Above all, let gratitude be expressed to Almighty God who throughout the Council proceedings has never ceased to assist the ecumenical sessions with His help and heavenly guidance. Indeed, if we consider the enormous amount of work accomplished so far by the Council, we are amazed to see both the numerous points of doctrine expounded by this extraordinary teaching authority of the Church as well as its wise disciplinary rulings which, true to ecclesiastical tradition, give new scope for the work of the Church and will no doubt be remarkably salutary for the welfare of souls.

If we then turn our attention to the echoes aroused in public opinion by the conciliar proceedings, the fact that the Council has awakened such enormous interest in the world is no secondary source of joy. Indeed, the problems and teachings of the Church in our times seem to bear immeasurable weight with all men of good will who, with open hearts, are seeking the truth and endeavoring to contribute to the true welfare of mankind. This affords the Church an opportunity of establishing a fruitful dialogue with the world, that is to say with men and peoples of all religions and civilizations, in order to contribute towards the defence of human values and to a more suitable solution of human problems in the light of the Gospel message.

It may truly be said that the Catholic Church has appeared before all peoples bathed in resplendent light, like the city on the hilltop, the unvanquished guardian of divine truths and human dignity. Nor is it difficult to foresee new developments of the Faith in the future, that is to say, when the people of God will have entered more fully into the atmosphere of spiritual renewal created by the Council within the Church.

All this, while it brings comfort to those who have been the instruments of this effusion of God's manifold grace in the hearts of men, causes us to recognize our urgent duty of making all possible efforts to prevent any impediment in the path of the mighty flow of heavenly grace that is today bringing happiness to the city of God, and any diminution of this present vital impulse in the life of the Church.

This might come about if, after the end of the Council's discussion and decision phase, the apostolic efforts of sacred pastors should be relaxed and if their attention to the responsibilities incumbent upon them during the post-Council period should prove to be insufficiently alert. In fact, the successful results of the Council and its salutary effects on the life of the Church will depend not so much on the multiplicity of rules as on thoroughness and zeal in putting into practice, in the years to come, the decisions which have emanated from the assembly. This means that it will be necessary above all to prepare the hearts of the faithful to accept the new rulings; shaking the apathy of those who are too reluctant to adapt themselves to the new order and restraining the excessive zeal of others who exaggerate in the indulgence of personal initiative and might thus jeopardize the sound renewal that has been undertaken; keeping the innovations within the limits prescribed by lawful authority; and instilling into all the spirit of faith in their sacred pastors and that complete obedience which is at once an expression of true love of the Church and an infallible guarantee of unity and complete success.

These few remarks, venerable brothers, are sufficient to reveal to you the gravity and importance of the duty that awaits you from now on. You must now undertake a task of immense responsibility that undoubtedly demands prudence, perseverence and perspicacity of decision; but no less does it demand the ready and generous cooperation of the entire Christian flock entrusted to each one of you, for the ecumenical Council requires the cooperation of all since it concerns the spiritual life of all the Church's children.

In this common effort, there is no doubt that, before all, our dearly beloved priests, and particularly those who have the care of souls, will be of help to their pastors. The ecumenical Council, having issued wise norms in their regard, has offered them an incomparable instrument for a worthier and more effective exercise of their priestly duties. They should therefore welcome this instrument with goodwill and make use of it, moved by stronger resolutions to achieve sanctity and perform the duties of their sacred ministry diligently and generously. From our own pastoral experience we are well aware how many of Christ's workers, all truly worthy, are active in the fields of the Lord and making them fertile with their sweat. We are not unaware, moreover, of the difficulties and sacrifices in the lives of many of these, who often live in solitude and poverty, surrounded by the hostility of men. Let these sons, so dear to us, be assured that the thoughts of the vicar of Christ are ever with them and that he unceasingly prays to God on their behalf. Their sufferings, for the most part hidden, may perhaps pass unnoticed by men, but certainly not by God Who is preparing for them in heaven a just reward for their labors.

Our thoughts also turn with particular confidence to the invaluable contribution that all religious families will bring to this venture. In fact, the Church derives a great part of her vigor, her apostolic zeal and her ardor of sanctity from flourishing religious life. Today, as never before, the Church has need of the public and social testimony offered by religious life as well as of the help it can afford the diocesan clergy in the exercise of the apostolate. May the example of those who have actually given up the world—in this way clearly proving that the Kingdom of God is not of this world—therefore shine ever more brightly and may the apostolic spirit which animates them not be confined within the boundaries of their own communities but reach out to all the spiritual needs which mark, alas, this present epoch.

Finally, we place great confidence in the laity engaged in the apostolate, whom we regard with paternal affection. That the ecumenical Council has wished to give special attention to their condition and has exhaustively described their role and duties within the Church demonstrates sufficiently and clearly the important responsibilities that are now to be attributed to the laity. In point of fact, the pastoral work of priests cannot fully achieve its purposes if it be not accompanied by action on the part of the laity, whose duty it is to provide help for the Church in the exercise of the sacred ministry, to cooperate willingly in the work of the priest wherever there is a dearth of clergy and also to devise new methods whereby the Church may more adequately and effectively transmit the message of salvation to the men of our time. We therefore exhort these sons of ours, with paternal affection, to show themselves equal to the demands of this great hour of the ecumenical Council and willingly to fulfill the hopes and expectations with which the Church is looking to them.

Venerable brothers, we are happily confident that your sons in Christ, in the same way in which they have so far shared your concern for the outcome of the ecumenical Council, by praying with you, fearing with you, hoping with you and exulting with you, will now give you cause for deepest satisfaction by their generous resolutions to offer their cooperation when you return to your Sees. In fact we sincerely hope that on your return home there will be no lack of public ceremonies in your honor and suitable demonstrations of appreciation. Such manifestations are called for by the great undertaking that you have completed with us, with the greatest prudence, wisdom and concern. Those who, like yourselves, have opened up new prospects for the Church and most authoritatively pointed out to men the path of human dignity, brotherly love, unity and peace are fully deserving of such a tribute.

Thanks to you, a great hope has sprung up in the Church and in the world: blessed be those who cooperate with you to encourage, strengthen and completely fulfil it.

You are well aware, venerable brothers, of the inadequacy of human strength for the arduous and serious task that you must undertake after the Council. Therefore, the application of the conciliar decisions will not bear the desired fruit for the Church unless your efforts are supported by the help of the Divine Savior who said: "Without Me you can do nothing" and unless the action of the Holy Spirit still continues to penetrate, enlighten and invigorate the hearts of the sacred pastors.

Prayer, therefore—which is like the breath of the Church—and particularly prayer addressed to the Holy Spirit who guides the steps of Christ's followers, constitutes the very first duty during this last phase of the Council. This is the source from which the faithful must draw supernatural energy which will enable them to continue on the way full of hope which has already been opened up before them; to comply in full agreement with the decisions of the Church, who now more than ever before wishes to see her sons docile in obedience, ready in action and brave, if need be, in sacrifice; and to pray God, finally, for a numerous company of saints who, like St. Charles Borromeo, shall be an example and an encouragement to Christians in the faithful implementation of the conciliar decrees, since it is from such men that we must expect the true renewal of the Church so ardently desired by the Council.

For this purpose, venerable brethren, we ordain that before the conclusion of the ecumenical Council a triduum of solemn prayer be announced in all the dioceses of the Catholic world, in the parishes and religious communities. These prayers, which will be offered during the coming novena of the Immaculate Conception, will have the purpose not only of rendering to God the thanks due to him and begging for new help from heaven, but will also afford an opportunity of instructing the faithful in their new duties and of exhorting them, so that, by joining their efforts to your works, they may promptly put into the practice of private and public Christian life the salutary decrees of the ecumenical Council.

Finally, venerable brethren, may we be allowed to express the following wish: namely, that you yourselves arrange to send out to your faithful from this city the necessary invitations and exhortations to prayer, so that on the same day and at the same hour in which the ecumenical Council is being solemnly concluded in Saint Peter's Basilica, the entire Catholic family throughout the world, in fervent prayer, will be united in voice and spirit with the vicar of Christ and with its own pastors.

Sustained by this hope, in expectation of heavenly favors and as a token of our benevolence, to all of you, venerable brethren, to the clergy and the people entrusted to your care, we impart from our heart, in the Lord, the apostolic blessing.

Given in Rome, at Saint Peter's, on November 4th, feast of Saint Charles Borromeo, in the year 1965, the third of our pontificate.

PAULUS PP. VI

Address of the Pope

This public meeting of our Vatican Ecumenical Council is taking place less than three weeks before the end of the council itself. For this reason, in addition to the expected promulgation of important acts of the council, it offers us an opportunity of speaking with you on some practical points involved in the termination of that great event in the life of the Church which we have observed at regular intervals over four periods of intensive work.

We shall not speak on this occasion about the extraordinary value—religious, doctrinal, spiritual, pastoral or historical—of this council, nor about the mystery of wisdom and grace that it offers, and will long continue to offer, for our meditation. Neither will we speak about the new developments set in motion by the council's deliberation, whether they concern the Church herself or her relations with persons and institutions around her. These are all matters that we all carry in our minds as fruitful subjects for thought and action. We have already made some mention of them in previous discourses, most recently in our apostolic exhortation of Nov. 4.

We are not making an estimate of the council on this occasion: let it suffice for us to note at most the good order, freedom and harmony with which it has developed at every stage, and how your presence and participation have made this development an impressive one, fruitful by your labors and beneficial beyond all doubt.

No other council in God's Church has been held on such a scale, or has been accompanied by work done in greater earnest and greater tranquility. No other council has treated topics of greater variety or of wider interest: the Church's own life; our Christian brothers still separated from communion with her; non-Christian religions, or humanity as a whole which in this very council we have come to know better in the complex and formidable problems besetting it, and have come to love more strongly in order to promote its well being; peace and salvation. May God be praised, He alone, God our Father, all-high and all-good, through Jesus Christ, our sole, most loving Lord, in the Holy Spirit, the gentle Paraclete, who by His love nourishes, guides and strengthens us. May God be praised.

Let it suffice now to direct our thoughts to a few consequences that we said were related to the ending of the ecumenical council. This ending is rather a beginning for many projects, the establishment of organizations to collaborate with us in laying down the norms desired by the decrees of the council. It is our intention to proceed as soon as possible to establish them, since we are resolved to put into speedy execution the holy deliberations of this ecumenical synod.

We have already set up three post-conciliar commissions: one for the sacred liturgy, a second for the revision of the Code of Canon Law, and a third which is already endeavouring to implement the provisions of the decree on communications.

We have not waited for the approval of the schema on the pastoral duty of bishops in the Church in order to grant in full the request contained in it. Instead, we have already announced the institution of the episcopal synod which, God willing, we hope to convoke for the first time, if not next year, which will be entirely taken up by other post-conciliar concerns, at least in 1967, when we shall have to commemorate in a suitable manner the centenary of the martyrdom of the Apostle Peter, an observance which was already instituted in the last century by our predecessor of revered memory, Pius IX.

In the same way also we shall be eager to institute, as early as possible, the commissions which the council has voted to set up in order to complete the norms of the conciliar decrees or to carry out the special projects connected with their application (Cf. Decree on the Pastoral Duty of Bishops, n. 44). New offices will be opened for those new services which may be rendered necessary by the statutes of the council and by the demands of the renewal of the Church.

On our part we shall not be wanting in the will to bring to a happy conclusion the unfinished business resulting from the celebration of the ecumenical synod and to carry out the activities initiated by it, like those of the three secretariats now doing excellent work, namely, the one which is fostering the unification of all Christians in the same church, the second which is promoting relations with non-Christian religions, and the third entrusted with the study and care of non-believers. May the Lord sustain our will and grant us the strength and means to fulfill these new obligations.

This, however, venerable brothers, will take some time. In any case please do not interpret this as a lack of fidelity to the proposals which we are going to announce, if these and other developments of the central offices of Church government take place with reasonable gradualness and if they are so studied and carried out as to avoid the encumbrances of bureaucracy and useless financial burdens.

We do not want to form a new and artificial hierarchical concentration. But we want to involve the episcopate in the task of applying the conciliar regulations. As far as possible we want also to make use of the collaboration of the episcopate so as to fulfill better our apostolic duty of governing the Universal Church. The newly recognized power of episcopal conferences is an important fact in the organic growth of canon law, and as we have readily welcomed and promoted it, so too we hope it will confer a salutary and respected blessing on Holy Church in the various nations and regions and, far from dividing or separating among them the visible members of the Mystical Body of Christ, may it strongly unite them in harmonious and fraternal unity. This we will promote; and the central offices of ecclesiastical government, and foremost among these, the Roman Curia, will be of effective assistance to us and at the same time of valuable service to the whole structure of the Church.

With regard to the Roman Curia, permit us, at the conclusion of this great proof of the spiritual and organizational resources of the Catholic Church, to commend this body to your generous recognition. If the Catholic Church finds herself today in that state of well being in which, by God's grace, we can see her to be, she owes it in good measure to the services of this industrious and faithful instrument of the apostolic office. It would be wrong to consider it antiquated or inefficient, selfish or corrupt; we are bound to bear testimony to its efficient service. By the constant mercy of God the defects imputed in other times to this human organization which surrounds and serves the Roman pontiffs, no longer exist today. On the contrary, a religious spirit and a true love for Jesus Christ, fidelity and obedience, zeal for the Church and readiness to favor progress, are happily the guiding principles of the Roman Curia, rendering it well fitted for its important function and entitling it to the confidence of the whole Church.

We do not hereby intend to exclude the possibility that the Roman

Curia may need improving. Everything human, everything that is temporal can easily be weak and imperfect. Moreover, the higher a man's office and the greater the demands his task imposes on his moral integrity and Christian holiness, the more manifest and lamentable his shortcomings appear. We ourselves are the first to recognize this fact, and we have taken measures to ensure that the Roman Curia will be appropriately reorganized, in accordance with paragraph 9 of the recent Decree on the Pastoral Office of Bishops in the Church. We will likewise be the first to see to it that the genuine spirit of Jesus Christ penetrates and animates to an ever higher degree all those who have the honor of belonging to this body.

We can assure you, venerable brothers, that we have not been idle in this matter in recent times, although overburdened with so many other cares. The studies undertaken with a view to the reform of the Roman Curia have been advanced and have made good progress. We can say at once that apart from the replacement of personnel, there is no great necessity for structural changes. On the other hand, there is need for not a few reforms, for some simplifications and other improvements. The criteria that should animate this body will be determined and formulated with greater clarity. The desired transformation will seem slow and partial. But it cannot be otherwise if due respect is to be had for persons and traditions. But come this transformation surely will.

However, in order to give some tangible proof of our words, we can announce that within a short time a new statute will be published to legislate for the principal sacred congregation, that of the Holy Office.

But, venerable brothers, we must turn our minds not only to these necessary reforms, but also to that moral and spiritual renewal which is to make us more like our Divine Master and better prepared to carry out the duties of our respective vocations. It is to this that we must pay special attention: to our genuine sanctification and to our effectiveness in spreading among the men of our time the message of the Gospel.

Now it seems to us extremely important that we should consider what our attitude should be in the time after the council. The feelings aroused by the holding of the council passed, in our opinion, through three successive stages. The first of these was marked by enthusiasm; and it was only right that it should have been so. Wonder, joy and hope, and an almost messianic vision greeted the announcement of the long-awaited and yet unexpected council; a breath of spring at first passed over the minds of all.

The second stage followed, that of the actual development of the council, and was characterized by confrontation with problems. Such a stage was a necessary accompaniment of the work of the council which, as you are well aware, was truly immense, to the special credit of the members of the commissions and subcommissions. In these the work of the council "periti" (experts), and of certain ones in particular, was most exacting and profoundly wise. To accord them some public recognition, it was our wish that some of their number should be associated with us today in the celebration of the Divine Sacrifice.

In this second stage, however, in some sectors of public opinion, everything seemed open to discussion and was in fact discussed. Everything was seen as complex and difficult. An attempt was made to subject everything to criticism, with impatience for novelty. There was uneasiness, and currents of opinion made themselves felt. It was a time of fears, of the audacious and arbitrary. Here and there, doubts were cast, even on the canons of truth and authority, until the voice of the council began to make itself heard: a voice that was calm, deliberate and solemn.

And in this last phase of the council its weighty and encouraging words will say what form the life of the Church should take. So there comes the third stage: that of ideas and plans, of acceptance and execution of the conciliar decrees.

And this is the period for which each one must dispose himself. Discussion is coming to an end, and understanding is beginning. The disturbance wrought by ploughing a field is followed by the well ordered labors of cultivation. The Church is settling down with the new norms she has received from the council. Fidelity is their characteristic. In these norms there is a new element, that of increased awareness of the ecclesial communion, of her marvelous structure, of the greater charity which should unify, vivify and sanctify the hierarchical communion of the Church.

This is the period of the true "aggiornamento" proclaimed by our predecessor of venerable memory, John XXIII. This word, which described his goal, certainly did not have the meaning for him which some try to give it, as if it allowed for the "relativization," according to the spirit of the world, of everything in the Church—dogmas, laws, structures, traditions. His sense of the doctrinal and structural stability of the Church was so vital and strong that it was the basis and foundation of his thought and of his work. From now on "aggiornamento" will signify for us a wisely undertaken quest for a deeper understanding of the spirit of the past council and the faithful application of the norms it has happily and prayerfully provided.

We think that it is along these lines that the new psychology of the Church must develop: clergy and faithful will find a magnificent spiritual work to be done for the renewal of life and action according to Christ our Lord. We invite our brothers and our sons to this work: may those who love Christ and the Church be with us in a clearer profession of the meaning of the truth which is proper to the doctrinal tradition begun by Christ and the Apostles. May they be with us in our profession of the meaning of ecclesiastical discipline and of the deep and sincere union which gives us all confidence and a sense of solidarity as members of one body.

And in order that we may all be strengthened in this spiritual renovation, we propose to the Church to recall with devotion the words and the examples of our last two predecessors, Pius XII and John XXIII, to whom the Church herself and the world owe so much. And we are arranging that to this end there be canonically begun the processes of beatification of these holy and eminent supreme pontiffs who are so dear to us. This will be an answer to the desire that has been expressed by innumerable voices in favor of each of these popes. In this way history will be assured the patrimony of their spiritual legacy. Thus it will be ensured that for no motive other than the cult of true holiness—which is the glory of God and the edification of His Church—will the authentic image of these well beloved figures be preserved for our veneration and for that of succeeding generations. The procedure cannot, obviously, be rapid; but it will be carried out with constancy and care. May God grant that it lead us where even now we hope to arrive.

The imminent conclusion of the council would naturally make us think of summing up the benefits which it has already brought to fruition. In the field of doctrine, the council has bequeathed to the Church splendid documents, rich resources for speculative and practical progress. In the field of charity, the council has brought all of us together here, even from the ends of the earth, that we might know one another, that we might pray, study, and deliberate together, that in union we might profess our loyalty to Christ and to His Gospel, and that we might increase our ability to love—to love one another, to love our separated brethren, to love the poor and suffering, to love the pensive, toiling world, to love the whole of humanity. But time does not permit so sweeping a synthesis. All of us will have other occasions for such a broad study; our successors will also have their chance.

For the present, let us conclude simply by expressing our plan, a plan which would serve as a spur to enshrine forever the memory of the council. Our proposal is to erect in Rome, in a location dictated by pastoral needs, a new church which will be dedicated to Mary Most Holy, Mother of the Church, whose daughter she is, the daughter first in time, in privilege, and in blessings.

Secondly, we announce our intention of declaring a special jubilee for the entire Church lasting from the closing of the council until next Pentecost. The purpose of the jubilee will be to afford preachers the opportunity to spread the message of truth and of charity, the message proclaimed by the council itself, and to stimulate in the faithful their sense of union around the pastors of their own dioceses. We encourage all to enjoy and to take advantage of "the ministry of reconciliation" (2 Cor. 5, 18) which every man of good will can see opened and offered to him in the most liberal manner possible. As soon as it can be done, information and norms regarding the jubilee will be published.

And now it is time for us to conclude our discourse, to bring to a close the solemn meeting which we celebrate today, and to thank all of you for your attendance and participation in these sacred ceremonies which are both weighty and wondrous. We greet all of you in the Lord, and in His most holy name we bless you.

Pope Paul's Address at Prayer Service of Observers and Council Fathers at St. Paul's Outside the Walls

DECEMBER 4, 1965

Gentlemen, dear observers, or rather allow us to call you by the name which has come to life in these four years of the Ecumenical Council: brothers, brothers and friends in Christ.

We are about to separate. The Council is ending. We should like at this moment of farewell to be the interpreter of the venerable Council Fathers who have come with us this evening to pray with you and to take their leave of you.

Each of us is about to take the road of return to his own home and we shall be alone once more. Allow us to confide to you this intimate impression: your departure produces a solitude around us unknown to us before the Council and which now saddens us. We should like to see you with us always!

This obliges us to renew our thanks for your presence at our Ecumenical Council. We have greatly appreciated this presence. We have felt its influence. We have admired its nobility, its piety, its patience and its affability. And this is why we shall preserve a grateful memory of your coming. And in thinking back on the courtesy of these human and Christian relations, we shall know how to appreciate more, in its

true value, the historical significance of your presence, to search into its
religious content as well as into the mystery of the divine plans which
it seems to hide and indicate at the same time.

And therefore, your departure will not put an end for us to the
spiritual and cordial relations to which your presence at the Council
has given birth. It does not close for us a dialogue began silently, but
obliges us, on the contrary, to examine how we can follow it up
profitably. The friendship lasts. And what also lasts as the first fruit of
the conciliar meeting is the conviction that the big problem of reintegra-
tion into the unity of the Church, evident to all who have the happiness
and responsibility to call themselves Christians, must be examined in
depth, and that the hour has come for this. Many of us already knew
this. Now the number of those who also think so has increased, and this
is a great advantage.

If we want to make up a balance sheet of the fruits which have
ripened during and because of the Council concerning the question of
unity, we can first of all register the fact of an increased awareness of
the existence of the problem itself, a problem which concerns and
obligates us all. We can add another fruit, still more precious: the hope
that the problem—not today, certainly—but tomorrow—can be resolved
slowly, gradually, honestly and generously. That is a great thing!

And this shows that other fruits have ripened too. We have come
to know you a little better, and not only as the representatives of your
respective confessions. Through you we have come into contact with
Christian communities which live, pray and act in the name of Christ,
with systems of doctrines and religious mentalities, and—let us say it
without fear—with Christian treasures of great value.

Far from arousing our jealousy, this rather increases our fraternity
and desire to reestablish the perfect communion between us desired by
Christ. And this leads us to discover still other positive results on the
road to our peace.

We have recognized certain failings and common sentiments that were
not good. For these we have asked pardon of God and of you. We have
discovered their unChristian roots and have proposed to ourselves to
change them, on our part, into sentiments worthy of the school of
Christ; to abstain from preconceived and offensive controversy and not
to bring into play questions of vain prestige; to try, rather, to keep in
mind the often-repeated exhortations of the Apostle at whose tomb we
are this evening: "lest perhaps there be found among you contentions,
envyings, animosities, dissentions, detractions, gossiping, arrogance, dis-
orders" (2 Cor. 12:20). We want to resume human, serene, benevolent
and confident relations.

And you know the steps we have tried to take in this direction. Suffice
it to remember the meetings during these years that representatives of
the Holy See and ourselves have had the honor and the joy to have with

so many of the members of your communities. Significant among all these was the unforgettable interview that Providence arranged for us to have with Patriarch Athenagoras in Jerusalem at the beginning of last year. This was followed by other moving visits from representatives of different Christian confessions, which for centuries had had no contact with the Catholic Church and especially with the Apostolic See. We consider these fraternal meetings as an historical event of great importance and we wish to see in them the prelude to more consoling developments.

But that is not all. You know, brothers, that our Ecumenical Council itself has gone forward to meet you in many ways: from the consideration which the Council Fathers have not ceased to show for your presence, so dear to them, to the unanimous effort to avoid any expression lacking in consideration for you; from the spiritual joy of seeing your elite group associated with the religious ceremonies of the Council to the formulation of doctrinal and disciplinary expressions able to remove obstacles and to open paths as wide and smoothed as possible for a better evaluation of the Christian religious inheritance which you preserve and develop.

The Roman Catholic Church, you can see, has shown its good will to understand you and to make itself understood. It has not pronounced anathemas, but invitations. It has not put any limits to its waiting, any more than to its fraternal offer to continue a dialogue in which it is engaged.

It would have liked, with Pope John XXIII, to whom goes the merit of this conversation which has again become trusting and fraternal, to celebrate with you, with some of those among you, the decisive and final meeting. But it realizes that in this is a too human haste and that in order to reach full and authentic communion there is still a long way to go, many prayers to be made to the Father of Lights (James 1:17), many vigils to keep. May we at least at the end of the Council record a victory: we have begun to love each other once more. And may the Lord will that, at least in this, the world may recognize that we are truly His disciples, because we have reestablished between us a reciprocal spiritual love (cf. John 13, 35).

You are about to leave. Do not forget the charity with which the Roman Catholic Church will continue to think of you and to follow you. Do not think it insensible and proud if it feels it its duty to preserve jealously the "trust" (cf. Tim. 6:20) which it has carried with it since its beginnings. And do not accuse it of having betrayed or deformed this trust if, during the course of its age-old, scrupulous and loving meditations, it has uncovered treasures of truth and life which it would be a breach of faith to renounce. Think that it is exactly from Paul the Apostle, from his ecumenicity that it received its first formation of dogmatic teaching; and you know with what unrelenting firmness (cf. Gal. 1:6 ff.). And think that truth dominates us and frees us all, and also that truth is close to love.

We were told, many years ago, about a charming and symbolic episode from the life of one of the great Oriental thinkers of modern times, and we tell it to you as we remember it. It seems to us it was about Soloviev. At one time, while staying in a monastery, he had been having a spiritual conversation until a late hour with a pious monk. Finally, wishing to return to his cell, he went out into the corridor on which opened the doors of the cells, all alike and all equally closed. In the dark he was not able to identify the door of the cell which had been assigned to him. On the other hand, he felt it impossible to return to the cell of the monk he had just left and he did not want to disturb anyone else during the rigorous monastic silence of the night. Thus the philosopher resigned himself to pass the night walking slowly up and down the monastery corridor, suddenly become mysterious and inhospitable, absorbed in his thoughts. The night was long and dreary but at last it passed and with the first light of dawn the tired philosopher easily recognized the door to his cell which he had passed time and time again during the night. And he remarked: It is often thus with those who search for truth. They pass right by it during their wakefulness without seeing it, until a ray of the sunlight of divine wisdom makes the consoling revelation so easy and happy.

The truth is near. Beloved brothers, may this ray of divine light allow us all to recognize the blessed door.

This is our hope. And now let us pray together at the tomb of St. Paul.

Joint Declaration
Issued by Pope Paul VI and Patriarch Athenagoras I

DECEMBER 7, 1965

1. Grateful to God who mercifully favoured them with a fraternal meeting at those holy places where the mystery of salvation was accomplished through the death and resurrection of the Lord Jesus, and where the Church was born through the outpouring of the Holy Spirit, Pope Paul VI and Patriarch Athenagoras I have not lost sight of the determination each then felt to omit nothing thereafter which charity might inspire and which could facilitate the development of the fraternal relations thus taken up between the Roman Catholic Church and the Orthodox Church of Constantinople. They are persuaded that in acting this way, they are responding to the call of that divine grace which today is leading the Roman Catholic Church and the Orthodox Church, as well as all Christians, to overcome their differences in order to be again "one" as the Lord Jesus asked of his Father for them.

2. Among the obstacles along the road of the development of these fraternal relations of confidence and esteem, there is the memory of the decisions, actions and painful incidents which in 1054 resulted in the sentence of excommunication leveled against the Patriarch Michael

Cerularius and two other persons by the legate of the Roman See under the leadership of Cardinal Humbert, legates who then became the object of a similar sentence pronounced by the Patriarch and the synod of Constantinople.

3. One cannot pretend that these events were not what they were during this very troubled period of history. Today, however, they have been judged more fairly and serenely. Thus it is important to recognize the excesses which accompanied them and later led to consequences which, in so far as we can judge, went much further than their authors had intended and foreseen. They had directed their censures against the persons concerned and not the Churches; these censures were not intended to break ecclesiastical communion between the sees of Rome and Constantinople.

4. Since they are certain that they express the common desire for justice and the unanimous sentiment of charity which moves the faithful, and since they recall the command of the Lord: "If you are offering your gift at the altar, and there remember that your brother has something against you, leave your gift before the altar and go, first be reconciled to your brother" (Matthew 5, 23–24), Pope Paul VI and Patriarch Athenagoras I with his synod, in common agreement, declare that:

a) They regret the offensive words, the reproaches without foundation, and the reprehensible gestures which, on both sides, have marked or accompanied the sad events of this period.

b) They likewise regret and remove both from memory and from the midst of the Church the sentences of excommunication which followed these events, the memory of which has influenced actions up to our day and has hindered closer relations in charity; and they commit these excommunications to oblivion.

c) Finally, they deplore the preceding later vexing events which, under the influence of various factors—among which, lack of understanding and mutual trust—eventually led to the effective rupture of ecclesiastical communion.

5. Pope Paul VI and Patriarch Athenagoras I with his synod realize that this gesture of justice and mutual pardon is not sufficient to end both old and more recent differences between the Roman Catholic Church and the Orthodox Church. Through the action of the Holy Spirit, those differences will be overcome through cleansing of hearts, through regret for historical wrongs, and through and efficacious determination to arrive at a common understanding and expression of the faith of the Apostles and its demands.

They hope, nevertheless, that this act will be pleasing to God, who is prompt to pardon us when we pardon each other. They hope that the whole Christian World, especially the entire Roman Catholic Church and the Orthodox Church will appreciate this gesture as an expression of a sincere desire, shared in common, for reconciliation, and as an invitation to follow out, in a spirit of trust, esteem and mutual charity, the dialogue which, with God's help, will lead to living together again, for the greater good of souls and the coming of the kingdom of God, in that full communion of faith, fraternal accord and sacramental life which existed among them during the first thousand years of the life of the Church.

Address of the Pope

PUBLIC SESSION, DECEMBER 7, 1965

We are concluding today the Second Vatican Council. We bring it to a close at the fullness of its efficiency: the presence of so many of you here clearly demonstrates it; the well-ordered pattern of this assembly bears testimony to it; the normal conclusion of the work done by the Council confirms it; the harmony of sentiments and decisions proclaims it. And if quite a few questions raised during the course of the Council itself still await appropriate answers, this shows that its labours are now coming to a close not out of weariness, but in a state of vitality which this universal Synod has awakened. In the post-conciliar period this vitality will apply, God willing, its generous and well-regulated energies to the study of such questions.

This Council bequeathes to history an image of the Catholic Church symbolised by this hall, filled, as it is, with shepherds of souls professing the same faith, breathing the same charity, associated in the same communion of prayer, discipline and activity and—what is marvellous— all desiring only one thing: namely, to offer themselves like Christ, our Master and Lord, for the life of the Church and for the salvation of the world. This Council hands over to posterity not only the image of the

Church but also the patrimony of her doctrine and of her commandments, the deposit received from Christ and meditated upon through centuries, lived and expressed now and clarified in so many of its parts, settled and arranged in its integrity. The deposit, that is, which lives on by the divine power of truth and of grace which constitutes it, and is, therefore, able to vivify anyone who receives it and nourishes with it his own human existence.

What then was the Council? What has it accomplished? The answer to these questions would be the logical theme of our present meditation. But it would require too much of our attention and time: this final and stupendous hour would not perhaps give us enough tranquillity of mind to make such a synthesis. We should like to devote this precious moment to one single thought which bends down our spirits in humility and at the same time raises them up to the summit of our aspirations. And that thought is this: what is the religious value of this Council? We refer to it as religious because of its direct relationship with the living God, that relationship which is the raison d'être of the Church, of all that she believes, hopes and loves; of all that she is and does.

Could we speak of having given glory to God, of having sought knowledge and love of Him, of having made progress in our effort of contemplating Him, in our eagerness for honouring Him and in the art of proclaiming Him to men who look up to us as to pastors and masters of the life of God? In all sincerity we think the answer is, yes. Also because from this basic purpose there developed the guiding principle which was to give direction to the future Council. Still fresh in our memory are the words uttered in this Basilica by our venerated predecessor, John XXIII, whom we may in truth call the originator of this great Synod. In his opening address to the Council he had this to say: "The greatest concern of the ecumenical Council is this: that the sacred deposit of Christian doctrine be guarded and taught more effectively . . . The Lord has said: 'Seek first the Kingdom of God and His justice.' The word 'first' expresses the direction in which our thoughts and energies must move" (Discorsi, 1962, p. 583).

His great purpose has now been achieved. To appreciate it properly it is necessary to remember the time in which it was realized: a time which everyone admits is orientated towards the conquest of the kingdom of earth rather than of that of heaven; a time in which forgetfulness of God has become habitual, and seems, quite wrongly, to be prompted by the progress of science; a time in which the fundamental act of the human person, more conscious now of himself and of his liberty, tends to pronounce in favour of his own absolute autonomy, in emancipation from every transcendent law; a time in which secularism seems the legitimate consequence of modern thought and the highest wisdom in the temporal ordering of society; a time, moreover, in which the soul of man has plumbed the depths of irrationality and desolation;

a time, finally, which is characterised by upheavals and a hitherto unknown decline even in the great world religions.

It was at such a time as this that our Council was held to the honour of God, in the name of Christ and under the impulse of the Spirit, Who "searcheth all things," "making us understand God's gifts to us" (cfr. I Cor. 2, 10–12), and Who is now quickening the Church, giving her a vision at once profound and all-embracing of the life of the world. The theocentric and theological concept of man and the universe, almost in defiance of the charge of anachronism and irrelevance, has been given a new prominence by the Council, through claims which the world will at first judge to be foolish, but which, we hope, it will later come to recognise as being truly human, wise and salutary: namely, God is— and more, He is real, He lives, a personal, provident God, infinitely good; and not only good in Himself, but also immeasurably good to us. He will be recognized as our creator, our truth, our happiness; so much so that the effort to look on Him, and to centre our heart in Him which we call contemplation, is the highest, the most perfect act of the spirit, the act which even today can and must be at the apex of all human activity.

Men will realize that the Council devoted its attention not so much to divine truths, but rather, and principally, to the Church—her nature and composition, her ecumenical vocation, her apostolic and missionary activity. This secular religious society, which is the Church, has endeavoured to carry out an act of reflection about herself, to know herself better, to define herself better and, in consequence, to set aright what she feels and what she commands. So much is true. But this introspection has not been an end in itself, has not been simply an exercise of human understanding or of a merely worldly culture. The Church has gathered herself together in deep spiritual awareness, not to produce a learned analysis of religious psychology, or an account of her own experiences, not even to devote herself to reaffirming her rights and explaining her laws. Rather, it was to find in herself, active and alive, in the Holy Spirit, the word of Christ; and to probe more deeply still the mystery, namely, the plan and the presence of God above and within herself; to revitalize in herself that faith which is the secret of her confidence and of her wisdom, and that love which impels her to sing without ceasing the praises of God. *Cantare amantis est* (Song is the expression of a lover), says St. Augustine (*Serm.* 336; P.L. 38, 1472).

The Council documents—especially the ones on divine revelation, the liturgy, the Church, priests, religious and the laity—leave wide open to view this primary and focal religious intention, and show how clear and fresh and rich is the spiritual stream which living contact with the living God causes to well up in the heart of the Church, and flow out from it over the dry wastes of our world.

But we cannot pass over one important consideration in our analysis of the religious meaning of the Council: it has been deeply committed to the study of the modern world. Never before perhaps, so much as on this occasion, has the Church felt the need to know, to draw near to, to understand, to penetrate, serve and evangelize the society in which she lives; and to get to grips with it, almost to run after it, in its rapid and continuous change. This attitude, a response to the distances and divisions we have witnessed over recent centuries, in the last century and in our own especially, between the Church and secular society—this attitude has been strongly and unceasingly at work in the Council; so much so that some have been inclined to suspect that an easy-going and excessive responsiveness to the outside world, to passing events, cultural fashions, temporary needs, an alien way of thinking . . ., may have swayed persons and acts of the ecumenical synod, at the expense of the fidelity which is due to tradition, and this to the detriment of the religious orientation of the Council itself. We do not believe that this shortcoming should be imputed to it, to its real and deep intentions, to its authentic manifestations.

We prefer to point out how charity has been the principal religious feature of this Council. Now, no one can reprove as want of religion or infidelity to the Gospel such a basic orientation, when we recall that it is Christ Himself who taught us that love for our brothers is the distinctive mark of his disciples (cf. Jn. 13. 35); when we listen to the words of the apostle: "If he is to offer service pure and unblemished in the sight of God, who is our Father, he must take care of orphans and widows in their need, and keep himself untainted by the world" (James 1, 27) and again: "He has seen his brother, and has no love for him: what love can he have for the God he has never seen?" (I Jn. 4, 20).

Yes, the Church of the Council has been concerned, not just with serself and with her relationship of union with God, but with man—man as he really is today: living man, man all wrapped up in himself, man who makes himself not only the centre of his every interest but dares to claim that he is the principle and explanation of all reality. Every perceptible element in man, every one of the countless guises in which he appears, has, in a sense, been displayed in full view of the Council Fathers, who, in their turn, are mere men, and yet all of them are pastors and brothers whose position accordingly fills them with solicitude and love. Among these guises We may cite man as the tragic actor of his own plays; man as the superman of yesterday and today, ever frail, unreal, selfish, and savage; man unhappy with himself as he laughs and cries; man the versatile actor ready to perform any part; man the narrow devotee of nothing but scientific reality; man as he is, a creature who thinks and loves and toils and is always waiting for something, the "growing son" (Gen. 49, 22); man sacred because of the innocence of his childhood, because of the mystery of his poverty, because of the dedication of his suffering; man as an individual and man in society; man who lives in the glories of the past and dreams of those of the future; man the sinner and man the saint; and so on.

Secular humanism, revealing itself in its horrible reality, anticlerical, has, in a certain sense, defied the Council. The religion of the God Who became man has met the religion (for such it is) of man who makes himself God. And what happened? Was there a clash, a battle, a condemnation? There could have been, but there was none. The old story of the Samaritan has been the model of the spirituality of the Council. A feeling of boundless sympathy has permeated the whole of it. The attention of our Council has been absorbed by the discovery of human needs (and these needs grow in proportion to the greatness which the son of the earth claims for himself.). But we call upon those who term themselves modern humanists, and who have renounced the transcendent value of the highest realities, to give the Council credit at least for one quality and to recognise our own new type of humanism: we, too, in fact, we more than any others, honour mankind.

And what aspect of humanity has this august senate studied? What goal under divine inspiration did it set for itself? It also dwelt upon humanity's ever twofold facet, namely, man's wretchedness and his greatness, his profound weakness—which is undeniable and cannot be cured by himself—and the good that survives in him which is ever marked by a hidden beauty and an invincible serenity. But one must realise that this Council, which exposed itself to human judgment, insisted very much more upon this pleasant side of man, rather than on his unpleasant one. Its attitude was very much and deliberately optimistic. A wave of affection and admiration flowed from the Council over the modern world of humanity. Errors were condemned, indeed, because charity demanded this no less than did truth, but for the persons themselves there was only warning, respect and love. Instead of depressing diagnoses, encouraging remedies; instead of direful prognostics, messages of trust issued from the Council to the present-day world. The modern world's values were not only respected but honoured, its efforts approved, its aspirations purified and blessed.

You see, for example, how the various countless languages of peoples existing today were admitted for the liturgical expression of men's communication with God and God's communication with men: to man as such was recognised his fundamental claim to enjoy full possession of his rights and his transcendental destiny. His supreme aspirations to life, to personal dignity, to his just liberty, to culture, to the renewal of the social order, to justice and peace were purified and promoted; and to all men was addressed the pastoral and missionary invitation to the light of the Gospel.

We can now speak only too briefly of the very many and vast questions, relative to human welfare, with which the Council dealt. It did not attempt to resolve all the urgent problems of modern life; some of these have been reserved for a further study which the Church intends to make of them, many of them were presented in very restricted and general terms, and for that reason are open to further investigation and various applications.

But one thing must be noted here, namely, that the teaching authority of the Church, even though not wishing to issue extraordinary dogmatic pronouncements, has made thoroughly known its authoritative teaching on a number of questions which today weigh upon man's conscience and activity, descending, so to speak, into a dialogue with him, but ever preserving its own authority and force; it has spoken with the accommodating friendly voice of pastoral charity; its desire has been to be heard and understood by everyone; it has not merely concentrated on intellectual understanding but has also sought to express itself in simple, up-to-date, conversational style, derived from actual experience and a cordial approach which make it more vital, attractive and persuasive; it has spoken to modern man as he is.

Another point we must stress is this: all this rich teaching is channeled in one direction, the service of mankind, of every condition, in every weakness and need. The Church has, so to say, declared herself the servant of humanity, at the very time when her teaching role and her pastoral government have, by reason of the Council's solemnity, assumed greater splendour and vigour: the idea of service has been central.

It might be said that all this and everything else we might say about the human values of the Council have diverted the attention of the Church in Council to the trend of modern culture, centered on humanity. We would say not diverted but rather directed. Any careful observer of the Council's prevailing interest for human and temporal values cannot deny that it is from the pastoral character that the Council has virtually made its program, and must recognise that the same interest is never divorced from the most genuine religious interest, whether by reason of charity, its sole inspiration (where charity is, God is!), or the Council's constant, explicit attempts to link human and temporal values with those that are specifically spiritual, religious and everlasting; its concern is with man and with earth but it rises to the kingdom of God.

The modern mind, accustomed to assess everything in terms of usefulness, will readily admit that the Council's value is great if only because everything has been referred to human usefulness. Hence no one should ever say that a religion like the Catholic religion is without use, seeing that when it has its greatest self-awareness and effectiveness, as it has in Council, it declares itself entirely on the side of man and in his service. In this way the Catholic religion and human life reaffirm their alliance with one another, the fact that they converge on one single human reality: the Catholic religion is for mankind; in a certain sense it is the life of mankind. It is so by the extremely precise and sublime interpretation that our religion gives of humanity (surely man by himself is a mystery to himself) and gives this interpretation in virtue of its knowledge of God: a knowledge of God is a prerequisite for a knowledge of man as he really is, in all his fulness; for proof of this let it suffice for now to recall the ardent expression of St. Catherine of Siena, "In Your nature, Eternal God, I shall know my own." The Catholic religion is man's life because it determine's life's nature and destiny; it gives life its real meaning, it establishes the supreme law of life and infuses it with that mysterious activity which we may say divinizes it.

Consequently, if we remember, venerable brothers and all of you, our children, gathered here, how in everyone we can and must recognise the countenance of Christ (cf. Mt. 25, 40), the Son of Man, especially when tears and sorrows make it plain to see, and if we can and must recognise in Christ's countenance the countenance of our Heavenly Father, "He who sees me", our Lord said, "sees also the Father" (Jn. 14, 9), our humanism becomes Christianity, our Christianity becomes centred on God; in such sort that we may say, to put it differently: a knowledge of man is a prerequisite for a knowledge of God.

Would not this Council, then, which has concentrated principally on man, be destined to propose again to the world of today the ladder leading to freedom and consolation? Would it not be, in short, a simple, new and solemn teaching to love man in order to love God? To love man, we say, not as a means but as the first step toward the final and transcendent goal which is the basis and cause of every love. And so this Council can be summed up in its ultimate religious meaning, which is none other than a pressing and friendly invitation to mankind of today to rediscover in fraternal love the God "to turn away from Whom is to fall, to turn to Whom is to rise again, to remain in Whom is to be secure, to return to Whom is to be born again, in Whom to dwell is to live" (St. Augustine, *Solil.* I, i, 3; P.L. 32, 870).

This is our hope at the conclusion of this Second Ecumenical Vatican Council and at the beginning of the human and religious renewal which the Council proposed to study and promote; this is our hope for you, brothers and Fathers of the Council; this is our hope for the whole of mankind which here we have learned to love more and to serve better.

To this end we again invoke the intercession of Saint John the Baptist and of Saint Joseph, who are the patrons of the ecumenical Council; of the holy Apostles Peter and Paul, the foundations and columns of the holy Church; and with them of Saint Ambrose, the bishop whose feast we celebrate today, as it were uniting in him the Church of the East and of the West. We also earnestly implore the protection of the most Blessed Mary, the Mother of Christ and therefore called by us also Mother of the Church. With one voice and with one heart we give thanks and glory to the living and true God, to the one and sovereign God, to the Father, to the Son and to the Holy Spirit. Amen.

Closing Address of the Pope
CLOSING CEREMONY, DECEMBER 8, 1965

Your Eminences, venerable brothers, representatives of governments, gentlemen of the city of Rome, authorities and citizens of the entire world! You, observers belonging to so many different Christian denominations, and you, faithful and sons here present, and you also scattered across the earth and united with us in faith and charity!

You will hear shortly, at the end of this holy mass, a reading of some messages which, at the conclusion of its work, the ecumenical Council is addressing to various categories of persons, intending to consider in them the countless forms in which human life finds expression. And you will also hear the reading of our official decree in which we declare terminated and closed the II Ecumenical Vatican Council. This is a moment, a brief moment of greetings. Then, our voice will be silent. This Council is completely terminated; this immense and extraordinary assembly is disbanded.

Hence, this greeting which we address to you has particular significance, which we take the liberty of pointing out to you, not to distract you from prayer, but to occupy the better your attention in this present celebration. This greeting is, before all, universal. It is addressed to all of you assisting and participating here in this sacred rite: To you, venerable brothers in the episcopate; to you, representatives of nations, to you, People of God. And it is extended and broadened to the entire world. How could it be otherwise if this Council was said to be and is ecumenical, that is to say, universal? Just as the sound of the bell goes out through the skies, reaches each one within the radius of its sound waves, so at this moment does our greeting go out to each and everyone of you. To those who receive it and to those who do not, it resounds pleadingly in the ear of every man. From this Catholic center of Rome, no one, in principle, is unreachable; in principle, all men can and must be reached. For the Catholic Church, no one is a stranger, no one is excluded, no one is far away. Every one to whom our greeting is addressed is one who is called, who is invited and who, in a certain sense, is present. This is the language of the heart of one who loves; every loved one is present! And We, especially at this moment, in virtue of our universal pastoral and apostolic mandate, We love all, all men.

Hence, We say this to you, good and faithful souls, who, absent in person from this gathering of believers and of nations, are here present in spirit with your prayer. Also of you, the Pope is thinking, and with you he celebrates this sublime moment of universal communion. We say this to you, those who suffer, like prisoners of your infirmities and who, if you were without the comfort of our heartfelt greeting would, because of your spiritual solitude, experience a redoubling of your pain.

This we say especially to you, brothers in the episcopate, who through no fault of your own, were missing from the Council and now leave voids in the ranks of your brother bishops and still more in their hearts and ours, voids which give us such sufferings and which condemn the injustices which shackle your liberty. And would that this was all that was wanting to enable you to come to our Council. Greetings to you, brothers, who are unjustly detained in silence, in oppression, and in the privation of legitimate and sacred rights owed to every honest man, and much more, to you who are the workmen of nothing but good, piety and peace. Oh hindered and humiliated brethren, the Church is with you. She is with your faithful and with all those who have a part in your painful condition! May this also be the civil conscience of the world! Lastly, our universal greeting goes out to you, men who do not know us, men who do not understand us, men who do not regard us as useful, necessary or friendly. This greeting goes also to you, men who, while perhaps thinking they are doing good, are opposed to us. A sincere greeting, an unassuming greeting but one filled with hope and today, please believe that it is filled with esteem and love.

This is our greeting. But please be attentive, you who are listening to us. We ask you to consider how our greeting, differently from what ordinarily happens in day to day conversation, would serve to terminate a relationship of nearness or discourse, our greeting tends to strengthen, and, if necessary, to produce a spiritual relationship whence it draws its meaning and its voice. Ours is a greeting, not of farewell which separates, but of friendship which remains, and which, if so demanded, wishes to be born. Even it is precisely in this last expression that our greeting, on the one hand, would desire to reach the heart of every man, to enter therein as a cordial guest and speak in the interior silence of your individual souls, the habitual and ineffable words of the Lord: "My peace I leave with you, my peace I give unto you, but not as the world gives it." (John, 14, 27.) Christ has His own special way of speaking in the secrets of hearts and on the other hand, our greeting wants to be a different and higher relationship because it is not only a two-sided exchange of words among us people of this earth, but it also brings into the picture another present One, the Lord Himself, invisible but working in the framework of human relationships. It invites him and begs him to arouse in him who greets and in him who is greeted new gifts of which the first and highest is charity.

Behold, this is our greeting. May it rise as a new spark of divine charity in our hearts, a spark which may enkindle the principles, doctrines and proposals which the Council has organized and which, thus inflamed by charity, may really produce in the Church and in the world, that renewal of thoughts, activities, conduct, moral force and hope and joy which was the very scope of the Council. Consequently, our greeting is in the ideal order. Is it a dream? Is it poetry? Is it only conventional and meaningless exaggeration, as often happens in our day to day expression of good wishes? No. This greeting is ideal, but not unreal. Here we would ask for a further moment of your attention. When we men push our thoughts and our desires toward an ideal conception of life, we find ourselves immediately in an utopia, in rhetorical caricature, in illusion or delusion. Man preserves an unquenchable yearning towards ideal and total perfection, but by himself he is incapable of reaching it, perhaps not in concept or much less with experience or reality. This, we know, is the drama of man, the drama of the fallen king.

But note what is taking place here this morning. While we close the ecumenical Council, we are honoring Mary most holy, the Mother of Christ, and consequently, as we declared on another occasion, the Mother of God and our spiritual mother. We are honoring Mary most holy, the immaculate one, therefore innocent, stupendous, perfect. She is the woman, the true woman who is both ideal and real, the creature in whom the image of God is reflected with absolute clarity, without any disturbance, as happens in every other human creature.

Is it not perhaps in directing our gaze on this woman who is our humble sister and at the same time our heavenly mother and queen, the spotless and sacred mirror of infinite beauty, that we can terminate the spiritual ascent of the Council and our final greeting? Is it not here that our post-conciliar work can begin? Does not the beauty of Mary immaculate become for us an inspiring model? A comforting hope?

Oh, brothers, sons, and gentlemen who are listening to us, we think it is so: for us and for you. And this is our most exalted and, God willing, our most valuable greeting.

Papal Brief Formally Closing Council

DECEMBER 8, 1965

Pope Paul VI: To the perpetual memory of the event:

The Second Vatican Ecumenical Council, assembled in the Holy Spirit and under protection of the Blessed Virgin Mary, whom we have declared Mother of the Church, and of St. Joseph, her glorious spouse, and of the Apostles SS. Peter and Paul, must be numbered without doubt among the greatest events of the Church. In fact it was the largest in the number of Fathers who came to the seat of Peter from every part of the world, even from those places where the hierarchy has been very recently established. It was the richest because of the questions which for four sessions have been discussed carefully and profoundly. And last of all it was the most opportune, because, bearing in mind the necessities of the present day, above all it sought to meet the pastoral needs and, nourishing the flame of charity, it has made a great effort to reach not only the Christians still separated from communion with the Holy See, but also the whole human family.

At last all which regards the holy ecumenical Council has, with the help of God, been accomplished and all the constitutions, decrees, declarations and votes have been approved by the deliberation of the synod and promulgated by us. Therefore we decided to close for all intents and purposes, with our apostolic authority, this same ecumenical Council called by our predecessor, Pope John XXIII, which opened Oct. 11, 1962, and which was continued by us after his death.

We decide moreover that all that has been established synodally is to be religiously observed by all the faithful, for the glory of God and the dignity of the Church and for the tranquility and peace of all men. We have approved and established these things, decreeing that the present letters are and remain stable and valid, and are to have legal effectiveness, so that they be disseminated and obtain full and complete effect, and so that they may be fully convalidated by those whom they concern or may concern now and in the future; and so that, as it be judged and described, all efforts contrary to these things by whomever or whatever authority, knowingly or in ignorance, be invalid and worthless from now on.

Given in Rome at St. Peters, under the (seal of the) ring of the fisherman, Dec. 8, on the feast of the Immaculate Conception of the Blessed Virgin Mary, the year 1965, the third year of our pontificate.

Declaration on the Relation of the Church to Non-Christian Religions

PROMULGATED OCTOBER 28, 1965

✠

1. In our time, when day by day mankind is being drawn closer together, and the ties between different peoples are becoming stronger, the Church examines more closely her relationship to non-Christian religions. In her task of promoting unity and love among men, indeed among nations, she considers above all in this declaration what men have in common and what draws them to fellowship.

One is the community of all peoples, one their origin, for God made the whole human race to live over the face of the earth. One also is their final goal, God. His providence, His manifestations of goodness, His saving designs extend to all men, until that time when the elect will be united in the Holy City, the city ablaze with the glory of God, where the nations will walk in His light.

Men expect from the various religions answers to the unsolved riddles of human existence, which today, even as in former times, deeply stir the hearts of men: What is man? What is the meaning, the aim of our life? What is moral good, what is sin? Whence suffering and what purpose does it serve? Which is the road to true happiness? What are death, judgment and retribution after death? What, finally, is that ultimate inexpressible mystery that encompasses our existence: whence do we come, and where are we going?

2. From ancient times down to the present, there is found among various peoples a certain perception of that hidden power which hovers over the course of things and over the events of human history; at times some indeed have come to the recognition of a Supreme Being, or even of a Father. This perception and recognition penetrate their lives with a profound religious sense.

Religions that are bound up with an advanced culture, however, have struggled to answer the same questions by means of more refined concepts and a more developed language. Thus, in Hinduism, men contemplate the divine mystery and express it through an inexhaustible abundance of myths and through searching philosophical inquiry. They seek freedom from the anguish of our human condition either through ascetical practices or profound meditation or a flight to God with love and trust. Again, Buddhism, in its various forms, realizes the radical insufficiency of this changeable world; it teaches a way by which men, in a devout and confident spirit, may be able either to acquire the state of perfect liberation, or attain, by their own efforts or through higher help, supreme illumination. Likewise, other religions found everywhere try to counter the restlessness of the human heart, each in its own manner, by proposing "ways", comprising teachings, rules of life, and sacred rites.

The Catholic Church rejects nothing that is true and holy in these religions. She regards with sincere reverence those ways of conduct and of life, those precepts and teachings which, though differing in many aspects from the ones she holds and sets forth, nonetheless often reflect a ray of that Truth which enlightens all men. Indeed, she proclaims, and ever must proclaim Christ, "the way, the truth, and the life" (Jn. 14, 6), in whom men may find the fulness of religious life, in whom God has reconciled all things to Himself.

The Church, therefore, exhorts her sons, that through dialogue and collaboration with the followers of other religions, carried out with prudence and love and in witness to the Christian faith and life, they recognize, preserve and promote the good things, spiritual and moral, as well as the socio-cultural values found among these men.

3. The Church regards with esteem also the Moslems. They adore the one God, living and subsisting in Himself, merciful and all-powerful, the Creator of heaven and earth who has spoken to men; they take pains to submit wholeheartedly to even His inscrutable decrees, just as Abraham, with whom the faith of Islam takes pleasure in linking itself, submitted to God. Though they do not acknowledge Jesus as God, they revere Him as a prophet. They also honour Mary, his virgin mother; at times they even call on her with devotion. In addition, they await the

day of judgment when God will render their deserts to all those who have been raised up from the dead. Finally, they value the moral life and worship God especially through prayer, almsgiving and fasting.

Since in the course of centuries not a few quarrels and hostilities have arisen between Christians and Moslems, this sacred synod urges all to forget the past and to work sincerely for mutual understanding and to preserve as well as to promote together for the benefit of all mankind social justice and moral welfare, as well as peace and freedom.

4. As this sacred synod searches into the mystery of the Church, it remembers the bond that spiritually ties the people of the New Covenant to Abraham's stock.

Thus the Church of Christ acknowledges that, according to God's saving design, the beginnings of her faith and her election are found already among the Patriarchs, Moses and the prophets. She professes that all who believe in Christ—Abraham's sons according to faith—are included in the same Patriarch's call, and likewise that the salvation of the Church is mysteriously foreshadowed by the chosen people's exodus from the land of bondage. The Church, therefore, cannot forget that she received the revelation of the Old Testament through the people with whom God in His inexpressible mercy concluded the Ancient Covenant. Nor can she forget that she draws sustenance from the root of that well-cultivated olive tree onto which have been grafted the wild shoots, the Gentiles. Indeed, the Church believes that by His cross Christ Our Peace reconciled Jews and Gentiles, making both one in Himself.

The Church keeps ever in mind the words of the Apostle about his kinsmen: "theirs is the sonship and the glory and the covenants and the law and the worship and the promises; theirs are the fathers and from them is the Christ according to the flesh" (Rom. 9, 4–5), the Son of the Virgin Mary. She also recalls that the Apostles, the Church's mainstay and pillars, as well as most of the early disciples who proclaimed Christ's Gospel to the world, sprang from the Jewish people.

As Holy Scripture testifies, Jerusalem did not recognize the time of her visitation, nor did the Jews, in large number, accept the Gospel; indeed not a few opposed its spreading. Nevertheless, God holds the Jews most dear for the sake of their Fathers; He does not repent of the gifts He makes or of the calls He issues—such is the witness of the Apostle. In company with the Prophets and the same Apostle, the Church awaits that day, known to God alone, on which all peoples will address the Lord in a single voice and "serve him shoulder to shoulder" (Soph. 3, 9).

Since the spiritual patrimony common to Christians and Jews is thus so great, this sacred synod wants to foster and recommend that mutual understanding and respect which is the fruit, above all, of biblical and theological studies as well as of fraternal dialogues.

True, the Jewish authorities and those who followed their lead pressed for the death of Christ; still, what happened in His passion cannot be charged against all the Jews, without distinction, then alive, nor against the Jews of today. Although the Church is the new people of God, the Jews should not be presented as rejected or accursed, as if this followed from the Holy Scriptures. All should see to it, then, that in catechetical work or in the preaching of the word of God they do not teach anything that does not conform to the truth of the Gospel and the spirit of Christ.

Furthermore, in her rejection of every persecution against any man, the Church, mindful of the patrimony she shares with the Jews and moved not by political reasons but by the Gospel's spiritual love, decries hatred, persecutions, displays of anti-semitism, directed against Jews at any time and by anyone.

Besides, as the Church has always held and holds now, Christ underwent His passion and death freely, because of the sins of men and out of infinite love, in order that all may reach salvation. It is, therefore, the burden of the Church's preaching to proclaim the cross of Christ as the sign of God's all-embracing love and as the fountain from which every grace flows.

5. We cannot truly call on God, the Father of all, if we refuse to treat in a brotherly way any man, created as he is in the image of God. Man's relation to God the Father and his relation to men his brothers are so linked together that Scripture says: "He who does not love does not know God" (1 Jn. 4, 8).

No foundation therefore remains for any theory or practice that leads to discrimination between man and man or people and people, so far as their human dignity and the rights flowing from it are concerned.

The Church reproves, as foreign to the mind of Christ, any discrimination against men or harassment of them because of their race, colour, condition in life, or religion. On the contrary, following in the footsteps of the holy Apostles Peter and Paul, this Sacred Synod ardently implores the Christian faithful to maintain "good fellowship among the nations" (1 Pet. 2, 12), and, if possible, to live for their part in peace with all men, so that they may truly be sons of the Father who is in heaven.

Constitution on Divine Revelation

PROMULGATED NOVEMBER 18, 1965

1. Hearing the word of God with reverence and proclaiming it with faith, the sacred synod takes its direction from these words of St. John: "We announce to you the eternal life which dwelt with the Father and was made visible to us. What we have seen and heard we announce to you, so that you may have fellowship with us and our common fellowship be with the Father and His Son Jesus Christ" (1 John 1:2–3). Therefore, following the footsteps of the Council of Trent and of the First Vatican Council, this present council wishes to set forth authentic doctrine on divine revelation and how it is handed on, so that by hearing the message of salvation the whole world may believe, by believing it may hope, and by hoping it may love.

CHAPTER I
Revelation Itself

2. In His goodness and wisdom God chose to reveal Himself and to make known to us the hidden purpose of His will (see Eph. 1:9) by which through Christ, the Word made flesh, man might in the Holy

Spirit have access to the Father and come to share in the divine nature
(see Eph. 2:18; 2 Peter 1:4). Through this revelation, therefore, the
invisible God (see Col. 1:15; 1 Tim. 1:17) out of the abundance of His
love speaks to men as friends (see Ex. 33:11; John 15:14–15) and lives
among them (see Bar. 3:38), so that He may invite and take them into
fellowship with Himself. This plan of revelation is realized by deeds and
words having an inner unity: the deeds wrought by God in the history
of salvation manifest and confirm the teaching and realities signified
by the words, while the words proclaim the deeds and clarify the mystery
contained in them. By this revelation then, the deepest truth about God
and the salvation of man shines out for our sake in Christ, who is both
the mediator and the fulness of all revelation.

3. God, who through the Word creates all things (see John, 1:3) and
keeps them in existence, gives men an enduring witness to Himself in
created realities (see Rom. 1:19–20). Planning to make known the way
of heavenly salvation, He went further and from the start manifested
Himself to our first parents. Then after their fall His promise of redemption aroused in them the hope of being saved (see Gen. 3:15) and from
that time on He ceaselessly kept the human race in His care, to give
eternal life to those who perseveringly do good in search of salvation (see
Rom. 2:6–7). Then, at the time He had appointed He called Abraham
in order to make of him a great nation (see Gen. 12:2). Through the
patriarchs, and after them through Moses and the prophets, He taught
this people to acknowledge Himself the one living and true God, provident father and just judge, and to wait for the Savior promised by
Him, and in this manner prepared the way for the Gospel down through
the centuries.

4. Then, after speaking in many and varied ways through the
prophets, "now at last in these days God has spoken to us in His Son"
(Heb. 1:1–2). For He sent His Son, the eternal Word, who enlightens all
men, so that He might dwell among men and tell them of the inner-
most being of God (see John 1:1–18). Jesus Christ, therefore, the Word
made flesh, was sent as "a man to men." He "speaks the words of God"
(John 3:34), and completes the work of salvation which His Father gave
Him to do (see John 5:36, 17:4). To see Jesus is to see His Father (John
14:9). For this reason Jesus perfected revelation by fulfilling it through
his whole work of making Himself present and manifesting Himself:
through His words and deeds, His signs and wonders, but especially
through His death and glorious resurrection from the dead and final
sending of the Spirit of truth. Moreover He confirmed with divine
testimony what revelation proclaimed, that God is with us to free us
from the darkness of sin and death, and to raise us up to life eternal.

The Christian dispensation, therefore, as the new and definitive
covenant, will never pass away and we now await no further new public

revelation before the glorious manifestation of our Lord Jesus Christ (see 1 Tim. 6:14 and Tit. 2:13).

5. "The obedience of faith" (Rom. 13:26; see 1:5, 2 Cor. 10:5–6) "is to be given to God who reveals, an obedience by which man commits his whole self freely to God, offering the full submission of intellect and will to God who reveals," and freely assenting to the truth revealed by Him. To make this act of faith, the grace of God and the interior help of the Holy Spirit must precede and assist, moving the heart and turning it to God, opening the eyes of the mind and giving "joy and ease to everyone in assenting to the truth and believing it." To bring about an ever deeper understanding of revelation the same Holy Spirit constantly brings faith to completion by His gifts.

6. Through divine revelation, God chose to show forth and communicate Himself and the eternal decisions of His will regarding the salvation of men. That is to say, He chose to share with them those divine treasures which totally transcend the understanding of the human mind.
As a sacred synod has affirmed, God, the beginning and end of all things, can be known with certainty from created reality by the light of human reason (see Rom. 1:20); but teaches that it is through His revelation "that those religious truths which are by their nature accessible to human reason can be known by all men with ease, with solid certitude and with no trace of error, even in this present state of the human race."

CHAPTER II
Handing on Divine Revelation

7. In His gracious goodness, God has seen to it that what He had revealed for the salvation of all nations would abide perpetually in its full integrity and be handed on to all generations. Therefore Christ the Lord in whom the full revelation of the supreme God is brought to completion (see Cor. 1:20; 3:13; 4:6), commissioned the Apostles to preach to all men that Gospel which is the source of all saving truth and moral teaching, and to impart to them heavenly gifts. This Gospel had been promised in former times through the prophets, and Christ Himself had fulfilled it and promulgated it with His lips. This commission was faithfully fulfilled by the Apostles who, by their oral preaching, by example, and by observances handed on what they had received from the lips of Christ, from living with Him, and from what He did, or what they had learned through the prompting of the Holy Spirit. The commission was fulfilled too, by those Apostles and apostolic men who under the inspiration of the same Holy Spirit committed the message of salvation to writing.

But in order to keep the Gospel forever whole and alive within the Church, the Apostles left bishops as their successors, "handing over" to them "the authority to teach in their own place." This sacred tradition, therefore, and Sacred Scripture of both the Old and New Testaments are like a mirror in which the pilgrim Church on earth looks at God, from whom she has received everything, until she is brought finally to see Him as He is, face to face (see 1 John 3:2).

8. And so the apostolic preaching, which is expressed in a special way in the inspired books, was to be preserved by an unending succession of preachers until the end of time. Therefore the Apostles, handing on what they themselves had received, warn the faithful to hold fast to the traditions which they have learned either by word of mouth or by letter (see 2 Thess. 2:15), and to fight in defense of the faith handed on once and for all (see Jud. 3). Now what was handed on by the Apostles includes everything which contributes toward the holiness of life and increase in faith of the people of God; and so the Church, in her teaching, life and worship, perpetuates and hands on to all generations all that she herself is, all that she believes.

This tradition which comes from the Apostles develops in the Church with the help of the Holy Spirit. For there is a growth in the understanding of the realities and the words which have been handed down. This happens through the contemplation and study made by believers, who treasure these things in their hearts (see Luke, 2:19, 51) through a penetrating understanding of the spiritual realities which they experience, and through the preaching of those who have received through episcopal succession the sure gift of truth. For as the centuries succeed one another, the Church constantly moves forward toward the fulness of divine truth until the words of God reach their complete fulfillment in her.

The words of the holy Fathers witness to the presence of this living tradition, whose wealth is poured into the practice and life of the believing and praying Church. Through the same tradition the Church's full canon of the sacred books is known, and the sacred writings themselves are more profoundly understood and unceasingly made active in her; and thus God, who spoke of old, uninterruptedly converses with the bride of His beloved Son; and the Holy Spirit, through whom the living voice of the Gospel resounds in the Church, and through her, in the world, leads unto all truth those who believe and makes the word of Christ dwell abundantly in them (see Col. 3:16).

9. Hence there exists a close connection and communication between sacred tradition and sacred Scripture. For both of them, flowing from the same divine wellspring, in a certain way merge into a unity and tend toward the same end. For Sacred Scripture is the word of God inasmuch as it is consigned to writing under the inspiration of the divine Spirit,

while sacred tradition takes the word of God entrusted by Christ the Lord and the Holy Spirit to the Apostles, and hands it on to their successors in its full purity, so that led by the light of the Spirit of truth, they may in proclaiming it preserve this word of God faithfully, explain it, and make it more widely known. Consequently it is not from Sacred Scripture alone that the Church draws her certainty about everything which has been revealed. Therefore both sacred tradition and Sacred Scripture are to be accepted and venerated with the same sense of loyalty and reverence.

10. Sacred tradition and sacred Scripture form one sacred deposit of the word of God, committed to the Church. Holding fast to this deposit the entire holy people united with their shepherds remain always steadfast in the teaching of the Apostles, in the common life, in the breaking of the bread and in prayers (see Acts 2, 42, Greek text), so that holding to, practicing and professing the heritage of the faith, it becomes on the part of the bishops and faithful a single common effort.

But the task of authentically interpreting the word of God, whether written or handed on, has been entrusted exclusively to the living teaching office of the Church, whose authority is exercised in the name of Jesus Christ. This teaching office is not above the word of God, but serves it, teaching only what has been handed on, listening to it devoutly, guarding it scrupulously and explaining it faithfully in accord with a divine commission and with the help of the Holy Spirit; it draws from this one deposit of faith everything which it presents for belief as divinely revealed.

It is clear, therefore, that sacred tradition, sacred Scripture and the teaching authority of the Church, in accord with God's most wise design, are so linked and joined together that one cannot stand without the others, and that all together and each in its own way under the action of the one Holy Spirit contribute effectively to the salvation of souls.

CHAPTER III

Sacred Scripture: Its Inspiration and Divine Interpretation

11. Those divinely revealed realities which are contained and presented in sacred Scripture have been committed to writing under the inspiration of the Holy Spirit. For holy mother Church, relying on the belief of the Apostles (see John, 20:31; 2 Tim. 3:16; 2 Peter 1:19-20, 3:15-16), holds that the books of both the Old and New Testaments in their entirety, with all their parts, are sacred and canonical because written under the inspiration of the Holy Spirit, they have God as their author and have been handed on as such to the Church herself. In composing the sacred books, God chose men and while employed by Him they made use of their powers and abilities, so that with Him

acting in them and through them, they, as true authors, consigned to writing everything and only those things which He wanted. Therefore since everything asserted by the inspired authors or sacred writers must be held to be asserted by the Holy Spirit, it follows that the books of Scripture must be acknowledged as teaching solidly, faithfully and without error that truth which God wanted put into the sacred writings for the sake of our salvation. Therefore "all Scripture is divinely inspired and has its use for teaching the truth and refuting error, for reformation of manners and discipline in right living, so that the man who belongs to God may be efficient and equipped for good work of every kind" (2 Tim. 3:16–17, Greek text).

12. However, since God speaks in sacred Scripture through men in human fashion, the interpreter of sacred Scripture, in order to see clearly what God wanted to communicate to us, should carefully investigate what meaning the sacred writers really intended, and what God wanted to manifest by means of their words.

To search out the intention of the sacred writers, attention should be given, among other things, to "literary forms." For truth is set forth and expressed differently in texts which are variously historical, prophetic, poetic, or of other forms of discourse. The interpreter must investigate what meaning the sacred writer intended to express and actually expressed in particular circumstances by using contemporary literary forms in accordance with the situation of his own time and culture. For the correct understanding of what the sacred author wanted to assert, due attention must be paid to the customary and characteristic styles of feeling, speaking and narrating which prevailed at the time of the sacred writer, and to the patterns men normally employed at that period in their everyday dealings with one another.

But, since holy Scripture must be read and interpreted in the same spirit in which it was written, no less serious attention must be given to the content and unity of the whole of Scripture if the meaning of the sacred texts is to be correctly worked out. The living tradition of the whole Church must be taken into account along with the harmony which exists between elements of the faith. It is the task of exegetes to work according to these rules toward a better understanding and explanation of the meaning of sacred Scripture, so that through preparatory study the judgment of the Church may mature. For all of what has been said about the way of interpreting Scripture is subject finally to the judgment of the Church, which carries out the divine commission and ministry of guarding and interpreting the word of God.

13. In sacred Scripture, therefore, while the truth and holiness of God always remains intact, the marvelous "condescension" of eternal wisdom is clearly shown, "that we may learn the gentle kindness of God, which words cannot express, and how far He has gone in adapting His language with thoughtful concern for our weak human nature." For the words of God, expressed in human language, have been made like

human discourse, just as the word of the eternal Father, when He took to Himself the flesh of human weakness, was in every way made like men.

CHAPTER IV
The Old Testament

14. In carefully planning and preparing the salvation of the whole human race the God of infinite love, by a special dispensation, chose for Himself a people to whom He would entrust His promises, First He entered into a covenant with Abraham (see Gen. 15:18) and, through Moses, with the people of Israel (see Ex. 24:8). To this people which He had acquired for Himself, He so manifested Himself through words and deeds as the one true and living God that Israel came to know by experience the ways of God with men. Then, too, when God Himself spoke to them through the mouth of the prophets, Israel daily gained a deeper and clearer understanding of His ways and made them more widely known among the nations (see Ps. 21:29; 95:1-3; Is. 2:1-5; Jer. 3:17). The plan of salvation foretold by the sacred authors, recounted and explained by them, is found as the true word of God in the books of the Old Testament: these books, therefore, written under divine inspiration, remain permanently valuable. "For all that was written for our instruction, so that by steadfastness and the encouragement of the Scriptures we might have hope" (Rom. 15:4).

15. The principal purpose to which the plan of the old covenant was directed was to prepare for the coming of Christ, the redeemer of all and of the messianic kingdom, to announce this coming by prophecy (see Luke 24:44, John 5:39; 1 Peter 1:10), and to indicate its meaning through various types (see 1 Cor. 10:12). Now the books of the Old Testament, in accordance with the state of mankind before the time of salvation established by Christ, reveal to all men the knowledge of God and of man and the ways in which God, just and merciful, deals with men. These books, though they also contain some things which are incomplete and temporary, nevertheless show us true divine pedagogy. These same books, then, give expression to a lively sense of God, contain a store of sublime teachings about God, sound wisdom about human life, and a wonderful treasury of prayers, and in them the mystery of our salvation is present in a hidden way. Christians should receive them with reverence.

16. God, the inspirer and author of both Testaments, wisely arranged that the New Testament be hidden in the Old and the Old be made manifest in the New. For, though Christ established the new covenant in His blood (see Luke 22:20; 1 Cor. 11:25), still the books of the Old

Testament with all their parts, caught up into the proclamation of the Gospel, acquire and show forth their full meaning in the New Testament (see Matt. 5:17; Luke 24:27; Rom. 16:25–26; 2 Cor. 14:16) and in turn shed light on it and explain it.

CHAPTER V
The New Testament

17. The word of God, which is the power of God for the salvation of all who believe (see Rom. 1:16), is set forth and shows its power in a most excellent way in the writings of the New Testament. For when the fulness of time arrived (see Gal. 4:4), the Word was made flesh and dwelt among us in His fulness of graces and truth (see John 1:14). Christ established the kingdom of God on earth, manifested His Father and Himself by deeds and words, and completed His work by His death, resurrection and glorious Ascension and by the sending of the Holy Spirit. Having been lifted up from the earth, He draws all men to Himself (see John 12:32, Greek text), He who alone has the words of eternal life (see John 6:68). This mystery had not been manifested to other generations as it was now revealed to His holy Apostles and prophets in the Holy Spirit (see Eph. 3:4–6, Greek text), so that they might preach the Gospel, stir up faith in Jesus, Christ and Lord, and gather together the Church. Now the writings of the New Testament stand as a perpetual and divine witness to these realities.

18. It is common knowledge that among all the Scriptures, even those of the New Testament, the Gospels have a special preeminence, and rightly so, for they are the principal witness for the life and teaching of the incarnate Word, our savior.

The Church has always and everywhere held and continues to hold that the four Gospels are of apostolic origin. For what the Apostles preached in fulfillment of the commission of Christ, afterwards they themselves and apostolic men, under the inspiration of the divine Spirit, handed on to us in writing: the foundation of faith, namely, the fourfold Gospel, according to Matthew, Mark, Luke and John.

19. Holy Mother Church has firmly and with absolute constancy held, and continues to hold, that the four Gospels just named, whose historical character the Church unhesitatingly asserts, faithfully hand on what Jesus Christ, while living among men, really did and taught for their eternal salvation until the day He was taken up into heaven (see Acts 1:1). Indeed, after the ascension of the Lord the Apostles handed on to their hearers what He had said and done. This they did with that clearer understanding which they enjoyed after they had been instructed by the glorious events of Christ's life and taught by the light of the Spirit

of truth. The sacred authors wrote the four Gospels, selecting some things from the many which had been handed on by word of mouth or in writing, reducing some of them to a synthesis, explaining some things in view of the situation of their churches, and preserving the form of proclamation but always in such fashion that they told us the honest truth about Jesus. For their intention in writing was that either from their own memory and recollections, or from the witness of those who, "themselves from the beginning were eye-witnesses and ministers of the Word" we might know "the truth" concerning those matters about which we have been instructed (see Luke 1:2–4).

20. Besides the four Gospels, the canon of the New Testament also contains the epistles of St. Paul and other apostolic writings, composed under the inspiration of the Holy Spirit, by which according to the wise plan of God, those matters which concern Christ the Lord are confirmed, His true teaching is more and more fully stated, the saving power of the divine work of Christ is preached, the story is told of the beginnings of the Church and its marvelous growth, and its glorious fulfillment is foretold.

For the Lord Jesus was with His apostles as He had promised (see Matt. 28:20) and sent them the advocate Spirit who would lead them into the fullness of truth (see John 16:13).

CHAPTER VI
Sacred Scripture in the Life of the Church

21. The Church has always venerated the divine Scriptures just as she venerates the body of the Lord, since, especially in the sacred liturgy, she unceasingly receives and offers to the faithful the bread of life from the table both of God's word and of Christ's body. She has always maintained them, and continues to do so, together with sacred tradition, as the supreme rule of faith, since, as inspired by God and committed once and for all to writing, they impart the word of God Himself without change, and make the voice of the Holy Spirit resound in the words of the prophets and Apostles. Therefore, like the Christian religion itself, all the preaching of the Church must be nourished and regulated by sacred Scripture. For in the sacred books, the Father who is in heaven meets His children with great love and speaks with them; and the force and power in the word of God is so great that it stands as the support and energy of the Church, the strength of faith for her sons, the food of the soul, the pure and everlasting source of spiritual life. Consequently these words are perfectly applicable to sacred Scripture: "For the word of God is living and active" (Heb. 4:12) and "it has power to build you up and give you your heritage among all those who are sanctified" (Acts 20:32; see 1 Thess. 2:13).

22. Easy access to sacred Scripture should be provided for all the Christian faithful. That is why the Church from the very beginning accepted as her own that very ancient Greek translation of the Old Testament which is called the septuagint; and she has always given a place of honor to other Eastern translations and Latin ones, especially the Latin translation known as the vulgate. But since the word of God should be accessible at all times, the Church by her authority and with maternal concern sees to it that suitable and correct translations are made into different languages, especially from the original texts of the sacred books. And should the opportunity arise and the Church authorities approve, if these translations are produced in cooperation with the separated brethren as well, all Christians will be able to use them.

23. The bride of the incarnate word, the Church taught by the Holy Spirit, is concerned to move ahead toward a deeper understanding of the sacred Scriptures so that she may increasingly feed her sons with the divine words. Therefore, she also encourages the study of the holy Fathers of both East and West and of sacred liturgies. Catholic exegetes then and other students of sacred theology, working diligently together and using appropriate means, should devote their energies, under the watchful care of the sacred teaching office of the Church, to an exploration and exposition of the divine writings. This should be so done that as many ministers of the divine word as possible will be able effectively to provide the nourishment of the Scriptures for the people of God, to enlighten their minds, strengthen their wills, and set men's hearts on fire with the love of God. The sacred synod encourages the sons of the Church and Biblical scholars to continue energetically, following the mind of the Church, with the work they have so well begun, with a constant renewal of vigor.

24. Sacred theology rests on the written word of God, together with sacred tradition, as its primary and perpetual foundation. By scrutinizing in the light of faith all truth stored up in the mystery of Christ, theology is most powerfully strengthened and constantly rejuvenated by that word. For the sacred Scriptures contain the word of God and since they are inspired, really are the word of God; and so the study of the sacred page is, as it were, the soul of sacred theology. By the same word of Scripture the ministry of the word also, that is, pastoral preaching, catechetics and all Christian instruction, in which the liturgical homily must hold the foremost place, is nourished in a healthy way and flourishes in a holy way.

25. Therefore, all the clergy must hold fast to the sacred Scriptures through diligent sacred reading and careful study, especially the priests of Christ and others, such as deacons and catechists who are legitimately active in the ministry of the word. This is to be done so that none of them will become "an empty preacher of the word of God outwardly,

who is not a listener to it inwardly" since they must share the abundant wealth of the divine word with the faithful committed to them, especially in the sacred liturgy. The sacred synod also earnestly and especially urges all the Christian faithful, especially Religious, to learn by frequent reading of the divine Scriptures the "excellent knowledge of Jesus Christ" (Phil. 3:8). "For ignorance of the Scriptures is ignorance of Christ." Therefore, they should gladly put themselves in touch with the sacred text itself, whether it be through the liturgy, rich in the divine word, or through devotional reading, or through instructions suitable for the purpose and other aids which, in our time, with approval and active support of the shepherds of the Church, are commendably spread everywhere. And let them remember that prayer should accompany the reading of sacred Scripture, so that God and man may talk together; for "we speak to Him when we pray; we hear Him when we read the divine saying."

It devolves on sacred bishops "who have the apostolic teaching" to give the faithful entrusted to them suitable instruction in the right use of the divine books, especially the New Testament and above all the Gospels. This can be done through translations of the sacred texts, which are to be provided with the necessary and really adequate explanations so that the children of the Church may safely and profitably become conversant with the sacred Scriptures and be penetrated with their spirit.

Furthermore editions of the sacred Scriptures, provided with suitable footnotes, should be prepared also for the use of non-Christians and adapted to their situation. Both pastors of souls and Christians generally should see to the wise distribution of these in one way or another.

26. In this way, therefore, through the reading and study of the sacred books "the word of God may spread rapidly and be glorified" (2 Thess. 3:1) and the treasure of revelation, entrusted to the Church, may more and more fill the hearts of men. Just as the life of the Church is strengthened through more frequent celebration of the Eucharistic mystery, similarly we may hope for a new stimulus for the life of the Spirit from a growing reverence for the word of God, which "lasts forever" (Is. 40:8; see 1 Peter 1:23–25).

Declaration on Religious Freedom

On the Right of the Person and of Communities to Social and Civil Freedom in Matters Religious

PROMULGATED DECEMBER 7, 1965

1. A SENSE OF the dignity of the human person has been impressing itself more and more deeply on the consciousness of contemporary man, and the demand is increasingly made that men should act on their own judgment, enjoying and making use of a responsible freedom, not driven by coercion but motivated by a sense of duty. The demand is likewise made that constitutional limits should be set to the powers of government, in order that there may be no encroachment on the rightful freedom of the person and of associations. This demand for freedom in human society chiefly regards the quest for the values proper to the human spirit. It regards, in the first place, the free exercise of religion in society. This Vatican Council takes careful note of these desires in the minds of men. It proposes to declare them to be greatly in accord with truth and justice. To this end, it searches into the sacred tradition and doctrine of the Church—the treasury out of which the Church continually brings forth new things that are in harmony with the things that are old.

First, the council professes its belief that God Himself has made known to mankind the way in which men are to serve Him, and thus be saved in Christ and come to blessedness. We believe that this one true religion subsists in the Catholic and Apostolic Church, to which the Lord Jesus committed the duty of spreading it abroad among all men. Thus He spoke to the Apostles: "Go, therefore, and make disciples of all nations, baptizing them in the name of the Father and of the Son and of the Holy Spirit, teaching them to observe all things whatsoever I have enjoined upon you" (Matt. 28:19–20). On their part, all men are bound to seek the truth, especially in what concerns God and His Church, and to embrace the truth they come to know, and to hold fast to it.

This Vatican Council likewise professes its belief that it is upon the human conscience that these obligations fall and exert their binding force. The truth cannot impose itself except by virtue of its own truth, as it makes its entrance into the mind at once quietly and with power.

Religious freedom, in turn, which men demand as necessary to fulfill their duty to worship God, has to do with immunity from coercion in civil society. Therefore it leaves untouched traditional Catholic doctrine on the moral duty of men and societies toward the true religion and toward the one Church of Christ.

Over and above all this, the council intends to develop the doctrine of recent popes on the inviolable rights of the human person and the constitutional order of society.

2. This Vatican Council declares that the human person has a right to religious freedom. This freedom means that all men are to be immune from coercion on the part of individuals or of social groups and of any human power, in such wise that no one is to be forced to act in a manner contrary to his own beliefs, whether privately or publicly, whether alone or in association with others, within due limits.

The council further declares that the right to religious freedom has its foundation in the very dignity of the human person as this dignity is known through the revealed word of God and by reason itself. This right of the human person to religious freedom is to be recognized in the constitutional law whereby society is governed and thus it is to become a civil right.

It is in accordance with their dignity as persons—that is, beings endowed with reason and free will and therefore privileged to bear personal responsibility—that all men should be at once impelled by nature and also bound by a moral obligation to seek the truth, especially religious truth. They are also bound to adhere to the truth, once it is known, and to order their whole lives in accord with the demands of truth. However, men cannot discharge these obligations in a manner in keeping with their own nature unless they enjoy immunity from external coercion as well as psychological freedom. Therefore the right to religious freedom has its foundation not in the subjective disposition of the person, but in his very nature. In consequence, the right to this immunity continues to exist even in those who do not live up to their obligation of seeking the truth and adhering to it and the exercise of this right is not to be impeded, provided that just public order be observed.

3. Further light is shed on the subject if one considers that the highest norm of human life is the divine law—eternal, objective and universal —whereby God orders, directs and governs the entire universe and all the ways of the human community by a plan conceived in wisdom and love. Man has been made by God to participate in this law, with the result that, under the gentle disposition of divine Providence, he can come to perceive ever more fully the truth that is unchanging. Wherefore every man has the duty, and therefore the right, to seek the truth in matters religious in order that he may with prudence form for himself right and true judgments of conscience, under use of all suitable means.

Truth, however, is to be sought after in a manner proper to the dignity of the human person and his social nature. The inquiry is to be free, carried on with the aid of teaching or instruction, communication and dialogue, in the course of which men explain to one another the truth they have discovered, or think they have discovered, in order thus to assist one another in the quest for truth.

Moreover, as the truth is discovered, it is by a personal assent that men are to adhere to it.

On his part, man perceives and acknowledges the imperatives of the divine law through the mediation of conscience. In all his activity a man is bound to follow his conscience in order that he may come to God, the end and purpose of life. It follows that he is not to be forced to act in a manner contrary to his conscience. Nor, on the other hand, is he to be restrained from acting in accordance with his conscience, especially in matters religious. The reason is that the exercise of religion, of its very nature, consists before all else in those internal, voluntary and free acts whereby man sets the course of his life directly toward God. No merely human power can either command or prohibit acts of this kind. The social nature of man, however, itself requires that he should give external expression to his internal acts of religion: that he should share with others in matters religious; that he should profess his religion in community. Injury therefore is done to the human person and to the very order established by God for human life, if the free exercise of religion is denied in society, provided just public order is observed.

There is a further consideration. The religious acts whereby men, in private and in public and out of a sense of personal conviction, direct their lives to God transcend by their very nature the order of terrestrial and temporal affairs. Government therefore ought indeed to take account of the religious life of the citizenry and show it favor, since the function of government is to make provision for the common welfare. However, it would clearly transgress the limits set to its power, were it to presume to command or inhibit acts that are religious.

4. The freedom or immunity from coercion in matters religious which is the endowment of persons as individuals is also to be recognized as their right when they act in community. Religious communities are a requirement of the social nature both of man and of religion itself.

Provided the just demands of public order are observed, religious communities rightfully claim freedom in order that they may govern themselves according to their own norms, honor the Supreme Being in public worship, assist their members in the practice of the religious life, strengthen them by instruction, and promote institutions in which they may join together for the purpose of ordering their own lives in accordance with their religious principles.

Religious communities also have the right not to be hindered, either by legal measures or by administrative action on the part of government, in the selection, training, appointment, and transferral of their own ministers, in communicating with religious authorities and communities abroad, in erecting buildings for religious purposes, and in the acquisition and use of suitable funds or properties.

Religious communities also have the right not to be hindered in their public teaching and witness to their faith, whether by the spoken or by the written word. However, in spreading religious faith and in introducing religious practices everyone ought at all times to refrain from any manner of action which might seem to carry a hint of coercion or of a kind of persuasion that would be dishonorable or unworthy, especially when dealing with poor or uneducated people. Such a manner of action would have to be considered an abuse of one's right and a violation of the right of others.

In addition, it comes within the meaning of religious freedom that religious communities should not be prohibited from freely undertaking to show the special value of their doctrine in what concerns the organization of society and the inspiration of the whole of human activity. Finally, the social nature of man and the very nature of religion afford the foundation of the right of men freely to hold meetings and to establish educational, cultural, charitable and social organizations, under the impulse of their own religious sense.

5. The family, since it is a society in its own original right, has the right freely to live its own domestic religious life under the guidance of parents. Parents, moreover, have the right to determine, in accordance with their own religious beliefs, the kind of religious education that their children are to receive. Government, in consequence, must acknowledge the right of parents to make a genuinely free choice of schools and of other means of education, and the use of this freedom of choice is not to be made a reason for imposing unjust burdens on parents, whether directly or indirectly. Besides, the right of parents are violated, if their children are forced to attend lessons or instructions which are not in

agreement with their religious beliefs, or if a single system of education, from which all religious formation is excluded, is imposed upon all.

6. Since the common welfare of society consists in the entirety of those conditions of social life under which men enjoy the possibility of achieving their own perfection in a certain fullness of measure and also with some relative ease, it chiefly consists in the protection of the rights, and in the performance of the duties, of the human person. Therefore the care of the right to religious freedom devolves upon the whole citizenry, upon social groups, upon government and upon the Church and other religious communities, in virtue of the duty of all toward the common welfare, and in the manner proper to each.

The protection and promotion of the inviolable rights of man ranks among the essential duties of government. Therefore government is to assume the safeguard of the religious freedom of all its citizens, in an effective manner, by just laws and by other appropriate means.

Government is also to help create conditions favorable to the fostering of religious life, in order that the people may be truly enabled to exercise their religious rights and to fulfill their religious duties, and also in order that society itself may profit by the moral qualities of justice and peace which have their origin in men's faithfulness to God and to His holy will.

If, in view of peculiar circumstances obtaining among peoples, special civil recognition is given to one religious community in the constitutional order of society, it is at the same time imperative that the right of all citizens and religious communities to religious freedom should be recognized and made effective in practice.

Finally, government is to see to it that the equality of citizens before the law, which is itself an element of the common good, is never violated, whether openly or covertly, for religious reasons. Nor is there to be discrimination among citizens.

It follows that a wrong is done when government imposes upon its people, by force or fear or other means, the profession or repudiation of any religion, or when it hinders men from joining or leaving a religious community. All the more is it a violation of the will of God and of the sacred rights of the person and the family of nations when force is brought to bear in any way in order to destroy or repress religion, either in the whole of mankind or in a particular country or in a definite community.

7. The right to religious freedom is exercised in human society: hence its exercise is subject to certain regulatory norms. In the use of all freedoms the moral principle of personal and social responsibility is to be observed. In the exercise of their rights, individual men and social groups are bound by the moral law to have respect both for the rights

of others and for their own duties toward others and for the common welfare of all. Men are to deal with their fellows in justice and civility.

Furthermore, society has the right to defend itself against possible abuses committed on the pretext of freedom of religion. It is the special duty of government to provide this protection. However, government is not to act in an arbitrary fashion or in an unfair spirit of partisanship. Its action is to be controlled by juridical norms which are in conformity with the objective moral order. These norms arise out of the need for the effective safeguard of the rights of all citizens and for the peaceful settlement of conflicts of rights, also out of the need for an adequate care of genuine public peace, which comes about when men live together in good order and in true justice, and finally out of the need for a proper guardianship of public morality.

These matters constitute the basic component of the common welfare: they are what is meant by public order. For the rest, the usages of society are to be the usages of freedom in their full range: that is, the freedom of man is to be respected as far as possible and is not to be curtailed except when and in so far as necessary.

8. Many pressures are brought to bear upon the men of our day, to the point where the danger arises lest they lose the possibility of acting on their own judgment. On the other hand, not a few can be found who seem inclined to use the name of freedom as the pretext for refusing to submit to authority and for making light of the duty of obedience. Wherefore this Vatican Council urges everyone, especially those who are charged with the task of educating others, to do their utmost to form men who, on the one hand, will respect the moral order and be obedient to lawful authority, and, on the other hand, will be lovers of true freedom—men, in other words, who will come to decisions on their own judgment and in the light of truth, govern their activities with a sense of responsibility, and strive after what is true and right, willing always to join with others in cooperative effort.

Religious freedom therefore ought to have this further purpose and aim, namely, that men may come to act with greater responsibility in fulfilling their duties in community life.

9. The declaration of this Vatican Council on the right of man to religious freedom has its foundation in the dignity of the person, whose exigencies have come to be more fully known to human reason through centuries of experience. What is more, this doctrine of freedom has roots in divine revelation, and for this reason Christians are bound to respect it all the more conscientiously. Revelation does not indeed affirm in so many words the right of man to immunity from external coercion in matters religious. It does, however, disclose the dignity of the human person in its full dimensions. It gives evidence of the respect which Christ showed toward the freedom with which man is to fulfill

his duty of belief in the word of God and it gives us lessons in the spirit which disciples of such a Master ought to adopt and continually follow. Thus further light is cast upon the general principles upon which the doctrine of this declaration on religious freedom is based. In particular, religious freedom in society is entirely consonant with the freedom of the act of Christian faith.

10. It is one of the major tenets of Catholic doctrine that man's response to God in faith must be free: no one therefore is to be forced to embrace the Christian faith against his own will. This doctrine is contained in the word of God and it was constantly proclaimed by the Fathers of the Church. The act of faith is of its very nature a free act. Man, redeemed by Christ the Savior and through Christ Jesus called to be God's adopted son, cannot give his adherence to God revealing Himself unless, under the drawing of the Father, he offers to God the reasonable and free submission of faith. It is therefore completely in accord with the nature of faith that in matters religious every manner of coercion on the part of men should be excluded. In consequence, the principle of religious freedom makes no small contribution to the creation of an environment in which men can without hindrance be invited to the Christian faith, embrace it of their own free will, and profess it effectively in their whole manner of life.

11. God calls men to serve Him in spirit and in truth, hence they are bound in conscience but they stand under no compulsion. God has regard for the dignity of the human person whom He Himself created and man is to be guided by his own judgment and he is to enjoy freedom. This truth appears at its height in Christ Jesus, in whom God manifested Himself and His ways with men. Christ is at once our Master and our Lord and also meek and humble of heart. In attracting and inviting His disciples He used patience. He wrought miracles to illuminate His teaching and to establish its truth, but His intention was to rouse faith in His hearers and to confirm them in faith, not to exert coercion upon them. He did indeed denounce the unbelief of some who listened to Him, but He left vengeance to God in expectation of the day of judgment. When He sent His Apostles into the world, He said to them: "He who believes and is baptized will be saved. He who does not believe will be condemned" (Mark 16:16). But He Himself, noting that the cockle had been sown amid the wheat, gave orders that both should be allowed to grow until the harvest time, which will come at the end of the world. He refused to be a political messiah, ruling by force: He preferred to call Himself the Son of Man, who came "to serve and to give his life as a ransom for the many" (Mark 10:45). He showed Himself the perfect servant of God, who "does not break the bruised reed nor extinguish the smoking flax" (Matt. 12:20).

He acknowledged the power of government and its rights, when He commanded that tribute be given to Caesar: but He gave clear warning that the higher rights of God are to be kept inviolate: "Render to Caesar the things that are Caesar's and to God the things that are God's" (Matt. 22:21). In the end, when He completed on the cross the work of redemption whereby He achieved salvation and true freedom for men, He brought His revelation to completion. For He bore witness to the truth, but He refused to impose the truth by force on those who spoke against it. Not by force of blows does His rule assert its claims. It is established by witnessing to the truth and by hearing the truth, and it extends its dominion by the love whereby Christ, lifted up on the cross, draws all men to Himself.

Taught by the word and example of Christ, the Apostles followed the same way. From the very origins of the Church the disciples of Christ strove to convert men to faith in Christ as the Lord; not, however, by the use of coercion or of devices unworthy of the Gospel, but by the power, above all, of the word of God. Steadfastly they proclaimed to all the plan of God our Savior, "who wills that all men should be saved and come to the acknowledgement of the truth" (1 Tim. 2:4). At the same time, however, they showed respect for those of weaker stuff, even though they were in error, and thus they made it plain that "each one of us is to render to God an account of himself" (Romans 14:12), and for that reason is bound to obey his conscience. Like Christ Himself, the Apostles were unceasingly bent upon bearing witness to the truth of God, and they showed the fullest measure of boldness in "speaking the word with confidence" (Acts 4:31) before the people and their rulers. With a firm faith they held that the Gospel is indeed the power of God unto salvation for all who believe. Therefore they rejected all "carnal weapons": they followed the example of the gentleness and respectful-ness of Christ and they preached the word of God in the full confidence that there was resident in this word itself a divine power able to destroy all the forces arrayed against God and bring men to faith in Christ and to His service. As the Master, so too the Apostles recognized legitimate civil authority. "For there is no power except from God," the Apostle teaches, and thereafter commands: "Let everyone be subject to higher authorities. . . . He who resists authority resists God's ordinance" (Romans 13:1–5). At the same time, however, they did not hesitate to speak out against governing powers which set themselves in opposition to the holy will of God: "It is necessary to obey God rather than men" (Acts 5:29). This is the way along which the martyrs and other faithful have walked through all ages and over all the earth.

12. In faithfulness therefore to the truth of the Gospel, the Church is following the way of Christ and the apostles when she recognizes and gives support to the principle of religious freedom as befitting the dignity of man and as being in accord with divine revelation. Throughout the ages the Church has kept safe and handed on the doctrine received

from the Master and from the apostles. In the life of the People of God, as it has made its pilgrim way through the vicissitudes of human history, there has at times appeared a way of acting that was hardly in accord with the spirit of the Gospel or even opposed to it. Nevertheless, the doctrine of the Church that no one is to be coerced into faith has always stood firm.

Thus the leaven of the Gospel has long been about its quiet work in the minds of men, and to it is due in great measure the fact that in the course of time men have come more widely to recognize their dignity as persons, and the conviction has grown stronger that the person in society is to be kept free from all manner of coercion in matters religious.

13. Among the things that concern the good of the Church and indeed the welfare of society here on earth—things therefore that are always and everywhere to be kept secure and defended against all injury—this certainly is preeminent, namely, that the Church should enjoy that full measure of freedom which her care for the salvation of men requires. This is a sacred freedom, because the only-begotten Son endowed with it the Church which He purchased with His blood. Indeed it is so much the property of the Church that to act against it is to act against the will of God. The freedom of the Church is the fundamental principle in what concerns the relations between the Church and governments and the whole civil order.

In human society and in the face of government the Church claims freedom for herself in her character as a spiritual authority, established by Christ the Lord, upon which there rests, by divine mandate, the duty of going out into the whole world and preaching the Gospel to every creature. The Church also claims freedom for herself in her character as a society of men who have the right to live in society in accordance with the precepts of Christian faith.

In turn, where the principle of religious freedom is not only proclaimed in words or simply incorporated in law but also given sincere and practical application, there the Church succeeds in achieving a stable situation of right as well as of fact and the independence which is necessary for the fulfillment of her divine mission.

This independence is precisely what the authorities of the Church claim in society. At the same time, the Christian faithful, in common with all other men, possess the civil right not to be hindered in leading their lives in accordance with their consciences. Therefore, a harmony exists between the freedom of the Church and the religious freedom which is to be recognized as the right of all men and communities and sanctioned by constitutional law.

14. In order to be faithful to the divine command, "teach all nations" (Matt. 28:19-20), the Catholic Church must work with all urgency and

concern "that the word of God be spread abroad and glorified" (2 Thess. 3:1). Hence the Church earnestly begs of its children that, "first of all, supplications, prayers, petitions, acts of thanksgiving be made for all men. . . . For this is good and agreeable in the sight of God our Savior, who wills that all men be saved and come to the knowledge of the truth" (1 Tim. 2:1–4). In the formation of their consciences, the Christian faithful ought carefully to attend to the sacred and certain doctrine of the Church. For the Church is, by the will of Christ, the teacher of the truth. It is her duty to give utterance to, and authoritatively to teach, that truth which is Christ Himself, and also to declare and confirm by her authority those principles of the moral order which have their origins in human nature itself. Furthermore, let Christians walk in wisdom in the face of those outside, "in the Holy Spirit, in unaffected love, in the word of truth" (2 Cor. 6:6–7), and let them be about their task of spreading the light of life with all confidence and apostolic courage, even to the shedding of their blood.

The disciple is bound by a grave obligation toward Christ, his Master, ever more fully to understand the truth received from Him, faithfully to proclaim it, and vigorously to defend it, never—be it understood—having recourse to means that are incompatible with the spirit of the Gospel. At the same time, the charity of Christ urges him to love and have prudence and patience in his dealings with those who are in error or in ignorance with regard to the faith. All is to be taken into account —the Christian duty to Christ, the life-giving word which must be proclaimed, the rights of the human person, and the measure of grace granted by God through Christ to men who are invited freely to accept and profess the faith.

15. The fact is that men of the present day want to be able freely to profess their religion in private and in public. Indeed, religious freedom has already been declared to be a civil right in most constitutions, and it is solemnly recognized in international documents. The further fact is that forms of government still exist under which, even though freedom of religious worship receives constitutional recognition, the powers of government are engaged in the effort to deter citizens from the profession of religion and to make life very difficult and dangerous for religious communities.

This council greets with joy the first of these two facts as among the signs of the times. With sorrow, however, it denounces the other fact, as only to be deplored. The council exhorts Catholics, and it directs a plea to all men, most carefully to consider how greatly necessary religious freedom is, especially in the present condition of the human family. All nations are coming into even closer unity. Men of different cultures and religions are being brought together in closer relationships. There is a growing consciousness of the personal responsibility that every man has. All this is evident. Consequently, in order that relationships of peace and harmony be established and maintained within the whole of mankind, it is necessary that religious freedom be everywhere provided with an effective constitutional guarantee and that respect be shown for the high duty and right of man freely to lead his religious life in society.

May the God and Father of all grant that the human family, through careful observance of the principle of religious freedom in society, may be brought by the grace of Christ and the power of the Holy Spirit to the sublime and unending and "glorious freedom of the sons of God" (Rom. 8:21).

Index

✠